Partner and I

Polly Porter and Molly Dewson in Maine in the early 1920s.

Partner and I:
Molly Dewson, Feminism, and New Deal Politics

❖❖❖

SUSAN WARE

Yale University Press
New Haven and London

Designed by James J. Johnson
and set in Goudy Old Style type
by Eastern Graphics, Binghamton, New York.
Printed in the United States of America by
Halliday Lithograph Corporation, West Hanover, Massachusetts.

Library of Congress Cataloging-in-Publication Data

Ware, Susan, 1950–
  Partner and I.

  Includes index.
   1. Dewson, Molly, 1874–1962. 2. Politicians—
United States—Biography. 3. Democratic Party (U.S.)—
Biography. 4. Women in politics—United States—History
—20th century. 5. New Deal, 1933–1939. 6. United
States—Politics and government—1933–1945. I. Title.
E748.D49W37   1987   324.2′092′4   86–33972
ISBN 0–300–03820–8 (cloth)
      0–300–04621–9 (pbk.)

10   *9*   *8*   *7*   *6*   *5*   *4*   *3*   *2*

Contents

Acknowledgments

With each book I write, I have more people to thank. Don Ware has read practically every word I have written, and his suggestions improved the style and content of the manuscript; his unflagging belief in my career during the years I worked on this project made an enormous difference in my life. Just as supportive, both personally and professionally, has been Barbara Miller Solomon, who not only read the draft but encouraged me as I struggled with the problems of writing women's biography as an independent scholar.

During the initial stages of the project, I had the great fortune to link up with a Cambridge-area group of women historians writing biography. My association with Ann Lane, Barbara Sicherman, Joyce Antler, and Janet James provided me with models of scholarship and underscored the importance of friendship and support to women's professional careers. I am especially grateful for the time that Joyce took from the final stages of her biography of Lucy Sprague Mitchell to help me with the last unresolved questions of mine. Joan Jacobs Brumberg, whom I met while I was writing the book, has earned my respect as a loyal friend and tireless critic who always challenged me to do more. I would also like to thank Frank Freidel and Aida Donald for their perceptive readings of earlier versions of the book.

This book was shaped by interviews with various people who knew Molly Dewson and Polly Porter. It could not have been written without the help of Dewson's great-niece, Virginia Bourne, who welcomed me, my husband, and whatever dog we had in tow to Moss Acre on several occasions. By giving me the freedom to roam the house and grounds, she allowed me to experience for myself how "the aunts" lived. Her willingness to loan me family letters, daybooks, and especially the Porter-Dewson scrapbooks has made an enormous contribution to the book. I also profited from conversations with two of Polly Porter's god-children, Marion Hall Hunt and Peter Dobkin Hall. Historians them-selves, they shared with me sources and memories of the women they remembered as "Aunt Moll and Aunt Poll." Boston attorney James Barr Ames, a Castine neighbor of Molly and Polly, also shared his recol-lections with me and provided me with copies of their wills. Clara Beyer, the last of Dewson's cohort from the New Deal, confirmed dur-ing several interviews Molly Dewson's central role in the social welfare aspects of the New Deal and offered me clues on the Porter-Dewson partnership. India Edwards, Harriet Allen Kerr, Maurine Mulliner, and Carolyn Wolfe kindly shared copies of their correspondence with Dewson.

Biographies take a long time to write, and I am grateful to several institutions for help during the years I was completing this book. The Radcliffe Research Scholars program, jointly administered by the Schlesinger Library and the Henry A. Murray Research Center at Rad-cliffe College, funded the initial research for the book. An American Council of Learned Societies / Ford Fellowship supplied additional funding. Affiliations as a fellow at the Charles Warren Center at Har-vard and as a Visiting Scholar at Radcliffe College provided me institu-tional bases while I was writing various drafts. I am especially grateful to President Matina Horner for her role in arranging my Radcliffe appointment.

The people at the Yale University Press have made the process of turning manuscript into book a pleasant one. I would like to single out my editor, Chuck Grench, and my manuscript editor, Stephanie Jones, for their help in the final stages of the project. Rick Stafford of the Fogg Art Museum at Harvard did the photographic reproductions.

Finally, I would like to thank my colleagues and graduate students at New York University for their support and interest in the book. Their belief in my abilities as a teacher and a scholar at a critical junc-ture in my career gave me a future that, I hope, will include many more exciting projects.

Introduction

Molly Dewson—Boston-bred and Wellesley-educated—was America's first female political boss. At the height of her power in 1936, she controlled eighty thousand women as director of the Women's Division of the Democratic National Committee. During the depression decade of the 1930s, she built the Women's Division into one of the most effective components of the newly revitalized Democratic party, winning places for women in politics and government on an unprecedented scale. These breakthroughs gave women their own New Deal.

Male politicians had never seen anything like her. She strode into their offices, a tall, sturdy, middle-aged woman with New England Yankee written all over her face. Yet, instead of speaking with a cultured upper-class accent, she greeted her astonished and then bemused colleagues in a deep foghorn voice that boomed across the room. She quickly earned the nicknames "Queen Molly," "The General," and, in a pun on her initials, "More Women Dewson." To the extent that she paid attention to her appearance, she was definitely the tweedy type, favoring tailored suits with long jackets and deep pockets, sensible low shoes, no makeup, and pince-nez perched precariously on her nose. Wags noted that she bore a certain physical resemblance to her beloved commander-in-chief, Franklin Delano Roosevelt.

It was not just Molly Dewson's appearance that confounded the politicians: it was her style. "Don't talk to anybody, just act" summed up her compact philosophy. She had a down-to-earth practical manner that male politicians liked. Unlike many political greenhorns, she was not afraid to compromise; if a public fight seemed counterproductive, she found ways to achieve her goals behind the scenes. While she was at best a mediocre public speaker, one-on-one she overwhelmed her antagonists with a combination of bravado, humor, and combativeness. James Farley, chairman of the Democratic National Committee during the 1930s, called her the most persistent woman he had ever met. Yet, after relentlessly badgering her male colleagues, she could relax with them at the end of the day telling what were quaintly referred to as "off-color" jokes. She cited her age (she was sixty-two in 1936) as the key to her ability to work so effectively with men: "Fortunately, I was old enough to be their aunt, and men are at their best with their mothers and favorite aunts."[1] She did not add the obvious corollary: she was too old for male politicians to think of her as a suitable object for their sexual attention.

Molly Dewson never became just one of the boys. Hers was a politics with a feminist twist, bridging nineteenth-century ideals of womanhood and twentieth-century modes of political activism. In the vanguard of suffragists who entered public life after the nineteenth amendment, she learned to work effectively in the male realm of politics, but she never forgot that women often brought a different agenda to current affairs. With many women of her generation she shared the belief that women were more concerned than men with fundamental values such as economic security, peace, and humanitarian reform. The depression decade of the 1930s proved an ideal time to push such an issue-oriented approach to political action.

There had been women in politics before the 1930s, but Molly Dewson represented a new breed of activists who came to politics by way of women's suffrage and women's voluntary reform organizations. Rather than promoting women as candidates for public office, they worked on the issue of access—getting women appointed in prominent government positions, demanding formal roles in the party hierarchy, building up local women's political organizations. They also stressed the importance of bringing women into politics on the strength of issues, not personalities—an orientation which characterized women's political activism both before and after the winning of the vote.

While early suffragists-turned-politicians enjoyed some success on the state and local level in the 1920s, Molly Dewson was one of the first women to have a crack at national influence and power in New Deal Washington. At the base of her approach to power was a cooperative impulse—a willingness, almost an imperative, to collaborate with like-minded women on issues of common concern. Harboring no ambition for elected office, she entered politics not for personal gain but in order to promote the issues she believed in as a social reformer and a feminist. Eschewing the limelight usually sought by national political figures, she preferred to work quietly and effectively behind the scenes. Throughout the 1930s, her impact on national politics and government derived less from her institutional base at the Democratic National Committee than from her intimate association with Franklin and Eleanor Roosevelt, her fruitful collaboration with other women scattered throughout the burgeoning government bureaucracy, and the supportive climate of the early New Deal. Two of her closest allies were First Lady Eleanor Roosevelt and Secretary of Labor Frances Perkins.

Throughout her career, Molly Dewson was an activist, not a philosopher. No one could ever have accused her of being intellectual or the least bit introspective: "I get all the facts I can and then I just put it in my subconscious to percolate" was how she humorously described her decision-making process.[2] Her open-ended mandate to build up the Women's Division of the Democratic Party allowed her to set her own priorities, a circumstance which suited her both temperamentally and politically. She worked most effectively when initiating a plan or meeting an impending deadline; once a project was running smoothly, she looked around for something else to do. During the social and economic upheavals caused by the depression, she found no shortage of challenges. She added a new twist to the adage of a far more traditional political boss, Tammany leader George Washington Plunkitt: "I seen my opportunities and I took 'em."[3]

Born in 1874, Molly Dewson did not find the niche that best utilized her multiple talents until somewhat late in life. Her initiation into partisan politics came through Eleanor Roosevelt, whom Dewson had met in New York City reform circles in the 1920s. Eleanor was already deeply involved in Democratic women's politics, both in New York State and on the national level. During the 1928 presidential campaign, she asked her new friend to handle a ticklish situation in the St. Louis headquarters. Molly had never participated in Democratic politics before, but she quickly agreed. Her official assignment took only a few days, but she stayed for the duration of the campaign. Not until the 1940s would another Democratic campaign be conducted without her on the Roosevelt team.

Dewson's entry into politics at the behest of a friend was typical of how women were recruited for political activity in the immediate postsuffrage era. Men often prepared for careers in public service by way of law or business, but there were no parallel routes for women. It would have been inconceivable for Molly Dewson to begin grooming herself for political life when she graduated from Wellesley College in 1897: women at that time did not contemplate such careers because they simply did not exist. And yet when Eleanor (and later Franklin) Roosevelt called, she was as ready as any woman could have been to exert national leadership in the realm of women's politics.

Molly Dewson was part of a generation of college-educated women who gained political experience during the Progressive era on such issues as the minimum wage and women's suffrage and then went on to wield power at the state and national levels in the postsuffrage era. Whether acting as a social worker, a reformer, or a Democratic politician, Dewson's overriding priority was to improve the economic and social security of American citizens, especially women and children. Tracing a direct line from Progressive reform to the New Deal, her career reflected the values and tactics of public-spirited women who looked to the government to provide solutions for the pressing social problems of modern industrial life.

For this generation of women reformers, a commitment to improving the general welfare overrode attention to the specific problems of women. Yet, despite her ideology, in which women's issues were secondary, it is hard not to be struck by the woman-centeredness of Molly Dewson's life. At every significant stage she was surrounded by women or working on women's issues or both. Upon graduating from Wellesley, she worked at Boston's venerable Women's Educational and Industrial Union, where she did research on women workers. She headed a parole department for delinquent girls at the Massachusetts state school at Lancaster and helped win the first minimum wage for women workers in the country. She participated in the women's suffrage campaign and went to France during World War I with a group of female social workers. During the 1920s, she worked with Florence Kelley, one of the most dynamic women reformers of the twentieth century, again on the issue of the minimum wage for women. Drawn into partisan politics, she organized women's activities in every Democratic campaign from

1928 to 1940. In the 1930s, she was the principal architect of a women's network which made significant contributions both to Democratic politics and to the New Deal's relief, reform, and recovery programs. She chose to spend her life with another woman, Polly Porter, and most of her friendships and associations were with like-minded single or professional women.

Molly Dewson's fifty-two-year relationship with Polly Porter supplies important clues for understanding the changing priorities and shifting affiliations of her career. After the death of her mother in 1912, she decided to make a home with Porter, a younger woman who had served as her intern at the Lancaster Parole Board from 1909 to 1912. During the next seven years, the Porter-Dewsons (as they called themselves from the very start) ran a dairy farm in central Massachusetts and then served together overseas with the Red Cross during World War I. Upon their return, they shared a home in New York's Greenwich Village and a large summer house in Castine, Maine. Although today we would probably label them as lesbians, they used the word *partners* to describe their commitment to each other. Their partnership exemplifies the choices of many late nineteenth- and early twentieth-century educated women who built their emotional lives around other women rather than men. Longstanding and intense female friendships were a socially acceptable vehicle to a full personal and professional life without the constraints of marriage and heterosexual convention.

Molly Dewson was thirty-eight, Polly Porter twenty-eight, when they began their lifelong association in 1912. In effect, Polly Porter acted as an emotional and material support system for her companion and friend. Porter's substantial inheritance from her family's International Harvester holdings allowed the two women to enjoy a privileged lifestyle, especially before the Great Depression. Polly's wealth also freed her partner from the necessity of steady paid employment. Unencumbered by the need to support herself, Dewson could pick and choose her professional commitments, and she often pursued her interests on a volunteer basis.

The Porter-Dewson partnership had enormous consequences for Molly Dewson's career. After 1912, Molly made almost all her career decisions based upon the impact they would have on her relationship with Polly Porter. (After a short stint as a social worker, Polly decided not to pursue a professional career.) Dewson accepted only work that would leave her free to spend the summer in Castine with Polly and their circle of friends and family. Nor did she accept professional commitments which would disturb their settled Greenwich Village lifestyle during the rest of the year: even much of her political work during the New Deal was conducted from New York, not Washington. Significantly, when Dewson did move to Washington in 1937 to serve on the Social Security Board, Porter refused to relocate. The resulting strain on their relationship caused Molly to resign her high-level New Deal appointment after only nine months. From 1938 until Dewson's death in 1962, the two women lived contentedly together without further separations.

Molly Dewson's relationship with Polly Porter was the most important emotional commitment of her adult life. She might have followed a more direct path to career advancement had she not always weighed the impact of professional opportunities on her personal life —yet she had no desire to put career success ahead of personal commitment. She saw the two parts of her life as mutually supportive, not in opposition. That she consciously juggled her personal life with the demands of an active if varied career shows that she was aware of the importance of maintaining an equilibrium between her private and public worlds.

Her personal choices had a wider significance. As Molly Dewson successfully made her way in the man's world of politics and public life, she never left the woman's world which nurtured her, both personally and professionally. Dewson was not alone in this dual orientation: such a congruence between informal friendships and public activism characterized many women's participation in public life in the early twentieth century. Reform-minded women felt at home in the company of other women, whether they combined marriage with a commitment to reform and feminism (as did Frances Perkins and Eleanor Roosevelt) or whether, like Molly Dewson and so many others, they chose not to marry.

Recognition of the importance of women's friendships and communities marks the beginning of what may be called a new political history of women, a story in which Molly Dewson played a leading role. Denied access to traditional sources of political power and accustomed to working with other members of their sex, women developed alternative ways of wielding influence in the public sphere. The key instruments were networks that brought together reformers, political activists, and traditional women's organizations on issues of common concern. Such models of cooperation and association provided both a base of support in a world often hostile to women's aspirations and a powerful tool with which to influence the shape of public policy in twentieth-century America.[4]

From the perspective of her settled Castine retirement in the 1950s, Molly Dewson ruminated on her place in twentieth-century women's history. During her lifetime she had observed the "slow but steady development" of women, of which her career was but one example. "Yet I expect now and then some young woman might care to contemplate women's slow emergence from family and domestic affairs alone, to public concerns as shown step by step in one person's life. Of course no one life touches more than a tiny part of the social, economic and political field but it is somewhat indicative of the way the generation after the great pioneers applied their principles."[5] The late nineteenth and early twentieth centuries had indeed seen a growing number of women enter the public domain previously reserved for men. Molly Dewson, in her early attempts to forge a role for herself as a social reformer, and in her efforts during the New Deal to increase women's political participation, represented one example of this important transformation in the lives of American women.

Molly Dewson placed herself within a generational framework that helps to explain significant shifts in the history of American women. Identifying herself as a member of the generation that followed the great pioneers who first made a place for themselves in the public sphere, she acknowledged a debt to women such as Jane Addams, Julia Lathrop, Sophonisba Breckinridge, and Florence Kelley for making the path to a public career easier for younger women like herself. Consciously locating herself within a tradition of women in public life, she then proceeded to add another chapter to that story with her long career.

A key element of Dewson's consciousness, and one shared by many women of her generation, was the conviction that women were indeed different from men. Their familial and domestic experiences gave them a different perspective on life. This gender consciousness, which grew directly out of the nineteenth-century concept of separate spheres for the sexes and the rich history of women's religious and reform societies, was a source of great strength and power for women of Molly Dewson's generation.[6] Although this ideological orientation grew out of the conventional stereotype that limited women to the domestic sphere, it meant that gender was a positive element in women's self-definition and encouraged them to collaborate with other women on common causes. This sense of feminist solidarity found perhaps its greatest flowering in women's suffrage and Progressive reform movements in early twentieth-century America.[7]

By 1920, this collective female consciousness was fading. As women's organizations lost momentum in the wake of the suffrage victory, new models of assimilation and integration into male institutions competed for attention. By the 1920s, many young women no longer wanted to be viewed as creatures with special needs and sensibilities: they wanted to be treated as men's equals. Yet women found that the price of attempting to integrate themselves into the male world was high. They lost the power bases they had had in women's settlement houses and in the social reform and women's suffrage movements, which had given them the confidence and the tools, in a society not exactly friendly to women's aspirations, with which to attack the problems of modern industrial life and to protest discrimination against women.

While no broad-based women's movement existed in the period between the struggle for suffrage and the activism of the 1960s, feminism was not necessarily dead. Women like Molly Dewson, whose political consciousness had been formed during the Progressive period but whose careers did not peak until the postsuffrage era, suggest the survival of a feminist impulse in public life after 1920. Dewson's dedication to raising women's issues within the context of the dominant political system represents a strand of mainstream feminism that links the women's suffrage campaign to the revival of feminism as a national issue in the 1960s. The suffragists who belonged to the National American Woman Suffrage Association, the administrators and politicians who participated in the women's network in the New Deal, and the women who founded the National Organization for Women in 1966 all sought to bring women into existing political structures. This strand of liberal feminism stretched from Carrie Chapman Catt to Molly Dewson and Eleanor Roosevelt and eventually to Betty Friedan.

Molly Dewson made enduring contributions to politics as well as to feminism. The style of her activism in the 1930s suggests that women, at least those of her generation, adapted a different approach to power and politics than did men, one which was more issue-oriented, more collaborative, and less concerned with competition and prestige. Molly Dewson became an effective political leader because she learned to play the game by the men's rules while remaining connected to bases of female support in women's voluntary reform organizations and among prominent women in public life. As she worked to increase women's participation in politics, she forged an effective style of feminist activism that allowed her to be both inside and outside the dominant political system.

Dewson had learned the lessons of networking and cooperation early, and this awareness stayed with her for the rest of her life. Later generations of women grew up among different values and priorities which made them less interested in the woman-centered existence that had so enriched Molly Dewson's life. This slackening of gender consciousness was a major factor in the decline of American feminism after 1920. Not until women once again recognized gender as a significant determinant in their lives would feminism emerge as a political and social force in American life. In this still unfolding story, Molly Dewson's values and strategies continue to hold a compelling relevance.

PART I

Progressive Patterns

CHAPTER ONE

A New England Girlhood

"I TOOK my first breath in a sparkling snowy land with lots of elbow room," Molly Dewson recalled with characteristic optimism. Mary Williams Dewson was born on February 18, 1874 in Quincy, Massachusetts, a town which she remembered as "steeped in history." She lived around the corner from the Adams homestead, and as a child watched the aged Charles Francis Adams, ambassador to the Court of St. James's during the Civil War and the son and grandson of American presidents, walk along its garden paths. She worshipped at the First Church of Christ in Quincy, the burial place of John Adams and John Quincy Adams, and visited nearby Merry Mount, the site of one of the earliest settlements in the Massachusetts Bay Colony.[1]

"My home seemed built on a rock of decency and self-respect," she later recalled. "We were not at the mercy of external things."[2] Yet a major economic upheaval, the Panic of 1873, had occurred just a year before Molly was born. Railroads defaulted on their bonds and eighteen thousand businesses collapsed within the next two years. Agricultural prices plummeted, and three million Americans were thrown out of work as steel mills and founderies fell idle. The dislocation and economic confusion created by rapid industrialization in America had little direct impact on Molly Dewson's childhood, however. Only later did she connect the events of the 1870s with the course of her career. As unemployment mounted during the Great Depression of the 1930s, she observed to her good friend Felix Frankfurter, "The situation of the workers has not been so bad since the early seventies. I always marvel why I was so much interested in this problem, but now I understand that I was birthmarked by it."[3]

Molly Dewson's sense of place and personal identity began with family roots that stretched back to the earliest New England settlements. Her mother's family arrived in 1637; her father was descended directly from Samuel Bass, who came to America from England in 1657. Molly's paternal grandfather, Francis Dewson, was an English sea captain in the China trade, as were two of her uncles. On her mother's side, her great-great-grandfather Colonel Joseph Williams earned his military title fighting the Indians and later participated in the Boston Tea Party and served in the General Court of the Commonwealth of Massachusetts. Colonel Joe, as he was called, built the ancestral home in Roxbury which Molly often visited as a child.[4]

The winding, narrow lanes from Quincy to Roxbury that Molly remembered were later widened into six-lane highways, and the old Williams farmhouse was torn down to make room for Boston's Franklin Field. But when Molly's grandfather Francis Williams was born in 1802, Roxbury was a country town. By 1836, five years after his marriage to Mary Ann Hardwick, he had relocated to nearby Quincy, where he converted a famous Quincy landmark known as James Brackett's Tavern into a family home. Francis Williams ran a successful tannery in Quincy; he was the first in a long line of Williams and Dewson men who drew their livelihoods from the leather business. At his death in 1875, he left an estate of a hundred thousand dollars.[5]

Elizabeth Weld Williams, Molly's mother, was born in 1836, the second of Francis and Mary Ann Williams's five children. She was a small yet well-proportioned woman whose hip-length hair was coiled into a thick bun at her neck. She held herself so erect when riding in a buggy that her back never touched the seat. "Her fine, lithe figure, her neat aspect and her lively, handsome face with its clear cut Yankee features" guaranteed her many suitors. One of them was Edward Henry Dewson.[6]

Much less is known of his early life than hers. He was born in Dorchester, Massachusetts, in 1832. Some people called him Ned, others Henry; his daughter later could not remember which was more common. He left school at thirteen and around 1855 entered the leather business with Francis Williams in Boston. One day the elder Williams decided to bring his new business associate home to meet his family in Quincy. Family lore claimed that it was love at first sight for Edward Dewson, but the children could never get their mother to give them her side of the courtship. All she volunteered was that her future husband had proposed while they were driving into Boston for a band concert.

Elizabeth Weld Williams and Edward Henry Dewson were married in Quincy on September 2, 1857. She was twenty-one, he twenty-five. Francis Williams gained not only a son-in-law but a permanent business associate as well. Soon after the wedding, he made E. H. Dewson a full partner in the firm.[7]

The Dewsons began married life in Roxbury, where their first child, Francis Williams, was born in 1859. They subsequently moved to a far larger home in Quincy, a gift from Grandfather Williams. Built in 1836 on fifteen acres of land originally owned by the Adams family, the six-bedroom brown-shingled house was solid and ample, encircled by a wide piazza. The house at 235 Adams Street remained in the Dewson family for the next sixty-five years, and the remaining five children were born and raised there: George Badger (1861), William Inglee (1863), Edward Henry, Jr. (1865), Ellen Reed (1871), and Mary Williams (1874).

The substantial estates that lined Adams Street gave their residents the feeling of living in the country, although they were only several blocks from Quincy Center and a mere twenty-minute ride from downtown Boston on the Old Colony railroad. The writer Henry Adams, who divided his childhood between Beacon Hill and Quincy, captured this contrast: "Town was restraint, law, unity. Country, only seven miles away, was liberty, diversity, outlawry, the endless delight of mere sense impressions given by nature for nothing, and breathed by boys without knowing it."[8] Young girls like Molly Dewson also breathed this air of freedom.

By the time the Dewson family moved to Quincy in 1859, however, the town was undergoing a fundamental transformation that threatened its rural character. The railroad magnate Charles Francis Adams, Jr., whose lavish home on President's Hill was directly across from the Dewsons', traced this change to the growth of the granite industry after 1820: "The silence of the west Quincy Hills was now broken by the sharp ring of the sledge on the drill, and loud blasts told of quarries from which gangs of busy men were taking huge blocks of stone to be carried off on the newly-devised railway, which opened only the year before, [and] was daily examined by curious visitors from far and near." As the old traditions gave way, "Quincy became a species of sleeping apartment, conveniently near to the great city counting-room."[9]

Access to the Boston "counting-rooms" that Charles Francis Adams deplored was especially important for the men in the Dewson and Williams families. By 1850, the thriving commercial and financial hub of Boston had emerged as the leading wholesale leather center in the United States, spurred in large part by the phenomenal growth of the shoe industry. By the 1880s, Massachusetts shoe centers like Lynn produced well over half the shoes sold in the country.[10]

Dewson, Williams and Company were consignment merchants; that is, they sold leather to the boot and shoe industry, which then cut and stitched the pieces into a finished product. The consignment business was characterized by strong seasonal and yearly fluctuations and a fickle market attuned to consumer demands for new styles and fashions. Turnover and business failures were common.

With forty years of trade experience, E. H. Dewson held a respected position in the Boston leather community. This standing was undergirded by an extensive network of family connections within the leather trade. The firm employed several of Francis Williams's sons and the husband of his youngest daughter. For a while Edward Dewson's brother James was their hidebroker in New York. The family connection was strengthened by the two sons, George and William, that Edward Dewson brought into the leather trade with him.[11] There was never any thought, however, of the two Dewson daughters entering the family trade.

Although the leather business provided a steady, indeed ample, living for the Dewsons, family life was disrupted by the periodic illnesses of Molly's father. Apparently Edward Henry Dewson was never a healthy man. When Elizabeth announced their engagement, her friends inquired solicitously, "Is he well enough to marry?" Her new husband avoided conscription into the Quincy Civil War regiment and was not required to furnish a substitute, as was his brother-in-law Stedman Williams. His health took a turn for the worse during the war years, and in 1863 the doctors prescribed a long sea voyage. Shortly after his third son was born, he signed onto a ship captained by his brother James, and they sailed around Cape Horn to San Francisco. Her mother's friends thought she would never see her husband again, but he returned, although his health had not improved.[12]

Edward Dewson's illness was usually described by the family as

neuralgia, but his symptoms suggest neurasthenia, another nervous disease that was frequently diagnosed in the nineteenth century. The medical practitioner George M. Beard coined the term in 1868 to describe
nervous exhaustion or a general weakness of the nervous system. Phy-
sicians speculated that the competitive and aggressive nature of nineteenth-century life was placing enormous demands on nervous systems
of Americans, strains which were causing a dramatic rise in the inci-
dence of this disease.[13]

Molly's father manifested many of the symptoms associated with
neurasthenia, including neuralgia, spinal pain, insomnia, headache,
and chronic indigestion. He was excitable and moody: some days he
would chatter away and crack jokes, but others he would be too de-
pressed to get out of bed. Just as telling were the frequent references to
his general lack of energy and vitality and his inability to withstand
much physical or mental exertion. Often when he came home from
work in Boston, he was so tired that he had to lie quietly on the couch
until suppertime.[14]

The volatile leather business was an unfortunate career choice for
a person characterized by a high-strung sensibility and a general lack of
physical stamina. The patterns of Edward Dewson's illness roughly corresponded to the upturns and downswings of the business economy. In
1893 there was a major economic depression and he suffered a complete
breakdown. As the economy slowly improved after 1893, his health
mended. Luckily for the family, his two sons and other family members
who also worked in the leather business took up the slack, making it
easier for the Dewsons to weather the economic and psychological de-
pressions of the late nineteenth century.

The connection between Edward Dewson's health problems and
the business cycle suggest that neurasthenia had social as well as physical causes.[15] Never in good health, habitually deficient in energy
(which was a character trait thought necessary for growth and prosperity in industrializing America), Edward Dewson always seemed something of a misfit in the highly competitive world of late nineteenth-
century America. His illness was a socially accepted excuse to opt out of
the male mystique of success, rugged individualism, and upward economic mobility that characterized nineteenth-century ideology.

If Molly's father felt ill at ease with male gender roles, her mother
embodied the ideology of nineteenth-century womanhood.[16] Elizabeth
Dewson's entire world revolved around home, family, and religion.
What better image of her than Molly's memory of her mother and sev-

eral other "full-skirted" ladies reading aloud from Louisa May Alcott's *Little Women.*[17]

Much of Mrs. Dewson's time was devoted to uncomplaining care of her sick husband. "Father was not well, times were often unsettled and hard," Molly explained, "so mother found a minimum on which we could live and keep fit and stuck to it. She never spent an unnecessary cent. In the back of her mind she thought any unnecessary expense is just so much more of a burden on father." Molly's mother ministered to her husband's needs without making him feel patronized or burdensome. "Father had to be very careful as to what he ate," Molly remembered. "We never had mince pies, and in those days mince pies were good, for either Father would have to remember his limitations or be tempted to fall. Mother saw to it that there were no opportunities for a fall."[18] Elizabeth Dewson thus resembled the "ministering angel" so often found in nineteenth-century popular fiction.[19]

In spite of her husband's illness, Elizabeth and he had what was by all accounts a mutually satisfying marriage. In their more than forty years together, Molly remembered, "I never heard a cross, disagreeable or impatient word between them. As far as I could see my father was completely satisfied with his wife and although personal relationships were not discussed in those days he conveyed to her without soft words their unbreakable unity." In return, her mother "adored father and [thought that] what he did was right and best."[20]

In many ways, the division of power and responsibility in the Dewson marriage reflected the clearly defined gender roles then prevalent in middle-class America. He, as the head of the household, took on the role of breadwinner and participant in civic and political affairs. She had complete responsibility for the domestic sphere, including supervision of the maid, cook, and hired man as well as the primary care of the children. Contradicting the notion of totally separate spheres for the sexes, however, both husband and wife seem to have derived their primary satisfaction from domesticity and family life.[21]

Religion played an important unifying role for the Dewson family, although it meant different things to different family members. Edward Dewson enhanced his stature as a community leader through the First Church of Christ, the place of Unitarian worship favored by the old families that comprised Quincy's elite.[22] Molly vividly remembered going to this church every Sunday. From her pew she could see the plaques honoring the presidents John Adams and John Quincy Adams and their wives Abigail and Louisa Catherine, who were buried in the church. Molly seems to have been more affected by the architecture and the historical ambience of the church than the weekly sermons. Her Unitarian upbringing reinforced her identification with the New England heritage, but she was never very devout in her youth. This lack of interest in organized religion characterized her adult life as well.

Molly's mother, however, was a "devoutly religious woman" whose Unitarianism was the most important element in her life after her home and family. As president of the Women's Alliance, Elizabeth Dewson prepared the monthly communion service with her daughters Nell and Molly as "her quiet decorous aides." One of the oldest pieces in the communion set was a small silver cup from the late seventeenth century, inscribed with the name of Deacon Samuel Bass, a direct ancestor of Edward Dewson.[23]

The family also shared a love of reading aloud. Edward Dewson read the Bible to his family every day, first thing in the morning during the summer and after supper on cold winter evenings. He also read from favorite Unitarian writers such as William Ellery Channing and Ralph Waldo Emerson or from the pages of *Harper's Magazine*, to which the family had a charter subscription. Far less of an intellectual than her husband, Mrs. Dewson would knit or mend in her favorite Shaker rocking chair as she listened. Molly enjoyed these shared family moments as well: "When I was a very little girl I loved to sit on father's lap, my cheek against the smooth broadcloth of his Prince Albert, and listen to him read aloud. Even if I did not wholly understand I liked the sound of his voice."[24]

Although Molly maintained the family custom of reading aloud for the rest of her life, she was "no bespectacled student." She was a tall and athletic child, skinny but full of energy, who loved to roam outdoors, especially along the Furnace Brook which bordered the Dewsons' property. With four older brothers and approximately forty male cousins and playmates, she had plenty of opportunities for the strenuous activity usually reserved for boys. In short, she was a nineteenth-century tomboy, in spiritual kinship with Jo in Louisa May Alcott's *Little Women*.[25]

She pitched on the boys' softball team in primary school and excelled at golf, but tennis became Molly's favorite sport in her teens. She recounted proudly, "I earned my first A no. 1 tennis racket by carrying milk and by picking currants at two cents a box" for Aunt Mame, her mother's crippled younger sister who lived nearby with her husband, Timothy Reed.[26] A childhood friend, Susan Sharp Adams, described

Molly in a tournament in Wellesley Hills: "You wore a blue serge skirt, a white silk sailor blouse with wide collar, and a red silk four-in-hand tie. Hair parted in the middle and braided in a heavy braid and tied with black ribbon four inches from the krimpy ends. Every time you reached down to pick up a tennis ball on your racquet, the braid flopped front, and you jauntily tossed it back."[27] But such stylish tennis attire was hardly the Dewson norm. Molly cared not one whit about her appearance, and her mother (who was also uninterested in fashion) usually let her be.

The young Molly showed a similar disdain for the usual girls' games. Instead of dolls, she kept an army of paper soldiers ("I knew 'The Boys of Seventy-Six' by heart and refought its battles on mother's floor") and stabled a rocking horse in her mother's closet. "Mother's room was the important part of the house to me," she remembered, "perhaps because of its closet, perhaps because in that sanctuary the noise and confusion of play went unnoticed, perhaps because mother was always there with me." On the few occasions when Molly was naughty, the closet was her "jail" and she stood at the window and made faces at the assembled children mocking her from below.[28]

Throughout her childhood, Molly recalled, the house on Adams Street boasted a "constant stream of brothers and sisters, nephews and nieces, cousins and friends, who came for a week or a month or a summer, and the welcome lasted." "The Dewsons were great huggers," she boasted, "real masters of the art of making you feel desirable and desired."[29] For the rest of her life, she kept in touch with her brothers and sister, their children, grandchildren, and even great-grandchildren through an ever-widening system of family round robins she initiated when she was young.

Yet, when it came to talking about feelings, the family, especially her mother, was not so open. Once, when one of her daughters-in-law was seven months pregnant, Elizabeth Dewson still had not mentioned the future grandchild. The daughter-in-law unburdened herself to Molly, who then asked her mother why she had never said anything. Her mother replied seriously, "She would have to tell me about it first." Obviously such a mother would have had difficulty discussing sexual hygiene or marital relations with her daughters. Perhaps other women relatives, such as dearly loved Aunt Mame, filled the void. In the probable absence of any guidance from their mother, menstruation became a private sisterly topic between Nell and Molly.[30]

By all accounts, Molly Dewson benefited from a happy and secure childhood. As the youngest child, and clearly her father's favorite, she enjoyed freedoms not allowed to older siblings.[31] In fact, the only cloud over her childhood was anxiety about her father's illness. "There were days when he could not bear to have me come near he suffered so from neuralgia," she recalled of her early years. As she matured, she felt guilty when she contrasted her own energy with his sickness and lack of vigor, telling her mother that she wished she could "change insides" with him because she was so strong and he so weak. At times, she even feared that she might be the cause of his illness: "Don't let Father get sick, he always does when I come home, undue excitement," she told her sister when she returned home from Wellesley her freshman year.[32]

Dewson's childhood observations of her father may have influenced her own conduct as an adult. Throughout her life, she exhibited a pattern that mirrored his illnesses. At certain stressful points in her career, she threw herself into projects so completely that she jeopardized her usually robust health. She literally burned out, and then had to retreat to Castine (and Polly Porter) to recover her physical and mental equilibrium. While certainly not a case of neurasthenia, this pattern of strenuous activity followed by rest and recuperation in many ways replicated the rhythm of her father's illness.

Molly Dewson consciously created one false myth about her childhood. Later in life, she repeatedly mentioned the reverses that her father's leather business had faced during her youth and college years; yet her recollections of genteel middle-class poverty were highly exaggerated. To be sure, business fluctuated from year to year, especially after the depression of 1893, but the results of the 1890s downturn were hardly catastrophic. The family let the hired man go and gave up their horse and carriage—sacrifices no doubt, but certainly no threat to their comfortable middle-class lifestyle. Edward Dewson continued to serve on industry and church boards, they staffed their house on Adams Street with two servants, and they paid yearly tuition bills of 350 dollars for their daughter's college education.

This retrospective emphasis on financial insecurity was almost certainly triggered by Molly's acquaintance with some quite wealthy women at Wellesley. And her association with Polly Porter, whose family lifestyle was clearly more lavish than the frugal New England economies practiced by Molly's, no doubt led her to reevaluate her childhood. That she later portrayed her family's temporary financial difficulties in melodramatic terms confirms how little she understood her privileged class background, especially in contrast to the distressed conditions under which a substantial majority of Americans toiled in the late nineteenth century.

But her most compelling reason for creating this myth of poverty was probably the need to justify—to herself and to society—her decision to attend college and seek a professional career. This need reflected in part the ambiguous legacy concerning gender roles that Molly Dewson had received. Many elements in her childhood fostered a sense of confidence, assurance, and self-respect. She was never confined to dolls, dresses, or decorous behavior but instead was encouraged to follow her tomboy urges and roam the Quincy countryside. The love and support of both her parents encouraged her healthy self-esteem. Yet what options or role models did such a confident and emotionally secure girl have in the 1880s and 1890s?

The tradition of strong New England women provided one model to emulate. Molly Dewson grew up in a part of the country where women had always been central to community and religious life. Frances Perkins, a contemporary of Dewson's who would later join her in the Roosevelt administration, celebrated the strong women who had populated her childhood in nearby Worcester: "I had been brought up in a group where the women were very well-treated, very well-advantaged and where they had their own property." She added, "I don't think people realize how much professional and cultural life women had if they wanted it before the days of women suffrage."[33]

Molly Dewson similarly was surrounded by strong New England women who provided her with a model of family life and good works. "None of the women of this type were communicative about their inner life or personal thoughts nor did they pry into yours or care for gossip," Molly recalled, "but you could rely on their doing the right and decent thing and on their being interested and kind, thoughtful, and considerate by nature as well as by conviction. They were comfortable, peaceful women to live beside even with all their energy and activity." These women, Molly asserted, were "the kind of woman that way down deep in my heart I have admired most."[34]

Molly contrasted her mother's life with that of the close family friend Elizabeth Cabot Putnam. Elizabeth Dewson was the archetypal New England wife: "mother of many children, heart of her family, supporter of the church, maintainer of standards, who gave this part of America its quality." Elizabeth Cabot Putnam, familiarly known as Miss Lizzie, was "the Boston spinster aunt full of social work being developed to care for the aftermath of the industrialization of New England," al-

ways mislaying her bonnet as she strode off "with her vigorous determined step to help some young girl in a bad spot." Molly emphasized
that Miss Lizzie was "no unattractive, disappointed woman." She would
have made a grand Boston matron if the Civil War had not robbed her
of suitors; not being a wife and mother, she had simply taken on extra
work for such causes as prison and moral reform.[35]

Although women like her mother and Elizabeth Cabot Putnam offered appealing role models, they had distinct limitations for the young
and ambitious Molly Dewson. It could not have escaped her attention
that, with six children, a sick husband, and a household to run, Elizabeth Dewson had little time for anything but domestic affairs. Molly
had all the energy that her father lacked, and she also had a strong desire to do something useful with her life. Sometime in her adolescence,
she began to realize that perhaps she was not cut out to be the selfless
New England mother and that she probably would never marry.

The alternative model of a spinster aunt dedicated to good works
was in many ways just as problematical to Molly as marriage and family.
Molly did not stand to inherit enough money to allow her to support a
life of charity and good works without being financially dependent on
her family. By the late nineteenth century, moreover, the traditions of
volunteerism and Christian benevolence were giving way to a new emphasis on professionalism and training. Fortuitously, by the 1890s there
were more options for middle-class women than there had been just several decades before. The expansion of collegiate education and professional opportunities for women provided Molly with the means to
support herself if she chose not to marry. On a deeper level, her quest
to gain a college degree and forge a professional career brought Dewson the fulfillment and satisfaction she had seen in the New England
women of her youth, but in a decidedly twentieth-century manner.

CHAPTER TWO

The Education of Molly Dewson

"WHEN I was seventeen, I told my father I 'ached' to know more and wanted to go to college. I had never consciously met a woman college graduate but I had chanced on a Bryn Mawr catalogue."[1] Like many women graduates of her generation, Molly Dewson relied on a moment of epiphany to explain her decision to attend college. Instead of Bryn Mawr in distant Pennsylvania, however, she and her family settled on nearby Wellesley College.

Many aspects of Molly Dewson's adult life had roots in her years at Wellesley. She was an ambitious young woman who arrived on campus determined to make the most of the opportunities there. She self-consciously and deliberately cultivated faculty members and built a strong academic record. She wangled an invitation into one of the college's most prestigious social clubs, used her athletic prowess to consolidate her position as a leader of the class of 1897, and had her first taste of politics when she successfully campaigned for election as senior class president. By the time she graduated, she had demonstrated many of the same leadership qualities that she exhibited later during her career.

The impact of Wellesley College on Dewson's development extended far beyond her academic and extracurricular success on campus. Access to higher education provided her with the professional tools to strike out in new directions different from her Quincy upbringing.

Wellesley gave Molly Dewson her start as a social reformer by opening her mind to a broader understanding of the social and economic problems accompanying America's rapid industrialization. Her determination to show the contributions educated women could make to American culture and society provided the foundation for the feminism that guided her career. Finally, the Wellesley faculty—all women—offered her a model of professional achievement and personal satisfaction that represented an attractive and welcome alternative to the patterns of marriage and family traditionally held out to women. The legacy of Molly Dewson's years at Wellesley testifies to the overarching importance of a college education to women of her generation.

Molly Dewson's childhood provided a supportive backdrop for her successes at Wellesley. Although Edward and Elizabeth Dewson had had little formal education themselves, they provided excellent educational opportunities for all their children. Even though the enlightened pedagogy of Francis Parker had given the Quincy school system a national reputation by the 1870s and 1880s,[2] there was never any question of the Dewson children attending public schools. Two sons prepped at the prestigious Adams Academy in Quincy and the third at English High School in Boston; George Dewson graduated from Harvard in 1883 and Edward Dewson, Jr., from the Massachusetts Institute of Technology two years later. The daughters as well as the sons were encouraged to pursue their education: Nell and Molly were sent to Miss Ireland's on Louisburg Square in Boston, where they attended classes alongside other daughters of the New England business and professional elite.[3]

Catharine Innes Ireland was one of the strong, principled New England women Molly Dewson admired so much. Born in 1838, Ireland first taught history at the private girls' school run by Harvard professor Louis Agassiz and his wife, Elizabeth, in Cambridge. She then taught at Miss Clapp's School, where she befriended the young Alice James, before finally opening her own school in Boston in the 1870s. By the time she retired from teaching in 1893, Ireland had influenced three generations of Boston women.[4]

Although Miss Ireland's offered a demanding curriculum, it was not strictly college preparatory. Molly's older sister, Nell, spent several stimulating years there but never considered continuing her education. Instead, she returned to Quincy for a round of parties and social engagements that she probably hoped would lead to courtship and marriage.

But the years passed and Ellen did not marry. She lived at home and began to teach school in Milton. Not until her early thirties did she finally marry a local widower and establish a home and family of her own.[5]

If Molly had followed Ellen's example, she would have returned to Quincy on graduation from Miss Ireland's at age seventeen and considered the few options available to women, such as marriage or teaching. But those traditional routes held no appeal for her. Unlike her sister, Molly never showed much interest in boys or dating. Instead, inspired by the intellectual excitement she had experienced at Miss Ireland's, she planned to continue her education. Whether she decided to go to college after chancing upon a Bryn Mawr catalogue, as she later claimed, or whether the process was more cumulative is in the end irrelevant.

In the 1890s a young woman's decision to go to college was still a momentous one. Schools such as Wellesley, Vassar, and Smith had been founded a scant twenty years before; the doors of coeducational institutions such as Cornell and the University of Michigan had been open to female undergraduates barely as long. In 1890, only 2.2 percent of American women aged eighteen to twenty-one attended college and less than three thousand women actually received degrees. (Thirteen thousand men received degrees in 1890.) Many people still believed that higher education would "unsex" young women, destroy their general and reproductive health, and make them unfit for their "true" roles as wives and mothers. And, in fact, college women did tend not to marry, or at least to marry at a later age than women with less education.[6]

Unlike feminists such as M. Carey Thomas, who had to battle their fathers for permission to attend college, Molly Dewson met no resistance. Edward Dewson supported women's rights and women's education, and he had no inclination to deny his favorite child her wish for further education.[7] We do not know what kind of discussions took place between father and daughter: did he confess his regret that his formal education was so limited? did they discuss the financial strain paying her tuition might put on the family? had they concluded that Molly probably would not marry and should prepare herself for some useful work? Her father probably did try to deflect Molly's attention away from Bryn Mawr to nearby Wellesley, only an hour's train ride from the love and security of her supportive family.

At seventeen, however, Molly was considered too young to enter Wellesley College, whose average student matriculated at the age of nineteen. On the recommendation of a family friend, she enrolled for two years at Dana Hall, the preparatory school for Wellesley located near its campus. Successful completion of Dana Hall's curriculum of Latin, Greek, mathematics, English literature, French or German, and history exempted students from the entrance examinations required of freshmen.[8]

Dana Hall was shaped by Julia and Sarah Eastman, who set the tone for their school the way Miss Ireland had for hers. Julia Eastman was a writer of children's literature, and her younger sister Sarah had taught history at Wellesley from 1875 until Dana Hall was founded in 1881. When Molly Dewson arrived in 1891, the school enrolled sixty-two boarders and twenty-five day students. The yearly tuition and board was 450 dollars, 100 dollars more than Wellesley's.[9]

Molly Dewson loved Dana Hall. She captioned a picture of Ferry Cottage, where she boarded, "my second home." Her popularity with other students grew steadily, and she was elected junior class president; she also excelled at athletics, introducing basketball to the campus. At Dana Hall, she made a symbolic break from the reigning Republicanism of her family by starting a Cleveland for President Club in 1891. (She supported his stand on free trade.) Dewson maintained her allegiance to the Democratic party for the rest of her life.[10]

The main attraction of Dana Hall was its proximity to Wellesley College. College functions and social events were often open to Dana Hall students, and there was a constant stream of visitors back and forth. This interaction between preparatory school and college no doubt eased Molly's transition to the demanding role of college under-graduate in the 1890s. In many ways, she had the privilege of six years of college instead of four.

Wellesley College had been founded in 1875 by Henry and Pauline Durant to incorporate their religious evangelicism with support for higher education for women. Perhaps the most radical aspect of the experiment was the Durants' commitment to an entirely female professoriate. In its early years, however, Wellesley was more like a seminary than a college. Of the 314 students who enrolled when Wellesley opened its doors in 1875, only 30 passed the stiff entrance exams.[11]

From its tentative beginnings, the college took a major step forward when Alice Freeman, only twenty-six years old, assumed the presidency in 1881. Freeman was a charismatic teacher and administrator. Drawing on her experience as one of the first woman graduates of the University of Michigan, she molded Wellesley into her image of what a woman's college ought to be. She revamped the departmental structure, giving more power to department heads, and she secularized and liberalized the college. One of her lasting contributions was the hiring of outstanding faculty such as Carla Wenckebach, Katharine Lee Bates, Mary Whiton Calkins, and Vida Scudder, scholars who had taken advantage of the new opportunities for graduate training for women in the United States and abroad. This community of educated women shaped the college into the early twentieth century.

Alice Freeman resigned the Wellesley presidency in 1887 to marry the Harvard professor George Palmer, but she did not sever her connections with the college. As an active member of its board of trustees, she hand-picked the next three presidents. During the tenures of Helen Shafer (1887–94), Julia Irvine (1894–99), and Caroline Hazard (1899–1911), many of Freeman's goals were met: the religious requirement for faculty was dropped, as was required domestic work for students; an elective curriculum was introduced, and incompetent faculty purged. Of Wellesley's thirteen full professors in 1890, only six were left by 1900. While such changes were cause for some bitterness in the Wellesley community, the reforms significantly improved the intellectual and social tenor of the college.

Visitors arriving at Wellesley College in its early days entered "the park" (as the campus was then known) through a mile-long drive that led to College Hall. This impressive five-story structure, completed in 1875 in the shape of a papal cross, dominated the three-hundred-acre campus from its perch overlooking Lake Waban. College Hall provided living quarters for 216 women, both students and faculty; dining and social rooms; a library; twenty-eight classrooms; an assembly hall; and most of the college's administrative and departmental offices, as well as laboratories. By the 1890s, several small dormitories and ancillary academic buildings had been added, but almost all the life of the college continued to occur within the confines of College Hall.

When Molly Dewson arrived on campus in September 1893, she settled into a College Hall room with two other freshmen. At first she was a bit homesick, especially one forlorn Sunday just three weeks into the term when she missed a visit from her brother George even though she had skipped chapel to watch for his arrival. Initially she also found the academic work rather overwhelming, confessing her feelings of inadequacy to her sister, Nell: "I guess I might as well have begun teaching last year instead of having all this money spent on me for I am so stupid I never shall learn anything and it will be a miracle if I get thro' mid years." When she survived her midyear examinations ("Allah be praised!" she wrote), her fears of flunking out disappeared. Soon she settled into "a medley of work and play" that characterized the rest of her college years. [12]

Molly Dewson's coursework at Wellesley was a mixture of required courses and electives. Requirements of Bible, French, and Physiology and Hygiene held few rewards: she had nothing more positive to say of Bible at midyear than that they "were just getting the poor wanderers into Canaan." The rhetoric course was more bearable, but only because it was taught by the charismatic English professor Sophie Chantal Hart. The same held true for mathematics, in which Dewson was instructed by Professor Ellen Hayes, Wellesley's most outspoken feminist and no doubt quite a shocking figure to a class of freshmen. She wore short hair and short skirts and was an ardent supporter of women's suffrage and temperance. (By contrast, most Wellesley students sported the standard collegiate dress of a simple shirtwaist blouse and long dark skirt, and few, if any, had bobbed their hair.) Molly was delighted when she caught an error Hayes had made in class: "She owned up beautifully. I have not ceased to smile yet."[13]

While Dewson concentrated her courses in history, economics, and English literature, she did not neglect the sciences. The early women's colleges were noted for their strong science offerings, and she dabbled in geology and mineralogy. During her junior year she took Mary Whiton Calkins's Philosophy 7, one of the first courses in experimental psychology offered in this country. She especially liked her chemistry professor, Charlotte Roberts, who had graduated from Wellesley in 1880; Molly pronounced her "jolly and full of the old boy."[14]

Molly Dewson made a consistently favorable impression on her professors. While not a brilliant thinker or a gifted writer, she stood out in the classroom. (Her class rank cannot be determined because Wellesley students did not receive letter grades or class rankings until 1912.)[15] During her four years at college, she profited from her association with many of the stars on the Wellesley faculty, but two stood out.

Molly Dewson always remembered Professor Elizabeth Kendall of the History Department as the best teacher she ever had—"one of the milestones." She was fascinated with Kendall's "romantic life": the daughter of a diplomat, and an intrepid world traveler, Kendall staked a claim with two other women out West, studied history at Oxford, and received a law degree from Boston University. Molly described her as "the most refined and nicely dressed—with corsets—person of all the faculty," and soon she was reporting home that "of all the things I love, my history takes precedence."[16] After Molly's freshman midyear exam, Professor Kendall asked her if she was planning to go on with history, and Dewson replied that she hoped to make it her specialty. "She said that was right for I show aptitude and ability for it. I could have hugged the dear soul upon the spot, but just got red way up under my hair and fell out of the room." She never forgot the encouragement she had received, and she reciprocated by taking all six courses that Kendall offered.[17]

Elizabeth Kendall's Constitutional History of England, which Dewson took her junior year, was one of the college's most popular courses. The culmination of the first semester's work was a public enact-ment of a Parliamentary debate, staged with robes and wigs. Students took this debate quite seriously: Molly warned her family as she pre-pared her first brief that "you will hear little else this year." The 1896 debate topic was the Disestablishment and Disendowment of the Church of Wales, and Molly played Sir Michael Hicks, complaining, "It makes me about sick for I am on the conservative side."[18] She never mentioned the final outcome of the debate. Probably her side lost, since she rarely missed an opportunity to report a triumph to her family.

The other Wellesley teacher who had enormous impact on Molly Dewson was economics professor Katharine Coman. Coman was one of several turn-of-the-century Wellesley faculty who combined their intel-lectual interests with participation in reform movements. A graduate of the University of Michigan, where she was a close friend of Alice Free-man Palmer, Coman came to Wellesley in 1883 to teach political econ-omy and history; in 1900 she organized a separate department in eco-nomics and sociology. Throughout her tenure at Wellesley, she was active at Denison House, the Boston settlement house which also drew on the energies of Wellesley faculty Emily Greene Balch and Vida Scudder. Admired as one of the college's most stimulating teachers, she used no textbooks and preferred not to lecture. Another innovation was field work.[19]

What a treat it was for Dewson to work with Katharine Coman. Coman approached political economy more through history than the-ory, an orientation that Dewson came to share. Since Coman was on leave in 1895–96, however, Molly missed the chance to take her course on socialism, reputed to be her finest because it was so near to her heart. In Coman's place, the college hired a young doctoral candi-date from Harvard, one of the few male teachers that Dewson had in the otherwise predominantly female community.[20]

If one course stood out during Molly's four years at Wellesley, it was Professor Coman's graduate-level seminar, "Statistical Study of Certain Economic Problems."[21] Dewson and her classmate Grace Dennison were the only students enrolled, and most of the course consisted of independent work and field trips. Molly's final paper on pauperism in New York State made extensive use of statistical tables to discuss the relative advantages of the administration of state poor relief by a board or a single head. The statistical techniques she learned had a clear impact on her later career, she told Professor Coman sixteen years later:

It gave me enough insight into the principles and practice to encourage me to present my work the first years out of college in statistical form. It was approved. Without the incentive and little experience I gained from you I might not have tried to do this. Since then, in whatever field of social work I have been I have found this ability invaluable. . . . I am very grateful to you for this bit of technical training for which I would never have taken the time later.

Dewson was also grateful for the fact that Coman took her students seriously. "It always seemed such grown-up work," she recalled. "Partly, I suppose, because it was closely related to the things of life, and partly because you demanded a more grown-up and thoughtful point of view."[22]

Molly Dewson's course of study at Wellesley demonstrated the value of a liberal arts education as the foundation for a woman's successful professional career. Within Wellesley's broad curriculum, she found ample opportunities to concentrate on her special interests in history, political economy, and sociology. Through her coursework with professors Coman, Kendall, and others, she received a solid grounding in the political and constitutional history of England and the United States. She learned about the social and economic consequences of industrialization and mastered basic political theory as well as the tenets of socialism. Finally, her coursework gave her training in the methods of statistical research, field work, and social investigation.

This liberal arts education also helped Dewson broaden her social vision. Her sheltered upbringing in Quincy had presented few opportunities to observe the difficult living and working conditions of many Americans. At college, she began to confront, at least on an intellectual level, the problems of modern industrial life. Her courses with Kendall, Coman, and Balch opened her eyes to the existence of the disadvantaged and the downtrodden, and her grounding in political history and theory introduced her to a range of strategies for political change.

The development of her social sympathies at Wellesley only went so far, however. She learned about the problems of the poor, but she did not yet have actual contact with them. Despite the influence of professors like Katharine Coman and Vida Scudder, Dewson did not join other student volunteers at Denison House in Boston's South End.[23] She was quite content to remain on the Wellesley campus and deal with these problems on an abstract level. Throughout her career, in fact, she styled herself more as a social researcher than as a settlement worker who lived among the poor.

Her Wellesley education provided Molly Dewson with the direction of her future career, but this was only the most tangible result. Her friendships with women faculty were another dividend, one with important personal implications. Quincy had plenty of New England mothers and spinster aunts, but few women with doctorates. The Wellesley professoriate represented a new kind of late nineteenth-century woman, that is, women who had made a commitment to a professional career. Here was an alternative lifestyle that not only provided intellectual stimulation, but middle-class gentility and gracious living. Such lessons were not lost on impressionable students struggling to plot their personal and professional futures.

The collective lifestyle of the Wellesley College faculty has been skillfully documented by the historian Patricia Palmieri.[24] In the early years of the college, not a single member of the Wellesley faculty was married. When two women lived together in a settled relationship, however, (Katharine Lee Bates and Katharine Coman, and Vida Scudder and Florence Converse were two such pairs), it was called a "Wellesley Marriage."[25] With such arrangements the faculty created a lifestyle that allowed them intellectual stimulation, companionship, friendship, and love, all without marriage or men.

While a student, Molly Dewson had ample opportunities to observe her professors outside the classroom. One night she was invited to play charades in the chemistry lab: "Dr. Roberts and Miss Woolley were as funny as mortals could be. It was a lark seeing that side of the faculty." (In return, she invited her chemistry professor to watch her play in the college tennis tournament.)[26] She also received frequent invitations to the home that professors Katharine Lee Bates and Katharine Coman shared in Wellesley. When Coman traveled abroad with her mother on her sabbatical, Bates asked several of Coman's students over for dessert to hear her letters. About this evening, Molly declared, "Really I had such a good time, so non-collegey."[27]

Not all members of the Wellesley College community, it must be admitted, were so well-liked by Molly. She had little respect, for example, for the college physician who told her roommate to rub vaseline on the end of her nose to help a bad sore throat. She saved her best sarcasm, however, for Dean Margaret Stratton. The crowning incident occurred after Thanksgiving vacation:

Yesterday in chapel old Dean Stratton—the one I told you who giggled behind her fan and is so self-important—gave out some notices and in one of them she said at the 7.30 service Sunday night we will give prayer for Turkey. She was terribly solemn and I don't know how it started—but it was the first service after Thanksgiving and other tho'ts were fresh in our minds—and a surpressed giggle went over the chapel like a flash. My wasn't the old lady mad. She had begun another notice but she stopped short and just glared. I tho't she was going to descend and pulverize some one on the spot. Poor little Ada Belfield in the front row of the Seniors about four feet from the Dean was petrified. That made it funnier—i.e. to see the Dean speechless with wrath —but fearing she would break a blood vessel we stopped.

After some reflection, Molly added: "The question, however, is still unsettled in my mind as to why the prayer for Turkey and not Armenia."[28]

Such notes of irreverence were, however, quite rare in Molly Dewson's letters home. On the whole, she respected and admired the professors and administrators who made up the Wellesley community and enjoyed her encounters with them both inside and outside the classroom. Probably most students did not have as much contact with professors as did the ambitious Miss Dewson: she consciously sought them out, not just for friendship, but for the help they might give her in the future through job leads and letters of recommendation.[29]

Yet it is wrong to see Molly Dewson's friendships with faculty as strictly self-serving. She occasionally buttered up some of her professors, to be sure, but she was not insincere or fawning. She thrived on the intellectual stimulation their classrooms offered and admired their intelligence and personal qualities. As a community of single educated women who combined professional work with satisfying personal lives, the Wellesley College faculty provided important role models for a student who was already disinclined to follow the traditional route of marriage and family.

Molly Dewson's years at college strengthened her ties to her family.[30] So supportive were they of her aspirations that her college experience was practically a family affair. Frequent visits and a steady stream of letters between Quincy and Wellesley kept Molly securely in the family orbit throughout her college years.

Edward Dewson was especially proud of his daughter's accomplishments at Wellesley. When she was having trouble with a required math course her freshman year, he counseled, "I appreciate and fully sympathize with you in the difficulties in Math, but my dear, give them the best that is in you, and . . . if the result seems unfortunate, you will always feel sure of the love and deepest sympathy of your dear Mother and Father, and if successful, their love, admiration, and approval." He also let her know how much he missed the intellectual stimulation of their conversations at home. "But Molly dear come home and talk higher education, and student government," he wrote, " and though I am aware you may say to your self, Father knows but little about such matters, you will go away feeling that Father is no lunatic except on the subject of equal rights for women."[31]

Molly also remained close to her sister, Nell, during her years at college. She often scribbled informal notes to her that were not intended to be shared with the family: less concerned with showing off her ability to write a good letter, such sisterly communication shared news and gossip. One recurring topic was boys—Nell's boyfriends, that is, not Molly's, who never had anything to report in that department.[32] Nell was also a frequent visitor to the Wellesley campus, where she attended parties, watched Molly play in tennis matches, or just met mutual friends. The ease with which noncollegiate sisters participated in campus social activities suggests that the line between women who went to college and those who did not was not yet strictly drawn.

Without Nell, in fact, Molly might not have been able to go to college. By helping out with the household chores—she did all the sewing, including Molly's wardrobe—Nell relieved her younger sister of that duty. Nell's role as the daughter at home was especially important during their father's illnesses, which became increasingly debilitating during Molly's years at Wellesley.

While Molly Dewson kept in close touch with her family, her years away from home gave her a degree of independence rarely available to young women in the 1890s. She approached her extracurricular activities with the same determination that characterized her academic work: this ambitious young woman was out to make a name for herself among her peers just as she did with her professors.

In the 1890s Wellesley's social life took place almost entirely within the college's exclusively female community—there was no running back and forth to Harvard and Yale as later generations of Wellesley students would do. In fact, when the class of 1897 wanted to invite men to the junior prom, the faculty and administration vetoed the proposal as "unladylike."[33] So the women held the party without the men.

Early college women went to great trouble to develop rituals and traditions as a way of conferring legitimacy on their status as pioneers in higher education.[34] One such tradition at Wellesley was Float Day, which featured brightly-costumed crew teams serenading spectators on the shores of Lake Waban. Japanese lanterns, fireworks, and bands completed the atmosphere. During the 1890s as many as six thousand people attended, arriving on special trains from Boston. Molly usually got tickets for her parents, siblings, and various Quincy friends and relatives. Float Day provided a good opportunity to show the wider community that college women were still refined and attractive young ladies despite their intellectual attainments.[35]

Such ceremonies, with their costumes, orations, and pageantry, were quite popular with the students. Each class also produced an annual satirical play. In Molly's senior year, her class's tale centered around two knights and a monastery. The head of the monastery was Signora Julia Della Irvina (representing President Irvine). The Inquisitor-General was Francesca Domina (based on Latin professor Frances Lord). The Prior General of the Order of the Abbreviated Habit stood for Ellen Hayes—"she's our woman's righter." Saint Katerina was the beloved Katharine Lee Bates. And Doctor Carlus, Prior of the Shaven Brothers, was Fraulein Carla Wenckebach, who "wears her hair as well as the rest of her German faculty cut short." Such occasions provided the opportunity to poke some harmless fun at favorite (and not so favorite) faculty.[36]

Other parties, while not officially sanctioned as class events, were equally elaborate, often including dance cards to keep track of (female) partners. To celebrate one girl's birthday, Molly and a group of friends organized a dress ball where "elaborate toilets" were required. "Evy, Edith, and I with two Juniors represented the masculine element. There was no flaw in us, except that my trousers were too tight to sit down."[37] The birthday party was not the only occasion when Molly Dewson dressed up as a man. Later that year, she hurried back from a weekend in Quincy to attend a "Fairy Cotillion." "I am going to wear my dress suit, and Ethel is going to make me wings and I am going to be a dude fairy." Her costume, she boasted, transformed her into quite a "gallant youth" and she was the only one there in regular men's clothing. "In the evening" she reported, "I kept on my suit, and walked with one of the girls to call at Stone Hall. We met several people, but they thought I was a real man, which was all the more amuzing [sic]. I felt rather queer out-of-door in that rig without even a macintosh. . . . We were over the lakeside porch and the fairies draped themselves over the balustrade and me in the most interesting manner."[38]

Molly Dewson saw nothing especially odd about her behavior. The absence of men on campus made it common for women students to dress as men for plays or social gatherings. Dewson, a tall and gangly young woman who never displayed much interest in conventional feminine adornments, was often chosen, or perhaps she volunteered, to play a man's role. Although she had masses of long hair that she braided into a bun, her wire-rimmed pince-nez gave her a rather severe appearance. Never the least bit coquettish and seemingly oblivious to the possibility of romantic involvement with men, she conveyed a certain brusqueness not usually cultivated by young women of her times. In short, she had a forceful personality and felt no qualms about taking the male part.[39]

In Molly's letters home she never mentioned the phenomenon known as "smashing," where two young women formed intense emotional bonds expressed in explicitly passionate language. One description of smashing comes from Vassar in the 1870s: "When a Vassar girl takes a shine to another, she straightway enters upon a regular course of bouquet sending, interspersed with tinted notes, mysterious packages of 'Ridley's Mixed Candies,' locks of hair perhaps, and many other tended tokens, until at last the object of her attentions is captured, the two become inseparable, and the aggressor is considered by her circle of acquaintances as—SMASHED."[40] Although several girls developed crushes on Dewson when she was at Dana Hall, she never seems to have entered into any such relationship at college.[41] She had many close friends at college, but no "particular" friend.

A small group called Phi Sigma, which Molly joined her sophomore year, provided many of these close friends. Phi Sigma and Zeta Alpha were the two literary societies established on campus in 1889; other societies were devoted to politics, the classics, and the arts, and there was also the popular Shakespeare club, which staged plays. Each semester Phi Sigma chose a subject, such as the short story, Dante, or the poetry of Shelley, for its discussion program. Molly was delighted with the topic her junior year—the evils of the industrial system—because it tied in so closely with her coursework in political economy and history. In fact, she probably had a hand in its choice.[42]

Society members wielded a disproportionate influence on campus and collegiate affairs. Like sororities on coeducational campuses, the societies comprised the recognized social elite at Wellesley. Only fifty-four women in Dewson's class, fewer than one-third of the graduating seniors, belonged to the seven societies. Rivalries between different societies, often a factor in elections for class officers, even affected the classroom. When Elizabeth Kendall's Constitutional History class elected speakers for the Parliamentary debate, all eight were society girls, including Molly. "Wasn't it funny," she remarked ingenuously to her brother, for she had just ranked the societies by their social prestige. Zeta Alpha had never counted like Phi Sigma and Shakespeare: "ZA always has had the girls from N.Y. City and you know how girls of the type of Boston and Phil. look to a New Yorker, and of course she preferred that style society. But with the exception of three or four genuine ones among the gay birds they have never counted like Shakes and us."[43]

Molly Dewson was always a bit of a snob, and she was especially status-conscious at Wellesley. She commented pointedly to her mother soon after arriving on campus, "By the way you spell College with a capital C and two E's not an a. Excuse my speaking of it but I thought you might like me to." For the first time in her life, she was exposed to very wealthy girls who had unlimited money to spend on clothes and amusement. Lest her parents think she was squandering money on frivolous amusements, she kept a careful account of her expenditures at school.[44] Molly's lack of cash did not necessarily crimp her social life, however. "Now one of my grandest accomplishments is the cheerful way in which I eat," she reported humorously. "Frequently I am asked to spreads to enliven their general tone." After being treated to a grand dinner of oysters and lobster at a well-known Boston restaurant, she reported, "Nothing like having wealthy friends."[45]

With such attention to money on campus, Molly had realized early that the societies were the key to prestige there. Prospective members were usually tapped at the end of freshman year, but she had been passed over. Overcoming this disappointment, she literally took matters into her own hands. Taking a rarely used route, she applied directly for membership in Phi Sigma her sophomore year and was initiated into the select group in May of 1895. Yet she was always in a bit over her head with this crowd: she never won election to a Phi Sigma office and, unlike the wealthy girls who gave lavish gifts to the society, she had to be careful that her contributions did not strain her modest budget. Nevertheless, she guarded her privileges jealously. When Nell came to visit, she received careful priming from her unctuous little sister: "All the Phi Sigma girls with a pin on you are to be cheerful to."[46]

Molly Dewson also used her athletic prowess to earn the respect of her peers. A natural athlete, she made the most of Wellesley's spacious campus and extensive sports facilities. Women's colleges in the late nineteenth century stressed physical fitness to counter the argument that higher education was detrimental to women's health, and Molly led the kind of strenuous outdoor life that Theodore Roosevelt would have appreciated: rowing before breakfast, skating, sleigh rides, bicycling, golf, tennis, and basketball.[47]

While she loved nothing better than to end the day with a round of basketball, she first had to pass a required physical examination where, she confided in dread to Nell, the physician measured each student "in every conceivable place." She stood 5 feet 8 ½ inches tall and weighed a skinny 133 ¼ pounds. "I felt like a horse, and wanted to show her my teeth and ask her to guess my age," Molly protested sarcastically. It also took her a while to get used to the required gym outfits, about which she was more self-conscious than dressing in men's clothing for parties: "The bloomers are most ample and it feels very queer to go around in them. We wear our skirts over them until we get in the Gym."[48]

Molly's favorite sport at college was tennis. A highly competitive player, she had little trouble winning both her class championship and the all-college tournament each of her four years. She relished these championships because they brought honor to her class, but an added incentive was the prize offered to the winner. One year a Boston sporting goods store put up a Sears tennis racquet; another time the prize was ten dollars in cash. Molly used her winnings to buy books that formed the nucleus of her permanent library. The junior year championship provided her with Stubbs's three-volume *Constitutional History of England*, Stevens's *History of France*, and *The Religious Aspects of Philosophy*; her senior year victory meant a two-volume set of Adam Smith's *The Wealth of Nations* and a nine-volume Browning.[49]

Her only tennis defeat during four years at Wellesley came at the hands of a Radcliffe woman her junior year. Dewson first had to secure permission for the Wellesley team to challenge Radcliffe from President Julia Irvine, who said, "This is the opening wedge of inter-collegiate athletics, isn't it" but laughingly gave her approval. "We want Radcliffe to perceive that we are not boors," Molly remarked tellingly.[50] Wellesley lost three of the four matches before a mob of spectators. "Their champion Miss Humphrey is the best girl player I ever saw," Molly reported to Nell; "they were in grand practice and hard as rocks." All the defeated Wellesley team could do was vow a rematch in the fall.[51]

Her defeat at the hands of Radcliffe notwithstanding, Molly's athletic exploits helped solidify her standing as a class leader: two days after the Radcliffe match, she was elected president of the senior class.[52] For Molly, this election capped four years of active participation in student affairs. While not a top vote-getter in the election for freshman class officers, Dewson had a group of followers who put her name forward on successive ballots. This strategy paid off the next year when she was easily elected sophomore class president, garnering seventy votes to her nearest opponent's eighteen. But Molly turned down that honor in order to leave more time for her studies. (It did not stop her four days later from successfully defending her college tennis championship.) She settled for a spot on the executive committee her junior year. Her main contribution to student government was known as the "Dewson amendment" to the class constitution: the adoption of the Australian or secret ballot for class elections.[53]

When she pushed through the new ballot system, she deliberately excluded the coveted office of class president, who continued to be chosen by open discussion and voting. Even though the class of 1895 took thirty-six ballots to elect their president, Molly never expected to be the focus of a bitter three-week struggle two years later. Her classmate Geneva Crumb saved a ballot in her scrapbook, labeling it "a genuine relic of the famous struggle over '97's senior president."[54]

At its base the fight was between two rival societies. Zeta Alpha members were "breaking their necks" to get Elizabeth Evans in: "Edith Howland has been circulating the worst gossip about me, and another one of the Z.A.s has been letting me have it. My backers are a little hot, but have not slandered Eliz. yet, so my only chance is that the undecided part of the class will get soured on the treatment I'm getting." "Altogether it's a very dirty job and I wish I were well out of it," Molly wrote to her family—but she never really seriously considered withdrawing her name from contention.[55]

Several weeks and numerous ballots later, Elizabeth Evans conceded the election. "They considered themselves beaten and wanted to get out of the field," Molly suspected. The end of the deadlock triggered cheers, serenades, and this timely stanza: "Ninety-seven, Ninety-seven / Buried so long in Lecture Room I / Welcome now to the dew and the sun / Dew-son, see that pun?" Bouquets of flowers arrived in such profusion that Molly's College Hall room resembled a conservatory. Professor Roberts loaned her chemistry beakers to display the flowers, and Molly kept her door open to perfume the hall.[56]

The election brought a letter from her father which must have given her much pleasure. "My precious Molly," he began, "Until you received this honor, I was not aware of how much I desired it for you. . . . To be able to feel that we have won in some measure the respect and love of our associates is one of the greatest prizes in life. It will be with you when all besides fails. You cannot fully appreciate it now, it may take many years, but it will be a great comfort. I feel sure you will try to live up to the ideals that appear before you." Several days later Edward Dewson seemed to compensate for his business troubles by savoring the triumphs of his favorite child. It "relieves a bit of the friction down here in South St. to have you appreciated," he lovingly told his daughter.[57]

The twenty-three-year-old from Quincy, Massachusetts, who had come to college hoping to make her mark certainly felt enormous satisfaction at the respect she had gained during her four years at Wellesley. By graduation, she had amassed honors and tributes for her work in the classroom, on the playing fields, and in the student government. She was not the most brilliant member of the class of 1897 and was certainly far from the most beautiful or wealthy. But she was the one her classmates chose for their most prestigious office.

It would be more than thirty years from Dewson's election as president of the Class of 1897 until her entry into Democratic politics in the late 1920s. Yet her Wellesley classmates had her pegged. The prediction in the 1897 Wellesley classbook, expressed as historical reportage, remains prophetic:

It seems absurd to tell an American audience what became of Molly Dewson; but for the sake of any present who might not know that the famous person of that name belonged originally to '97 (a fact which '97 is likely to enlarge upon), we simply mention that President Dewson of the United States and President Dewson of '97 are one and the same—with allowances, of course, for some years of development. Molly was Belva Lockwood,—a little belated, but still in the ring, —and the campaign which resulted in her election is one of the glories of American history.[58]

Molly Dewson never became a lawyer like Belva Lockwood, nor did she run for political office. But she did become a trusted advisor to President Franklin D. Roosevelt and had a significant impact on the political and reform activities of the New Deal. Forty years later, the class prophecy proved itself not far off the mark.

CHAPTER THREE

A Progressive Apprenticeship

IN a class book published by Wellesley College in 1910, Molly Dewson wrote exuberantly to her fellow classmates: "We used to play at choosing the period in which we would rather have lived. But what time could be more thrilling than our own, when in every city and town are springing up hundreds of sane, alert people to fight under scientific leadership the problems of their community with sympathy and sense?"[1] Dewson thus placed herself squarely within the Progressive reform tradition that animated early twentieth-century America. Coming of age during that period fundamentally shaped the course of her career.

Historians continue to debate the scope and definition of Progressivism, but most agree that during the early twentieth century there was a nationwide efflorescence of reform activity on the municipal, state, and federal levels.[2] Spurred by concern over the consequences of massive immigration, awareness of the terrible working conditions in the nation's factories and shops, and shock at the poverty that haunted urban family life, citizens realized that the old traditions of private charity and benevolence were no longer adequate to meet the problems of modern industrial and urban life. The rapid concentration of economic and political power in a small number of wealthy corporations raised fears of monopoly, while the corruption of many urban political machines was interpreted as an impediment to good government, indeed a threat to democracy. Many turn-of-the-century reformers gravitated toward in-struments of the state—local ordinances and municipal reorganization, state legislation, federal regulation, court action—to redress the wide array of alarming conditions.

Recent strands of Progressive historiography have focused on the roles that business leaders and a new professional elite played in shaping the era's reform agenda. But just as important to the story were the con-tributions of reform-minded middle-class women who injected their so-cial welfare concerns into the political dialogue of the day. During the Progressive era more women participated in public life than ever before. Their increased access to higher education and growing professional ex-pertise, the politicization of the middle-class women's club tradition, and the temperance, settlement house, and suffrage movements pro-pelled women to the center of the public debate over the tactics and goals of Progressive reform. The settlement leaders Jane Addams of Hull House and Lillian Wald of Henry Street, the industrial medicine pioneer Alice Hamilton, and the protective legislation activist Florence Kelley of the National Consumers' League all developed national repu-tations. On a local level, public-spirited women participated in the fer-ment of urban life by arguing that the city was simply an extension of the home and that women's domestic expertise and humanitarian view-point was invaluable in identifying and overcoming the dislocations caused by urbanization and industrialization.

This backdrop of Progressive activism, especially by women, pro-vided the supportive climate in which Molly Dewson began her profes-sional life. In the fifteen years after her graduation from Wellesley in 1897, she laid the foundation for her career as a social reformer. During this apprenticeship, she held three positions: research assistant at the Women's Educational and Industrial Union in Boston, Superintendent of Probation for the Lancaster State Industrial School for Girls, and ex-ecutive secretary of the Massachusetts Commission on the Minimum Wage. Although she spent more time tabulating statistics than inter-acting with the poor, her exposure to the difficulties faced by impover-ished young women fundamentally reoriented Dewson's life away from an individual casework approach to poverty and toward ameliorating such conditions through state intervention. Many of the causes that she worked on during her apprenticeship, such as the minimum wage and protective legislation for working women, remained her primary focus well past the New Deal.

These fifteen years were also an important period of maturation for

Molly Dewson. Her new style of dress reflected her widening professional responsibilities: having abandoned the shirtwaist uniform of her college days, she now dressed in the floor-length dark skirts, long, tailored suit jackets, and plain blouses favored by the professional women of the day. The self-confidence—bordering on cockiness—that had served her well in childhood and adolescence occasionally proved a liability in the professional realm. "No one with so strong a personality as Miss Dewson's can help being,—like a flame or a bright light—felt by others," commented one of her coworkers in 1903. "It will necessarily be years before Miss Dewson can so fully control her energies as to be perfectly sympathetic and perfectly absorbent of other's individuality."[3]

Here the help of two women, Elizabeth Glendower Evans and Elizabeth Cabot Putnam, proved crucial. Realizing Molly's special talents, they encouraged her while at the same time trying to polish her rough edges. "We must not clip her wings too close,—must not wound her unjustly," Putnam admonished Evans. "It is the coming man and the coming woman whom we want to put forward, as you have Miss Dewson." Molly's two early mentors, both strong women in their own right, helped the headstrong young woman develop an effective personal and professional style.[4]

The Boston reformer Elizabeth Glendower Evans offered Molly Dewson her first job. Boston's Women's Educational and Industrial Union (WEIU) had become interested in why young female workers preferred shop and factory employment to domestic service, and Evans contacted Wellesley College to see whether a prospective graduate who had specialized in economics would be interested in conducting a study. Professor Katharine Coman recommended Molly Dewson as the most highly qualified. Molly met Evans in the main reception room of College Hall one early June morning in 1897 and immediately accepted the position.[5]

The WEIU offer ended a job search that had consumed much of Dewson's senior year. Her family's financial situation was deteriorating because of her father's failing health (Edward Dewson died in 1898), and she had to find a job. Teaching was the obvious route for most college women of her generation, but it held little appeal for Molly. She unenthusiastically prepared for it, however, by taking (along with two-thirds of her senior class) Professor Carla Wenckebach's course on pedagogy and then signing up with a placement agency that handled teaching positions.[6] She interviewed for several positions, including one at Milwaukee-Downer College for Women in Wisconsin. Though

Dewson went eagerly to her Milwaukee interview, her enthusiasm quickly dimmed. "The building is barely standing, the work scarcely up to Sophomore year at college and the place imbued with a tremendous religious fervor—at which I groan."[7]

Not only did Evans's job offer save Molly Dewson from exile in Milwaukee, but it marked the beginning of a significant friendship which lasted until Evans's death in 1937. Their fifteen years of most active association began with Dewson's employment at the WEIU from 1897 to 1900. It continued at the State Industrial School for Girls, of which Evans was trustee, and on the Minimum Wage Commission in 1911–12, where Dewson served as Evans's trusted lieutenant. She always remained grateful to Evans for those "busy happy early days when you were training me for life."[8]

Evans's upbringing hardly predestined her for the causes she embraced in her long career. Born in 1856, her childhood was shaped by her father's early death, after which her family lived with her relative William Howard Gardiner, a prominent and wealthy Bostonian. She was educated in private schools. Elizabeth met Glendower Evans in 1877, and they married in 1882. They had only four years together, however, and no children, before his death in 1886. From then on, she called herself Elizabeth Glendower Evans in his memory.

Seeking useful work after her husband's death (a substantial inheritance freed her from the necessity of paid employment), Evans turned to family friend Dr. Charles Putnam, who suggested she become a trustee of the State Industrial School for Boys and Girls, as was his sister Elizabeth Cabot Putnam. Together Putnam and Evans brought the latest progressive techniques for juvenile rehabilitation to the Massachusetts penal system. Later Elizabeth Glendower Evans led the Massachusetts fight for the minimum wage in 1911 and 1912. She was also active in labor struggles, the fight for women's suffrage, and the cause with which her name is most widely associated, the Sacco and Vanzetti case.[9]

Molly Dewson was lucky to have such a well-connected mentor in her early years. Although Evans later observed that Dewson had "the best mind I think I ever encountered and admirable political judgment,"[10] when they first met, Molly had no experience in real-world employment or politics. Sensing Molly's great potential, over the next fifteen years Evans actively steered opportunities in the direction of her young protégé, chances that might not have come Molly's way without Evans's ever-watchful intercession. The attention Evans paid to this young woman's career confirms the importance of mentoring to women's professional achievement.[11]

Dewson was also fortunate that her first job was with the WEIU, a worthy introduction to the tradition of women's voluntary associations that would shape and nurture her career. The WEIU had been founded in 1877 "to increase fellowship among women in order to promote the best practical means of securing their educational, industrial and social advancement." Started by forty-two women, its membership had grown to thirteen hundred by the 1890s. While the WEIU hoped to appeal to women of all classes and backgrounds, the well-to-do used its services and facilities more often than did poor women. By the 1890s, the WEIU (usually referred to simply as the Union) had moved into headquarters at 264 Boylston Street.[12]

The Union combined the social functions of a women's club with activism in the expanding field of civic and municipal reform. The Committee on Domestic Reform that hired Molly Dewson had been formed in November 1896 by Elizabeth Glendower Evans, Alice Goldmark Brandeis, and the labor and settlement worker Mary Kenney O'Sullivan. This group had originally planned to mount a general investigation of women's labor conditions, but after consulting with the lawyer Louis Brandeis (Alice's husband), they chose to concentrate their attention on domestic service. The initial goal of the Domestic Reform League was to interest women in domestic work, which was chronically undersupplied, as an alternative to work in shops and factories, where there was a labor glut and working conditions were poor. Obviously self-interest was involved on the part of the WEIU reformers, many of whom no doubt grouped themselves among the legions of middle-class housewives who voiced the perennial complaint that "good help is hard to find." At the same time, they believed that young women would be better off learning domestic skills in other (that is, middle-class) women's homes than on their own facing the temptations of modern urban life.

To implement their reform plans, the committee hired an agent in early 1897 to contact women workers directly and offer them positions in service, primarily with suburban housewives recommended by local ministers and women's clubs. Working women displayed little interest in such offers, and only one factory worker was satisfactorily converted into a domestic servant. The committee's work stalled in frustration.[13] At this point Elizabeth Glendower Evans visited the Wellesley campus and hired Molly Dewson to undertake an investigation of the factory women's reticence.[14] Reporting for work on August 23, 1897, the newest WEIU staff member approached her assignment for the Domestic Reform League as if she were still in Katharine Coman's graduate economics seminar. She talked to employers in manufacturing establishments and retail shops about what working women expected from their jobs. She contacted 216 shop and factory employees for individual interviews. Then she tabulated the material, using a schedule prepared by the Massachusetts Bureau of Statistics of Labor. The conclusions were strikingly uniform: young women liked housework only if they were doing it for themselves; they hated the long hours, the isolation, and the lack of independence that went with employment in another woman's household. Domestic service was thus considered a last resort by turn-of-the-century working women.[15]

Dewson's investigations of domestic service were published in the *Massachusetts Labor Bulletin*.[16] These reports display her mastery of the statistical analysis she had studied at Wellesley and confirm an observation she later made to her New Deal colleague Lorena Hickok: "I always preferred figures to adjectives." Despite her dislike of adjectives, her ability to combine statistical material with descriptive narrative became one of Dewson's strongest proselytizing weapons throughout her career.[17]

Orientation toward the mistresses rather than the maids mirrored another ongoing WEIU project in which Molly Dewson participated: the School of Housekeeping, an early manifestation of the home economics movement. Originally established in 1897 by the WEIU, the School of Housekeeping was taken over by the newly founded Simmons College in 1902. Conceived to study both the theoretical basis and practical applications of the science of housekeeping, the undertaking reflected the high value that Progressive reformers placed on the home.

The school optimistically directed its efforts at both middle-class housewives and working-class women, but its attempts to interest potential domestic servants in a five-month training course met with the same lack of success that had befallen the recruitment efforts of the Domestic Reform League. Despite free tuition, domestic servants had little incentive to complete the arduous program since any woman, trained or not, could get a job in service. Far more successful was the School of Housekeeping's program to train the employers, that is, housewives. The curriculum included courses on household sanitation, chemistry of foods, home economics, home sociology, house architecture, and principles of housework, marketing, and sewing. Tuition was fifty dollars, and the only other requirement was a knowledge of general chemistry.[18]

A distinguished associate of the school in its early days was Ellen Swallow Richards, who served as a lecturer on the chemistry of foods and household management. In 1870 Richards was the first woman to be admitted to the Massachusetts Institute of Technology; opening opportunities for women in science remained a special focus throughout her life. After 1890, much of her energy went into developing the field of home economics.[19]

It was Richards who approached Molly Dewson in 1898 about teaching a course on household economics at the School of Housekeeping. Dewson asked what books would be useful for the course, and Richards replied that there was only one: *Domestic Service* (1890) by Vassar professor Lucy Salmon. Since there was so little material available, Molly decided to write her own text. Looking ahead several years, she called it *The Twentieth Century Expense Book*. The book, with the copyright in Dewson's name and including a foreword by Ellen Richards, was published in 1898 and eventually went through three editions.[20]

The Twentieth Century Expense Book was not really a book but an annotated ledger for keeping track of household expenses. Dewson later remarked that she was bored with people who complained of the high cost of living; thus, her ledger contained the usual items in a budget, such as housing, food, and clothing, as well as a section she called "The Higher Life." She broke this down into "mental" (education of children, books, magazines, lectures), "moral" (church and charity), "aesthetic" (music, art, flowers), "physical" (athletics, sports, Turkish baths, and hairdressers), and "social" (theater, clubs, amusements, travel) categories. The final section, whimsically entitled "Fines for Disobeying Nature's Law," included physician's fees, medicine, and dentistry. "The Old Bostonians rather enjoyed this section," she later recalled, "but they were most highly entertained because I did not have a section for bearing and raising babies."[21] In an otherwise comprehensive budget for household management, the omission of entries for childrearing costs was, for a single woman still of a marriageable age, a rather revealing slip.

Dewson always thought *The Twentieth Century Expense Book* was a "rare bit," and there remains something rather ironic in this twenty-five-year-old unmarried college graduate who had never run a home of her own teaching other women how to do it.[22] So, while students kept their accounts, Dewson plotted the expenditures of her mother's household in Quincy, where she was still living. She found two things of interest. The Quincy ledger invariable listed more guests than those of her students, primarily because the Adams Street residence was often full of relatives or visiting Unitarian ministers. She also noted that, in three years of keeping accounts, her mother's expenditures for food, service, and maintenance never varied by more than ten dollars a year, no matter how many visitors she entertained or who was living at home. Elizabeth Dewson had determined the standard of living that family circumstances could support and stuck to it. If only her students could do the same, Molly must often have thought.[23]

The three years that Dewson spent with the Domestic Reform League and the School of Housekeeping were formative ones. The WEIU introduced her to many of the causes to which she devoted the rest of her career and gave her her first experience with a voluntary organization dominated by women. Her work at the Union also exposed her in a limited way to an aspect of modern life—poverty—that she had only read about at Wellesley. Yet her exposure was still limited compared with that of college-educated women who chose to live in the settlement houses that dotted the nation's slums during the Progressive era. At the WEIU, Molly Dewson remained primarily a researcher, not a participant, although her work there did serve as a transition between college and her next job as a probation officer for delinquent girls. Once again, Elizabeth Glendower Evans was instrumental in lining up this new challenge for her talented protégé.

The Massachusetts State Industrial School for Girls at Lancaster, with which Molly Dewson was associated between 1900 and 1911, was founded in 1856. It was the first reform school for girls in the United States. The Lancaster school was not a prison, or at least it was not conceived as one. Drawing on a long tradition of protective and rescue work by women's religious and benevolent groups, its purpose was to give another chance to young women who had made "false starts" during adolescence. The school was located in the rural countryside between Boston and Worcester, in a deliberate attempt to remove these young women from the temptations of city life. Girls could be sent to Lancaster as early as age seven, but the average age of commitment was closer to fifteen. Most girls were committed by their parents, either for "stubbornness" (a term that covered a variety of misdeeds) or for "tendencies toward lewd or immoral conduct." The root cause of their problems, however, was invariably the terrible poverty that afflicted their families. The historian Barbara Brenzel has aptly called these young women "daughters of the state."[24]

From its beginning in 1856, the state industrial school pursued a two-stage plan for rehabilitating girls. Upon being committed, a young woman was sent to Lancaster for instruction in housekeeping and domestic arts. At age sixteen or seventeen, most girls were placed with a family, for whom they worked for wages while remaining under the supervision of the state. Such training was intended to adapt a girl for the station in life to which she was encouraged to aspire: a servant in a simple household, and eventually a wife and mother in a humble home of her own. It was hoped that by the age of twenty-one the girl would have outgrown her turbulent youth and settled down as a respectable married member of the community.

It was the second, probationary stage of the Lancaster program in which Molly Dewson became involved. When Elizabeth Cabot Putnam discovered that young women placed out from Lancaster were supervised by male agents from the State Board of Charity, she organized a corps of women volunteers to act as auxiliary visitors. Throughout the 1880s and 1890s, these women expanded their responsibilities, but they still lacked official status. Board members Evans and Putnam agreed that Dewson was the perfect person to oversee the establishment of a permanent women's probation department separate from the State Board of Charity.[25]

When Dewson joined the Lancaster staff in 1900, the entire probation department was contained in a tiny basement room at 63 Marlborough Street in Boston, which was provided rent-free by Putnam's brother Charles, a Boston physician. After Dewson's promotion in 1904 to the position of superintendent of probation and parole, a title which reflected the permanent reorganization of the department, the operation moved into more spacious quarters at 198 Dartmouth Street.[26] Under Dewson's tenure, the number of paid visitors grew from two in 1900 to eleven in 1910, all covered by civil service and earning between six hundred and one thousand dollars a year. At the same time, the reliance on volunteer visitors decreased. Another manifestation of the growing professionalization of the parole operation was the appearance of interns from the newly opened Boston School for Social Workers in 1908.[27]

The superintendent of probation position was a quite impressive one for a woman social worker just several years out of college to hold. At a time when government employment was still something of a nov-

elty for women, Molly Dewson landed a responsible state position with
excellent long-term prospects. An additional bonus was a substantial
salary increase.[28] But probably most appealing to Molly was how the
job fit her still untested image of herself as a college-trained social
worker: "The social worker helps make life normal where it is sadly out
of joint. . . . The joy and the pith of social work lies in this personal
contact, the following through of individual lives."[29] She welcomed
the challenge to test her philosophy in action.

In many ways, however, Dewson functioned more as a bureaucrat
and administrator than as a caseworker. One of her primary responsibilities was to gather statistical material for yearly reports to the trustees on
the three to four hundred girls who were typically under her charge.
Such information was useful not only for making decisions on the future
of individual girls but for identifying trends and patterns such as parents'
ethnicity and relationships between causes of commitment and age.
Molly Dewson the social scientist was intrigued by this large data base:
"My warm interest in getting the girls started in a reasonable life never
prevented me from analyzing and registering statistically the results of
our work."[30]

An individualized approach, which took into account each girl's
personality, family situation, background, and potential, was the hallmark of Molly Dewson's approach to delinquency. The visitor from the
probation department supplied "the keystone to the arch." Superintendent Dewson knew exactly the kind of visitor she wanted: practical yet
idealistic and imbued with the "mothering spirit." In staff meetings and
training sessions, Dewson emphasized that there were no rigid rules
about the extent of visitor's roles. Sometimes a girl might not need supervision for several months; during a crisis, she might need to be seen
every day. Anything from a call at the office to an hour in an art museum, a trip to the girl's home, or help with job hunting counted as a
visit. What mattered most was personal attention.[31]

As superintendent of probation, Molly Dewson imparted to her
staff a constellation of values and attitudes about gender, heredity, and
class that were shared by many Progressive reformers and social workers
at the time. Among these was the antagonism, often loosely disguised
as paternalism, that Dewson displayed towards girls classified as mentally defective or feebleminded. "A striking proportion of the girls in
industrial schools and prisons are high grade feebleminded girls, who
do badly because they are defective, and not because they are vicious,"
she told her Wellesley classmates. Such women were not considered

suitable prospects for rehabilitation, and in effect Dewson simply wrote them off: "For them the expensive training of an industrial school is not warranted. They are a clog in the wheels." Permanent institutional care, she felt, was the "only humane solution."[32]

Dewson's obsession with "feeblemindedness" among the Lancaster girls reflected the strength of eugenics, nativism, and anti-immigrant prejudice in later nineteenth- and early twentieth-century scientific and intellectual thought.[33] The eugenics movement promulgated a belief that both mental and physical traits were hereditary, warning that unless checked, future generations with supposed inherited deficiencies would pollute and overwhelm the old American stock. Illegitimate children were very much an issue in girls' reform schools, and such racist diatribes increased the paranoia. Since, in Dewson's view, feebleminded girls were "born to be victims if exposed to temptation," she felt that placing them under permanent custodial care was necessary to save the state "great expense from the breeding of defective and diseased children."[34] While Dewson no doubt believed that her concern for these women was both sincere and scientific, one may suspect that some girls were labeled feebleminded primarily because they proved difficult to rehabilitate. By writing off the most recalcitrant cases, Dewson and her staff could have inflated their official success rates.[35]

Dewson's position as the first superintendent of parole at the nation's oldest reform school for girls guaranteed her an entree into Progressive reform circles. In 1908, the publication of "Feeblemindedness and Juvenile Delinquency: A Study from Experiences" (coauthored with Elizabeth Glendower Evans) in the influential journal *Charities and the Commons* further enhanced Dewson's growing professional reputation. She was invited to give lectures about the Lancaster probation experiments to audiences across the country, and she shared her experiences at meetings of the National Conference on Charities and Correction in St. Louis, Boston, and Cincinnati. Most thrilling was an invitation to speak at Chicago's School of Public Administration, where she had the chance to stay at Hull House.[36]

These widening contacts with a nationwide network of Progressive reformers brought Dewson several job offers. The state of Kentucky approached her about reorganizing their parole department. Louis Brandeis wanted her to become the executive director of a project to provide financial security for retired workers. In an entirely different field, she was even, for a time, considered for a deanship at Radcliffe College.[37]

A challenging possibility surfaced in 1911. Florence Kelley, the general secretary of the National Consumers' League and one of the Progressive era's most influential women leaders, had heard about Dewson from her friend Elizabeth Glendower Evans. Kelley came to Boston to urge Evans's young protégé to put her name in for a position on the staff of the commission set up to investigate the Triangle Shirtwaist fire of March 25, 1911, in which 146 working women were killed when they were unable to escape from a burning factory because its owners had bolted shut the emergency exits. Dewson decided not to apply for the position because she did not want to leave Boston. In one of those links that would connect the lives of this Progressive generation of women reformers, the job went instead to Frances Perkins.[38]

Around the time of Florence Kelley's inquiry, Dewson received an offer in Boston which she did not need to refuse. This new position, as executive secretary of the Massachusetts commission set up to investigate the minimum wage, came once again through the intercession of Elizabeth Glendower Evans.

To Americans now thoroughly accustomed to the guarantees of the welfare state, it is difficult to imagine how controversial the minimum wage seemed in the early twentieth century. At that time, the federal government did almost nothing to protect the economic and social welfare of American citizens; the few attempts by states to regulate working conditions were usually struck down by the courts as an unconstitutional restraint of trade and the freedom of contract. In an age still philosophically committed to laissez-faire individualism and the Horatio Alger ethic of hard work as the ticket to upward social mobility, all workers, male or female, had to make it on their own.[39]

The minimum wage was a comparatively new approach to alleviating the appalling conditions of industrial life and urban poverty. Australia and New Zealand set up the first minimum wage boards in the 1890s, and England enacted a similar law in 1909, but the United States remained for a time untouched by these developments. Then, in 1908, Florence Kelley visited Beatrice Webb, one of the proponents of minimum wage legislation in England, and learned about pending legislation in other European countries. Kelley was determined to make the minimum wage—or "living wage," as it was then often called—a high priority of the National Consumers' League. Reformers were heartened when the Supreme Court upheld the regulation of the hours of female laundry workers in the pathbreaking case of *Muller v. Oregon* (1908); they hoped that acceptance of a minimum wage would be the next step in improving conditions for working women and that this protection would eventually be extended to male workers as well.[40]

The minimum wage movement came to Boston through the combined efforts of Florence Kelley, Elizabeth Glendower Evans, and the Boston Women's Trade Union League. In October 1910, the Boston Women's Trade Union League (WTUL) called a meeting on the working conditions of the 350,000 women employed in the Commonwealth of Massachusetts. A British Member of Parliament described the workings of the new English law, and Florence Kelley outlined the efforts to establish a minimum wage law in this country. The WTUL membership was so excited about this new approach to the problems of low wages and urban poverty that it immediately resolved to introduce a minimum wage bill into the state legislature in 1911.[41]

The politics were not quite so simple. There was strong opposition to the minimum wage in Massachusetts, and the political leadership in the legislature would only go so far as to create a commission to look into the question. The investigatory body, required to include one woman as well as representatives of labor and management, was instructed to report its findings by January 1912. The legislative leadership no doubt saw this as a stalling technique; Elizabeth Glendower Evans, the woman selected for the panel, had other ideas.[42]

One of her first actions was to raise several thousand dollars from public-spirited citizens to augment the legislature's stingy appropriation of two thousand dollars for the six-month fact-finding commission. Her next step was to convince Molly Dewson to take a leave of absence to become the commission's executive secretary. Finally, since the appropriation was too small to cover rental of office space, she lent her Beacon Hill townhouse to the commission staff for six months, reserving for herself only the library and one bedroom. Her right-hand woman Molly Dewson contrasted the frantic pace of the commission's operation with its genteel surroundings: "We swarmed like locusts over every available inch, resigning the dining room table only long enough for her cook, the president of the union of domestic servants, to serve every one luncheon. How well I remember the piles of cold corned beef and kidney beans we seasoned with shop talk!" "Working like beavers," they met the mid-January deadline.[43]

The 1905 state census listed 380,675 gainfully employed women in Massachusetts, obviously too large a sample for a six-month survey. Therefore, Dewson and her staff of ten researchers decided to restrict their study to the four occupations which employed the largest number of women workers in the Bay State. For the cotton textile industry, the commission drew on material in the recently published federal study of female and child labor. The commission also scrutinized women workers in the confectionary industry, retail stores, and laundries. In "public-spirited cooperation," factories opened their books to researchers —the first time payrolls were made available to outsiders, Dewson believed. A total of 6,900 individual wage schedules were examined, and personal data were gathered through interviews and other sources for 4,672 additional women workers. When the material on cotton workers was included, the commission had information on 15,728 women wage earners in Massachusetts.[44]

The overwhelming conclusion was that pitifully low wages prevailed for women workers in early twentieth-century Massachusetts and, by extension, throughout the rest of the country. More than 65 percent of candy workers, 29 percent of saleswomen, 41 percent of laundry workers, and 38 percent of textile cotton workers earned less than six dollars a week. Even though the Massachusetts commission did not cite an absolute minimum wage, a 1915 study called eight dollars a week the bare minimum necessary for subsistence for women workers in urban areas.[45]

The final report contained enough tables and charts to overwhelm the most numerically oriented reader, but Dewson attempted to present the material in human terms wherever appropriate. Following a device that she had perfected at the WEIU and the parole board, she supplied vignettes of women at work, like the story of a bundle girl named Annie. The victim of sporadic employment, low wages, and the sudden deaths of several family members in industrial accidents, Annie cried bitterly when Dewson questioned her about her life: "But you know, no girl *can* live on $6 a week, let alone the $2.50 which was all I had when I first had to support myself. No girl *can* get by on that. And it's awfully lonely without any of your own people."[46]

Despite the dramatic impact of this report, those who favored the proposed minimum wage law still had to overcome widespread antipathy to government interference in the workplace, a philosophy which was especially strong in the conservative business and social climate of Massachusetts. When a bill modeled on the commission's recommendations was introduced, it was denounced as "socialistic, as revolutionary, as subversive of the conservative traditions of the Commonwealth and as fatal to the continuance of our industries." It languished in committee. What finally broke the logjam were the major labor upheavals of

1912, especially the three-month textile strike in Lawrence led by the
Industrial Workers of the World (familiarly known as the Wobblies).
The specter, so close to home, of class conflict spurred on by radicals
pushed the Massachusetts legislature to enact a compromise minimum
wage measure in the hope of avoiding future labor strife.[47]

The 1912 Massachusetts law, the first minimum wage in the
United States, established a permanent three-member commission with
authority to investigate women's wages on an industry-by-industry basis and to recommend acceptable pay levels. The law only applied to
women workers and children under eighteen; the hostility to regulatory
labor legislation was still so strong that no one dared to include men in
the coverage. Nor were its recommendations legally binding. Since the
commission lacked the power to compel compliance, enforcement depended on an educated public's willingness to force employers to follow
the suggested wage guidelines.[48]

While the noncompulsory aspect of the Massachusetts bill was a
disappointment, reformers nevertheless saw this law as a great advance
in social legislation. Eight other states enacted minimum wage legislation in 1913, and by 1923 fourteen states had such laws on their books.
Most of them granted their commissions legal authority to set manda-
tory minimum wage levels for women.[49]

In the wake of the passage of the minimum wage law, Molly Dewson found herself at an important crossroad in her professional career.
She showed little inclination to return to her job as Lancaster's superintendent of probation, from which she was technically on leave. She
had been working for the Commonwealth of Massachusetts for almost
twelve years, longer than she would ever stay in any job again. During
her tenure with the Lancaster board, she had established her department on a firm foundation and infused her workers with the spirit to
tackle a difficult job. Now that the operation was running smoothly,
she felt less challenge in that work.

In 1912, she was asked to become the executive secretary of the
permanent Massachusetts Commission on the Minimum Wage, a job
offer which would have provided her with a perfect excuse not to return
to Lancaster. But she turned this job down, citing her mother's declining health.[50] Another factor no doubt was Dewson's recognition that
the minimum wage position was not well suited to her personality and
administrative style. She had flourished in the hectic excitement sur-
rounding the deadline for submitting the legislative report; the routine

administration of a noncompulsory minimum wage bill would likely
have proved far less stimulating for her.

Molly Dewson's goal-oriented personality would not allow her to
be confined for long to a government bureaucracy or indeed to any
single organization. Throughout her career, she enjoyed tasks in their
early and formative stages: she loved the excitement of starting from
scratch, of fighting an uphill battle for a cause she believed in. Once
the problem was solved or the challenge lost in routine administration
or a maze of bureaucratic regulations, it was time to move on. She followed this pattern not only at Lancaster and with the minimum wage
commission, but under Florence Kelley at the National Consumers'
League in the 1920s and at the Women's Division of the Democratic
National Committee during the New Deal.

The events of 1911–12 marked a critical turning point in Molly
Dewson's career. After a decade of dealing with delinquent girls on a
case-by-case basis, she had grown increasingly frustrated by larger social
problems, such as poverty, disease, low wages, and poor working conditions, over which she had no control. She could help a girl gain confidence, but pride and self-esteem could not feed a hungry stomach.

Assisting in the passage of legislation like Massachusetts's minimum wage statute offered a compelling alternative to dealing with social problems on an individual basis. The enactment of a minimum
wage for women could potentially guarantee women workers a wage
they could live on and thereby break the cycle of poverty that ruled
their lives. And a minimum wage law could reach more than 350,000
women, not just the 300–400 girls she supervised at Lancaster. From
1912 on, Dewson invariably looked to the state and federal governments to enact legislation to correct the glaring social ills she saw all
around her.[51] This fundamental reorientation of her philosophy away
from social work and toward government intervention was the most significant lesson she learned during her fifteen-year apprenticeship. Not
coincidentally, this insight set her on the road that would lead eventually to Franklin Delano Roosevelt and the social welfare legislation of
the New Deal.

CHAPTER FOUR

Polly

"**I** MAY not always have been considered the most conservative member of '97, but I have qualified now," Molly Dewson reported to her Wellesley classmates in 1910. "I am still living with my mother in the house where I was born, and I am working for the same employer who interviewed me in the College Hall reception room in 1897."[1] Was this dutiful daughter living at home the same woman who had been proving her professional competence in the widening social welfare networks of Progressive America? These two images are not mutually exclusive. For many college graduates, work and independence, on the one hand, and continuing ties to family and kin, on the other, were not irrevocably opposed. In fact, a supportive family and home life could provide the emotional and physical base for the transition from college to career.[2]

Molly Dewson never doubted that she would live at home after college if, as she hoped, she found employment in the Boston area. One of her primary reasons for working was to replenish her family's finances after the expense of her college education. She would have been foolish to squander her tiny salary from the WEIU on an apartment in the city—and it would not have been considered respectable for a young single woman like herself to live alone there. Had she left her family, she would most likely have chosen a settlement house like Denison House in Boston's South End, where she could have lived with like-minded social reformers in a setting reminiscent of a college dormitory. Yet familial duties and emotional claims—especially the imminent death of her father and, afterward, the need to watch over her widowed mother—pulled her home to Quincy in 1897. She did not leave the family home until she was thirty-eight.

Elizabeth Dewson remained vigorous and alert. "Until she was in her seventies she never walked upstairs but always ran," Molly bragged. The Dewson children gave their widowed mother watchful care in her old age: perhaps too watchful, Molly later thought. At least one of them was always on hand in the evening to play whist or read aloud or to accompany Elizabeth Dewson to church on Sunday. After Ellen married and moved to Providence, Molly's brother Bill and his wife Harriet moved into the family home and Harriet assumed the main burden of housekeeping.[3]

Despite the differences in their personalities and lives, Molly built a dependable daily rapport with her mother. Mrs. Dewson especially enjoyed meeting the friends that Molly brought home. One frequent visitor was Lucy Ward Stebbins, who worked at the Parole Department from 1903 to 1905. Stebbins represented the kind of woman Dewson sought for her corps of professional visitors: college-educated (Radcliffe, 1902), with a graduate degree in social economics. Lucy and Molly quickly hit it off, and they took a trip together to England and Scotland in 1906. The daughter of Reverend Horatio Stebbins, the noted pastor of San Francisco's First Unitarian Church, Lucy also remained a special favorite of Molly's mother because of their shared Unitarian heritage.[4]

Lucy Stebbins stayed on the staff of the Parole Board for only two years before joining Boston's Associated Charities as a social worker. She later returned to Berkeley, where she became dean of women at the University of California. Soon after Stebbins left, Dewson began an even more important friendship with one of her visitors—a young volunteer named Polly Porter who began work in 1909.

The parole board had never seen anything like Mary G. Porter. She was by far the most smartly dressed intern the Boston School for Social Work had sent their way: the cut of her clothes and the expensive leather in her shoes and purse set her apart from many of the other woman, who had to work for their livings. Polly was attractive, impulsive, and conspicuously wealthy. Soon she and Molly became "fast friends."[5]

Polly Porter entered Molly Dewson's life at a critical juncture. Dewson was thirty-six when they met (Polly was ten years younger) and

still living at home. No doubt the uncertainties that troubled her professional life from 1910 to 1912—her growing frustration with the Lancaster job, her decision to turn down the permanent minimum wage
position, her uncertainty about her future plans—were linked to unresolved questions haunting her personal life. The Adams Street household had at first provided a comfortable domestic setting for a busy
young professional woman who divided her time between a job in Boston and a wealth of other social work commitments,[6] but by 1910 or so
the benefits of living at home had begun to wear thin. Her mother's
health was failing, and Molly had probably realized that staying on in
Quincy with her brother Bill and his wife would not provide her with
enough companionship and stimulation to last the rest of her life.[7] By
now she knew that she would never marry, not that it had ever been
much of an option. Her growing friendship with Polly thus hinted at an
alternative life.

Perhaps as early as 1910, but certainly by the summer of 1911,
Polly and Molly took a trip together to Polly's family home in Castine,
Maine. Dewson boldly if enigmatically signed the guest book, "What is
the only machine? A Ford," providing the first record of the more than
fifty summers she would spent in that house with Polly. Back in Boston,
the two women kept up a busy social schedule, attending the symphony, the opera, and many theatrical and musical productions
together. They "skated home" after a performance of Messiah by the
Handel and Haydn Society at Symphony Hall, as Molly carefully documented in the playbill she preserved in a theater scrapbook. And Molly
also saved the catalogue of a 1911 Museum of Fine Arts exhibit of the
work of Claude Monet. At the very bottom, in tiny handwriting quite
unlike her usual bold scrawl, was penned "w. Polly."[8]

In 1910 Porter took an apartment on Beacon Hill at 101 Mount
Vernon Street, and Dewson often stayed there if she had evening activities in the city. This pied-à-terre came in especially handy in late 1911
when she was working long hours on the minimum wage report. Elizabeth Glendower Evans recalled: "She migrated from my house, which
had been used as a headquarters while the work was in process . . . to a
room I don't know where, in which she and her friend, Mary Porter,
buried themselves." Already acquaintances like Evans considered Molly
and Polly inseparable.[9]

Polly Porter was also a frequent visitor to the Dewson home in
Quincy. It was almost as if Molly were showing off her newly chosen
mate to her family—perhaps to tell her mother that she would not be

alone once her mother was gone. Whatever Molly's motives, Mrs. Dewson gave her blessing to the relationship: "Of Polly she said dreamily during her last days as she watched her playing on the steps with Sun Yat Sen, our chow, 'She is a good woman.' This is mother's highest compliment for she did not go in for hyperbole." Dewson added tellingly, "As Polly's mental picture of herself at twenty-eight had not expanded in this direction I enjoyed her reaction to the compliment."[10]

The year 1912 brought important professional and personal changes for Molly Dewson. She decided to turn down the offer to join the Massachusetts Commission on the Minimum Wage as its executive secretary. She felt she had worked herself "ragged" and needed time to recuperate.[11] In the first manifestation of a pattern that grew more pronounced as her career progressed, she took an extended trip to Quebec in February to recover her health and rethink her professional options. Deciding that she needed a change after twelve years of steady employment with the Commonwealth of Massachusetts, she resigned her position as superintendent of parole. She then nursed her mother through her final illness and spent more and more time with Polly.

Although she and Polly began investigating options for living together in 1911, this devoted daughter continued to put her mother's welfare first.[12] For all her outward appearance of modern womanhood, Molly was probably more entrapped by what Jane Addams called "the family claim" than she ever admitted to herself. In the end, however, she never had to make a choice between Polly and her mother. Elizabeth Dewson died on December 28, 1912, at the age of seventy-eight.[13] Now Molly was finally free to leave the family home.

The life that Molly and Polly envisioned for themselves was a far cry from the problems of delinquent girls that first brought them together. In the summer of 1912, they pooled their resources to buy a farm in the central Massachusetts town of South Berlin, telling friends that they wanted to try their hands at "cow farming." Their joint decision to move to rural Massachusetts suggests both their spirit of adventure and the freedom that Polly's inheritance gave them to make a total break with the past.[14]

More than anything else, the farm represented a commitment to a life together. As early as Christmas of 1912, they began to build a common library with the distinctive imprint "Porter-Dewson" stamped on each book.[15] As the new year dawned in 1913, they were finally free to live together on their own terms, unhampered by professional or familial responsibilities. These were two women in love.

Polly Porter had traveled a far different road to the South Berlin farm than had her partner.[16] Mary Gurley Porter was born in Chicago on March 25, 1884, the first child of Mabel and William D. Porter; a brother, William Deering Porter, Jr., was born six years later. Polly spent her early life in Evanston, Illinois, where her family lived just several blocks from Lake Michigan. She was a strikingly attractive young girl, with smooth skin, luxuriously thick dark braids, and a penetrating gaze. Family photographs usually show her with one of the many pets —a Skye terrier, a Pomeranian puppy, a pug, a pigeon—she adopted in her childhood.

The Porters led a secure and extremely comfortable life, largely because of their family connections with the International Harvester fortune. William Deering, the man responsible for this business and commercial success, had founded one of the country's largest dry goods commission houses (Deering Milliken) in Portland, Maine, after the Civil War. In the 1870s, Deering embarked on a new career when he invented a piece of farm machinery that helped change American agriculture. In 1902, his company, Deering Harvester, merged with the McCormick Reaper Company to form International Harvester, a conglomerate which quickly took over 80–90 percent of farm implement sales in the United States. Through these business activities, William Deering amassed a sizable fortune. He gave more than a million dollars to Northwestern University and was also a special patron of the Garret Theological Seminary, a leading member of the First Methodist Church in Evanston, and a founder of Wesley Hospital in Chicago.[17]

William Deering was Polly Porter's great-uncle. The links go back to Maine in the 1830s and 1840s. William Deering and William Reed Porter, Polly's paternal grandfather, had been childhood friends in Paris, Maine, and Porter married William Deering's older sister, Elizabeth Hannah Deering. William and Elizabeth Porter had three daughters and one son, William Deering Porter, who was born in 1848. He was Polly's father.[18]

The Deerings left Maine in 1873 for Chicago, where the headquarters of the newly founded Deering Harvester Company were located. In the late 1870s, William Deering Porter followed them. Joining his uncle's firm as a clerk, he lived with his uncle and cousins Charles and James in the Deering family home in Evanston.[19] Around 1882 Porter and his new wife, Mabel Gurley, took up residence just several blocks from the Deering mansion, and Polly's father remained associated with Deering Harvester for the rest of his career. Although hardly a dynamic entrepreneur or financier (not unlike Edward H. Dewson), he increased his wealth substantially through stock options and real estate investments before his death in 1904 at the age of fifty-six.[20]

The Deering family ties to Maine led the Porters to build a summer home near the Penobscot Bay village of Castine in the 1890s. They purchased fifty acres of land "off the neck," an area three miles outside the town, and commissioned the Chicago architectural firm of Handy and Cady to draw up plans for a massive shingled "cottage" which they called Moss Acre. No member of the Porter family set foot in Castine until the house was completed, which caused the Castine residents to wonder what species these outlandishly wealthy Midwesterners could be. When the Porters arrived by boat with a full entourage of family members, servants, and dogs, the whole town turned out at the dock.[21]

Moss Acre was, in a word, ample. The enormous square house had three full floors framed by two chimneys; its brown shingled exterior, soon weathered by the harsh Maine climate, was set off by dark green trim. The long veranda, also painted dark green and anchored by a massive door, offered an unsurpassed view of the Penobscot Bay and the Camden Hills. The interior was dominated by a huge living room which stretched along the entire south side of the house; upstairs there were seven bedrooms and baths. In addition to the main house, there were separate servants quarters, a stable, a laundry, and a garage.

In the early days, life at Moss Acre was conducted on a lavish scale. The Porters kept so many dogs that local delivery wagons were afraid to approach the house. One early visitor remembered being greeted by a pack of three Great Danes, several collies, some medium-sized dogs, a dachshund named Doc, and a very small beast called Dixon Draw the Sword.[22] Parties were frequent, and the house was always full of visitors, many of whom arrived in chartered yachts at Moss Acre's private dock. Guests could sample Moss Acre's tennis court, laid out near the shoreline with the Penobscot Bay as a backdrop, or they could swim or ride. The Porters kept a stable full of horses, each stall labeled with a painted plaque: Daisy, Granny Dunn, Israfel, and Strong Heart were Polly's favorites. For years afterward, townspeople remembered young Polly riding sidesaddle into town dressed in a white linen riding outfit. So much did Polly love to ride that the mounting block at the entrance to Moss Acre was chosen as the headstone for her grave.[23]

Polly's family spent time in Evanston and Castine, with occasional interludes in Buffalo, New York, and Camden, South Carolina. Polly loved the long childhood summers in Maine the best. She grew close to the family of James Barr Ames, dean of the Harvard Law School, whose property abutted the Porters'. She also played with the Hutchins children in nearby Brooksville. Edward Hutchins was a prominent Boston lawyer, and his daughter Grace was one of Polly's earliest friends.

Polly's life changed dramatically when, in her late teens, she lost both her parents. Her mother died in 1902 in Paris while the family was on an extended European trip. And Polly's father died suddenly two years later, leaving her an orphan at nineteen. Polly and Bill Porter split an inheritance of almost three hundred thousand dollars, a sizable sum of money in those days for two teenagers.[24] Bill was not yet of legal age, so his income was controlled by a guardian in Chicago. A similar arrangement continued when he came of age, since he was regarded as a rather slow child—in the Maine vernacular, "he didn't have all his seabags."[25] He married late in life and had no children.

Polly Porter's trust funds were also placed outside her control, an arrangement quite common for young women with property. Financial control, it was thought, must rest with men. Her half of the inheritance thus went into an irrevocable trust from which she could receive income, but she could not touch the principal. Moreover, until she reached twenty-one, she could receive no more than six thousand dollars a year no matter how much income the trust earned. If the capital from this settlement had been well invested, the trust fund could have grown substantially over the years. Unfortunately, the assets were too heavily concentrated in International Harvester stock, and the trust income eventually failed to keep pace with the rising cost of living. But back in the early 1900s Polly was flush and friends remember that she spent money like water.[26]

After her father's death, Polly chose not to return to Evanston, and instead joined her thirteen-year-old brother who was in school in the Boston area. Too young to live on her own, she moved into the Cambridge home of Dean and Mrs. James Barr Ames and stayed with them for several years.[27]

Wealthy young orphans, especially one as stunningly beautiful as Polly Porter, often have many suitors, and Polly never lacked for male companionship. Her scrapbooks from the late 1890s on were filled with snapshots of eligible young men, but she never became seriously enough involved with one to consider marriage.[28] From an early age, she may have preferred emotional attachments to women. One of her closest friends during adolescence and early adulthood was a striking blonde woman named Bunny Marsh, who appeared frequently with Polly in family photographs.[29]

Since Polly showed no signs of wanting to settle down in an early marriage, she had to find something to do with her life. Her education had been spotty, alternating between Evanston and Buffalo with a short stint at a French finishing school in 1901–1902; she had not been back to school since her father's death. After living with Dean and Mrs. Ames for several years, Polly and her brother Bill rented rooms in a house on Brattle Street owned by the Harvard professor George Baker, who was noted for his theater workshops for aspiring playwrights. Polly toyed with the idea of becoming an actress and at one point enrolled in a dramatic school with a friend named Irma Lerner. In the end, however, she decided to continue her education and enter the field of social work.[30]

When Polly Porter enrolled at the Boston School for Social Workers in 1908, she became a member of the first cohort of students to receive formal training in the new profession of social work. The Boston School for Social Workers opened in 1904 under the joint supervision of Simmons College and Harvard University. Social work was in its infancy, and the Simmons-Harvard experiment was in the forefront of providing professional training in this new field. The school was jointly directed by Jeffrey Richardson Brackett, a Harvard graduate who had become interested in social reform while in college, and Zilpah Smith, formerly with Associated Charities in Boston. The classrooms and offices were located near the Boston Common and the new Park Street subway.[31]

Polly Porter's brief attendance at the Boston School for Social Workers substituted for the higher education she never received. To gain admission to the program, students had to show proficiency equivalent to a college education; women without a formal degree registered for courses at Simmons College; the few men enrolled took courses at Harvard. Polly attended lectures and conferences three mornings a week and did specialized reading in economics, psychology, the family, care of delinquent children, and the problems of poverty.[32]

An important part of each student's training was field work. In 1909, Polly Porter was assigned to an internship at the Parole Department of the Lancaster School for Girls, where her supervisor was Molly Dewson. Polly never completed the requirements for her social work degree at Simmons and did not officially graduate.[33] Instead she stayed on as a volunteer visitor at the Parole Board for several years after her internship ended, resigning in 1912 when Molly quit her position as superintendent of probation. With the exception of a stint with the American Red Cross in France during World War I, she never again worked as a professional social worker and, in fact, after 1912 she never again held a job. From that point on, her life remained bound up with Molly Dewson's.

Polly Porter's relationship with her former Lancaster supervisor was the principal commitment of her adult life. Always a rather dependent person who had trouble making her own decisions, she had been drifting since her parents died. Then along came Molly, a woman ten years her senior who was strong, funny, outgoing, and who liked to take charge. Molly made Polly feel secure and wanted after the lonely and aimless years of her early adulthood. At first some of Polly's family friends were not sure that the forward, indeed somewhat overbearing Miss Dewson was an entirely suitable friend for the shy Miss Porter. Many of the conservative Castine residents were shocked by the earthy barnyard tales Molly told about their Berlin farm. But when they saw how Polly blossomed in Molly's company, the objections were withdrawn.[34]

Yet it is misleading to paint the Dewson-Porter relationship primarily in terms of the rewards Polly received from Molly's companionship. As Polly reminded visitors to Castine during their long years of retirement, Molly chose her as a partner—a gentle rebuke to their friends who unthinkingly assumed that the attraction and benefits of the relationship were lopsided.[35] While Molly appeared to the world as a successful and self-reliant modern woman, she had needs too, needs which Polly fulfilled. Molly was at a crossroad in her personal life; the death of her mother deprived Molly of the stable home that had nurtured her since college. At a crossroad, too, in her professional career, she had left one job behind but had no plans for the future. She had saved some money, and she inherited a small amount when her mother died, but not enough to last very long. Money had always been a source of concern to Molly, especially after her experience at Wellesley. The appearance in her life of an attractive young woman with a $150,000 trust fund was not to be ignored by a woman like Dewson who understood the discomforts of genteel poverty.

Of course, Molly was not just interested in financial security. She shared Polly's devotion. Her career demonstrates that from 1912 on she considered every decision affecting her professional life in terms of its impact on her partnership with Polly Porter. Since Molly was clearly an ambitious woman, whose quest for power took her to the upper echelons of the New Deal bureaucracy in the 1930s, there could be no stronger testament to the primacy that she placed on her commitment to her partner.

Polly Porter's and Molly Dewson's decision to live together was not an uncommon one among middle-class women in the late nineteenth and the early twentieth centuries. The social phenomenon of two unmarried women living together in a long-term relationship became so familiar that the term *Boston marriage* was coined to describe it. Such a relationship with a companion or friend offered elite women a socially accepted alternative to the traditional route of marriage and children. Often these women were independently wealthy, since only access to the money and property that went with a privileged class background could substitute for a husband's income. In most cases, at least one of the women involved in such a romantic friendship was a career woman or feminist: this arrangement thus allowed women to pursue their professional callings free of the responsibilities of managing children and a large household. Such a commitment also gave these women more freedom. It was still considered rather improper for a single woman to live by herself in a city, but societal fears of women's independence and worries about their vulnerability were assuaged when women chose the security of living in pairs.[36]

The late nineteenth and early twentieth centuries were dotted with such couples, made up primarily of members of the first several generations of professional and college-educated women. The relationship between Molly's professors Katharine Lee Bates and Katharine Coman fit this mold, as did that of fellow faculty members Vida Scudder and Florence Converse. Mount Holyoke's president Mary Woolley and English professor Jeannette Marks were another academic couple whose relationship was forged at Wellesley while Dewson was a student. Jane Addams of Hull House shared her life for forty years with Mary Rozet Smith; Alice James found a devoted companion and friend in Katherine Loring; the radical labor writer Grace Hutchins spent her life with her fellow activist Anna Rochester; and Frieda Miller of the Women's Bureau shared hers with the labor organizer Pauline Newman.[37]

Several aspects of turn-of-the-century American society and culture made it something of a golden age for female friendships. In an era which boasted such illustrious single women as Jane Addams and Alice Hamilton, women who chose not to marry were respected for their choices rather than pitied for their state of singlehood. Moreover, since women were presumed to lack a sexual drive, family, friends—and the public—rarely suspected that two women living together might share a sexual relationship. Only in the 1920s did the work of sexologists such as Freud, Krafft-Ebbing, and Havelock Ellis begin to alter the American understanding of the role of sexuality in modern life. At that time, being normal began increasingly to mean being actively heterosexual. Along with these new concepts came a tendency to reinterpret women's feelings for other women in a decidedly negative light: love between women became identified as perverse, distorted, and unnatural.[38]

While these new attitudes would doom many women's relationships after the 1920s, or at least force them to be viewed in more explicitly sexual terms, such disapproval was less prevalent in an earlier time. When Molly and Polly chose to live together, their families and friends applauded this as an ideal solution for two unattached women who would probably otherwise live out their lives in lonely spinsterhood.

In many ways, Dewson and Porter's relationship mirrored a conventional heterosexual marriage. From the very beginning, Molly took charge of the relationship. She handled the money and made all the financial decisions, even though Polly's inheritance represented their primary source of income. Her career shaped where they lived and how they spent their time. She took responsibility for most of the heavy work around the house and for mechanical things like taking care of the automobiles they both loved to drive. Polly managed the day-to-day affairs of the household, adding small "feminine" touches to their life like fresh-cut flowers every morning. When company came, she often stayed in the background, barely entering into the conversation.

The exaggerated role divisions of the Porter-Dewson partnership, which were most pronounced in their early years together, made them seem like an odd couple to many who met them and even to friends who had known them for a long time. The public side, however, was only the tip of the iceberg. While we cannot reconstruct the exact dimensions of their relationship, the nuances and shadings of their shared life suggest that the attraction may have been far deeper and more complex than family and friends suspected. Between these two women existed a private understanding, a territory that remained hidden from the rest of the world. It was this private mutual affection, rather than the public aspects of their shared life, that kept the partnership intact for more than fifty years.

Since Molly and Polly were rarely separated, few letters exist to document their feelings for each other or chart the ways in which they manifested their love. (Even if letters existed, Polly's sense of privacy would likely have led her to burn them after Molly's death.) But several scraps of evidence from their service in France during World War I, one of the few times they were apart, do suggest the depth of their feelings. They had pet names for each other—Polly called Molly "Puisye" and Molly signed herself "Aunty Whitewash."[39] "Puisye I love you very much," Polly began one letter, "and I was thoroughly interested in your letter from Paris—but no more of that now—it is business hours—and to business therefore!" On another occasion when they were both finding the wartime separation difficult, Polly wrote lovingly to her absent partner: "Little danger that the Puisye will become unnecessary to me—I should be like a ship without sails and a pilot without a north star were she not part of my life."[40]

Such demonstrations of devotion and affection from Porter to Dewson raise the issue of whether there was an erotic or sexual dimension to this relationship. Should we call these two women lesbians? The partnership fits the definition of lesbianism formulated by the historian Blanche Wiesen Cook: "Women who love women, women who choose women to nurture and support and to create a living environment in which to work creatively and independently, are lesbians."[41] Whether they ever engaged in sexual activity is impossible to determine, although they always shared a bedroom wherever they lived or traveled. (Moss Acre had six other bedrooms, so they must have enjoyed the companionship of sleeping in the same room.) In the end, of course, what is important is not what they did in bed, but that they chose each other, loved each other, and expressed that love through a lifetime of shared partnership. While the term *lesbian* had not entered the popular consciousness in the early twentieth century and thus was never used by Dewson, Porter, or their friends to characterize their relationship, the word does—in the broad sense in which Blanche Cook uses it—convey the depth and intensity of their emotional commitment to each other. Such woman-identified love shaped their lives until they were parted by Molly Dewson's death in 1962.

The Porter-Dewson partnership went through several stages. In their first decade, the two women shared many interests and usually worked together, whether it was at the Parole Department, on their farm, in the women's suffrage campaign, or in France during World War I. They proudly identified themselves as the Porter-Dewsons, and their friends treated them as a more or less inseparable twosome. So accepted were they as a couple that Molly could offhandedly begin a letter to the suffrage leader Maud Wood Park in 1920 with the sentence, "Partner and I have been bursting with pride and satisfaction ever since you were elected chairman of the League of Women Voters," without ever referring to Polly by name.[42] In these early years, their relationship consistently replicated the original circumstances under which they met on the Parole Board: Molly always held the more responsible position, while Polly kept to the background.

By the 1920s, the patterns of Dewson's and Porter's life together were changing. They no longer shared active professional interests. Polly gave up her social work career and opened a kennel to raise sheltie dogs. Molly meanwhile started her rise to prominence that would culminate in the New Deal. Their social life, however, continued to revolve around other like-minded women, mostly unmarried professional women who lived alone or in pairs. And their bond to each other grew even stronger. In the 1930s Molly Dewson described her partner in an offhand yet very loving way: "And, moreover, she doesn't care a whoop about politics and is bored by public questions. Fortunately, however, she still likes me and we run four establishments in common. . . . Now, how do you feel about Porter and Dewson?"[43]

The relationship entered a final stage after Dewson's retirement from public life in 1938. For the next quarter century, the women lived happily together in Greenwich Village and Castine, Maine, unencumbered by the political and professional responsibilities that had filled Dewson's life in the 1920s and 1930s. Now Molly and Polly devoted their time primarily to each other and to their friends. By the 1940s, any of the asymmetry that had characterized the early years of their relationship had disappeared, replaced by a mutual trust and equality that had grown steadily through the decades of their shared life.

Toward the end of her life, Polly Porter wrote a reflective letter to her godchild, a young woman then very much caught up in relationships with young men. "Aunt Poll" was sympathetic to this interest in boys but offered her own perspective: "As to love between a man and a woman I have never yet been able to fathom what creates it, what makes it grow. I am inclined to feel that it is passion—passion that sometimes falls upon sustaining soil, hence must seek, on and on for fulfillment—or that, sometimes, finds itself completely mated and then no longer hears 'the call of the wild,' but settles down into complete companionship, this time not only of the pulsating womb but of the spirit itself. Well, well, God knows? I at least have never found the true answer. . . . In the meantime, lots of love to you—not the puzzling kind of love, but the dependable kind."[44]

Polly Porter here posited two kinds of love: the temporary passion that sometimes joins men and women, and a more dependable, more satisfying love between friends and partners of either sex, such as some find in marriage and she found with Molly Dewson.[45] Such love based on "complete companionship" freed Molly Dewson and Polly Porter to grow together, sustaining a fifty-year partnership that enriched and strengthened their lives. As Molly and Polly shared the long evenings of their retirement in Castine, how thankful they must have been for the chain of events that had brought a young and insecure Polly Porter to the offices of the Parole Board so many years before.

CHAPTER FIVE

The Farmer-Suffragettes

IT is the spring of 1913 in the small central Massachusetts town of South Berlin. Two unmarried women have just moved into the old Lamson place down on River Road. The women seem serious about farming: they are building up a herd of Guernsey cows and have invested in a DeLavelle milk separator. Whenever they meet local townspeople at the store or at farm auctions, they seem knowledgeable about dairy herding and cattle management. And yet everyone in South Berlin realizes that Molly Dewson and Polly Porter are not typical Massachusetts farmers.

For one thing, they spend money at a fantastic rate. Before they moved in, they extensively remodeled the farm house, increasing its space by one-quarter. (Their architect had just finished restoration of the Paul Revere House in Boston's North End.) Even the house they built for their tenant farmer is luxurious by local standards. And the cars: not just one, but two. The stylish Buick they use to flit around the countryside far surpasses the serviceable Ford that local farmers might aspire to.[1]

The Berlin townspeople are also a bit dubious about these two women living off by themselves on this farm. Where are their husbands? Where are their families? That women can live so happily and self-sufficiently without men raises disturbing questions for the people of this conservative farming community. To top it off, the two women

have not been in Berlin more than a year or two before they become active suffragists, touring the Worcester County countryside in their cars
to drum up support for the alien idea of giving women the vote. The
neighbors' nickname for them of "farmer-suffragettes" reflects a mixture
of derision, humor, and most of all, amazement: what will these two
women do next?[2]

The Porter-Dewson farm was located in gentle farming country
which ran along the Assabet River near Worcester. Boston was an easy
thirty-five-mile drive on the Boston Post Road, and their farm was readily accessible by train. It was situated just ten miles south of the Lancaster State Industrial School for Girls; the women had no doubt fallen in
love with this rural setting on their frequent trips out to the reform
school. Their piece of property was 110 acres, 40 acres of cleared fields
and the rest in pasture and woods. Fruit trees and an orchard produced
apples, pears, quinces, and grapes, and the open fields were excellent
for growing hay. But the land was best suited for pasture and grazing,
and Dewson and Porter devoted most of their attention to dairy farming.[3] As Christmas gifts in 1912, they exchanged such treatises as *Dairy
Cattle and Milk Production* and *The Management and Feeding of Cattle*,
each marked with the inscription "Porter and Dewson, December 25,
1912."[4]

The farm house was a special attraction. On a bend in the road between Berlin and Hudson, the house sat on high ground looking down
toward the Assabet River. Built in 1790, the farm house was still bordered by its original stone wall. The white frame house was square and
substantial, set off by distinctive green shutters and trim mirrored by
green shutters on top of the cupola of their white-painted barn. The
fireplace of the large living room provided a cozy setting for cold winter evenings; upstairs there were four bedrooms and a bathroom with
"first class fixtures and hot and cold water." An added benefit was the
Kelsey hot air furnace.[5]

While Molly and Polly thought of themselves as farmers, they
were not exactly roughing it: a hired man milked and tended the cows,
and extra hands were hired in the fall to help with the haying and
harvesting. Since the women would have been lost without full-time
household help (neither knew how to cook), they employed several local farm girls to do the domestic work around the house. The farm
turned a small profit, but farm income alone would never have sustained their rather grand lifestyle. Polly's trust fund bridged the gap.

The Porter-Dewsons' conspicuous lifestyle set them apart from their rural neighbors. In the winter of 1913, while the farm house was being remodeled, they took a three-month trip to Europe, skiing in Switzerland and then relaxing on a beach in Spain. Each summer, at a time when most farmers would be hard at work, Molly and Polly managed an extended trip to Castine. And they entertained an endless stream of visitors who arrived by train from Boston or New York. Molly's Wellesley classmate B. Z. Scott and Polly's childhood friends Irma Lerner and Constance Churchyard were frequent visitors, as were their Castine neighbors Dorothy Blake and Edward Hutchins. Bill Porter came by at least once a summer, as did Molly's sister Nell and her family from Rhode Island; Lucy Stebbins managed a trip all the way from California in 1916. Molly and Polly took great delight in showing off their unusual rural lifestyle to their friends.[6]

Freed from the daily chores of manual labor, Molly and Polly turned their attention to farm management. Their herd of twenty-five Guernsey cows produced grade A, bacteriologically tested milk and cream, and Dewson kept extensive records of each cow's milk production, the milk's bacteria content and butter fat level. Not unlike the statistical reports that she had kept of Lancaster girls on parole were her dutifully recorded observations about the age, health, and disposition of each cow and bull.[7]

Molly and Polly maintained their sense of humor in their new careers as gentlewomen farmers. All the cows had names and distinctive personalities to match. The Porter-Dewsons were fond of naming their animals after friends and acquaintances. The bossy cow Delinda was probably named for one of Dewson's nieces, the daughter of her brother George. They called another cow Sophonisba, surely in honor of Miss Breckinridge of the University of Chicago. Polly drew on her time at the Boston School for Social Workers to tag one cow Zilpah for the associate director Zilpah Smith; a bull was christened (perhaps somewhat dubiously) Jeffrey Brackett of Assabet after the program director. Dewson later proclaimed the efficacy of their method of selecting names: "When you name a child after someone I always maintain the child resembles the name giver—at least that is true with cows." That was not the only lesson Molly Dewson learned from her dairy farming. "Nothing is better political training than raising cattle," she said in a newspaper interview much later. "If you have ever led a young calf to pasture, it's simple enough to make any unmanageable political workers eat out of your hand."[8]

On the whole, the farm did well. The milk and cream production realized a profit of more than sixteen hundred dollars in 1915, and haying brought in a thousand dollars in a good year. Their hopes of building up a top Guernsey herd were dashed, however, when tuberculosis struck one-third of their stock. Polly carefully marked the records of the deceased cows and bulls with small crosses, just as she would later mark the passing of her beloved shelties in her Castine diary.[9]

Their Guernsey herd's health problems reminded these amateurs that dairy farming could be a risky proposition. But Molly and Polly were too interested in living well and having fun to get completely caught up in Jeffrey Brackett of Assabet's tuberculosis or Delinda's latest butter fat level. So, after a year or so in their snug Berlin farm house, Molly and Polly began casting about for other things to do. They turned their attention to the issue that was sweeping Massachusetts in 1915: women's suffrage.

The women's suffrage movement probably brought together more women working on feminist issues than did any other reform cause in American history. Although the demand for the vote was part of a broad spectrum of interest in women's emancipation that flourished during the early twentieth century, suffrage gradually emerged as the rallying cry for the entire women's movement. Activism increased dramatically around 1914, and suffragists finally celebrated victory in 1920 with the passage of the nineteenth amendment.[10]

The demand for the vote had first been raised by Elizabeth Cady Stanton at Seneca Falls, New York, in 1848, but throughout most of the nineteenth century women's suffrage was seen as a radical cause with little chance of success. But, as old pioneers like Stanton, Susan B. Anthony, and Lucy Stone were replaced by a younger group of suffrage leaders at the turn of the century, women's suffrage began to become more mainstream among American reform movements. Settlement leaders like Jane Addams stressed what women would do with the vote, such as clean up the cities with civic-minded "municipal housekeeping." This new emphasis made the vote seem less antagonistic to women's traditional roles in the home and made women's suffrage more acceptable to the general citizenry.[11]

The expanding roles that women had been playing in professional and civic life since the 1880s also gave new impetus to their demand for the vote. Women organized themselves into everything from temperance unions to women's clubs to socialist organizations. The belief that women belonged only in the domestic sphere eroded as women made important contributions to public life. The vote thus became a convenient symbol of women's new roles in the public sphere.[12]

Many women who participated in the suffrage campaign were fundamentally affected by the experience. Suffrage provided women with the kinds of exhilarating experience often described by men in periods of war or political upheaval. The growing consciousness of women's common concerns fostered a feminist solidarity unique in twentieth-century America.[13] The suffrage campaign also honed women's organizational skills. Because opposition by politicians was so fierce (they feared women would use their votes to sweep them from office), and because most of the public remained indifferent, if not hostile, women were forced to become extremely effective campaigners, lobbyists, and publicists. Once learned, these skills were put to use after the vote was won.

Participation in the suffrage campaign had a personal resonance for many women as well, especially those who were venturing into new areas such as education, the professions, and social reform. They were proud to be part of this great women's crusade, and the feelings of solidarity it engendered remained with them for the rest of their careers. Frances Perkins described this perspective: "The women learned to like each other in that suffrage movement. . . . The friendships that were formed among women . . . have been the most lasting and enduring friendships—solid, substantial, loyal—that I have ever seen anywhere."[14] The shared suffrage experience provided the foundation for many of the feminist networks which bound women together in the postsuffrage era.

Molly Dewson's experiences parallel those of her New Deal colleague and friend Frances Perkins. Suffrage fundamentally shaped her attitudes about women's roles in public life and social reform and profoundly influenced her later participation in the New Deal. The suffrage campaign gave her the opportunity to work with women she greatly admired, women who embodied the ideals of public-spirited womanhood that she strove to emulate in the 1920s and 1930s. At the same time, suffrage provided her with a stimulating interlude of political activity while she was on an extended leave from her professional career. "No work I have ever done was more entertaining," Dewson later recalled, "for woman suffrage has nothing to do with economics."[15]

Exactly when Molly Dewson first declared her support for votes for women cannot be determined. She never mentioned it during her years at Wellesley College, although several of her professors, especially the mathematics professor Ellen Hayes, were outspoken suffragists in the 1890s. Dewson had joined the Boston Equal Suffrage Association for Good Government by 1908, and the College Equal Suffrage League by 1910, but her involvement in both organizations was limited to paying dues. Dewson's only public association with the College Equal Suffrage League came at an afternoon tea in January of 1911, when she was one of seven college graduates who gave a five-minute talk on "Why I Believe in Votes for Women."[16]

Dewson squarely aligned herself with those who argued for the vote based on what women could accomplish with it. In an interchange of letters with the *Outlook* editor and presidential candidate Theodore Roosevelt in 1912, she claimed that women would use suffrage to uplift the tenor of government and public life.[17] "Women with their more truly practical and idealistic nature would be most valuable coworkers with men in matters of government," she wrote. She felt that this was especially true of social workers, who saw at close range the results of "defective government" in the tenements, streets, and factories and thus were interested in developing creative state policy for education, health, and industry. But to ensure the incorporation of women's point of view into public life, women must first be granted full rights of citizenship, including the right to vote.[18]

After responding to Theodore Roosevelt, Molly Dewson remained silent on the question of women's suffrage for several years. Then, in 1915, she and Polly volunteered their services to the Massachusetts Woman Suffrage Association (MWSA) as suffrage workers in Worcester county. Dewson took over District 10, with responsibility for the towns of Berlin, Hudson, Clinton, and Westborough. Polly Porter did not hold an official position, but she was Molly's constant sidekick. Together the two women kept a scrapbook of their 1915 suffrage activities. Filled with clippings about events in Worcester County as well as more general news about the suffrage cause, the scrapbook contained both pro- and antisuffrage clippings, with the latter carefully marked in red. The red ink predominated.[19]

One reason for the heightened level of suffrage activity in 1915 was the state referendum scheduled for November. In order to reach the male citizens who would decide whether to give women the vote, the MWSA mounted a statewide operation; Molly's and Polly's activities in Berlin represented the campaign at the local level. They opened a

"Votes for Women" shop in Hudson and created a window display of suffrage mottoes and banners. They wrote numerous letters to the editors of local Worcester County newspapers, and distributed "Suffrage Blue Birds" emblazoned with "Votes for Women, November 2."[20]

Some of their suffrage work was more social. The Berlin newspaper reported that Miss Dewson and Miss Porter had issued invitations for a "militant whist party" at the Unitarian Church one Saturday evening to build support for suffrage. Members of the Berlin Woman Suffrage League attended a garden party resplendent with "Votes for Women" sashes. Porter and Dewson also tried to convert the Berlin women's club into a suffrage group. Even though Molly was a director of the club and Polly the secretary, the Tuesday Club barely recorded a majority in support of suffrage.[21]

The farmer-suffragettes were willing to do almost any work for suffrage that involved driving their beloved automobiles. Molly and Polly relished the sensation they created as they cruised the Worcester countryside in a car covered with suffrage banners and emblems. The Northboro newspaper captured one such scene: "After riding through the main streets in an auto, with a bugler making merry, the party of suffragists drew up at the curbing on Church Street and Miss Dewson of Berlin introduced Mr. Vahey." Such dramatic arrivals were sure to attract a crowd.[22]

Another method of garnering publicity favored by Massachusetts suffragists was the open-air meeting. Polly Porter never spoke from the platform, and, except for cameo roles in an occasional suffrage play, she kept pretty much in the background. But Molly loved the limelight. Dewson pitched her talks to the low level of political sophistication found in these random audiences. "Women would be women just the same whether they had the ballot or not," she reassured listeners in Hudson. "Just as long as women live they will be women; they will work for home, husband, and children."[23]

Dewson and Porter were soon drawn into the organizational network that bound local suffrage workers to state and national groups. They signed up for a one-day conference in Worcester in February 1915 on suffrage techniques. In May, they attended a three-day MWSA conference in Boston, which ended with a "monster" rally on the Boston Common. They also represented the town of Berlin in the Suffrage Victory Parade in Boston in October 1915, decorating their car with special care for the occasion.[24] And both women were chosen as Massachusetts delegates to the National American Woman Suffrage

Association (NAWSA) convention held in Washington in December 1915.[25]

The national suffrage convention in Washington marked a significant turning point for the suffrage movement. At this convention, Carrie Chapman Catt took over national leadership of the NAWSA from Anna Howard Shaw. While Dewson thought Shaw "a super woman," "the best speaker by far for the suffrage cause," she thought even more highly of Catt, calling her the "keystone" of the suffrage movement and half joking in 1934, "without her I believe we still would be voteless!"[26]

As a lowly district leader from central Massachusetts, Dewson had little personal contact with such luminaries at the 1915 convention. But she did initiate friendships with younger and less well-known suffrage workers who would continue the struggle for women in politics in the postsuffrage era. Many of these women came to prominence in the New Deal. At the Washington convention Dewson first met Florence Ellinwood Allen, then the executive secretary of the College Equal Suffrage League. In 1934 Dewson was instrumental in Allen's nomination to the United States Court of Appeals and pushed hard, although unsuccessfully, to persuade Roosevelt to name Allen as the first woman to the United States Supreme Court. Dewson also met the noted Southern suffragist Nellie Nugent Somerville and her daughter Lucy; in 1934 she secured Lucy Somerville Howorth's appointment to the Veterans' Board of Appeals. During a visit to the Democratic National Committee headquarters in Washington, Dewson also made her first contact with Emily Newell Blair, who would rise to prominence in the Democratic party in the 1920s, and Sue Shelton White, a loyal worker at the Democratic National Committee in the early 1930s and later a lawyer for the Social Security Administration.[27]

After only a year on the suffrage circuit, Molly Dewson stood poised to break into a position of substantial leadership on the statewide level. Her rapid rise in the MWSA marked the first time that she had succeeded on her own rather than through the influence and intercession of her mentor Elizabeth Glendower Evans. At this point, the suffrage careers of the partners diverged. At first, they had been very much in it together: "Polly and Molly, the farmer-suffragettes," always a big hit with their cars and suffrage plays. But Dewson had far stronger organizational talents than Porter and felt more at ease in public than her shy partner. Polly continued to be active in women's suffrage until they left for France during World War I, but she participated more as Molly's companion than as a coworker. Meanwhile, Dewson had once again found an arena to exhibit the administrative and political skills she had developed in her years as superintendent of parole and on the minimum wage commission.

In 1915, much work remained to be done. Massachusetts suffragists had suffered an overwhelming defeat at the November polls; only 35.5 percent of the voters had favored the suffrage referendum.[28] Undaunted, activists kept up the suffrage agitation without missing a beat. Meanwhile the social worker-turned-farmer-turned-suffragist stepped up her involvement in the cause. When Teresa Crowley, chair of MWSA's Legislative Committee, resigned in September of 1916, Dewson agreed to assume this unsalaried position. She continued to live on the Berlin farm and happily drove the thirty-five miles into Boston for the weekly executive board meetings.[29]

As head of the Legislative Committee, Molly Dewson reacquainted herself with the halls of the Massachusetts legislature, which she last frequented during her days on the minimum wage commission.[30] Soon she began prodding the suffrage organization to lobby for social welfare measures similar to those she had advocated with the Parole Board and the Minimum Wage Commission, specifically a bill limiting working hours for women and children to eight hours a day. This showed how committed to legislative reform Dewson had become by 1916. Yet the proposal caused immediate controversy over the tactics and priorities of the suffrage movement. Elizabeth Glendower Evans put the matter succinctly: would the endorsement help or hinder the suffrage cause in Massachusetts?[31]

Those who wanted the MWSA to take a broader stand on social issues marshalled a variety of arguments, but theirs was an uphill, and ultimately unsuccessful, battle. MWSA president Alice Stone Blackwell pointed out that there was a precedent for endorsing causes other than suffrage, claiming that Massachusetts would never have passed its equal guardianship law if the MWSA had not lobbied for it. Wenona Pinkham, chair of the Organization Committee, argued that suffragists would never get the labor vote if they stayed aloof, a view seconded by Mabel Gillespie of the Women's Trade Union League. Since the suffrage amendment had gone down to defeat in 1915 by a 2–1 margin, suffragists were well aware of the need to cultivate new sources of support.[32]

But many in the Massachusetts suffrage organization remained unconvinced by these arguments. Former Legislative chair Teresa Crowley felt that the organization should not take a stand on the eight-hour bill unless a large majority of the membership favored it. Grace Johnson of the Congressional Committee felt it was much easier to sell straight suffrage to the voters than suffrage in conjunction with a host of other reforms. Like most suffragists, Johnson strongly supported the eight-hour bill, yet she feared that endorsing it in order to cement friendship with the unions and industrial workers would lay suffragists open to requests from other organizations on which there might not be such unanimity—such as prohibition or birth control. Johnson's doubts carried the day, and the motion to endorse the eight-hour bill was rejected both by the executive board and at an open meeting of the MWSA membership two weeks later.[33]

By 1917, a new issue challenged the suffrage movement. The United States formally entered World War I in April and many suffrage groups felt torn between working for the vote and supporting the American effort. While some radical suffragists bravely opposed the war for pacifist reasons, most mainstream suffragists, including Molly Dewson, lined up behind the Wilson administration. They were unwilling, however, to cease agitation for suffrage.[34]

The Massachusetts Woman Suffrage Association complied with this dual policy, and in 1917 Dewson found herself doing an increasing amount of suffrage-related war work. She headed a committee on the Elimination of Waste and Increase in Food Supply and lectured to women's groups and suffrage organizations on how they could help the war effort. She even got stuck on a committee planning soldiers' recreation at the Army encampment in Ayer. Her enthusiasm for the suffrage cause waned in direct proportion to the amount of war-related work she was called on to perform.[35]

Even though suffrage victory was still three long years away, by 1917 Molly Dewson's active involvement was drawing to a close. Perhaps she felt confident enough of its ultimate success to move on to new fields. Yet the imprint of these years on the rest of her career was unmistakable. Participation in the women's suffrage campaign fostered her deep commitment to expanding roles for women in public life, a goal she would vigorously pursue in the 1920s and 1930s. And the issue-oriented approach to politics that characterized the suffrage cause— which argued that women needed the vote to improve social and economic conditions in the United States—remained the hallmark of her political philosophy throughout her career. Finally, as in every major professional activity of Dewson's life, the suffrage campaign allowed her to work primarily with other women on issues of concern to women.

Molly Dewson's suffrage experiences also confirmed a pattern that stretched from the Progressive era through the New Deal: she always worked within the system, not on the picket lines or in protest demonstrations. In her suffrage activity she steadfastly sought the center, eschewing the militant confrontational tactics of organizations like Alice Paul's Congressional Union, which used picketing and hunger strikes to compel political change, in favor of the conventional means favored by the NAWSA, such as referenda, lobbying, and political education. When Dewson entered politics and government at a time of deep crisis in the 1930s, she still held firm to her belief that, at base, the American political system was sound. To be sure, she had suggestions for improvement, especially where women and working conditions were concerned, but she never lost her deep-seated belief in the capacity of the American political system to respond to challenge and change. Her participation in the suffrage movement, indeed her whole Progressive apprenticeship, imbued her with this optimistic faith.

CHAPTER SIX

Women at War

ON board the *S.S. Adriatic* after fifteen months in France with the Red Cross during World War I, Molly Dewson wrote her close friend Lucy Stebbins, "Here we are one day out of New York and my war experience is nearly over. It certainly has been the great adventure of my life. The anguish of war for me was between its declaration and the time I got to work. . . . What a God given thing it is to know what you think you should do and to be able to do it."[1]

Many other Progressives shared Dewson's support for America's part in the Great War. President Woodrow Wilson set idealistic stakes in his declaration of war aims: America would enter the European conflict to make the world safe for democracy, advance the cause of freedom against the forces of totalitarianism and autocracy, and bring American goals of idealism and national self-determination to the conduct of world affairs. In essence, Woodrow Wilson described America's entry into the war as the logical extension of Progressivism at home.[2]

Not everyone was convinced that war could be an uplifting experience, however. When fighting broke out in Europe, significant opposition to American entry into the war surfaced in this country. Many Americans wanted no part of this war, which they saw as a grab for territory on the part of the European superpowers. Pacifism ran especially high in 1915, when the Woman's Peace Party and the American

Union against Militarism rallied intellectuals and liberals against the war. Woodrow Wilson himself successfully ran for reelection in 1916 on the platform that he had kept America out of the war. In 1917, however, German submarine attacks on unarmed American ships finally drew the United States into the conflict.

The declaration of war proved especially troubling for many women activists who had called for nonviolent resolution of international conflicts. Once America joined the war effort, a strong emphasis on national unity made dissent and pacifism seem unpatriotic and unacceptable. A brave few, like Jane Addams, Crystal Eastman, Florence Kelley, and Emily Greene Balch, continued to oppose American participation in the war, a course that ruptured friendships and working relationships and led to public vilification of these women. Balch's stance even cost her her job at Wellesley. The militant wing of the suffrage movement, led by Alice Paul's Congressional Union, also opposed the war. They were arrested and jailed for picketing, chaining themselves to the White House fence, and burning President Wilson's speeches on war and democracy. The militant suffragists were among the first victims of a wave of repression that would later turn on labor groups and socialist organizations opposed to the war.[3]

Molly Dewson suffered no such conflicts of conscience over the war. Just as she supported the mainstream National American Woman Suffrage Association and eschewed Alice Paul's militant tactics, so too did she support the Progressive ideal of joining the war effort to make the world safe for democracy. Never a radical activist, disenchanted liberal, or even a critic of democratic capitalism, she always cooperated with the American political system rather than challenged it.

This is not to say that Molly Dewson volunteered for duty as soon as war was declared. Her hesitation came not from politics or pacifism, however, but from personal considerations. No matter how altruistic she seemed from the shipboard perspective of January 1919, she had been far less idealistic sixteen months earlier. "Farming in war time is not for us two," she confided to Lucy Stebbins in September of 1917. "In 1916 it was no expense. This year the scarcity and poorness of labor and its expense have discouraged Wynott [their tenant farmer] so he is going. We can get no one else. . . . Since we perforce have no farm and our maids have just left and more are hard to get we might as well seize the moment and close up for the winter and take a change."[4]

At this point, all Porter and Dewson had decided to do was take a leave of absence from farming and suffrage work. They held an auction at the South Berlin farm in mid-September, but 1917 turned out to be a poor time to sell a farm. So they planted their fields with winter rye that did not have to be harvested until the summer of 1918 and arranged for a Berlin family to take care of the house and remaining stock.[5]

Freed from farming responsibilities, Molly and Polly assessed their options. One inviting possibility was a six-month drive to California in the winter of 1917–18. Dewson asked Lucy Stebbins to map out a trip for them, cautioning, "Remember we are very far from Vanderbilts or Californians and have not laid by one cent for this trip." Molly and Polly were tempted by the prospect of a cross-country motor trip, but they kept putting off the final decision. "Partner is full of negations and it leaves it pretty hard to decide," Dewson confided to Stebbins. Soon both Porter and Dewson began to feel a little guilty about planning an extended vacation while the United States was at war: "Of course we almost feel as if we did a little work it would be more appropriate to war time so that our consciences may prick us against going anyway." By mid-October, they had cast their lot. "We just couldn't do it Lucy. We felt it would be like quitters this year to travel. If you were in N.Y. you'd think all the world was going to France." Somewhat less idealistically than they later described their decision, Molly and Polly prepared to sail for France.[6]

Most Americans found their lives touched and to some extent disrupted by U.S. participation in World War I, but only a few made war work a full-time commitment. Molly Dewson and Polly Porter signed on as social workers for the American Red Cross in France. They did not volunteer for service as young women emotionally caught up in the thrill of fighting in a foreign land (Molly was a mature forty-three and Polly thirty-three) or as a way to meet men. Their motivation was quite direct: there was a war on, and they had no intention of leaving it all to the men.

While the popular image of Red Cross work pictured women working in canteens and men driving ambulances at the front, most of what the Red Cross workers did was far less glamorous. An important priority for the Red Cross was providing for the needs of refugees displaced by the German occupation of French territory. The war was in its fourth year; many of its battles had been fought on French soil and had dislocated large segments of the population and destroyed much of the countryside. French citizens had lost their homes and belongings, their livelihoods, and often many members of their families. When refugees arrived in a new location, they literally had to rebuild their lives from

scratch. Trained social workers were brought in to help. Operating with
a budget of nine million dollars, approximately one-sixth of all Red
Cross expenditures in France during the war, such rehabilitation work
eventually aided almost two million French refugees. "You call Social
Security legislation a new idea?" Dewson later observed. "Why, it was
what we were striving to do back in 1917."[7]

Having signed their contracts with the Red Cross, Dewson and
Porter journeyed to New York, which was "flooded" with soldiers and
women going to France. The two women stayed at the Hotel Holley on
Washington Square West while waiting for their final orders and travel
plans; they filled their time by taking intensive French lessons. The volunteers also visited Abercrombie and Fitch to outfit themselves with
the obligatory Red Cross uniform: tailored suit jackets, long skirts, plain
blouses with neckties, and large square hats. This severely masculine
outfit was modeled on the style favored by professional women of the
day.[8]

Molly and Polly even had time to march in a massive suffrage parade in New York, which Dewson pronounced "superb" and "a thrill."
At the parade, Dewson ran into Carrie Chapman Catt, who expressed
cautious optimism about the upcoming New York referendum on
woman suffrage. To suffragists' delight, they won a narrow but conclu-
sive victory in New York in November 1917, the first breakthrough in a
major Northern industrial state. Dewson heard the news on the boat
train from LeHavre to Paris: "Our little car jambed [sic] with American
social workers . . . nearly blew off the track with joy." Dewson glowed
to Polly's brother Bill, "What do you think of the gallant men of New
York! . . . Well it certainly gave me about the best send off I could have
asked from my native land." If she had had any regrets about leaving the
suffrage campaign before its success was assured, she must have been
greatly heartened by the New York results. A victory in a state with a
significant proportion of foreign-born and immigrant voters could coun-
teract losses like the 1915 Massachusetts referendum. Catt's assessment
that the tide was turning was proving accurate. Right now Molly Dewson had only one thing to say: "Hooray!"[9]

The voyage to France took place without mishap, despite the
threat of submarine attacks by the Germans. The S.S. Rochambeau carried 450 passengers, two-thirds of them women; Dewson reported that
"the women and the Quakers and the Y.M.C.A. men swamp the military."[10] Passengers, packed four to a room, quickly become one big
family: "a ship load of good Samaritans with one idea and held together

by the 1% danger of submarines made something as novel as a peace-
ship." Vigilante groups patrolled the decks on submarine watches and
blackouts were observed at night, but Molly could never convince herself that she was in as much danger aboard ship as she was driving to
their Berlin farm from Boston on a rainy night. Only the Episcopalian
bishop was afraid: he "went around saying he had a message that he was
to be drowned for his sins. . . . Imagine his trying to start a panic—the
bishop! . . . But even at that he could not stampede this boatload of
women. We let the church lean on us."[11]

When Porter and Dewson disembarked at Le Havre in mid-No-
vember 1917, plans for using American social workers to ameliorate the
refugee crisis were not yet formed. Coordinating civilian relief plans in
the midst of a war whose outcome was still in doubt caused confusion
and delay. "Some small work it is making organizations go," Dewson
observed with a sigh. Bureaucratic snarls trapped Molly, Polly, and
their shipmates in Paris while they waited for their orders. Staying at
the American Red Cross Club for Women on the rue de Cambon, they
continued their French lessons and Molly passed her driver's test in a
broken-down Ford. Yet she was impatient to get down to work: "I shall
be glad to be out of Paris. It is jammed with Americans."[12]

Finally her orders came through: she and Polly had both been assigned to the Maine-et-Loire district as delegates for the Red Cross.
Dewson stayed there until January 1918, when she was transferred to
Bourg-en-Bresse, located in the south of France near the Jura Mountains and the Alps. By the end of the war, she had been promoted to
the position of director of general relief for the South Intermediate and
Southern Zones, a territory comprising about one-third of France. She
oversaw the headquarters in Lyons, and fifty people worked directly under her.[13]

Dewson quickly climbed the bureaucratic ladder, drawing on the
organizational and administrative talents she had been developing since
college. Her assignments took account of her personal needs as well.
When Molly and Polly originally signed on, the Red Cross offered to
match their previous salaries, but they decided to accept payments only
for expenses. "We hope to keep together and we thought as volunteers
we had a better chance." Although they both were initially assigned to
the Maine-et-Loire, Polly was soon posted to the industrial town of
St.-Etienne, many hours away from Dewson's new assignment in the
Jura Mountains. They were occasionally able to get together for weekends, but finally the separation proved too much for them, and Dewson

requested a transfer in June, 1918. "You may wonder why I am out of the Ain and the Drôme," she told her family. "Well Poll and I were a little sick of seeing so little of each other so I took a new job of Regionale Deleguée."[14] As field supervisor for the Bureau of Refugees, Dewson had responsibility for Puy de Dome, Haute Loires, Haute Alps, Basses Alps, and for Polly's department, the Loire. The logistics of the new assignment meant that Dewson and Porter could spend every weekend together, and, in their capacities as field supervisor and local delegate, talk daily on the telephone. This arrangement proved far more satisfactory to them.[15]

American Red Cross delegates were called on to perform many different tasks, but their primary responsibilities were running an employment bureau and relocation service for the displaced refugees. Dewson once jokingly described herself as a combination "furniture buyer and warehouse man and general express agent,"[16] which also applied to Polly Porter's duties. "I wish you could have seen me today," Polly wrote her brother, "careening around the streets of St.-Etienne, a watering pot under one arm, a shovel & hoe in my hand, and a willow baby crib on my head, starting a family off for the country!" Porter bragged that in one week she had provided her refugees with seventeen beds, ninety-six sheets, thirty-four blankets, nine buffets, five tables, seven stoves, and thirty-six chairs—practically enough to start her own store.[17]

A Red Cross delegate's work brought her into direct contact with the French people, both local citizens and French officialdom. While visiting one family whose tiny stove and bed were the only furnishings for a mother and her two children, Dewson noticed that the twelve-year-old daughter was sick. "I hauled her out over to the window and put a spoon in her throat and showed up some good white patches." She suspected tuberculosis and ordered a visit from the local doctor and free delivery of milk for the family. The pain and suffering of the people was as often emotional as physical. "We see the repatries on the train eager to see a husband whom they have not seen for three and a half years, and a week later when we call on them at home they have heard he was killed Nov. 1914 etc." Sometimes the stories were so pitiful that "the only solace is work until you can't think and then sleep."[18]

Fortunately, moments of elation matched the despair and devastation on the civilian front. "The cutest thing we ever did was to find his wife for an old man of 70," Dewson recounted cheerfully. Stranded in a small village, the man had been separated from both his wife and his luggage. The Red Cross sent him a suit and found his trunk. Locating his wife took a little longer: she had wound up in a village about four hours away by train. "We started her coming back and by chance we passed through the village the morning of her return. He was wreathed in smiles, clad in his new suit, and at the station waiting for her three hours before the train was due. The old cutey!"[19]

Relocating refugees and settling them into new lives involved long hours of work for Red Cross workers like Dewson and Porter. Trains arrived in Bourg-en-Bresse at 5:50 and 7:15 in the morning and 4:30 in the afternoon, a schedule which guaranteed long days. When the intensified German offensive after March 1918 drastically increased the flood of refugees, the Red Cross gave up hope of finding employment for the relocated French citizens and concentrated instead on meeting their basic needs for food and shelter. "We thought we were busy before the offensive, but now with all the people from the Oise and Somme flooding down here we just gape."[20]

Throughout the resettlement work, the American Red Cross delegates strove to keep open channels of communication and cooperation with the French government, at whose invitation they were operating. This involved working long hours with the local French officials, and it also involved speaking French. "My French, Lucy, well it's as great as ever," Dewson confessed to Stebbins. She had nearly flunked French at Wellesley during her freshman year. Now Molly struggled to master the language well enough to converse with the "mucky mucks," but, she admitted, "It takes more courage to speak French than to cross the ocean." She eventually learned to use her poor linguistic skills to her advantage. She often opened meetings by saying, "Je suis certaine que vous pouvez me comprehendre parce que je parle Français si magnifiquement." By the time she got to the word magnifiquement, she wrote, "they all giggle and we have arrived."[21]

Although Dewson learned to charm the local French citizens, she was not always so successful in dealing with the overlapping layers of bureaucracy comprised by the American Red Cross, the International Red Cross, the American Expeditionary Force, and the French government. Dewson called the French system "the most autocratic government that I ever met with in any country professing to have free institutions." Divided into eighty-three prefectures, each area was under the control of an appointed official. Dewson complained, "No man can even build a pigpen without his permission." Such institutional impediments made repatriation work even more difficult.[22]

Nor did she have many kind words for her compatriots who were running the American war effort in France. By the time she took over as director of general relief for Southern France in June 1918, she felt completely hemmed in by the army bureaucracy: "really these funny old business men, all tricked out in uniform, running around ordering and counter-ordering, and saluting and Majoring and Captaining, are a perfect scream. I never thought men were any smarter than women, and I now think their organizing ability is enough to make a dressmaker smile."[23]

If dealing with the bureaucracy sometimes wore Molly Dewson down, it almost did poor Polly Porter in. Polly was, to say the least, no born bureaucrat, and she found it much more difficult than her partner to find her niche in France. Polly took a rather unorthodox approach to running her operation. Red Cross chief Edward Devine was amused neither by her reference to military requirements as "rigamarole" nor by the infrequency of her reports. She in turn had little sympathy for her overworked superiors in Paris: "It may be annoying to have Paris bombarded and Amiens about to fall, but all this is entirely obliterated for us by our local mole hills." And she was not content to wait patiently in St.-Etienne for the bureaucracy to answer her questions. Once she got so exasperated that she "ran away" to Lyons to find out for herself what was going on: "They just *will not* answer your letters satisfactorily from head quarters and there are certain things I *must* know so I have decided, whether they like it or not, and they certainly won't like it, to appear in person and commandeer the information I must have!"[24]

Polly Porter always underestimated her capabilities. When she was first posted to St.-Etienne, she cried in despair, "So there I am—in the dirtiest, dreariest city in France, with a perfectly overwhelming job on my hands and quite, quite unable to swing it." In fact, however, she did a good job at her post. "Polly is in great condition, industrious and contented," Molly reported to Bill Porter. "It's been a good thing for her to come to France. She is always so much better off when occupied." The Red Cross came to a similar assessment of Porter's usefulness: "Miss Porter knows the people well enough by this time," one official wrote, "and is known by them—and liked—and in spite of her unwillingness to own it, she has grown to like the work she is doing here."[25]

But it was precisely Polly's inability to take satisfaction from her work that made her so testy and ready to take offense. Characteristically she began one letter to her absent partner, "Delicious little fire burning on the hearth, room neatly swept—a tasty little lunch at the Orgeas'

neatly tucked away inside me—but me voilà—cross as a bear!" A
coworker ("curse take her," Polly wrote) was hounding her for an ac-
counting of a shipment of blankets; a group of officials was scheduled to
arrive from Lyons, "and it is my sorry fate to spend the afternoon clos-
eted with Ludvic—little, fat, inane fool! He is going to tell me exactly
what to do about my furniture—his round baby face puckers into wrath
and distress as it begins to dawn upon him just how much stuff I have
here!" The final straw was that Ludvic always called her Miss Holmes:
"You know how gratifying it is to me not to have an identity of my
own!!" In a postscript, Polly admitted that Ludvic had not been so bad
after all, but she always expected the worst, and that trait did not make
for a happy bureaucrat.[26]

Polly Porter's stay in France was not all woe, however. In many
ways, she and Molly managed to enjoy themselves in spite of the war.
They used their weekends together to explore the French countryside
(territory they would visit again under more settled conditions in
1927), and Polly acquired a taste for French cinema. She was even
elected vice-president of St.-Etienne's "Union française pour le suffrage
des femmes."[27]

Just as they did back on the Berlin farm, Molly and Polly spent
many of their happiest moments zipping from village to village in an automobile on official Red Cross business. "We feel very much at home
here because we are to have a little Ford!" Polly told her brother. But
this was not just any Ford—it was their own station wagon, which they
shipped over from the Berlin farm. It arrived packed like a piano, the
only casualty of the transatlantic crossing being a broken brake. Parts
were hard to find, and Dewson and a crew of mechanics struggled to
keep the car running in spite of the battering it took on the French
country roads. Their not-so-trusty Ford set the stage for a series of mis-
adventures. "Rather let me picture my little partner Polly, coming back
from Roanne with a nurse, bursting a tire, stopping and unable to start
the Ford, getting a soldier to push. Still stuck, soldier decamped with
Miss Smythe's nurse's cape in the dark, and the two spent the night beside the road."[28]

Despite the grim conditions all around her, Molly Dewson approached her war work in the cheery frame of mind she used to describe
Polly's adventures on the road. "Oh, this is a funny, funny life! I can't
write the serious side," she admitted. "I never should have earned my
salt on the Sob Squad." She adopted the same tone when sharing tales
of her Red Cross service with her Wellesley classmates: "We certainly

took off our coats, pulled up our sleeves, screwed our hair into a knob on the back of our heads, and sailed in. But I would not bother '97 with any miseries but just tell them how I piloted an all but brakeless Ford down the Juras, coming home triumphant but at dizzying speed on high; how I slept on the floor of the train corridor but one sardine in a box of foreign soldiery, which however by daylight and examination of the head in my lap proved to be Italian speaking, 100 per cent Americans from New York City; and how I made a joke book for relief workers that always broke the ice in a French Committee meeting. Oh those good old faithful jokes in my terrible French!"[29]

Another comic theme was men, a topic usually absent from Dewson discourse. She was especially fond of describing the foibles of men in uniform, comparing a country at war to the awkwardness of a sixteen-year-old boy. She complained loudly about the business and military men who liked to chase Red Cross workers: "Really I never did so believe in early marriages and every one staying at home before. This running here and there, eating with a bunch of old brokers every night, does not amuse me." One night Dewson climbed a church rampart by moonlight with a "lit" U.S. sergeant. "Better with my sedate company than with another," she observed pragmatically.[30] In Lyons, an expert on contagious diseases "camped out" at her desk until she agreed to have dinner with him. She professed ulterior motives for accepting this date: typhoid was affecting her district, and she hoped to pump him for information. That task accomplished, the next night she ducked out of her office through a side door to avoid his persistent attention. If her brother and his wife had any fears that forty-four-year-old Molly might be contemplating romance, Dewson reassured them: "Do not think, however, George and Minnie, that this dyed in the wool old maid is thrown off her balance." The moral was clear: "Really a decent American man is better at home."[31]

The light, almost frivolous tone that Dewson adopted in her letters home was quite common among Americans stationed in France. Few doughboys were subjected to the sustained heavy fighting or the monotonous yet terrifying trench warfare that sapped the morale of their British and German counterparts. Often members of the American Expeditionary Force experienced the war more as tourists and spectators than as soldiers. Their letters home, like Molly Dewson's, discussed the war less than the beauty of the French countryside, the antiquity of its buildings and culture, and their inevitable chafing at military discipline. "What most strikes the reader of these personal war records," concluded the historian David Kennedy, "is their unflaggingly positive, even enthusiastic tone."[32]

Molly Dewson could observe the French scene so cheerfully because she lived in reasonably comfortable surroundings. "It is enormously easier than staying at home. I have plenty to eat though restricted in certain directions. I even have a bath every day." Her accommodations varied from place to place: one household she shared with five Red Cross workers came with a maid. By contrast, her flat in Lyons was cold, damp, and full of bedbugs—her colleagues took fifty-eight nits from her hair. (Lest her family worry, she added in the next breath, "It is a gay little dashing life.") Despite the wartime travel restrictions, she managed to move quite freely around France, with frequent business trips to Paris and a rendezvous with Polly almost every weekend. Travel by rail was not simple (Dewson described the trains as packed "like [for] a Harvard-Yale game, but not so polite a crowd"), but if passengers were willing to sit overnight, they usually could get where they wanted. Dewson's official Carte d'Identité and her distinctive Red Cross uniform often helped to get her a seat.[33]

Dewson's spirits sagged occasionally. She unburdened herself to her fellow suffragist Grace Johnson: "France lies so beautiful so tranquil under the summer sun it seems as though here was the birthplace of peace. Never a heart on the sleeve, never a sign but this eternal terrible mourning—how I hate it—no hysteria, no bearing up—just this same everyday attitude toward life. It might almost deceive you. You might forget that a few hundred miles away the Germans are still pushing pushing on."[34] The ravages of war coincided with the pain of separation from Polly, one of the few times they were apart in more than fifty years. Molly was just as lonely for Polly's companionship as Polly was for the woman she called the sails of her ship, her own North Star.[35] Dewson titled a snapshot of herself sitting by the side of a road looking exhausted and forlorn, "MWD at her lowest ebb."[36]

The war news by the early fall of 1918 was considerably more optimistic than it had been in the spring: the massive influx of American troops and supplies had finally tipped the balance toward the Allies. By chance Molly Dewson was attending a meeting at the Red Cross headquarters on the Place de la Concorde in Paris on November 11, 1918, the day the Armistice was declared. For the rest of her life, she loved to tell of being in the midst of the French and American crowds as they celebrated the Allied victory and the return of peace.[37]

The armistice ended the war but not the urgent need for relief and rehabilitation. Dewson was the one woman chosen along with eleven men to oversee Red Cross civilian relief in the areas of the north now returned to France. (Polly irreverently referred to this delegation as "you & your 11 fat gentlemen friends.") Dewson supervised the transfer of supplies and material from the southern sector of France to the north. Polly Porter, left to close down her operation in St.-Etienne, reconciled herself to this final four-week separation: "Just the same you little, old coal-black Puissye, I don't begrudge you the change."[38]

Dewson's trip to the Laon area in mid-December 1918 gave her first-hand exposure to the devastation wrought by the German occupation.[39] The American Red Cross wanted Dewson to stay on in France, offering her and Polly positions as assistant managers of their warehouse operation in Verdun. (In an offhand manner that would have galled Polly, the Red Cross official said, "I am taking it for granted that you can answer for her.")[40] But the two volunteers were eager to return home: "We are folding our tents now," Molly said in early December. She was especially tired of wartime restrictions: "Papers! Oh heavens but it will be nice to go where you please when you please once again. For the free born the rules of the military are necessary but tiresome." Molly and Polly traveled to Liverpool to board the S.S. *Adriatic* back to America. They disembarked in New York on the last day of January 1919, fifteen months after they began their wartime service.[41]

For the United States the war was over almost as soon as it began, a stark contrast to the years of stalemate and devastation experienced by the European combatants. Molly Dewson never had any doubts about the necessity of fighting the war: "Peace was a dream that the world was no where near ready for," she wrote. "We were too selfish for peace, and our selfishness was not sufficiently organized."[42] Polly never recorded her feelings on the righteousness of World War I, but she was deeply moved by the experience. For the rest of her life she considered herself a pacifist.

The war cemented the Porter-Dewson partnership. By 1919 there was little question in their minds, or among their friends, that they would spend the rest of their lives together. Their experiences also strengthened friendships with other women who, like themselves, had gone off to war. B. Z. Scott, a Wellesley classmate of Dewson's who served with the Y.W.C.A. in France, and Margaret Curtis, a Boston social worker who became chief of the Bureau of Refugees for the Red Cross, remained friends of Molly's and Polly's for life.[43] So did Marie-Thérèse Vieillot, a French Red Cross colleague who worked with them in the Loire district. Vieillot, who later studied at both Simmons and the New York School of Social Work, was still coming to Castine for occasional summer visits after the Second World War. One lazy July day in 1952, Dewson made place cards out of old French postcards for a "World War I Reunion Lunch" that included her partner, Marie-Thérèse Vieillot, and B. Z. Scott.[44]

For all the benefits of war work, Molly Dewson's time in France was tinged with a certain amount of regret. When Molly and Polly first arrived in France, "we were wild to go up behind the front handing out doughnuts and cigarettes to the soldiers, but not for us. They appealed to us to stand by the ship." At first, repatriation work had been interesting: "all the fun was being with the French and the refugees and out and around turning handsprings." But as Dewson gained more administrative responsibility in the Red Cross, her position was "getting to be a stupid old organizing job. It has been stupid as death for two months, and I really don't know how long I can stick it out."[45]

Molly Dewson often remarked that she felt removed from the war: while she saw thousands of men in uniform, she never saw the war itself. "You feel more a part of the war than many here," she wrote somewhat wistfully to Lucy Stebbins in California. As the Armistice neared, she sounded a similar refrain to her sister in Rhode Island: "Well it looks as though the war was going to finish without my hearing as much noise of warfare as you have had off the U.S. Coast line."[46]

Even though Molly Dewson never got to the front lines to hand out doughnuts to the troops, her World War I work was a monumental break from the life she had been leading. Instead of sitting out the war on the sidelines of the home front, she and Polly Porter decided to become active participants. They went as a team, forgoing salaried positions to increase their chances of staying together, and saw their relationship strengthened as a result. Despite a few regrets, their war work qualified as "the great adventure" of their lives. For Dewson, the drama of the experience would be topped only by her service to Franklin and Eleanor Roosevelt in the New Deal. For now, she just felt good to be home in a world at peace.

PART II

A New Deal for Women

CHAPTER SEVEN

"When Red Roses Are Green": The National Consumers' League

HE year 1920 is often portrayed as a great divide in women's history.[1] The passage of the Nineteenth Amendment ended an arduous seventy-two year struggle and represented an important milestone for the nation's women citizens. Now, it seemed, women were the political equals of men.

Optimism and excitement surrounded the suffrage victory. Suffrage leaders envisioned a future in which women citizens would use their franchise to support the issues of greatest concern to them, especially the promotion of international understanding and the furthering of social and humanitarian justice. Organized politicians, foreseeing a doubled electorate, quaked in fear that women might use their votes to outlaw war, clean up politics, and reform the cities. Capitalizing on these fears of a potential women's bloc, politically savvy women won passage of several significant pieces of legislation in the immediate postsuffrage years. Most noteworthy was the 1921 Sheppard-Towner Act, which established federally funded maternal and infancy health care programs. Passage of this law was viewed as the first of many fundamental changes that women's suffrage would bring to political and social life.[2]

In many ways, this optimism proved exaggerated and short-lived. By the mid-1920s, women's political clout began to wane. The addition of women to the electorate did not double the voting turnout overnight; in fact, turnout relative to the number of voters declined in the 1920s. When the women's bloc failed to materialize, women had to shoulder the blame for their supposed apathy. Soon they were the victims of the widely held notion that the nineteenth amendment had not made any difference in politics and public life at all. In fact, much of the disappointment over the failure of women's suffrage to accomplish sweeping reforms was rooted in unrealistic expectations about what women could do with their votes. No one seemed to blame men for failing to cure the nation's ills at the ballot box, but women were held to a higher standard. Few were listening when Jane Addams responded to the question, "Is Woman Suffrage Failing?" by asking, "is suffrage failing?"[3]

The fate of women at the polls was intricately linked to broader patterns of political participation in modern American life. Women were not to blame for the drop in voter turnout: electoral participation had been declining since the turn of the century, well before the great majority of women won the vote.[4] Such changes were part of a broader transition from the nineteenth-century political culture characterized by intense party loyalty and high turnout (regularly as high as 75 percent of eligible voters) to a twentieth-century pattern of declining party affiliation and increased voter apathy. Anticipating the findings of the new political history by four decades, the feminist Suzanne LaFollette noted in 1926, "It is a misfortune for the woman's movement that it has succeeded in securing political rights for women at the very period when political rights are worth less than they have been at any time since the eighteenth century."[5]

Historians have also tended to accept 1920 as a crucial benchmark in recent women's history and to judge the postsuffrage era as somehow lacking excitement in comparison to the women's activism that characterized the suffrage mobilization.[6] In contrast to the apparent unity of the suffrage movement, the 1920s women's movement seemed fragmented and ineffective, especially because of disagreement among feminists over protective legislation and the Equal Rights Amendment. But such an interpretation is inadequate. The suffrage movement was not monolithic. The goals of Southern white women, immigrant labor organizers in New York City, and leaders in the Western states who already had the vote were quite different. The split between Alice Paul's Congressional Union and the National American Woman Suffrage Association was just one of the most public and spectacular instances of profound fissures within the ranks of suffragists.

Like the women's bloc (which was not very feasible in a two-party system, especially when voting is being systematically devalued), it was not realistic to hope for a unified women's movement, given the diversity of concerns women's groups brought to public life. After the false unity provided by suffrage, a more normal pattern returned in the 1920s as the women's movement broke into a variety of smaller units. But, rather than registering a decline in feminist activity, the 1920s (and the decades afterward) were characterized by continued vitality on the part of women's organizations. Women participated in a wide range of political movements and organizations: the club movement, traditional voluntary organizations, groups organized around racial, religious, or ethnic identities, peace groups, professional organizations, and partisan politics. Although some women's organizations declined or disbanded, such as the Women's Trade Union League or the National American Woman Suffrage Association, new ones—such as the Federation of Business and Professional Women's Clubs and the Women's Organization for National Prohibition Repeal—sprang up. The historian Nancy Cott has concluded that the level of women's organization at the end of the 1920s compared favorably to the level reached at the height of suffrage mobilization.

The idea that suffrage was somehow a disappointment and that the women's movement entered a period of decline after the passage of the nineteenth amendment has colored, even poisoned, descriptions of women's contributions to the postsuffrage era. Yet once the shibboleths about suffrage are swept away (predictions promulgated for the most part not by the suffragists but by politicians and political commentators), the decade appears in a different light. Voting is not the only or even the most appropriate measure of women's political mobilization. The limited act of casting a ballot was in fact a minor change, although symbolically it was of great importance. More important than voting after the 1920s was the continuation of women's political activities from the presuffrage era, especially the ongoing vitality of women's organizations. The political and social climate in the 1920s proved more hostile for women's issues than the Progressive era had, but we should not look on the decade as a period of unmitigated stagnation or disillusionment for women in public life.

Molly Dewson's career in the 1920s and 1930s adds an important chapter to the story of women's political activism in the years beyond suffrage. Rather than marking a decrease in her activism, the period after 1920 represented the flowering of her political talents. The modes in which she chose to exercise her political influence are instructive. She began the decade by returning to a women's voluntary organization, the National Consumers' League, as a vehicle to promote adoption of protective legislation. She then worked at two women's civic organizations —the Women's City Club and the New York Consumers' League— where she joined like-minded women who were interested in effecting reform. By 1928, Molly Dewson had taken a final step on the path that had begun with the successful suffrage fight less than a decade before: she entered partisan politics through the intervention of her good friend and colleague Eleanor Roosevelt. Once Franklin Delano Roosevelt won election to the White House in 1932, Dewson inaugurated a program of issue-oriented educational organizing within the Women's Division of the Democratic party that drew directly on her suffrage experience.

Molly Dewson was fortunate to have belonged to a generation of women who won the right to vote early enough in their careers to forge new roles for women in politics and public life. This generation belonged to two eras: one in which women were marginal to the political scene, and one in which they were beginning, however tentatively, to establish themselves as a permanent presence in the American political system. Dewson's political career exemplifies the ways women used their new franchise and highlights the priorities and problems that they faced as they made their way in the "man's world" of politics.

When Molly Dewson disembarked from the S.S. *Adriatic* on the last day of January, 1919, she had no firm plans. "Well and now I've turned another page," she wrote to Lucy Stebbins. "What [next]? But anyway I'm like all the let down European nations somewhat self indulgent and I'm not worrying one bit."[7] Dewson's attitude was typical of how she approached her career: confident that interesting challenges would keep coming her way, she did not hesitate to quit one activity before settling on the next. Polly's income freed her from the necessity of earning a living and allowed her to pursue this rather unconventional pattern of professional advancement. Dewson planned to keep busy in her chosen field—regulation of working conditions by means of legislation—but she did not worry about finding a "professional niche." In fact, she never did, even after she entered Democratic politics in the late 1920s. This was the career pattern that suited her best, both personally and professionally.

Molly and Polly savored their freedom from bureaucratic commitments after fifteen months of service in France. They picked up their

dogs in Castine and checked out the farm they still owned in South Berlin. There was no thought of returning to farming—a wise decision
since a severe depression struck agriculture in 1920–21. Neither did
they want to stay in Boston, a city they had come to feel was too pro-
vincial for their tastes. They stopped there just long enough to attend a
luncheon given in their honor by the Boston Equal Suffrage Association for Good Government.[8]

No doubt Massachusetts suffragists, on the verge of victory in
1919, hoped Dewson and Porter would stay around for the final stages
of the campaign, but the two women had decided to go West. Neither
had ever visited California, and Dewson expected to be "mad" about
the state she had heard so much about from Lucy Stebbins. They
shipped their car to Southern California and took the train out, accom-
panied by their chow, Fu T'ou. ("What will your mother think of a dog
visitor," Dewson joked to Stebbins.) Their travel agenda was loose and
flexible: "We are not in any hurry. It's all a question of how long the
money holds out." Arriving back in Castine in May after logging three
thousand miles, the Porter-Dewsons settled in for what had become
their annual summer vacation at Moss Acre. Dewson reported to her
Wellesley classmates, "It is a perfect lark and I am brown as a hobo."[9]

Summer in Castine was rejuvenating, but Dewson soon started
thinking about resuming her professional career. She had no dearth of
options. As late as 1921 the Red Cross was still trying to tempt her with
child welfare work in Central Europe. (They wondered, "Would it
make any difference . . . if Miss Mary Porter were asked to go also?")[10]
Homer Folks approached Dewson about a job with the New York State
Charities Aid Association, and Maud Wood Park sounded her out
about joining the national staff of the newly formed National League of
Women Voters. In addition, she received several offers to continue her
work with delinquent girls.[11]

The most challenging offer, and the one that Dewson chose to accept, came from Florence Kelley of the National Consumers' League
(NCL). The Consumers' League was the main voluntary association
pushing for the nationwide adoption of the minimum wage, Dewson's
major political interest since 1912, and Florence Kelley was a close
friend of Elizabeth Glendower Evans, Dewson's first mentor. In 1911,
she had tried to lure Dewson to New York to serve on the committee
investigating the Triangle Shirtwaist Factory fire. This time she was
successful.[12]

Florence Kelley stands out as one of the preeminent woman reformers of the Progressive generation, matched in influence and power only by Jane Addams. The daughter of an outspoken Pennsylvania congressman and a Quaker mother, Kelley graduated from Cornell University in 1882. She studied socialism at the University of Zurich (the first European university open to women), where she met and married a Russian medical student named Lazare Wischnewetsky, with whom she had three children. The marriage did not survive transplantation to America. In 1891 Kelley moved into the new Hull House in Chicago while she served as Illinois's first factory inspector. Like other professional women of her time, Kelley drew strength from the supportive settlement-house network for the rest of her life; her friendships with Jane Addams and Julia Lathrop were especially close. When Kelley accepted the general secretaryship of the newly formed National Consumers' League in 1899, she took up residence at New York's Henry Street settlement.[13]

No one who worked with Florence Kelley could fail to be touched by her total commitment to improving the conditions of modern industrial life. Under her leadership, the NCL served as a training ground for several generations of women reformers who went on to serve in the federal and state government.[14] Her coworker Frances Perkins recalled, "Countless times Mrs. Kelley's steely look and steady, 'Frances, you've got to do it' have meant the difference between doing it that year and not doing it at all." As Kelley once confided to her young assistant, "You know at twenty I signed on to serve my country for the duration of the war on poverty and on injustice and oppression, and I take it, Frances, that it will last out my life and yours and our children's lives." Newton Baker captured her force especially well: "Everyone was brave from the moment she came into a room."[15]

Although the National Consumers' League never had more than several thousand members, the group had an influence that far outweighed its often limited financial resources. The NCL placed a high priority on the promotion of labor legislation, especially laws protecting women and children in the work force. In 1908, the prominent Boston attorney Louis Brandeis and the NCL researcher Josephine Goldmark helped convince the U.S. Supreme Court to uphold legislation mandating a maximum ten-hour day for women workers in Oregon. Their successful brief in *Muller v. Oregon* devoted less attention to legal analysis than to the presentation of sociological data linking long hours and poor health in women. This soon became a standard NCL tactic.[16]

The National Consumers' League also worked to change public policy through legislative action. The organization was in the forefront of agitation for the minimum wage, limitations on night work by women, and the elimination of excessive hours and sweatshop conditions. It lobbied successfully for the creation within the U.S. Department of Labor of the Children's Bureau in 1912 and the Women's Bureau in 1920; these bureaus spearheaded further legislative initiatives such as the Sheppard-Towner Federal Maternity and Infancy Act of 1921, one of the first federally funded health care programs. The NCL also orchestrated the uphill and ultimately unsuccessful fight for a child labor amendment to the U.S. Constitution. By the 1920s, however, the organization had been hurt by the conservative political climate in force after the war, especially by the redbaiting that linked many reform groups with unpopular radical causes.[17]

Molly Dewson experienced Florence Kelley's force of personality firsthand during their close association from 1919 to 1924. Although Dewson's official title was Research Secretary, she was not overestimating her influence when she called herself Kelley's "right hand woman" in the early 1920s. Dewson contributed a succinct portrait of her new boss: "Facial expression, that of an indignant old fighter used to battle, enlisted for life. Appearance, about like Velásquez's Esopus, no interest in clothes, always in black, no stays." Kelley was not always an easy person to work for—Dewson later characterized her as a "smoking volcano that any moment would burst into flames." If Molly did not have something trenchant to contribute, Kelley would look up at her and say, "Are you feeling sick today?" Somehow she found the words.[18]

Since the staff of the Consumers' League was so small, Molly Dewson was often drawn into whatever activity was engaging Kelley's attention. In the early 1920s, an issue very much on Kelley's mind was a proposal put forward by Alice Paul and the National Woman's Party for a constitutional amendment to prohibit discrimination based on sex. Concluding that Paul's "terrifying draft for a federal amendment" would undermine the protective legislation which was the cornerstone of the NCL philosophy, Kelley spoke out sharply in opposition. Because of her commitment to the minimum wage for women, Molly Dewson also had reasons to oppose the amendment.[19]

The Equal Rights Amendment (ERA) was not a unifying cause for feminists in the 1920s. In fact, disagreement over the issue split the women's movement throughout the postsuffrage years. Arrayed on one side were the former militant suffragists led by the National Woman's

Party, who supported equal treatment for men and women under the law. On the other side were reform-minded women in groups like the Women's Trade Union League, the Consumers' League, and the League of Women Voters, who saw legislative initiatives, especially protective legislation, as the best way to advance women's interests.[20]

Much was at stake in this debate, and tensions ran high. The controversy concerned both ideology and tactics. The social reformers tended to stress the special conditions, such as maternity and family responsibilities, that limited women's ability to compete equally in the world. The Woman's Party saw men and women as equal and decried any devices which artificially set women apart as a special class.

The debate over the ERA also reflected differences within the women's movement over short-term tactics. Both sides agreed that, ideally, both men and women should enjoy protection such as limited work hours and minimum wage standards. But few courts were likely to extend such benefits to men in the conservative judicial climate of the 1920s. The social reformers therefore gave a higher priority to the continuation of protective legislation for women than to support for the abstract principle of legal equality. To their minds, half a loaf was better than none. The Woman's Party, on the other hand, pointed out the drawbacks of protective legislation. Prohibitions on night work, for example, kept women out of such lucrative trades as printing, and limitations on hours prevented them from working split shifts as conductors or telephone operators. Rather than suffer under laws designed to protect their interests, the Woman's Party argued, women should be free to make their own choices with regard to employment and career, even at the cost of short-term losses for certain groups of women who benefited from protective legislation. Throughout the 1920s and 1930s, these two groups faced each other in an uneasy standoff.[21]

Although Florence Kelley repeatedly tried to enlist Molly Dewson in the campaign against the ERA, Dewson's heart was never in the fight. Every time the subject came up, she replied that she greatly preferred research work and writing pamphlets on the minimum wage to battling with Alice Paul over the ERA. This was a matter as much of personality as of politics. Temperamentally Dewson was far more interested in pursuing a positive goal—such as promoting the minimum wage—than the negative one of opposing the proposal of another women's organization. Florence Kelley respected Dewson's judgment and eventually set her free to devote her energy and enthusiasm to the minimum wage.[22] Molly Dewson threw herself into promoting the minimum wage with a singleminded zeal similar to her total identification with Franklin Roosevelt and the New Deal in the 1930s. She quickly became so associated with the cause that, in a pun on her initials, her colleagues took to calling her "Minimum Wage" Dewson.

The shadow of unconstitutionality hung over all efforts to promote minimum wage legislation in the 1910s and 1920s. No matter how much education and advocacy the National Consumers' League could muster (as research secretary Dewson contributed some sharply argued pamphlets), the fate of the minimum wage still rested with the courts, and it was here that Dewson concentrated her efforts. In 1917, the Supreme Court had let stand by a 4–4 vote a lower court's ruling upholding Oregon's minimum wage law for women, but the ultimate status of minimum wage laws remained in doubt. *Adkins v. Children's Hospital* (1923), on which Molly Dewson worked full time for almost two years, provided such a definitive ruling.[23]

The District of Columbia's minimum wage law, which spawned this case, had a somewhat unusual legislative history. The law was enacted on September 19, 1918, by the United States Congress, which retained responsibility for governing the District of Columbia. This minimum wage legislation was an anomaly in a Congress that was preoccupied with the conduct of World War I and, as evidenced by the increasing repression of civil liberties in wartime, not especially noted for its support of progressive causes. In fact, the D.C. law was the last minimum wage statute enacted until the 1930s.

The purpose of the legislation was "to protect the women and minors of the District from conditions detrimental to their health and morals, resulting from wages which are inadequate to maintain decent standards of living." A Minimum Wage Board created to determine and then enforce standards set a minimum wage of $16.50 a week. No sooner had that standard been promulgated than the District of Columbia Children's Hospital filed suit to block its enforcement. Jesse Adkins, chair of the D.C. Minimum Wage Board, chose Harvard Law School professor Felix Frankfurter and the National Consumers' League to represent the Board.

The reformers met with initial success. The Supreme Court of the District of Columbia upheld the minimum wage law in 1920, and the U.S. Court of Appeals affirmed its decision by a 2–1 margin in 1921. Florence Kelley was ecstatic when she heard the news of the victory in the Appeals Court, singling Molly Dewson out for special praise: "I don't know how to congratulate you enough upon having a concrete result of such national importance to satisfy your mind. That is a satisfaction that I never get, and I'm moved to envy, along with my gratitude for your very hard and very effective work in our common cause."[24] Kelley hoped for a similarly positive ruling from the U.S. Supreme Court.

Kelley's optimism proved misplaced. An unusual set of circumstances upset the victory on which the reformers hoped to build their case to the Supreme Court. Justice Robb of the Court of Appeals had been ill during the oral arguments in February, and his place had been filled by a judge from the D.C. Supreme Court. Just a month after the June decision upholding the law, Justice Robb decided that he wanted to have the case reheard so he could sit on it. This unusual request was granted, and the case was argued again in October. A year later, by a 2–1 majority with Justice Robb tipping the balance, the law was declared unconstitutional. The stage was thus set for appeal to the United States Supreme Court.

Throughout this three-year legal battle, Molly Dewson collaborated closely with Felix Frankfurter, counsel for the Minimum Wage Board. They prepared three briefs, each one more elaborate than the last. The two-volume document submitted to the Supreme Court in 1923, an exposition of current economic and sociological research on women's working conditions modeled on the Brandeis brief in *Muller v. Oregon*, could probably have qualified as a doctoral dissertation had Molly Dewson gone on for a graduate degree in economics or sociology. Dewson was even listed on the cover of each brief alongside Frankfurter, a rare tribute to a nonlawyer for her central role in the appeal process.[25]

Since Felix Frankfurter lived and taught in Cambridge and Molly Dewson was happily settled in New York with Polly, much of the planning and execution of these briefs took place by mail. In fact, the two collaborators met for only one hour during the first stage of this complicated project. They soon developed an easy working relationship. While at first Molly signed her letters "Mary Dewson" and addressed her colleague as "Professor Frankfurter," they soon became "M.W.D." and "F.F." Dewson later recalled that Frankfurter "always treated me like one of his law students, who knew legal facts and whom he expected to do their own thinking." "Consider me as your Grade D student," she exclaimed, even though she was pushing fifty and was eight years older than Frankfurter.[26]

Like many other men with whom Molly Dewson worked, Felix

Frankfurter enjoyed her forthrightness and candor. While they were awaiting the first decision from the Court of Appeals, he poked fun at her prediction of the outcome: "Are you still betting that we will get two out of three?" (She was right.) He added more seriously, "I wonder if you know that it was a very real pleasure to work with you." Frankfurter was more fulsome in his praise to Florence Kelley, because "it is easier to tell you than to praise a New Englander to her face." After noting Dewson's "real quality of intellectual initiative and independence" as well as her imagination, understanding, and devotion, he concluded, "You are very lucky to have her."[27]

While the defendants awaited a decision from the Court of Appeals, Felix Frankfurter returned to his teaching and Molly Dewson worked on child labor for the NCL. In November of 1922 they got word that the Court of Appeals had ruled against them. Only momentarily pausing to regroup, the National Consumers' League readied itself for the final battle, proposing to take the case speedily to the United States Supreme Court. Molly Dewson wired Felix Frankfurter that she was "clearing the decks for action," and Florence Kelley solemnly informed a friend that all of Dewson's mail was coming to her desk because "Miss Dewson has taken the veil and retired from the world for many weeks" in order to prepare the Supreme Court brief.[28]

As Christmas approached, Molly was hard at work, she told Frankfurter, but "with only Mrs. Kelley and me in the office, and Mrs. Kelley making frequent trips to the West, it is terribly hard to stay behind 'the veil.' The fact that you do not expect a hearing until April has weakened our resistance to imperative calls." That false sense of security dissolved in January when the National Consumers' League learned that the case would be heard not in April or October as they had expected, but in late February. The brief was due on February 12th, just several weeks away.[29]

The next three weeks were probably the busiest in Dewson's career, surpassing even the final stages of the 1912 Massachusetts minimum wage report and the frantic pace of the 1936 presidential campaign. She later confessed to Eleanor Roosevelt that she "nearly committed hari-kari over the minimum wage briefs." During the week of January 22, Dewson worked every night until almost midnight, until two in the morning on Saturday, and three A.M. on Sunday. The next week was much the same. When she tallied up her evenings and weekends, she found she had worked more than twenty days of overtime in less than a month.[30]

Dewson was not the only one working long hours. Florence Kelley described the scene at NCL headquarters as "Merry Hell in general," adding, "Even Felix up in Cambridge is jumping high jumps twice daily." The office staff put in extensive overtime, bribed by Dewson's offer of double time off when the brief was finished. Still, they never would have made the deadline without the timely loan of proofreaders from the *New Republic*, the *Nation*, the *Freeman*, and the Russell Sage Foundation. Finally, on February 10th, Dewson could report to Kelley that the two-volume brief had gone to the printers and would be back in time to be filed on February 12th.[31]

"At first I thought there might not be a sufficient mass of evidence to be truly impressive," Molly Dewson told Felix Frankfurther when she began work on the *Adkins* brief, "and now I do not know but that I have too much." The Supreme Court brief topped off at 1,138 pages. Drawn from NCL material and state minimum wage commission reports, the brief represented one of the most complete legal and sociological documents ever compiled on the theory and practice of the minimum wage to date. Dewson's talent at collating masses of data and making them compelling to the lay reader, first demonstrated at the Women's Educational and Industrial Union and the Parole Board and refined for the 1912 minimum wage report, now found its most mature presentation in the *Adkins* brief.[32] Florence Kelley expected no less: "It exemplifies in an extraordinary degree the power which was revealed, a dozen years ago, in your Massachusetts report, of finding every conceivable significance in a medley of facts and showing the very last item, in a bright light, to the average reader."[33]

The final chance to convince the Supreme Court came at oral argument on March 18, 1923, and Molly Dewson journeyed to Washington to watch Felix Frankfurter present their case. Dewson reported to Marion Denman Frankfurter that her husband had been excellent in his presentation, but *"superb"* in his rebuttal. In just ten minutes, "with concentrated energy and terrific speed," he answered every point in a clear and convincing manner. "The court held its breath. It was a magnificent intellectual feat." After gushing so to Marion Frankfurter, Dewson cautioned, "Don't tell Mr. F.F. please for men have no understanding." She signed herself "your faithful reporter."[34]

But even Felix Frankfurter's brilliant oral argument did not sway the Court, which less than a month later struck down the D.C. law by a 5–3 vote. Justice Sutherland's majority opinion viewed the minimum wage as an arbitrary infringement of freedom of contract as protected by the due process clause of the Fifth Amendment. Referring back to *Muller v. Oregon*, the majority opinion claimed that special protection for women was no longer necessary now that women had gained equality through the Nineteenth Amendment and other social changes. Justices Taft, Sanford, and Holmes dissented, finding that regulation of wages of women workers constituted a valid exercise of the police power. "It will need more than the Nineteenth Amendment to convince me that there are no differences between men and women or that legislation cannot take those differences into account," Taft proclaimed.[35] Justice Brandeis abstained from the case because his daughter Elizabeth was the general secretary of the D.C. Minimum Wage Board. Molly Dewson thought that Brandeis should have kept his daughter off the board so that his vote could have counted on this crucial issue,[36] but he probably would have disqualified himself anyway based on his prior association with the Consumers' League. And, even if he had voted in favor of the law, the Court's decision would have stood. Suddenly minimum wage legislation, indeed all social legislation, was in doubt.

Adkins v. Children's Hospital generated much popular and scholarly comment, most of it negative. Editorials in the *New Republic, Nation,* and *Outlook* criticized its narrow legal reasoning and its ignorance of the conditions under which modern women toiled. Both the *Survey* and the National Consumers' League quickly convened symposia at which many leading scholars supported an amendment to the Constitution to limit the Supreme Court's authority to rule on cases involving social welfare legislation. A John Kirby cartoon appeared in the *New York World* in which Justice Sutherland held out the decision to a bedraggled figure labeled "Woman Wage Earner" and proclaimed, "This decision, madam, affirms your constitutional right to starve." It was left to Florence Kelley to remind people that not a single woman had participated in the judicial process.[37]

The atmosphere was glum at the headquarters of the National Consumers' League. *Adkins* was the only "Brandeis brief" that had failed to convince the courts. Molly Dewson was devastated.[38] After her months of preparation, how painful it must have been for her to read Justice Sutherland's haughty words, "A mass of reports, opinions of special observers and students of the subject, and the like, has been brought before us in support of this statement, all of which we have found interesting but only mildly persuasive."[39] Dewson took to "cussing" the Supreme Court opinion to Felix Frankfurter. He replied tersely, "Molly, you must learn that if the United States Supreme Court says a red rose is green, it is green. That's final."[40]

In the wake of the 1923 Adkins decision, the status of minimum wage laws in other states was in doubt, and court challenges loomed in Massachusetts, Wisconsin, Arizona, and California. In the fall and winter of 1923–24, Dewson worked on an amicus curiae brief in support of California's 1913 minimum wage law. The National Consumers' League entered the case (Gainer v. Dohrman) at the invitation of Katherine Philips Edson, a longtime Consumers' League activist and a member of California's Industrial Welfare Commission.[41]

Dewson quickly realized that the situation in California was quite different from that which had prevailed in the District of Columbia, notably in its ten years of successful operation and the far greater number of women affected by the California law. She concluded, "it became obvious that their 'red roses' were absolutely different from the 'green roses' of the District of Columbia case. Our amici brief was based on that difference." But the facts that Dewson painstakingly assembled in the Gainer brief were never ruled on, because the case was dismissed before it came to trial.[42] Because the possibility of an adverse decision had been so great, reformers were content with this outcome.

The Arizona minimum wage supporters were not so lucky. Even though the Supreme Court had signalled some support for protective legislation in 1924 by upholding a law limiting night work for women workers, it would not budge on the minimum wage. Relying solely on the Adkins precedent, the Supreme Court in 1925 ruled that the Arizona minimum wage for women was unconstitutional.[43] It continued striking down minimum wage laws for women until it reversed itself in the 1937 case of West Coast Hotel Co. v. Parrish; only in 1941 did the court approve hours and wages legislation for men as well. It took the Depression, the New Deal, and Roosevelt's court-packing plan, among other factors, to produce a Supreme Court which did not routinely rule against social legislation.[44]

Discouragement over the future of minimum wage legislation was probably the main reason why Molly Dewson resigned as NCL research secretary in 1924.[45] In February, even before she went to California to finish the Gainer brief, Molly Dewson told Florence Kelley that she wanted to leave. Further attempts to defend the constitutionality of minimum wage laws seemed futile, perhaps even counterproductive. If night work or maximum hours legislation faced court challenges, Dewson thought Josephine Goldmark had more experience in those areas. This left two other things Dewson could do, neither of which appealed to her: "I could still work for the passage of laws reducing the hours of labor. But few legislatures sit in 1925. Of course I could fight the Woman's Party program against protective laws for wage earning women. A publicity expert, however, could do it much more effectively."[46]

With the salutation "Dear Sister Dewson," Florence Kelley confessed that the letter of resignation did not come as a surprise: "You have not concealed your boredom." Kelley did not dispute Dewson's assessment of hard times on the social reform front: "The League has never offered any worldly rewards. Drudgery and delay—spade work with or without a following harvest—are inherent in it. And I see no prospect of change in that." She did note that forty-two legislatures would be in session in 1925, and asked, "If we do not make a nationwide drive for the 8 hours day in 1925, who will?" As to Dewson's claim that a publicity agent could do her job, Kelley dismissed this as "piffle." But Dewson's mind was made up, and in June the board of directors accepted her resignation with deep regret.[47]

Several factors influenced Molly Dewson's decision to leave the Consumers' League in 1924. The minimum wage situation certainly looked grim in 1923–24. Temperamentally, she lacked Florence Kelley's calm steadfastness in the face of long uphill battles. Health problems also played a role in her departure. When the pace quickened for the Gainer brief, Dewson told Felix Frankfurter that she did not want to ruin her health the way she had in the final weeks of the Adkins brief: "My doctor says I would be 57 kinds of a dumbbell if I did." As Florence Kelley later told Katherine Edson, "Mary Dewson, alas! left us after her return from California last summer when the brief was finished, suffering appallingly from an infected sinus. After a year of continuing suffering her health seems greatly injured and very slight progress made towards restored health." Kelley sympathized with Dewson's predicament: "She is such a dynamo—it is so hard for her to have the current even partly turned off." Yet Dewson remained in generally excellent health throughout the 1920s, suggesting that she used her illness as an excuse to extricate herself from a job she no longer found rewarding.[48]

Despite Dewson's feeling that it was time to move on, she never doubted that her five-year association with Florence Kelley at the National Consumers' League had been a fruitful and productive chapter in her career. Superficially, their working relationship replicated the mentorship that Elizabeth Glendower Evans had supplied in Boston from 1897 to 1912. Yet Elizabeth Glendower Evans had taken a rough and untested young woman under her wing: Florence Kelley confronted a mature, experienced fifty-year-old who was more her equal than her protégé. Molly's security in her professional and personal identity meant she could leave Florence Kelley's tutelage without regrets or hard feelings.

"It would be a great happiness to me," Dewson told Kelley with feeling when she resigned, "if I remained in your memory grouped with Josephine Goldmark and others of the faithful few." "I miss you horribly," Kelley had responded soon after.[49] Such bonds were not easily broken. While Kelley may have lost her right hand woman, she gained a far more valuable ally in the long run. By mid-decade, Molly Dewson was on a path that would lead her directly into the New Deal, a period of legislative reform that embodied much of what Florence Kelley advocated so tirelessly during the first third of the twentieth century.

The Porter-Dewson Scrapbooks

$\clubsuit \clubsuit \clubsuit$

"If there is ever a fire at Moss Acre," Molly Dewson instructed her trusted housekeeper, "the first thing you are to save is the scrapbooks." These meticulously assembled compilations of photographs and memorabilia, more than twenty volumes in all, document the life that Molly Dewson and Polly Porter shared for more than five decades. Forsaking the obligatory shots of relatives and Christmas celebrations, the two women used the scrapbooks to portray the fullness of the world they inhabited together, a world that was predominantly (although not exclusively) peopled with other women. In the scrapbooks are their friends and acquaintances, their extended family circle, their professional colleagues, their dogs, and even their cows. Most of all, the scrapbooks reveal the evolving and varied dimensions of the Porter-Dewson partnership. Photographs, rather than letters, document the love that bound these two women together.

Molly's neighborhood in Quincy, Massachusetts, provided the young girl with lots of companions during her energetic and athletic childhood. It was a life-style offering many advantages, including tennis, which was then coming into vogue among the upper classes. This shot is from the 1880s, when Molly (lower right) was in her early teens. Her sister Nell is the young woman holding a tennis racquet in the middle of the second row; her brother George wears the striped cap just behind his youngest sister. The young tennis player hardly looks like a future national politician, but even in the 1880s, her peers recognized her ambition.

Wellesley College in the 1890s provided a supportive atmosphere for a bright and ambitious young woman like Molly Dewson. She found its all-woman setting very much to her liking. In the group portrait, which she captioned "the inmates of Wood Cottage, 1896," Dewson stands out as the tall, rather severe young woman in a jacket and tie in the second to the last row. Note how the woman next to her, a close friend named Ada Belfield, has her arm linked with Molly's; many other Wellesley students showed similar displays of public affection. Dewson's striking graduation portrait, in which she chose to be photographed in a dark cape and hat, emphasizes her rather masculine demeanor at age twenty-three and reveals her lack of interest in traditional female adornments.

Even at age fourteen, Polly Porter was stunningly beautiful. Ten years Molly's junior, she met her future partner as an intern in the parole department of the Lancaster State Industrial School for Girls, which Dewson headed. The formal portrait of the parole department staff, with Dewson at the far left, shows the style of dress favored by professional women in 1912. But nothing can hide the beauty, or wealth, of Polly Porter (fourth from right). Her impeccably tailored suit with silk borders, matching hat, and expensive leather purse set her off from her colleagues, most of whom had to work for a living.

When Molly and Polly decided to live together in 1912, they gave up parole work and bought a dairy farm in western Massachusetts. They took their work seriously, as in this shot of them clearing land for a garden in front of their house. But they also exhibited a sense of humor, as the photograph of themselves captioned "Dairy-Maids" suggests. They found their roles as gentlewomen farmers very much to their liking.

One attraction of the farm, no doubt, was the quiet evenings the two partners shared in front of the fireplace, Polly reading aloud while Molly listened contentedly. They also threw themselves into the women's suffrage campaign, which throve even in rural Massachusetts. Here Polly is at the wheel of a "suffrage Ford," not a car at all, but a horse and buggy rigged up with suffrage propaganda. Few were more avid suffragists than Molly and Polly, especially since the campaign gave them the opportunity to cruise the countryside in one of their several automobiles.

When the United States entered World War I in 1917, the partners decided to give up farming and volunteer for duty in France. Having their passport photographs taken was the first step.

Serving in France with the American Red Cross was an adventure. Molly and Polly, aged forty-four and thirty-four respectively, put their social work training to use in rehabilitating French refugees, and their duties often brought them into contact with local military officials. Since they were assigned to different sectors of the war zone, they saw each other only occasionally, such as this weekend holiday at Pelussin in the Loire district. Soon the partners grew weary of this separation, and Molly arranged a transfer to a new job that would allow her and Polly to spend more time together.

When the two women returned from France, they indulged their passion for auto touring. In 1919–20, they drove cross-country with their chow, Fou T'ou. Often they would stop by the side of the road for a picnic, as seen in this photograph taken in the Imperial Valley. They launched another adventurous driving trip to Quebec in 1923, where they experienced "one blow out and three punctures in two days." Molly changed the tire, Polly took the picture.

The extended summer vacations that brought Molly and Polly to Moss Acre, Polly's family home in Castine, Maine, provided a respite from the hectic pace of life in New York City. One longtime Castine friend was labor activist Grace Hutchins, whose family lived in nearby Brooksville. Here Grace, Polly, and Molly enjoy a summer afternoon by the ocean.

In the 1920s and 1930s, Molly's and Polly's lives revolved primarily around other women. Polly opened a kennel in Connecticut with Katherine Lindsay, and Molly often helped out with the chores, here dressed comfortably in jodhpurs. Dewson remained an active sportsperson throughout her life, winning a tennis tournament at age fifty-four. She also kept up her golf, which required her to dress more formally than she did at the kennel.

During the 1920s, the political orientations and professional interests of the partners diverged. Polly was involved briefly in a group called Pioneer Youth of America, whose offices are shown above. Molly, meanwhile, was drawn into Democratic politics through her deepening friendship with Eleanor Roosevelt, whom she met in 1925. By 1932, Dewson was totally involved in Franklin Roosevelt's bid for the presidency. At the Chicago nominating convention, she posed for a campaign photograph with James Farley (right), Roosevelt's campaign manager, and a delegate from Nebraska.

After Roosevelt's successful election, Dewson took over the Women's Division of the Democratic National Committee. Here she is inducted into office by Jim Farley and Eleanor Roosevelt. Out of deference to Polly, Dewson ran women's politics out of New York, rather than Washington.

A major source of Molly's power was her close friendship with Franklin and Eleanor Roosevelt. Although Eleanor and Molly had plenty of opportunities to collaborate in New York and Washington, a special treat was E.R.'s visit to Moss Acre in 1935, where Polly and Molly welcomed Eleanor (far right), Marion Dickerman (center), and Malvina Thompson Schneider (far left).

Another close personal and professional friend in Washington was Secretary of
Labor Frances Perkins, shown here with Dewson at a 1938 reception at the Labor Department. At the time, Dewson was serving on the three-member Social
Security Board in Washington. Polly refused to relocate, so Molly rented a
small house in Georgetown, where she had two cats and two dogs to keep her
company, but no Polly. The strain on the partnership caused Dewson to resign
after only nine months on the job.

Dewson's service on the Social Security Board represented the last time she and Polly were separated. After Dewson's retirement, they divided their time between New York and Castine; after 1952, they moved permanently to Moss Acre, where they happily grew old together. Their love had grown stronger over their fifty-two-year partnership, a lifelong attachment (this photograph was taken in 1959) they lovingly preserved for future generations in the Porter-Dewson scrapbooks.

CHAPTER EIGHT

❖

A Small World:
New York in the 1920s

HEN Molly Dewson resigned from her job at the National Consumers' League in 1924, she was fifty years old and tired. The several years before her entry into Democratic politics in the late 1920s were one of the breathing spells which she, consciously or unconsciously, built into her life. "I seem to remember I wanted a rest," she observed about this gap.[1]

She picked an opportune time to pull back from the hectic pace of her career. With the Republicans firmly in control of the federal government and booming prosperity diverting attention away from structural weaknesses in the economy, the 1920s were not especially hospitable times for social reform. Undaunted, Molly Dewson merely scaled down her expectations. "Lack of enthusiasm for my profession and 'good works' does not wrinkle my billiard cloth either. . . . Work is a life long habit and I enjoy doing it just as one enjoys any easy, swift functioning to a necessary end, but since the war I have not been overstimulated by its contemplation." Dewson always maintained a flexible balance between her professional and personal lives. Now she temporarily emphasized the personal.[2]

In the 1920s, Molly Dewson and Polly Porter settled into a cosmopolitan lifestyle in New York which suited them perfectly. In 1927 Dewson humorously described to her Wellesley classmates how she spent her days:

I have renewed my youthful enthusiasms and play tennis, skate, raise puppies and kittens, calves and flowers. I wish you could see Lilly and Lucky (cows), Fu T'ou, Confudza and Shou Hu (chow dogs), and Marie Jeanne (Persian cat). The gold fishes died, alas! I love my lessons, too, Nationalism and Imperialism at Columbia, and French with a little French migrant who taught me in France during the war. By heroic efforts I don't *lose much* of the little I know of that beautiful but elusive language. As for travelling about, it is a passion. I am going to run around France in a Ford this summer, last winter I took a motor trip in North Africa and last summer a very beautiful one in Cape Breton. And friends! They are the essence of life.[3]

About the only social activity Dewson left out of her succinct self-portrait was her membership in the Cosmopolitan Club.

Molly and Polly never regretted their decision to leave Massachusetts for New York. "Molly was every inch the New Yorker," remembered her close friend Clara Beyer.[4] When the two women returned from World War I, they rented an apartment on Bank Street in Greenwich Village. Two years later they decided to put down roots and bought a two-bedroom cooperative apartment at 171 West 12th Street, where they remained until they retired to Castine in 1952. The building's twenty-four apartments were inhabited mostly by other unmarried women or pairs of women. Nancy Cook and Marion Dickerman, two women who were active in New York educational and political circles in the 1920s and who had a profound influence on the political education of Eleanor Roosevelt, lived across the hall.

The Dewson-Porter apartment was small but attractive. Oriental rugs covered the floors and a painting of Mount Moosilauke by Chauncy Ryder (who also lived in the building) hung on the wall. Molly and Polly shared the larger bedroom and bath; the study doubled as a guest room for their frequent visitors. The apartment was also inhabited by a menagerie of dogs or cats, animals with whimsical names such as Solemn Sister and Bad Girl. And, even in the middle of crowded Greenwich Village, Molly and Polly kept their trusty automobile, which was conveniently garaged around the corner.[5]

Molly and Polly spent about nine months of the year in New York, and then took an extended summer vacation, usually at Polly's home in Castine. Moss Acre was run on a fairly lavish scale well into the early 1930s, and guests filled every bedroom throughout the summer. For Molly, summers in Castine were essential: "You know I am a lazy old lady and can manage to work in the winter only when I have a long summer with my eight bow-wows." And Polly.[6]

While Dewson and Porter cherished their time together in Castine, wartime service in France and the trip west in 1919–20 had whetted their appetites for adventurous vacations. Dewson and Porter traveled extensively during the 1920s, more than at any other time in their lives. During the New Deal, Dewson was too absorbed in her political work to take time out for long vacations. And, by the time Molly retired from government in the late 1930s, both women felt too old (and too impecunious) to undertake such journeys. In the 1920s, there were no such constraints of time, energy, or money.

For the Porter–Dewsons, vacations were synonymous with traveling by car. In the fall of 1925 they took a motoring trip through Tunis and Algeria along the North African coast; the next year they drove from Maine to Cape Breton and back. In 1927 they took their first northern European trip since the war, touring the Dutch and French countryside in their Willys–Knight car. On average, they spent between three and four months abroad on each vacation. Obviously no pressing duties or commitments held them in the states.[7]

Dewson and Porter kept a travel diary of their 1927 European trip, which they entitled "Les Voyages des Mmes Porter–Dewson et son fidel chien Fu T'ou" (their favorite chow). Molly and Polly landed in Rotterdam, unloaded their car, and drove directly to Le Hague. They made a pilgrimage to the Peace House of the Women's International League for Peace and Freedom, but they were unimpressed: "not much," read the diary comment. As always, Dewson found European driving challenging: "motoring in cities [is] like driving a car on 5th Avenue sidewalks." They stayed in small hotels, sharing a bedroom. Once they reached southern and central France, they retraced the steps of their wartime service with the Red Cross, ending with sixteen days in Paris where Molly played detective to locate their French Red Cross friend Marie-Thérèse Vieillot.[8]

Molly and Polly enjoyed this trip so much they immediately began to plan another. They did not go abroad in the summer of 1928, however, because Dewson had banged her knee, which would have made driving difficult. (They took some of the money they saved to buy a radio and an electric refrigerator—"more durable satisfaction," she told Lucy Stebbins.)[9] But Dewson quickly hatched another plan for a European trip. Going into "retirement" for six weeks, Dewson wrote a description of their 1927 trip called "Motoring in France On Your Own: Two Women, a Dog, and an American Car." The piece covered itineraries and mileage, the logistics of shipping a car, and what to expect by way of local garages, repairs, and accommodations. She took a draft of this article to the head of the French Line in New York, who liked it so much that he agreed to publish the pamphlet in exchange for free passage for Dewson, Porter, their car, and Fu T'ou the following summer.[10]

The pamphlet was never published: Dewson surmised that the French Line publicity department felt that "our fresh and simple ideas did not harmonize with their stylized publicity for the well-to-do." Happily for Dewson and Porter, the French line did not renege on their offer of free passage. Dewson accepted with only the slightest twinge of guilt: "nor would I be squeamish about taking a free ride for no equivalent rendered if they had not let me in for thinking that I was earning it." They informed the French line that they wished to sail on the *Ile de France* in early June 1929 and return on the same boat in September. Dewson gloated, "We went as arranged in top style."[11]

Although Molly and Polly loved each other deeply and obviously took great delight in each other's company, friends did not always understand their bond. Clara Beyer, whose friendship with both women dated to the 1920s, characterized their relationship as "interesting," but conveyed the impression that Molly's friends put up with Polly mainly because she was so important to Molly. Polly was usually included in social gatherings, but she rarely entered into the conversation. Although she appeared quite bright and attractive, she remained an enigma to many of her partner's close friends.[12]

Polly Porter kept to the background in part because by the 1920s she and Dewson no longer shared professional interests. As Molly moved onto the boards of directors of civic organizations and participated in New York social welfare activities, Polly devoted much of her time to raising Shetland sheepdogs. In the 1920s, she bought a kennel in Westport, Connecticut, with her friend Katherine Lindsay, which they called Bagaduce Kennels, for the Maine river which flows into the Penobscot Bay near Castine. Polly usually spent at least one night a week up at Westport, and sometimes Molly came along for the ride.

Living in the shadow of a strong and self-confident woman like Molly Dewson, Polly Porter had to struggle to maintain her own identity. Despite the prevailing image of Polly as a shy, dependent woman, she had always been something of a free spirit—a close friend described her as very much "of the moment." In the 1920s, perhaps earlier, she began to characterize herself as a revolutionary, an anarchist, or a Communist. This fling with radicalism may have been one way to set herself apart from her more dominant partner. Clara Beyer remembered that, when Dewson was first getting involved in public life, people began asking questions about Polly Porter's political views. Porter and Dewson discussed this and, according to Beyer, Molly agreed "to accept her the way she was."[13]

Polly Porter probably came into contact with Communism through her longtime Castine friend Grace Hutchins, who was living in Greenwich Village in the 1920s with her friend Anna Rochester. In the early 1920s, Hutchins and Rochester were closely associated with the radical Christian pacifist organization called the Fellowship of Reconciliation; by 1927, they had joined the Communist Party. It might seem farfetched to suggest that Polly became a radical simply because of a childhood friendship, but Polly Porter had always been easily swayed by forceful personalities.[14]

One outlet for Porter's radicalism was an organization called the Pioneer Youth of America, with which she was associated in 1924 and 1925. Under the auspices of the New York Association for Child Development and various trade unions such as the International Ladies Garment Workers Union, the group organized clubs and camps for the children of workers in the New York area. Such children's clubs were an outgrowth of the movement for workers' education in the 1920s, which promoted continuing education for adult workers in an atmosphere sympathetic to organized labor. Polly's references to other volunteers as "Fellow Worker Rosenbaum," "Fellow Worker Lee," and "The Little Boss—Joshua Lieberman" initially suggested that this group followed a Communist-inspired model. Trade unionism and workers' education were controversial issues in the 1920s, and certainly to the left of the mainstream political activity favored by Molly Dewson, but they were independent of the Communist Party in this decade. *The Daily Worker*, for example, did not cover the activities of Pioneer Youth of America, while *The New York Times* did.[15]

Most of Molly's and Polly's friends did not take Porter's radical leanings very seriously. "Polly was no more a Communist than the man in the moon," Clara Beyer later commented, a view shared by other friends and family members. Polly never confronted the contradiction between her wealthy lifestyle and her political beliefs; she never studied Marxism or expressed any desire to go to the Soviet Union.[16] In the end, Polly Porter's radicalism emerges as an individualistic and private orientation, which fulfilled personal and intellectual needs she rarely discussed with anyone else. Perhaps the best way to view Polly's self-

declared revolutionary commitment is to accept a friend's characterization of her as a "poetic anarchist."[17]

Despite Polly's radicalism, which stood in stark contrast to Molly's
mainstream political views,[18] their partnership held firm, indeed grew
stronger as Polly emerged somewhat from Molly's shadow. In the 1920s,
the two women settled into a comfortable lifestyle in which their living
arrangements, social life, and professional contacts predominantly revolved around other like-minded women. These women worked with
men and had male friends, but most of them remained unmarried, living alone, with sisters, or in couples. They went to benefits together,
sat on the same boards and committees, and took vacations together.
This world held many rewards for women who chose not to marry and
had enough money to live independently of men.[19]

The apartment cooperative where Molly and Polly lived was such
a world. Across the hall lived Nancy Cook and Marion Dickerman,
and down a few flights were Katherine Lindsay, Porter's partner at the
Bagaduce Kennels, and her friend Edith Balmford. Grace Hutchins and
Anna Rochester lived together not far away in Greenwich Village.
Single women who played a large role in Dewson-Porter social activities
included Polly's friend Irma Lerner, Molly's Wellesley classmate Belle
Sherwin (she later became the president of the National League of
Women Voters), and professional women like Nelle Schwartz, Emily
Marconnier, and Dorothy Kenyon. A special friend was B. Z. Scott,
Dewson's closest chum from Wellesley, who lived with her two unmar-
ried sisters in New Canaan, Connecticut. Friends from Boston who of-
ten passed through included Margaret Curtis of the YWCA, a World
War I buddy; Constance Churchyard of the Windsor School; and
Dorothy Blake, Molly's and Polly's Castine friend.

Although women predominated in the Dewson-Porter social circle, the two women were far from anti-male. Polly was a close friend of
Columbia professors Vladimir Simkhovitch and Joseph P. Chamberlain; in fact, Polly, Molly, and B. Z. Scott considered Joe Chamberlain
such a good friend that they designated their tight little group "the
Lodge." In addition, both Molly and Polly kept up with an extended
network of family members and adopted kin throughout their lives.[20]

Molly Dewson had few, if any, regrets about her decision to remain single, but she still struck a defensive note to her Wellesley classmates in 1927: "Yes, I have no children. And I hope it will not be considered just sour grapes as it undoubtedly is, for me to plaintively hope
that at our reunion all '97's will think of themselves as human individu-

als rather than as proud progenitors or as part of some human conglomeration." As Freudian psychology was increasingly popularized after the 1920s, she realized that she was often perceived as a spinster who had missed out on the great female experiences of marriage and motherhood. In a way that had been absent earlier, she became a bit testy about her life choices.[21]

On occasion, Molly Dewson could be quite oblivious to the needs and desires of young women who wanted to combine professional work with marriage. When Clara Mortensen, the general secretary of the District of Columbia Minimum Wage Board, married Otto Beyer in 1920, she received this decidedly uncongratulatory note from Molly Dewson: "Your wedding announcement certainly gave me most mixed feelings. Even our short acquaintance has resulted in my wishing you all good luck and I can't help but be glad that you have found the right partner. *BUT* at the same time it is no joke for the M.W. [Minimum Wage] cause to have you leave your post until the M.W.B. [Minimum Wage Board] is safely on its feet. . . . Spare time from your wedding journey to tell me that you are modern and plan to return to it." The next spring, Dewson was still harping away at Clara: "Your husband is all to the good and I don't know how I should feel if I were you. Neither do I presume to imagine how he feels at being separated from his wife, but as for me, my feelings are as clear as a bell in regard to your staying in Washington. I can't bear to think of your leaving Washington for a domestic life or for the head of the Women in Industry Bureau of Pennsylvania, or for anything else, until this wave of reaction subsides."[22]

Clara Beyer opted not to follow Molly Dewson's advice. Over the next several years, she raised three children and kept up her professional career on a part-time basis. In 1928, when her youngest son was only three, Beyer returned to work for Grace Abbott at the Children's Bureau; in 1931 she became director of its Industrial Division. Beyer's promotion drew this comment from Dewson: "Well one woman whom we thought was lost to domesticity has been salvaged for the world's work." Molly Dewson was so used to functioning in a world unhampered by traditional female responsibilities that she sometimes had difficulty understanding women who made choices different from her own. Beyer responded plaintively, "I was patting myself on the back for participating, as I thought, in the world's work by bringing up three future leaders and here you come along and destroy my illusions. We poor married women have a hard time measuring up to standards set by our unencumbered sisters and when we think we have succeeded we are brought back to earth with a bang."[23]

While friends were the essence of Dewson's life in the 1920s, her work remained central to her personal and professional identity. After resigning from the Consumers' League in 1924, she did not stay unemployed for long. Just a month later, she was considering an offer from the Women's City Club of New York to become its civic secretary.[24] Dewson sounded out her friend Frances Perkins, who was a member of the club, about whether the job was right for her. Perkins was frank in her reply: "Now about the City Club job—if you want to hear me say that you can do it, you can have it in black and white that you can do it. It is as easy as pie as far as the job is concerned." She then added tellingly, "Getting on with the bunch of women is another matter. I think there is no question but what they will eat out of your hand, but they may worry you to death in the process."[25] Suitably forewarned, Dewson planned to start in the fall of 1924.

The Women's City Club had been founded in late 1915 to facilitate women's participation in the electoral process once they won the vote. When Dewson joined the staff in 1924, Ethel Dreier, a respected member of the New York reform community, had just taken over as president from the former suffragist Mary Garret Hay; the group's vice-presidents included social scientist Mary Van Kleeck and Eleanor Roosevelt. The membership was a mix of professional women and the wives and female kin of New York's social and economic elite. With the substantial financial resources these members could make available, the club bought a Stanford White–designed mansion at the corner of 35th Street and Park Avenue to serve as the clubhouse for its twenty-five hundred members.[26]

The Women's City Club took its civic obligations seriously. The club encouraged women with different political affiliations to work together harmoniously on common fields of endeavor, an orientation akin to the League of Women Voters. In many ways, the Women's City Club was closer to a study group than a political action committee. Molly Dewson did not hold any illusions about what such a heterogeneous mix could accomplish. "Such a club will not lead like a reform organization, nor lurch along like a partisan one, but it does count as a thoughtful and sincere force in public life."[27]

The position of civic secretary was quite openended, a situation, Frances Perkins noted perceptively, "that I take it is what you as an in-

dividual would require of a job."[28] Dewson plunged right in. She coor-
dinated the more than three hundred women who participated regularly
on such club committees as education, the budget, public health, housing, women in industry, legislation, and parks and playgrounds. Membership on these committees was equally divided between professional
women and what club president Ethel Dreier referred to as "just folks."[29]
One of the challenges facing the civic secretary was to teach nonpro-
fessional women to interpret facts and material analytically. Dewson
later used the skills she had learned with Democratic women voters
during the New Deal.

To increase the effectiveness of these civic-minded women, Molly
Dewson convinced Ethel Dreier to initiate a new club policy on legislation and lobbying. Dewson's eight "axioms" for getting legislation
passed reflected the lessons she had learned from Florence Kelley and
the National Consumers' League. If the club concentrated on a few
measures, Dewson argued, it would wield greater influence in behalf of
each measure selected. "Friends in the legislature can be lost by being
too often bothered about too many things," she reminded the board;
and legislators quickly learned to distrust lobbyists who were not thoroughly briefed and sincere in their advocacy. On the other hand, any
number of bills could be *opposed* without loss of influence.[30]

Under Molly Dewson's dynamic leadership, the Women's City
Club singled out several issues for its 1924–25 legislative program.
Topping the list was the Child Labor Amendment. In her capacity as a
representative of the club, Dewson served as the secretary of a coalition
of twenty-one organizations supporting ratification of the amendment.
She spent time in Albany, where she lobbied the state legislature, and
in New York City, where she tried to organize interest at the club. Unfortunately, it proved an inhospitable time to push this reform and
there was no action taken on it in New York.[31]

Wages and hours were the other priority item on the Women's
City Club agenda.[32] In New York state at that time women could work
a maximum of fifty-four hours per week. Reformers had been trying for
several years to lower the maximum to forty-eight. "The 48 hour week
bill was a storm center as it was last year and the year before," Dewson
reported to Women's City Club members. To promote the bill, Dewson
traveled to Albany to meet with allies in the Senate and also had several sessions with Governor Alfred E. Smith. Closer to home, Dewson
convinced the Legislative Committee of the Women's City Club to

commission a field survey of workers' attitudes toward the bill. By a wide margin, working women favored a 48-hour week even if it meant lower wages. But the bill did not pass until 1927.[33]

As civic secretary of the Women's City Club, Molly Dewson demonstrated her ability to transform a position with previously untapped potential into a vehicle for her own brand of political activism. As Frances Perkins predicted, Molly Dewson had no trouble getting these women to eat out of her hand. But many of Perkins's other predictions came true as well. While Dewson liked openended jobs, she found herself out of sympathy with the strictly nonpartisan stance of this organization; Dewson also found the group too heterogeneous to work together effectively. Compared to her old contacts at the National Consumers' League and the high-powered women she was meeting in New York State's Women's Democratic Committee, the Women's City Club was beginning to seem a little tame.[34]

Molly Dewson never said much about her time at the Women's City Club, but she resigned her position there after less than a year. She claimed health considerations as her sole reason for leaving, citing "her physical inability to undertake so large and exacting a position next year."[35] Yet no major medical crises occurred in this period of her life, and she and Polly set off on a four-month driving tour of Italy and Africa in the fall of 1925.

Despite whatever frustrations she experienced on the job, Molly Dewson's brief association with the Women's City Club had one monumental impact on the rest of her career: she met Eleanor Roosevelt through the club. She remembered their first meeting vividly: "My desk was in the large office of the President, Mrs. Edward Dreier, and one day she introduced me to a tall, slender woman who was hastening out of the room. 'This is our new Vice President, Mrs. Franklin D. Roosevelt,' she said. Mrs. Roosevelt stopped long enough to shake hands and give me a warm, friendly smile. . . . In that fleeting second, I felt her human warmth, sincerity and genuine interest in other persons. Of course she has grown with experience but basically she has never changed."[36]

Throughout 1925, the paths of Molly Dewson and Eleanor Roosevelt crossed frequently. Eleanor Roosevelt was quietly but capably moving into positions of leadership in a variety of organizations such as the Women's Trade Union League, the League of Women Voters, and the New York State Women's Democratic Committee. In February, when Eleanor testified on behalf of the Women's City Club at an Albany hearing on the Child Labor Amendment, Molly Dewson sat at her side.[37]

Dewson became a frequent guest at the Roosevelt home on East 65th Street, where she met Franklin Roosevelt, who was then contemplating a return to politics after his partial paralysis from polio in 1921. Dewson remembered, "He seemed rather to like the solicitous feminine fussing." One night the Roosevelts were dining at the apartment of Nancy Cook and Marion Dickerman, and they invited Molly over for coffee and dessert. She said to Franklin, "Before you go, do come across the hall to see our apartment." Dewson continued, "He was walking with crutches and to carry his straw hat at the same time was difficult. I took it from him and blurted out, 'You are too wonderful not to make a single complaint.' Even when incited to complain, he did not say a word, just smiled. When I told Mrs. Roosevelt, she said, 'He has never complained about his misfortune.'"[38]

Eleanor and Molly's friendship quickly deepened. For Christmas in 1925, Molly sent Eleanor a copy of Baudelaire's *Les fleurs du mal*, knowing how much Eleanor enjoyed reading French, which she had learned from her adolescent years at the Allenswood School in England. Eleanor replied warmly, "I love *Les Fleurs du Mal* and a thousand thanks to you for your sweet thoughts. May you have the happiest Xmas & do let us start the New Year by seeing more of each other."[39]

Molly also played a small part in the camping trip that Eleanor Roosevelt took with Nancy Cook, Marion Dickerman, and two of the Roosevelt boys in the summer of 1926. On the way back from Campobello, the entourage planned to spend a night with Molly and Polly in Castine. When Eleanor wrote to finalize these plans, she lavished love and affection on her new friend: "Of course you know that I love you and have the greatest admiration for the work you did this year." Molly returned these feelings.[40]

What are we to make of these flowery declarations of mutual love between Molly Dewson and Eleanor Roosevelt? Was there something more to their relationship than just friendship? Eleanor clearly possessed the capacity for deep friendships with other women: in the 1920s, her closest friends were Nancy Cook and Marion Dickerman, and in the 1930s she formed an intense emotional attachment to the journalist Lorena Hickok. There is no evidence, however, that Molly and Eleanor had anything approaching a love affair, either when they first met in the mid-1920s or at any later point in their relationship. Each woman continued to seek her primary emotional sustenance elsewhere, although it is clear that they felt deep affection for one another.

During the 1920s, Molly Dewson also forged a strong personal and professional bond with Frances Perkins, one characterized by a different level of intensity than her friendship with Eleanor Roosevelt. As Molly put it, "between us two cooperation has been of the head, not the heart."[41] Perkins and Dewson first worked together in 1922, when Dewson was at the National Consumers' League and Perkins was serving on the Industrial Commission of New York under Governor Al Smith. Interest in the field of labor legislation, combined with their shared New England heritage, drew these women together. Frances Perkins was a very private person, and even friendships with such dearly held people as Molly Dewson were kept at a certain distance. But the two women understood each other. In 1931, while riding between Albany and New York on the train, Perkins took a pencil and a piece of scratch paper and scribbled a touching note to Dewson in her indecipherable handwriting: "I've often thought that in case I were knocked out Franklin would look to you to help him reset the Labor Department." "I care more about this dept. & what it can do for the working people of N.Y. than for almost anything else," she noted, then she proceeded to list her most trusted workers and allies in the field. 'I'm O.K. nothing imminent," she added. "Just New England forehandedness." She signed off, "With love and complete trust in you as a sort of moral executor."[42]

Molly Dewson treasured this letter for the rest of her life. Coming so spontaneously from the usually reserved Perkins, it captures the special affection, shared commitment, love, and common ideals that joined such women in their pursuit of reform. As Eleanor Roosevelt observed, shared work "was one of the most satisfying ways of making and keeping friends."[43]

The bonds that linked Dewson, Perkins, and Eleanor Roosevelt extended to a small group of like-minded New Yorkers who were working on reform and women's issues during the 1920s. As Frances Perkins later recalled, New York in those days was "a small world": "The people who did anything were few in number, so that no matter what they did, whether it was art, music, the drama, social work, religion, they all touched each other sooner or later." For example, for many years representatives of reform and civic groups took the 8:30 A.M. Empire State Express to Albany to lobby the state legislature when it was in session. Out of this informal group emerged the Joint Legislative Conference, a coalition which advocated issues of interest to women in public life. Its membership, which included both Perkins and Dewson, represented the elite of New York reform circles, many of whom played roles in the New Deal.[44]

One gathering captured particularly well the bonds of friendship and solidarity that were forming among women in public life in the 1920s: a 1929 luncheon to honor Frances Perkins's recent appointment by governor-elect Franklin Delano Roosevelt as New York's industrial commissioner. She was the first woman to be appointed to such a position. "I take it that we are gathered not so much to celebrate Frances Perkins, the person, as we are to celebrate Frances Perkins as the symbol of an idea," said the guest of honor when she rose to speak. "It is an idea that has been at work among us for many years—the idea that social justice is possible in a great industrial community." She then paid tribute to those who had helped her:

How can I express what I owe the loyalty, the intelligence, and the wisdom of the women of this state, both organized and unorganized? There is, a little above the rest, that group, who stealing the phrase from dear Mary Dreier's Christmas card, have called ourselves—humorously, I hope—The Children of Light. That cordial, interlocking group of minds has meant much to all of us who have been welcomed to the inner conference of those who were trying to decide the best thing to do this year, and next year, and the year after, for the cause of industrial reform.[45]

"Really that luncheon was one of the great occasions of my life," Molly reported to Eleanor Roosevelt, who had been unable to attend.[46]

Soon after the luncheon, Frances Perkins added a special note of thanks to Dewson for her role in the affair. "I cannot tell you how much that lunch which you arranged for me has meant in my life and I want you to know not only that I am grateful for all that you did to make it a success but that it has given me a new insight into the beauty and loyalty and chivalry between women. How fine it is to play the game together all these years, isn't it?"[47]

That this "loyalty and chivalry" existed between women is an important part of the story. Women like Dewson and Perkins spent their formative years in woman-centered institutions, beginning with the women's colleges and moving on to reform groups like the National Consumers' League. They were profoundly shaped by their participation in the suffrage campaign. They learned to work easily and effectively with other women, seeing them as natural allies and collaborators on the issues they agreed were of greatest concern to their sex.

This ability and inclination to work closely with other women is especially significant in the context of the major changes taking place in the attitudes and expectations of American women in the 1920s. New attitudes about women's careers, an increased emphasis on hetero-sexual experience, the emergence of mass culture, and a political cli-mate more hostile to reform intersected in powerful new ways. Many young women coming of age in that decade, flush with feelings of equal-ity engendered by the suffrage victory, no longer believed that a sep-arate women's movement was necessary. The self-described "modern women" of the 1920s viewed the old suffragists as too strident and anti-male for their taste. Instead of collectively waging a battle for sex equality, which they believed had already been won, younger women wanted to enter male-dominated institutions such as politics or the professions. If they succeeded, they believed, it was because they were capable and competent; if they failed, it was their own fault, not society's.[48]

The goal of integrating women into the mainstream of American society was admirable, but it carried a heavy price. By identifying so closely with male values and standards, women lost touch with the female support networks that had nurtured the personal and public lives of earlier generations of women. After 1920, women like Molly Dew-son, Frances Perkins, and Eleanor Roosevelt became holdovers from a previous, more gender-conscious age. In many ways, women of Dew-son's generation were the last to have such an awareness of themselves as women in public life until the revival of feminism in the 1960s and 1970s once again brought gender consciousness to the fore.

It was precisely this tradition of loyalty and support among women that explains why, in 1928, Molly Dewson dropped everything to go on the presidential campaign trail solely because her friend Eleanor Roos-evelt asked for her help. Molly and Polly were enjoying their extended summer vacation in Castine when the telephone rang. It was New York calling, Mrs. Roosevelt on the line. "Harry Hawes says the women in the Midwestern Headquarters of the Democratic National Committee are fighting and I must come out, but I cannot possibly leave the head-quarters in New York. Will you go in my place? I know only two women whom it would be safe to send and you are one of them." Molly had never participated in an electoral campaign before, but Eleanor trusted her completely. In fact, she probably had targeted Dewson as a recruit for Democratic politics long ago.[49]

Once the pitch was made, Dewson said yes. She later recalled wistfully, "Scattered all over this country are, I imagine, a great many persons who have never been able to say 'no' to the Roosevelts, or even, 'I will think it over and telephone you.' I am no exception. That was on a Friday. The next morning, Miss Porter and I started on the two day trip by motor to New York. Monday, I reported at the Al Smith Headquarters for instructions, bought some dresses, and with a newspaper woman caught the evening train for St. Louis."[50]

The few days in St. Louis stretched into several weeks, and Dewson stayed on the Smith campaign staff through the November election. One telephone call from a trusted friend on a cool September day launched Molly Dewson's career as a Democratic politician.

CHAPTER NINE

Baptism into Politics

OLLY DEWSON often remarked that, before FDR, women's status in politics was "nebulous." Women political leaders had little power or independence. "Outside of a few exceptions they were just figureheads, symbols acknowledging that women had the vote. They waited for the go-ahead signal from the man who was responsible for their appointment." When women received any reward at all, it was based not on their ability but on "their looks, their money, or their late husband's service to the party."[1]

Dewson's rather bleak assessment showed how difficult it had proven to implement the goals women set when they won the vote in 1920. Women in politics never seriously considered the formation of a separate women's party—instead, they planned to enter the existing party structure and "bore from within." The suffragist Carrie Chapman Catt issued the clarion call in 1920: "The only way to get things in this country is to find them on the inside of the political party." She warned her audience, "You won't be so welcome there, but that is the place to be. . . . If you really want women's votes to count, make your way there."[2] For those who did not want to concentrate their political activity solely in the Democratic or Republican parties, the newly established League of Women Voters offered a vehicle for nonpartisan political activity that focused on issues, voter education, and preparation for citizenship.[3]

While the major political parties did not exactly welcome women after the passage of the Nineteenth Amendment, they did open ceremonial and occasionally substantive positions to them in the party hierarchy. The Republican National Committee tapped Harriet Taylor Upton and Pauline Morton Sabin, while Emily Newell Blair won appointment as the vice-chairman of the Democratic National Committee. In 1920 the Democratic National Committee agreed that each state should have an elected committeewoman as well as the traditional committeeman, a policy adopted by the Republicans four years later. Both parties established women's divisions; attendance by women at party conventions rose. Women who had access to political power on the state level in the postsuffrage era included Nellie Nugent Somerville in Mississippi, Sue Shelton White in Tennessee, Cornelia Bryce Pinchot and Emma Guffey Miller in Pennsylvania, Belle Moskowitz and Eleanor Roosevelt in New York, and Ruth Hanna McCormick in Illinois. No woman, however, emerged as a national figure in her own right.[4]

One measure of women's integration into politics was election to office, although this was not the high priority for women that it would later become. Several women were elected to Congress, and two (Nellie Tayloe Ross of Wyoming and Miriam Ferguson in Texas) served briefly as governors. Reflecting a political trend that has held true throughout the twentieth century, women were much more likely to participate at the local and state levels than the national. In 1929, 149 women were serving in state legislatures in thirty-eight states; by 1931, only Louisiana had failed to elect at least one female legislator.[5]

Moving into positions that were not just window dressing proved one of the hardest tasks for women in the 1920s. Belle Moskowitz, who served as a political advisor to Governor Alfred E. Smith throughout the decade, concluded in 1930: "the major political parties are still man-made and man-controlled. Few of their leaders can work with women on a basis of equality."[6] Partisan women were trying to function within structures run by men, unlike women activists in the birth control or peace movements, who could organize through the familiar voluntary organizations and use the lobbying tactics perfected over decades of activism in the women's movement. Women in politics were outnumbered, indeed outmanned.

Partisan women adopted a two-pronged strategy to overcome their liabilities. They made it clear that their ultimate goal was integration of women into the party structure on an equal basis with men, and they

supported measures to increase women's representation in the party hierarchy. But, knowing how difficult it would be to achieve that goal,
they simultaneously embraced a certain degree of separatism. The tactic
of concentrating political action within separate women's divisions
transcended party divisions. The traditional structures in both parties
were too formidable for individual women to make a difference without
the collective support of their sisters. And even then breaking in was far
from easy.[7]

One of the few places where women secured more than a token
position in politics was in the Democratic party in New York State. The
Women's Division of the Democratic State Committee attracted an
outstanding group of former suffragists determined to prove that women
could play vital roles in public life.[8] One of the most dynamic was
Nancy Cook, who, along with her friend Marion Dickerman, got
Eleanor Roosevelt involved in women's Democratic politics. Political
activity suited Eleanor Roosevelt's purposes perfectly in the 1920s, as
she simultaneously tried to keep her husband's name before the public
after his 1921 polio attack and also attempted to widen her own spheres
of interest and responsibility. Soon Eleanor Roosevelt was the dominant force at the Women's Division, so important that the party drafted
her to run the women's end of Al Smith's presidential campaign in 1928
along with former Wyoming governor Nellie Tayloe Ross. Alongside
the trio of Roosevelt, Cook, and Dickerman, Caroline O'Day (elected
to Congress in 1934), Agnes Leach, and Elinor Morgenthau (Henry
Morgenthau's wife and Eleanor Roosevelt's close friend) all became
prominent in Democratic women's circles, as did the former suffragists
Harriet May Mills and Mary Garret Hay.[9]

Molly Dewson was not yet part of this Democratic women's crowd
in 1928, although she knew many of these women from her work at the
Consumers' League and the Women's City Club. Perhaps her family's
longstanding Republicanism held her back—although that had not
kept her from declaring her allegiance to Democratic candidate Grover
Cleveland at Dana Hall in 1892. More likely, until the late 1920s she
felt more effective, or more comfortable, working for reform goals
through a voluntary organization rather than inside a political organization. In any case, even though she had not made the transition to
partisan politics in the 1920s as quickly as others, various factors—
especially her rapidly developing friendship with Eleanor Roosevelt—were pulling her toward more active partisan political
involvement.

By 1928, like many of her Democratic friends, Molly Dewson was convinced that Governor Al Smith of New York would make a fine president. She was impressed by his gubernatorial record, especially his commitment to the issues most critical to the National Consumers' League and the Women's Trade Union League. Although Molly Dewson supported prohibition and Al Smith most certainly did not, she respected his right to this view. And on the other controversial question of the 1928 campaign—Smith's Catholicism—she jabbed, "I would like to see the Church dictate to Smith!!" These positive opinions predisposed Dewson to agree when Eleanor Roosevelt asked her to go to St. Louis at the height of the 1928 presidential campaign.[10]

Eleanor recruited Molly to handle a tricky situation that had developed among the women at the Midwestern headquarters. The rival factions, each with its reigning queen, eyed each other suspiciously when Dewson stepped off the train in St. Louis. Dewson saw the situation as a riotous example of female politics run amok. On one side was Florence Farley, "a flighty flapper," whose "mental capacity is just nil": "All she wants is to have a good time and fuss around and gossip and play politics and build up a big machine for herself." Her adversary was "a terrible woman, adroit, smart, scheming," named Cunningham. Rather than trying to mediate between the two, Dewson cleverly arranged for both women to go on the road as speakers for the duration of the campaign. She made sure to send them to different states so that their paths would not cross, and thus literally made the problem go away. She boasted afterward to Eleanor Roosevelt, "Pretty fair for 4 1/2 days including Sunday?"[11]

Dewson's adroit handling of this affair greatly impressed the local Democratic leaders, who quickly convinced her to stay on to take charge of women's activities. Several women politicians at headquarters were disturbed that she assumed so much responsibility so quickly: "And she never had any political experience, and never was elected to any office, even precinct leader," sniffed Emily Newell Blair. Dewson responded drily to this charge that working in the Parole Department in Massachusetts for twelve years and lobbying for labor legislation did not exactly leave her a "complete greenhorn" in politics. She also felt that her perspective as a first-timer in partisan politics was important: "I had had no previous intimate contact with elections and went to St. Louis with 'fresh' eyes, returned full of what seemed to me the incredible stupidities of many current methods, and eager to talk about them." One of the images she recalled later was of boxes of campaign material sitting undistributed in a corner of the office headquarters the day before the election.[12]

Dewson found other incidents more deeply troubling. Al Smith's New York accent, unfamiliar mannerisms, immigrant background, and opposition to prohibition made him a convenient scapegoat for people worried about what they saw as disturbing changes in modern American life. The 1928 campaign brought to the surface bitter urban-rural tensions and ugly displays of anti-Catholicism. Years later Dewson told Frances Perkins about the hate mail and crank letters they received at the campaign headquarters, a real "chamber of Catholic horrors." She made the same point to Postmaster General Jim Farley in the 1930s: "Oh, no, Jim, a Catholic could not possibly be elected President now. You were not in the Bible Belt in 1928." (Only later did she realize that Farley had been sounding her out about his own presidential ambitions.) For her baptism into politics, Dewson picked one of the most divisive campaigns of twentieth-century political history.[13]

Dewson stayed in St. Louis until late October before returning to New York to help Eleanor Roosevelt weather the last-minute crush at national headquarters. Lucy Stebbins wanted her to continue out to California for a visit, but she declined, claiming that "it was not fair to leave P.P. so steadily with the pets," perhaps a discrete reference to Polly's displeasure with the time Dewson was spending away from her on political work. Polly's objections had grown so vociferous by the end of the 1932 campaign that Dewson was only half joking when she told her coworker Lavinia Engle that she was "attending to my partner to prevent a divorce."[14]

Although Al Smith never really had a chance in 1928, Democratic recruit Molly Dewson learned that working in an unsuccessful campaign could have its benefits. Basking in the thanks she had received from members of the Democratic National Committee, Molly demonstrated how quickly she was learning the political craft. "Since Mrs. Roosevelt seemed satisfied with my campaign efforts, like a good social worker I decided to cash in on them and asked her advice on how to interest Governor-elect Roosevelt on the legislative program of the New York Consumers' League of which at that time I was President." Eleanor said, "Go to Warm Springs to see Franklin before others talk to him." Dewson moved quickly. "I went as soon as my wire was answered."[15]

This trip to Warm Springs, and the results it produced, demonstrate Molly Dewson's growing friendship with Franklin Delano Roosevelt. Roosevelt greeted her with, "Let's get business out of the way and then I'll take you for a drive in my little car, and show you the grounds and the pool." Dewson told him she had two things on her mind: "One requires a long and tedious explanation and the other I can say in a sentence and I know it will interest you." The idea requiring the long exposition was the need for minimum wage legislation in New York, which she sketched in the briefest terms possible. Roosevelt appeared interested.

"And now for the plum," Dewson proceeded. "Since I have lived in New York, with the exception of Bernard Shientag, I have not been at all impressed with the Industrial Commissioners. Why don't you appoint Frances Perkins your Industrial Commissioner?" Eleanor Roosevelt had planted this idea, and Dewson thought her suggestion "really clicked."[16] Even though Al Smith adivsed otherwise ("Men will take advice from a woman, but it is hard for them to take orders from a woman," he told Roosevelt), the governor-elect went ahead with the appointment in early 1929.[17] This scenario—Eleanor and Molly working behind the scenes to get an appointment for Frances Perkins—was repeated when FDR named Perkins his secretary of labor in 1933.

By 1928, however, Molly Dewson had not yet settled for life on Democratic politics. Several crucial elements had not yet fallen into place. She was still unsure of her loyalty to Franklin Roosevelt—after all, she had worked in the Smith campaign, not Roosevelt's, and Franklin's election as governor in the midst of the Republican landslide had surprised almost everyone. But, finally, it would be the Depression, especially its disastrous impact on the labor standards that Dewson had worked for years to secure, that would point her irrevocably toward participation in New Deal politics.

After the Smith campaign, Molly Dewson returned to her familiar New York patterns.[18] The focus of her attention was the Consumers' League of New York, one of those gems of women's organizations that dotted New York City in the first third of the twentieth century. Its members, a small group of women interested in improving labor conditions for women and children, included the lawyer Dorothy Kenyon; Mary van Kleeck, head of the Industrial Division of the Russell Sage Foundation; and Nelle Schwartz, Frances Perkins's replacement on the New York Industrial Board. (Schwartz was also Dewson's tennis and golfing partner.) Eleanor Roosevelt was a member, but not a very active one. The group's relation to the National Consumers' League paralleled that of the New York and the National Women's Trade Union Leagues:

some overlap in membership, strong agreement on goals. The New York group served as the flagship of the larger national organization.[19]

The presidency of the Consumers' League of New York, which Dewson held from late 1927 until she resigned at the beginning of the 1932 presidential campaign, suited her temperament far better than did her previous job at the Women's City Club. The Consumers' League was a small, homogeneous organization, and Dewson bragged about its solid shape: "I believe that our program is excellent, our financial outlook encouraging, and the spirit of the Board high." Yet her presidency ran almost simultaneously with the worst years of the Great Depression, and she watched helplessly as hard times eroded or destroyed the labor standards that she had spent years promoting. One of the important lessons Dewson learned from the experience was that voluntary agreements were inadequate in the face of deteriorating economic conditions. Permanent government protection of the workplace would prove the only answer.[20]

The Consumers' League of New York promoted the protection of women and children by investigating industrial conditions and supporting model legislation to remedy the long hours, low pay, night work, and unsanitary working conditions that prevailed in industry in the late 1920s and early 1930s. Adopting an educational approach, it conducted investigations into specific industries where women workers predominated, studies similar to the ones Molly Dewson supervised in Massachusetts between 1897 and 1912. The main focus of the group during Dewson's presidency was candy making. The candy industry, with its poor working conditions, predominance of women workers, and appeal to consumers' sweet tooths, was a perfect educational tool. To publicize the terrible conditions in this industry, Dewson turned to a tactic first used by the National Consumers' League in 1903: listing establishments in which products were made under fair and hygienic conditions and urging consumers to patronize only these establishments. The "Candy White List" was the result.[21]

In order to devise a "white list" for the candy industry, the Consumers' League first engaged investigators to work incognito in the factories. After the results were made public, representatives of the Consumers' League negotiated with individual plants. If a factory met certain minimum standards (in 1928, a fifty-hour week at wages of fourteen dollars), it won inclusion on the list. Periodic reinspections by trained investigators guaranteed that standards were maintained at all times, not just when the Consumers' League was on the premises.[22]

President Dewson especially enjoyed tangling with the candy manufacturers. Since the Consumers' League endorsement meant business, she was dealing with manufacturers from an unaccustomed position of strength. She gloated, "It really was fun if you had lived a long life in this work to have them arguing with us and bringing up all these answers and we were sitting there enthroned with power and able to be very pleasant and fair and give them a long long hearing but to say we couldn't possibly accept a lower standard than $14." The Consumers' League proved tough negotiators. Of the fifty-seven establishments that won a spot on the Consumers' League list in 1928, forty-one did so by raising the wages of women workers.[23]

Given the shaky constitutional status of minimum wage laws in the 1920s, this approach represented an alternative way to guarantee a living wage for women workers. On the other hand, severe drawbacks limited its effectiveness. Because of the need for continual investigation, white lists were very expensive to maintain, and they benefited only a tiny minority of women workers in the state. Since candy manufacturers sold their goods in several states, moreover, it was hard to convince New York companies to maintain high standards, since their competitors across the river in New Jersey could then sell cheaper candy made under less hygienic, and less expensive, conditions. Furthermore, such lists were not legally binding, nor could the Consumers' League urge boycotts of nonparticipating establishments without running afoul of antitrust and libel laws. In the end, the Candy White List remained dependent on the good will of employers to maintain decent working conditions in return for the support of public-minded organizations like the Consumers' League.[24]

During the prosperous twenties, candy manufacturers could afford to go along with the Consumers' League guidelines. Once the Depression struck, however, the voluntary agreements were doomed to failure. In the downward spiral after 1929, candy manufacturers could not maintain their relatively high working and wage standards in the face of cutthroat competition, and wages dropped below the fourteen-dollar minimum. Dewson made a last-ditch effort to salvage the list by offering to lower the wage standards by 10 percent, but the manufacturers could not guarantee even that. The Consumers' League of New York had no choice but to allow the Candy White List to die.[25]

Deteriorating labor conditions emerged as the predominant concern of the Consumers' League in the early 1930s, both in New York and on the national level. The lesson from the Candy White List project pointed directly toward the New Deal: "Long experience in dealing with white lists and labels for other industries has proved that voluntary agreements cannot always be depended upon, especially in times of stress and depression when competition is keener," Dewson wrote. "We believe that only by the force of law can standards be maintained."[26] The Consumers' League now even more firmly committed itself to protective legislation as the best remedy for social and industrial problems.

In 1932, the National Consumers' League faced another critical challenge: adjusting to life without Florence Kelley. The woman Frances Perkins once addressed as "the head of the family in this enterprise which binds us all together" died on February 17, 1932, at the age of seventy-two.[27] When any one individual had dominated an organization as completely as did Florence Kelley, there were bound to be problems choosing a successor.

When Kelley became ill, Molly Dewson was named chair of an executive committee to run the Consumers' League in her stead. In this capacity, Dewson approached several trusted friends, explaining that the board was searching "very, very quietly" for a successor. She feared what might happen given a long hiatus in leadership: "temperamental defeatists among the League's friends would have time for action; our branches might be disheartened; our contributors might be discouraged; and there is need of us in this economic crisis."[28] Grace Abbott seconded the need to act quickly to find a new general secretary: "Unless the secretary gives it personality and can get a national hearing by her pen and voice and get the support of other leaders in this way, it cannot be very useful and I doubt that it could hold its present constituency." Both Dewson and Abbott were committed to finding a woman for the job. As Dewson reasoned, "I am presupposing a woman because I think we need a woman's approach to this problem. The League was created through one woman's instinctive vision and devotion. John Andrews and probably Dinwiddie may care about the workers but I am conscious only of the intellectual approach."[29]

Grace Abbott and Molly Dewson tried unsuccessfully to tempt the other with Florence Kelley's job, but when they and the Goldmark sisters withdrew from consideration, Lucy Randolph Mason emerged by default as the frontrunning candidate. Descended from several of Virginia's most distinguished families, Mason developed her social conscience during her work as the general secretary of the Richmond YWCA in the 1920s. In 1931, she had traveled to six Southern states, speaking on labor legislation for women and children on behalf of the

NCL. Mason's handling of that assignment impressed Kelley, who told Dewson that Lucy Mason was her personal choice as her successor.[30] Molly Dewson had been thinking along similar lines: "She seems pretty pale beside FK and you [Grace Abbott], but she has personality, devotion to industrial women, experience, prestige in her State and the South where I believe we should do a lot of work, and is, I understand, a good speaker and well respected by conservative men although they consider her 'advanced.'"[31]

Dewson's assessment of Lucy Mason proved remarkably accurate. She was an able worker and especially effective in the South. As a national leader, however, she lived up to the predictions of the Women's Bureau head Mary Anderson: "She is allright in her own bailiwick, but as a national figure would make no dent." In Mason's defense, the 1930s proved, in Molly Dewson's words, "a sad period" for the National Consumers' League. Besides being crippled by lack of funds during the Depression, the organization was undercut further by the dramatic success of the New Deal in the field of labor legislation. Lucy Mason eventually left the NCL in 1937 to join the newly formed Congress of Industrial Organizations, and she spent the next fifteen years crisscrossing the South as a roving labor organizer for the CIO.[32]

Would Molly Dewson have taken Florence Kelley's job if it had been offered her? The position was hers for the asking. If the job had opened up in the early 1920s, Dewson might have been tempted. By early 1932, however, she was completely absorbed in FDR's campaign for the presidency. There was no turning back from Molly Dewson's own "rendezvous with destiny."

CHAPTER TEN

F.R.B.C.
(For Roosevelt Before Chicago)

MOLLY DEWSON'S friendship with Franklin Delano Roosevelt grew more slowly than hers with Eleanor Roosevelt. With Eleanor, it all happened in a rush; with Franklin, it took several years to mature. But both relationships were among the most satisfying, both personally and politically, that Molly Dewson ever enjoyed.

When Molly first met Franklin through Eleanor in 1925, his political future was still very much in doubt. He seemed pleasant enough, but he had not yet demonstrated the grasp of social and economic conditions he later displayed in the New Deal. Dewson saw glimmerings of a deeper Roosevelt during his first term as governor of New York, when she was a frequent guest at the Governor's Mansion in Albany while lobbying for the Consumers' League. It was on one of these trips, she later claimed, that she "signed on for the duration" with FDR.

Dewson's decision was made during a fight for a bill to shorten the hours of women employed in retail stores. Dewson testified in favor of the bill as a representative of the Joint Legislative Conference, but the merchants were united in their opposition to the proposed legislation. Dewson returned to the Governor's Mansion tired and discouraged, and she poured out her disgust to Eleanor over a cup of tea in her sitting room. (Dewson called that room "the only pleasant spot in that great ark of a post Civil War monstrosity.") The governor rolled his wheelchair in, "looking fresh and cheerful as if he were going off for a week-end," Molly recalled. She continued: "Quick as a flash, Mrs. Roosevelt said, 'What are you going to do about the bill?' with what I thought was a touch of anxiety in her voice. 'Sign it of course,' he answered debonairly while he held out his hand for tea." Casting aside any previous reservations, Molly claimed, "it was then and there that without a word I signed on for the duration."[1]

As in describing her decision to attend college, Dewson relied on a moment of epiphany to explain her support for Franklin Roosevelt. The conversion was surely a more incremental process. The context, however, is instructive: it was Roosevelt's willingness to act positively on the social welfare issues Dewson was promoting at the Consumers' League that drew her into politics. Molly Dewson was a specialist in labor legislation, and Governor Roosevelt listened to her advice. Such common ground would be even more important in the New Deal.[2]

Many of Molly Dewson's elaborations of her support for Franklin Roosevelt were retrospective, written well after the New Deal had been accepted into the American political system. By then, there was no doubt that she identified completely with FDR: "I served Franklin Roosevelt with all that in me lay." She remained one of the most loyal of New Dealers right to the end, never losing faith in Roosevelt's desire to do what she considered right.[3]

When justifying her decision to support Roosevelt, Dewson repeatedly stated that he was far superior to any public figure that she had dealt with. Over the course of her career before the New Deal, she had worked with many men and women in social work, state legislatures, the labor movement, business and manufacturing, even farming, but, "then came Roosevelt." She listed his most compelling characteristics: "his personality, his charm, his manner of handling his fellow workers, Congressmen, the press and the radio public, his method of attacking problems, his willingness to settle for half a loaf and later come back for more, his way when deadlocked of temporarily shifting to another issue, and his stubbornness, himself an advocate of the balanced budget, in refusing to be embarrassed by spending right and left for relief." Other political figures possessed some of those qualities, but "no one man in my time combined so many valuable characteristics for getting things done."[4]

When Dewson recorded these views in her autobiography in the late 1940s, she could report no disappointments with Roosevelt in the field of labor legislation, and little anywhere else.[5] Yet it seems unlikely that Dewson formed quite so inflated a view of the man before he was tested by the Great Depression and World War II. To be sure, Roosevelt had compiled a strong record as governor of New York, distinguishing himself with his willingness to confront the deepening Depression with innovative state relief programs. In his two terms, he had proven willing to consult with social workers and reformers and to support labor legislation.[6] But his years of great leadership were still ahead of him. Tellingly, Dewson wrote to her old mentor Elizabeth Glendower Evans during the 1932 campaign, "He is no great man, but as I look the country over, I decided that he was the best man who could possibly be chosen for the Presidency. So I went to work for him."[7] Later in the 1930s, Dewson would never have penned such an expression of half-hearted support. She became a Roosevelt loyalist, conveniently repressing or revising her earlier doubts.

At base, what probably drew Molly Dewson to Franklin Roosevelt was a combination of style and shared ideology. Their personalities really clicked. She approached life with a combination of bravado, humor, and pragmatism, the very qualities that she admired in him as a leader. Moreover, she relished Roosevelt's "boyish, gay spirit," which again was very much like hers. A late-night card game at the Governor's Mansion in Albany demonstrated what kindred spirits these two politicos were. "Do you play rummy?" Franklin asked brightly. "Well, let's have a game." "His style of play was typical of his approach to real problems," Dewson wrote. "He was a friend of Lady Luck, bold, dashing, high spirited, awake to his opponent. He expected to win but I had a run of luck myself. I remember his surprised, amused, good-natured laughter."[8]

After her service in the 1928 presidential campaign, Dewson switched her attention to Democratic politics in the state of New York. When Governor Roosevelt came up for reelection in 1930, Eleanor Roosevelt drafted Molly Dewson to work at the New York State Women's Democratic Committee. Eleanor and Caroline O'Day planned strategy and tactics, and Nancy Cook ran the office. Molly answered miscellaneous letters, a potentially mundane task which she quickly elevated into a productive vote-getting strategy. "Every letter was an opportunity for winning a couple of votes or so," she recalled, "if I could find something for the writer to do that appealed to her and was within her powers." This concentration on writing personalized letters and giving women interesting tasks became the hallmark of her approach to women's politics in the New Deal.[9]

The 1930 campaign marked the first appearance of the Rainbow Fliers, one-page colored fact sheets distributed door-to-door during electoral canvassing. While Dewson could not take full credit for this innovation (Roosevelt's aide Sam Rosenman had a hand in the 1930 fliers), she immediately recognized its effectiveness from her suffrage days, when similar fliers had helped defeat suffrage opponent John W. Weeks, a Massachusetts senator, in 1918. In the campaign, the suffragists circulated a simple flier to the state's 350,000 registered voters that highlighted Weeks's votes against such popular issues as the income tax, the Federal Trade Commission, the direct election of senators, and the suffrage amendment. Dewson recalled, "Everyone was amazed but it was simple. . . . Just the facts and no comments—a sort of, if that's what you want vote for it." As she said concisely, "It paid."[10]

Frances Perkins also realized how heavily the innovations Democratic women brought to electoral politics in New York State drew on their experiences fighting for suffrage:

The women's organizations around New York and in some other states too, with a hard core of the same group that were for suffrage, have followed the same methods of organizing wherever they have gone into politics. . . . That is, they've done a grass roots organizing job and haven't depended upon big, overall banners and slogans, although they haven't been ashamed to use them and have been perfectly able to get up a big meeting. But they have known that the real work was done in the smaller meetings, in the house to house visitation, and in the organizing. If you could get a local woman to organize ten, you had ten votes and probably twenty for sure.[11]

This philosophy characterized women's politics in 1930 and beyond.

The 1930 campaign was Molly Dewson's first with Roosevelt's campaign manager, Jim Farley, the Irish Catholic politician who helped engineer Roosevelt's upset gubernatorial victory in 1928 and who headed the Democratic National Committee in the 1930s. Dewson and Farley did not get off to a very promising start. Molly and Frances Perkins wanted to set up a committee to work with the New York intelligentsia: foreshadowing later disagreements over the role of independent voters in Democratic politics, Jim Farley responded with "amused tolerance." "If you want to bother with that 1 1/2% of the voters, go ahead." Fortunately, Louis Howe, a trusted behind-the-scenes operator who had been Roosevelt's advisor since 1912, proved a more dependable ally, and the plan went ahead.[12]

That 1 1/2 percent of the electorate in fact proved unnecessary in the 1930 gubernatorial election, which Roosevelt won in a landslide. For the first time, a Democratic candidate carried upstate New York, including Roosevelt's home town of Hyde Park. This overwhelming victory in a state known for contributing presidential candidates made Franklin Roosevelt an overnight frontrunner for the 1932 Democratic nomination.

By this time, Molly Dewson had committed her energy to Franklin Roosevelt's growing presidential aspirations. She thus joined the select group who were "for Roosevelt before Chicago," that is, before the 1932 nominating convention. (Men in FDR's inner circle received cuff links inscribed "F.R.B.C.") In the spring of 1931, Eleanor Roosevelt, who played an important role both in her husband's political career and in Democratic women's politics, asked Molly Dewson to lend her name to a pro-Roosevelt letter that would be sent to selected Democratic women across the country. Molly protested that many names were better known than hers. "It gave me a shiver of apprehension that Roosevelt could do no better."[13] Dewson was selling herself short, however, for by 1931 she had built up many national contacts from her social work and reform activities. Frances Perkins realized what her colleague refused to admit: "She had very good access to women because she had been the secretary of the National Consumers' League. She had, through that, a connection with all kinds of organized women's clubs—the BPW clubs, the Federation of Women's Clubs. She had a good reason for going to see leading women in a community, or sending somebody to see them."[14] Dewson built on these contacts throughout her political career.

Another reason Dewson was attractive to the Roosevelt camp was her easy working relationship with Eleanor Roosevelt. "The nicest thing about politics is lunching with you on Mondays," Eleanor told Molly. These two women quickly settled into a pattern that prevailed throughout the New Deal: Molly Dewson functioned out front as an organizer and publicist, while Eleanor Roosevelt backed her up behind the scenes. Dewson was no mere front for Eleanor Roosevelt, however. It is testimony to the strong friendship and trust between these two women that they could work together in such a complementary and effective fashion. Eleanor summed up their understanding and mutual dependence: "I hate people to be grateful to me, just as much as you apparently hate them to be grateful to you so you need not worry. I love working with you for just the reasons I imagine you like working with me and you need not ever worry that I will not speak perfectly truthfully to you or that you should hesitate to say whatever you have on your mind to me."[15]

When Molly Dewson reported for work at the Friends of Governor Roosevelt headquarters after her 1931 summer vacation in Castine, she found herself working closely not only with Eleanor Roosevelt but also with Louis Howe, a true friend to women in politics. Dewson described him as "such a quaint, devoted, little gnome of a man—but a poet at soul!" At the Roosevelt campaign headquarters, Howe had the office next door to the one Eleanor and Molly shared. Two secretaries answered mail and received visitors. Jim Farley, who operated out of the nearby Biltmore Hotel, never visited their Madison Avenue offices, reflecting a clear division of tasks. Farley dealt with Democratic politicians across the country, while Howe oversaw what Dewson called "the brain workers"—those involved in publicity, research, and correspondence, including the Women's Division.[16]

The Friends of Roosevelt operation was chronically short of funds. Dewson was not paid for her full-time work on the campaign—but volunteering had characterized her professional life since she left the Women's City Club in 1925. Louis Howe told her in the summer of 1931, "We cannot pay you anything, but if we win, you will have a place in the Washington set-up." She grinned cheerfully and said nothing, thinking to herself, "To pull up my pleasantly settled roots at fifty-nine and go to Washington seemed fantastic."[17] She did not give it another thought.

A measure of Molly Dewson's growing importance in the Roosevelt campaign occurred in November 1931 when she learned she was to be sent "around the circle" (that is, to California and back) to talk to Democratic leaders. In July, Jim Farley, in his role as Exalted Ruler of the Elks, had made a productive Western trip to test the political waters for Roosevelt. Now (minus the Elks) Dewson was to do the same. The story is unclear as to whether Franklin or Eleanor Roosevelt originally suggested the trip, but it certainly was a novelty to send a female political organizer on the road in 1931.[18]

After a visit to Hyde Park to get her marching orders from Governor Roosevelt, Dewson set off. Her trip lasted from December 4 to January 9. Eschewing big meetings, public speeches, and news conferences, her schedule emphasized informal personal sessions with male and female Democratic leaders. "The men were all agreeable," she recalled, but "the few women they produced were, with a few exceptions, blades of grass."[19]

That there were so few women leaders for Dewson to meet reflected the sorry state of women's advancement in the Democratic party in 1932. Even the few effective women leaders like Mrs. Harrison Parkman, the vice-chairman in Kansas, were often ignored by the men. When Dewson arrived to talk to the Kansas governor, she was escorted not by Parkman, who had built a considerable women's organization in the state, but by a political nobody. At lunch, this young woman pointed out a very angry Mrs. Parkman sitting at a nearby table. Dewson introduced herself, figured out what had happened, and marched right over to Democratic headquarters to give the men there a piece of her mind. She left without even waiting for their reaction. They got the message and promised to give Parkman a larger role and more recognition.[20]

Dewson squeezed a full schedule of interviews and contacts into her month-long trip, but she managed to spend Christmas in the San Francisco Bay area with Lucy Stebbins. This 1931 trip was her fourth visit to California since she and Polly made their trip west after World War I. Stebbins arranged gatherings of prominent, politically minded Californians, and Dewson renewed her acquaintance with the Democratic leaders Henry and Lucretia Grady, whom she first met while working on the California minimum wage brief in 1924. She also entertained the twenty-eight students in Lucy Stebbins's social economics class at Berkeley. She attended two or three functions every day, exclaiming to her family, "How is that for one week!"[21]

The only Democrat in a family of twenty-eight Republicans, Molly described her activities with some trepidation. "You see I must admit that I am West primarily in the interest of the candidacy of Franklin D. Roosevelt. I fear this will cause great grief to all the family except John." She was right. Politics, considered somewhat unsuitable for well-bred women like herself, brought her much more into the public eye than her social welfare work had done, and for that reason, as well as because she was a Democrat, her family remained unsympathetic to her political activities throughout the 1930s. When the *Boston Sunday Globe* carried an article about women's activities in the 1932 campaign, it ran a picture of Dewson taken at the Chicago convention. It had been a very hot day, and Dewson had taken off her silk jacket. Her rather formal brother commented, "If you must go into politics at least you could dress like a lady." "Our poor families," his sister sighed, although with no intention of changing her behavior.[22]

Dewson's trip was by all accounts a successful one. Her reports, written nightly in longhand to Eleanor Roosevelt, were digested by the men on the Roosevelt staff as well. Yet on her return she found herself the target of some suggestive ribbing. Her expenses for this month-long trip came to only $446.29: $340.37 for travel, $14.45 for telephone calls, and $91.47 for personal items. Hearing of her miniscule request for reimbursement, Franklin Roosevelt became "facetious, even ribald," remarking pointedly, "You must have been well entertained by the Democratic men along the way." The fifty-nine-year-old Dewson took this comment in stride, although she later complained that Roosevelt had been "far too amused." In fact, Dewson was proud of her frugality, since she knew the national campaign committee was strapped for money.[23]

The success of her campaign swing, which convinced her that Roosevelt would not only be nominated but would win the presidency, emboldened Dewson to embark on a new plan of action. Remembering Howe's pledge that she would "be taken care of" if Roosevelt won, she decided, instead of taking a spot for herself, to promote Frances Perkins for his cabinet. In early 1932 Molly wrote Franklin that she was pleased about his reaction to her trip, and that she hoped he would reward her by considering Frances Perkins for his cabinet. She did not want an answer then, only Roosevelt's promise that he would begin thinking about it. "I did the same thing every time during the following ten months when words of appreciation were relayed to me."[24]

Frances Perkins soon heard of Molly's plan. "But, Mary," she protested, "Franklin would never do it." Dewson answered, "Maybe not, but many things I thought might never happen, happened through a little planning and some pleasant persistence." Dewson emphasized that she was not orchestrating this campaign out of personal friendship: "I just believed that here was the golden opportunity for pushing ahead the labor legislation program for which I had worked for so many years." She was certain that women "have been more successful in getting progressive labor laws passed and more effective in their administration than any men ever have been or could have been," and she wanted Frances Perkins to have the chance to prove her right.[25]

Although Dewson was already plotting the cabinet in Roosevelt's first administration, most of the work of the Friends of Governor Roosevelt was directed toward the nominating convention scheduled for Chicago in June of 1932. As the Democrats were called to order at noon on Monday, June 27th, Dewson prepared for her first dose of Democratic politics convention-style.[26]

Dewson's job at the Chicago convention was to look after the women delegates and to serve as floor manager for women. Between five and six hundred women attended as delegates, alternates, or National Committeewomen; other women political leaders came without official credentials. Louis Howe suggested that she open a reception room for women delegates at the hotel where the Roosevelt forces were headquartered, and he gave her money for "entertainment." "Drinks and cigars were not appropriate," she recalled, "nor was tea, for a heat wave had struck Chicago, but ices, sherbets, and little cakes plus comfortable chairs won great favor and an impressive attendance." Carefully chosen advocates circulated among those who dropped in, quietly pushing the Roosevelt candidacy to the undecided. Many committed Roosevelt supporters came by as well to meet the dynamic and intriguing Molly Dewson with whom they had been corresponding for the past year. Here at last was someone who took women's role in politics seriously.[27]

Some of the male leaders did not appreciate Dewson's work quite as highly as did the women. Jim Farley's office assigned her a convention seat in the third balcony, "a rather distant spot for action with the woman delegates," she observed drily. Rather than complain to Farley (one of her political maxims was that complaining women were ineffective), she swapped tickets with an ally from Maine, who had received a ticket for the speaker's platform. The Maine Committeewoman sat with her delegation, and Dewson now had access to the convention floor.[28]

Even though she acted as a floor manager for women, Molly Dewson had little to do with the last-minute political bargaining which won Roosevelt the nomination. After three inconclusive ballots, Roosevelt held a sizable lead over his rivals Al Smith and House Speaker John Nance Garner, but he was not picking up momentum. On the fourth ballot, California threw its support behind Roosevelt and the nomination was secured. Dewson was seated on the speakers' platform next to Florence Jaffray (Daisy) Harriman, the District of Columbia's leading female politician and a Consumers' League supporter as well. Harriman, who had supported Al Smith, did not approve of California's capitulation, and she said to Dewson, "I'd like to have seen them fight it out. I never liked a deal." Heated words were exchanged. Harriman's lapse of loyalty kept her on the fringes during Roosevelt's first term; not until 1937 was she offered a position as Minister to Norway.[29]

That Jim Farley assigned his floor manager for women a seat in the balcony suggested that he was not going to be much of an ally. "He did not help us carry out our plans, nor did he hinder us, except very rarely," Dewson remembered. (The contrast to Louis Howe was always sharp in her mind.) Although Farley and Dewson were both working for Franklin Roosevelt, they had entirely different styles and operated fairly independently of each other. This pattern, begun in 1932, continued for the rest of the New Deal. "It was Farley's job to see that the party 'bosses' were kept in line and had their stalwarts registered and voting, whereas it was my job, as I conceived it, to get the women organized, informed on the issues, and 'grasstramping'; to convert to the point of voting those previously too uninterested to go to the polls, or those too uncertain about Roosevelt to make him their candidate."[30] Since Dewson's approach worked better in smaller communities and rural areas, she did not encroach on Farley's territory in large cities with political machines. This division of turf allowed them to carve out an effective working relationship, but it was always based more on tolerance and personal respect than a common political ideology.

Secure in the approval of Louis Howe, Franklin Roosevelt, and Eleanor, and with the tacit support of Jim Farley, Molly Dewson set to work on organizing Democratic women. She followed a no-nonsense political philosophy:

I was going to make the men find working with women easy, pleasant, and profitable — if I could. Fortunately, I was old enough to be their aunt, and men are at their best with their mothers and favorite aunts. I was going to keep the women in a happy frame of mind by recognizing their abilities, giving them important work and due publicity, and not gossiping about one another. And, although I was going to see reporters when they came, I was not going to seek publicity myself and give the women cause for jealousy. I had a plan of action and I did not intend to be side-tracked by personal relationships.[31]

This style of operation remained Dewson's basic blueprint for women's Democratic politics throughout the New Deal.

Just as important was Dewson's commitment to what Frances Perkins called "educational organizing." Perkins noted, "She organized much as the woman suffragists had organized. That is, find really capable women in each community who will agree with you that Roosevelt would be a good President, and then organize around them."[32] The message was clear: focus on the individual voter.

As soon as Roosevelt won the nomination, Dewson caught the train from Chicago to Castine. She did not even stay for Roosevelt's "triumphant" address to the assembled delegates. "The pre-convention campaign had been long and strenuous and I was tired." More to the point, Polly Porter deserved some attention from her frequently absent partner. While Molly mended her personal fences in Maine in July and August, Florence Caspar Whitney and Eleanor Roosevelt ran the women's division in New York. Dewson had not sworn off politics for the summer, however: she kept up a voluminous correspondence from Castine, both with headquarters and with her developing network of women Democratic workers.[33]

By Labor Day, Molly and Polly were back in New York and Dewson was working full-time as director of the Women's Division at Roosevelt headquarters. Dewson's staff collected many of the top women in Democratic politics. Her executive secretary was her comrade from the 1928 campaign, Sue Shelton White. Mary Chamberlain directed publicity, Lavinia Engle ran the Speakers' Bureau, Elinor Morgenthau was in charge of radio, Emily Newell Blair handled the women's clubs, and Jo Coffin headed up the advisory labor committee. With the exception of Chamberlain's, all these positions were unsalaried.[34]

Dewson's staff was independent of the Democratic National Committee (DNC). Dewson's Women's Division was part of the Democratic National Campaign Committee, an ad hoc organization controlled by Roosevelt sympathizers. Given the acrimony of the preconvention campaign, Roosevelt did not want his fortunes during the national campaign in the hands of politicians who had been lukewarm about his candidacy. This necessitated bypassing the existing Women's Division of the DNC and finding a suitable role for its director, Nellie Tayloe Ross, whose years of service to women and the party could not be ignored. Dewson quickly named Ross to head an advisory committee and sent her on a national speaking tour (once again solving a ticklish personnel problem by sending a woman on the road). Other women chosen to serve on the advisory committee were Senator Hattie Caraway of Alabama, representatives Mary T. Norton of New Jersey and Ruth Bryan Owen of Florida, and Frances Perkins. Traditional politicians like Norton were at first a bit dubious about the prospect of working under a former social worker, but, as Dewson deadpanned, Norton "was a woman of independent judgment and could adapt herself to changed conditions."[35]

One name—that of Eleanor Roosevelt—was conspicuously absent from the Women's Division roster, even though Eleanor played a vital part in the campaign organization. Molly and Eleanor continued at their back-to-back desks in the small room they had shared before the convention, and Eleanor was there almost every day seeing to her stacks of correspondence. The candidate's wife also functioned as a liaison between the women and the men. As Dewson admitted in a marvelous bit of understatement, "Having through Mrs. Roosevelt a direct line to the Governor, to Louis, and to Jim, and having such a sympathetic operator, was an incalculable timesaver."[36]

When Molly Dewson, Eleanor Roosevelt, and the staff planned their post-convention strategy, they devised a structure that linked the Women's Division to an ever-growing network of local women Democratic leaders. Each state was to have a vice-chairman in charge of women's work, who would supply a contact in each county with whom the Women's Division could correspond directly. County contacts were especially important in rural areas, where they would serve as the main vehicles for distribution of campaign literature.

Often Dewson had to start "close to scratch" to build her contacts. Dewson had been delighted to receive a complete roster of county vice-chairman (the position customarily delegated to women) from the Michigan Democratic State Committee. She immediately contacted these women about the upcoming campaign, but was dismayed by the response: "I found one had died, some had moved, others were sick and hardly a single one considered her county vice-chairmanship was more than a recognition of herself or her husband, involving little if any responsibility."[37]

Fortunately, she had more success elsewhere. In Kansas, which had voted Republican in the last three national elections, every county had a woman vice-chairman who organized women down to the precinct level; Dewson's new-found ally from her western trip, Mrs. Harrison Parkman, was mainly responsible for the success of this organization. In Iowa, eighty-nine of ninety-nine counties had women leaders down to the precinct level, and the record was almost as good in Illinois and Indiana. With such an active organization in place, Dewson could initiate the lively correspondence which was her way of getting women involved and interested in Democratic politics. She tried to make her contacts as personal as possible, "keyed to person and place": "We hear you are doing great work in your district. Four years ago your county went 4872 for Hoover, 1763 for Smith. Working together we can reverse the vote this year." Both she and Sue Shelton White worked full-time on this correspondence. Dewson did not give a single speech during the campaign. She knew her talents lay elsewhere.[38]

Molly Dewson's attention to grassroots organizing and cultivating personal contacts with loyal Democratic women highlights an important aspect of her role as a politician. She had very little input toward defining the issues and platform of Roosevelt's campaign. Much of the time she functioned more like a traditional political organizer, albeit among women, than as someone who entered politics to work for her ideals. Superficially, Dewson's feminist politics turned out to be not all that different from conventional male-dominated politics. This was especially true in the 1932 campaign, which provided her with very little substance for the issue-oriented political organizing she would soon refine in the New Deal years. Yet the very fact that women were initiating other women into partisan politics and organizing them was an important break from the party's previous neglect of these voters.

Perhaps the most important corollary to Dewson's plan of action was the availability of campaign literature that was sharp, to the point, and convincing enough to convert independent voters. In the 1930 race for governor, the men in Roosevelt's campaign had produced a twelve-page brochure which Eleanor Roosevelt and her colleagues deemed completely unsuitable. "You surely don't expect us to send that to our women, do you?" Eleanor asked. "I don't know about you men, but we women have no time to waste reading through stuff like that."[39] The women turned instead to the Rainbow Fliers, which soon proved just as suitable to national campaigns as they had been to state politics.

These Rainbow Fliers, of which six million were distributed, were the mainstay of the women's campaign in 1932. Packets were sent to each woman precinct leader as soon as the Women's Division received her name. She also received a personal letter from Dewson asking her to call on her neighbors and tell them what Roosevelt planned to do if elected. "A respected neighbor who took the pains to call, explain her views, and leave the bunkless record, would be listened to," she reasoned, "even if the listener never read political talk in the papers or tuned in on political speeches on the air. And the fliers would be read by the men folks when they came back from work."[40]

Once again, however, women in politics had to tread carefully. Although the fliers were put together by the Women's Division, they carried only the label of the Democratic National Campaign Committee. Dewson explained, "We feared some men might be prejudiced by material put out over the Women's Division name." The scenario was repeated in 1936. Dewson claimed that the women made this sacrifice "cheerfully": "We considered [that] the collapse of the Hoover years created an emergency calling for the election of a leader like Roosevelt and that the recognition women might win by the fliers could be foregone."[41] Dewson's willingness to settle for what she could get allowed her to function successfully in the political world. No lost causes for her: she accepted any compromise that furthered her long-term goals.

Dewson offset the occasional compromises that she was forced to accept with a conscious attempt to extend to women some of the perquisites and attention usually reserved for male politicians. Even symbolic gestures provided an enormous boost to the egos of women who had been long ignored. State women's leaders were invited (at their own expense) to come to the New York headquarters to consult with Dewson and her staff just the way men flocked to see Jim Farley. They also were invited to the daily luncheon gathering of the Women's Division staff where, settled in a corner of the Biltmore Grill, "every noon we took up the day's events and problems." Dewson described the impact on the out-of-towners: "They caught the spirit."[42]

Dewson invented several other plans to increase women's participation in politics. One grew out of the fact that, during the Depression, many people had cars, but not everyone had money to pay for gas. This problem was especially acute in rural areas. The Gas Money Plan offered every county vice-chairman in a designated "fighting state" (one in which the election would be won or lost) ten dollars for gasoline, and another ten dollars if the organizing drives were successful. The Women's Division knew that, in order for their plan to be effective, the money had to be available during the summer months so women could lay the organizational groundwork before the hectic fall campaign season. Women politicians repeatedly stressed the importance of getting women organized before the traditional Labor Day kick-off for political campaigns ("Women do not go stale on a candidate," Dewson asserted), but the men at headquarters, who controlled the campaign's pursestrings, dragged their feet. In order to salvage the opportunity, Florence Caspar Whitney donated a thousand dollars for a summer's worth of gas money. The plan was a success.[43]

Lack of money also hampered other Women's Division activities, such as radio broadcasts and speaking tours. Because Dewson preferred patient local organizing to the one-shot appearance of a celebrity, she never relied very heavily on speakers. But she realized how exciting it could be for local morale to bring a well-known woman into town. So as not to waste money, she sent out only "our best and most seasoned" speakers. As in 1928, Nellie Tayloe Ross of Wyoming assumed the lead speaking role, aided by representatives Ruth Bryan Owen and Mary T.

Norton, Emily Newell Blair, and Frances Perkins. These five women "made up our top string."[44]

Unlike men, who in Dewson's eyes were inveterate free spenders when it came to politics, women were frugal. And they were generous with their own time and money. Minnesota activist Anna Dickie Olesen wrote to the Women's Division, "I am enclosing my expense account. It is over the $200 you sent. That amount I contribute. Wish I could give more. I was as economical as I could be. I took my own car and my brother to drive me into Iowa, Nebraska and Missouri or I could not have made those dates." Noting many similar contributions from women throughout the country, Dewson mused, "It has made me think of the old suffrage days when all we asked was an opportunity to serve."[45]

Molly Dewson was pleased with the 1932 election results and with her own work in the campaign. To her, the issue at stake was presidential leadership to pull the country out of the Depression. Yet Roosevelt's campaign platform hardly mapped out a blueprint of the New Deal. "The country needs and, unless I mistake its temper, the country demands bold, persistent experimentation," he proclaimed in one campaign speech. At the same time, he promised to cut federal expenditures by 25 percent in order to balance the budget. What Roosevelt really offered in 1932 was an attractive alternative to President Herbert Hoover, who was by then thoroughly discredited as a leader. For many voters, including independent voters and women who perhaps had not previously participated in politics, that was enough. In the end, Roosevelt won 22.8 million votes to Hoover's 15.7 million, sweeping the electoral college 472 to 59. Candidates of the Socialist and Communist parties garnered fewer than a million votes each, showing that Americans remained firmly committed to the two-party system despite the economic upheavals that had occurred.[46]

Novice politician Molly Dewson harbored a hope that a fundamental reorganization of the American political system would result from the 1932 election. She wrote to one woman leader right after the election, "My great ambition is to see the country divided into conservatives and liberals and I believe that if it is to be done in my lifetime it will be done now."[47] Later, she wrote along similar lines: "I believe a democracy is more likely to succeed when the voters divide into two parties, each holding as of the deepest importance one of the country's two major concerns; the interests of property, finance and business, and the interests of its people as human beings."[48] It is interesting that she separated business and financial interests from humanitarian and social concerns without using the framework of class struggle. Throughout the New Deal, she continued to display an antipathy toward business, but it was more for the roadblocks manufacturers put in the way of Roosevelt's social welfare programs than for business's oppression of the working class. Dividing the country into conservative and liberal camps was the closest she came to proposing fundamental changes in the political system, and she no doubt realized that the chances for success were slim at best.

As usual, once the campaign was over, Molly Dewson gave herself some time to unwind and be with her partner. At a ceremonial dinner in her honor in December, Dewson was presented with a chest of drawers from Val-Kill, the furniture factory managed by Eleanor Roosevelt, Nancy Cook, and Marion Dickerman. Molly was glad everyone was satisfied with her work, for she felt she had done her "darnedest." "Such is life," she wrote her family at Christmas, "perhaps too full for the greatest pleasure but who would be Mrs. Nero fiddling while Rome is burning."[49]

Molly Dewson was never one to sit long on the sidelines, but in December of 1932, and actually well into 1933, she had not decided what her future would hold. She wrote up a long report on the women's campaign, which she sent along with Eleanor to Warm Springs. She reminded Franklin, "I am counting on a quiet talk with you sometime before too long on the Democratic women." Whenever she was asked what she wanted by way of recognition, she mentioned the nomination of Frances Perkins as secretary of labor. But she never talked about her own political future. Perhaps she thought of nothing more than gracefully returning to the presidency of the Consumers' League of New York.[50]

That was certainly what Jim Farley had in mind. At the conclusion of the campaign, he wrote her a letter of thanks which ended, "I hope that you will come to Washington occasionally and help us in any way you can with our work there." Dewson drily observed, "He had not thought of me as part of his future." Franklin Roosevelt's note was more positive: "I hear nothing but words of praise from all sides for the way in which you handled your end of the work." He cited with approval her report on the Women's Division, adding, "from it let's hope we can build up a Women's organization which will be lasting and highly effective."[51]

Rereading Roosevelt's letter in the 1940s, Dewson concluded,

"Later events proved he intended to have me do this job for which I had no desire or thought. I liked my life in New York and I had no wish to go to Washington. But he left the idea in the air until he was ready for me to start work."[52] That may be how Dewson saw it in retrospect, but Franklin Roosevelt's statement of support probably was not much more heartfelt than Jim Farley's. It really did not matter. After a winter back at her old job at the Consumers' League, Molly Dewson was itching to get back into politics, whatever Roosevelt's plans: she had too much unfinished business on her agenda.

CHAPTER ELEVEN

Patronage Politics

IN the winter of 1932–33 came the cruelest despair of the Depression. Despite official statements from politicians and business leaders that prosperity was just around the corner, three years after the stock market crash of 1929 the economy was still contracting. In 1932, industrial production was at barely half the 1929 levels. Farmers had huge surpluses, but consumers could not afford to buy their products. Worse, between twelve and fifteen million American men and women were unemployed, as much as one-quarter of the workforce. The economy had come to a virtual standstill.[1]

The political system proved inadequate to deal with an economic crisis of this magnitude. Political leaders attempted to rekindle public confidence in the soundness of the economic system, but they had few constructive strategies for bringing an end to the Depression. The problem of relief for the unemployed became especially acute. During the 1920s, public welfare had been the responsibility of local and state governments supplemented by private charity. When those limited resources were exhausted by the unprecedented demands of the early 1930s, citizens had nowhere to turn but to the federal government. But President Hoover, who had supported a limited expansion of the federal government's role in stimulating the economy, balked at direct relief for the unemployed. Hoover's unpopularity made the election of a Democratic candidate in 1932 almost a certainty, but Franklin Roosevelt's plans for combating the Depression were no clearer than Hoover's had been. Moreover, the country had to wait four long months, which proved the harshest of the Depression, before Roosevelt took office.

Molly Dewson watched the Depression take its toll with a growing sense of frustration and anger. As head of the Labor Standards Committee of the National Consumers' League, she chaired a conference in December 1932 on the Breakdown of Industrial Standards. It was attended by representatives from more than fifty organizations.[2] Everywhere she looked she saw concrete evidence of the Depression's devastating impact on labor conditions: "Industrial standards built up inch by inch after years of struggle are going down like card houses before the demand of the unemployed for work at any price." Dewson and many other reformers saw federal action as the only possible solution.[3]

Molly Dewson also felt the impact of the Depression personally. "In 1929 I lost one-third of the little sum that was to carry me through my later years, although the money was cautiously [invested] as it should have been." In addition, Polly Porter's trust fund, which was amended in 1932 to include Dewson as a beneficiary, suffered a serious decline during the Depression. Polly and Molly were hardly destitute, but they had to manage on a reduced income for the rest of their lives. Never again would life be so lavish as it had been in the 1910s and 1920s.[4]

Like the presidential interregnum of 1932–33, Molly Dewson's political career was on hold over the winter. With Franklin Roosevelt's successful election in November, the Democratic National Campaign Committee was dissolved, and Molly's official political duties ceased. She saw little of Franklin and Eleanor Roosevelt between November and March. But Molly was not cut off. "So long as Mrs. Roosevelt is in the picture," she confided to Emily Newell Blair immediately after the election, " there is no question but that I shall be giving ideas on the organization of women."[5]

She continued in this transitional period to advocate Frances Perkins as secretary of labor. While many people assumed that Eleanor Roosevelt was behind this appointment, it was Molly Dewson who engineered nationwide support for the nomination, badgered the reluctant president, and won over a doubting Frances Perkins.[6] This appointment represented one of Dewson's most important contributions to the New Deal.

Molly Dewson worked so hard to get Frances Perkins into the cabinet because the appointment would fulfill one of her major political goals for the new Roosevelt administration: to show that FDR took women's contributions to politics and public life seriously and that he was willing to entrust women with unprecedented power and responsibility. To Dewson, this was a powerful feminist statement. She and her cohort never saw patronage as an end in itself, however. It was not just getting women jobs that mattered—it was what the women did with them. Frances Perkins, with her years of experience in New York state government and her rapport with Franklin Roosevelt, was the ideal candidate for such a bold statement in support of women's capabilities for high office.

Dewson stepped up her efforts on Perkins's behalf almost immediately after the election. In late November, she wrote directly to Franklin: "The desirability of it is on every one's lips"; the acclaim that greeted the recent appointment of Margaret Bondfield as secretary of labor in Great Britain "will be like child's piping compared with the huzzah you'll receive," she told him. She enclosed clippings of favorable press reports speculating on the Perkins nomination, which she marked simply, "FDR. Interesting Editorials. MWDewson." At the December dinner hosted by the Roosevelts in Dewson's honor, Franklin Roosevelt commented to Molly that Harry Woodring had sent over a whole stack of letters supporting his own candidacy for secretary of agriculture. Roosevelt contrasted this to the letters supporting Frances Perkins that had arrived "spontaneously" from people all over the country. Molly kept quiet—although the information hardly came as a surprise to her, since she had personally orchestrated the nationwide letter-writing campaign.[7]

Dewson mobilized a wide range of social welfare and political contacts, including her trusted lieutenant Clara Beyer of the Children's Bureau. Dewson got Beyer all fired up: "Go to it for Frances Perkins. Get your State Labor dept. leaders to write Gov. Roosevelt at Warm Springs. Anyone outside of N.Y. State who has standing and a letter head would be fine. Otto Beyer himself would be great. The Brookings School persons who have gone to other states are good material. NOW is the time." She commanded, "Make it an endless chain."[8]

As Dewson's campaign picked up momentum, she confronted Frances Perkins directly with her plans. Perkins initially expressed grave reservations: joining the cabinet would mean leaving New York and a job that she enjoyed; it would subject her to unwanted publicity; it would cause financial hardship. She told Josephine Goldmark, "This is a pipe dream. It is just something that you, as a Consumers' League person, think would be wonderful, but it wouldn't." At the same time, Perkins did confess to Lillian Wald that the idea "made my heart turn over with excitement and appreciation." Her professional pride was touched, but she was still wavering.[9]

Dewson came down hard on Perkins. "We have to have an understanding about some of these things. . . . I don't want to go and make a fool of myself any further if you're really going to turn me down." Dewson tried to impress her with the amount of support the appointment had already garnered. "I remember she made quite a point that she had sold the idea to quite a lot of people, including leading Democrats all over the country," Perkins recalled. "Particularly it was sold to the women of the country—not only Democratic women, but to all others. There was a great woman's response to the idea. It would be very humiliating to her and to everybody else, as well as a great disappointment if I backed out. She pled a duty to the sex."[10]

Molly parried each of Perkins's objections and pulled a few punches of her own. When Perkins said she did not think Roosevelt would appoint a woman, Dewson replied, "Well, the Women's Division has something to say about these things. We did an awful lot to elect him. I know I did and he knows I did." Perkins ventured that many people would oppose her because of her sex, but Dewson countered, "Just can that. That doesn't count. That will always be the case. Franklin has said to me that he thinks it would be a good idea to have a woman in the Cabinet. So there we are. He's not afraid of those who don't want a woman." Taking the offensive, Dewson played on Perkins's desire to see New York's strong record on labor legislation extended through the country: "You want all these things done. We're agreed. You have the idea. You've done them. You have no doubts. You can do it as nobody else can do it. What's more, you can get on with Roosevelt. He trusts you. He likes you. You're easy with him. You don't make him nervous. You've got all the equipment. You know how. You've got the personal relationship." Finally, Dewson played her trump card: "After all, you owe it to the women. You probably will have this chance and you must step forward and do it."[11]

By the time Frances Perkins survived this treatment, she had reason to agree with Felix Frankfurter that Molly Dewson was "a tactful tactician who, by force of her personality, made people enjoy doing what they *had not* planned to do at all." "She was strong," Perkins remembered, " and I think I said finally, with a groan, 'Well, all right, I

guess, only I don't think the President will do it. I still think he won't
do it.'"[12]

Then things stalled. Roosevelt named most of his cabinet in January and February, but he kept putting off the announcement of his
choice for secretary of labor. Whenever Perkins came up, he groaned in
mock horror, "Oh, the heat I'll have to take." It began to look as if the
appointment might not go through. Finally, on the evening of February
22, Perkins was summoned to Roosevelt's New York townhouse. Perkins called Dewson to ask her if she knew what was up. Dewson replied,
"Sure, I know what it's all about. You do too. Don't be such a baby.
Frances, you do the right thing. I'll murder you if you don't!"[13]

When Perkins arrived for her meeting with the president-elect,
Roosevelt asked her if Molly Dewson had told her what he had in mind.
Perkins replied, "Well, I never know if Molly is speaking the truth, or
just reflecting her own hopes and aspirations." Roosevelt then formally
asked Perkins to join his cabinet. Perkins in turn asked for his pledge of
support to unemployment relief, public works, hours and wages regulation, and several other issues about which she felt strongly. Roosevelt
assented. After checking with her husband, Perkins accepted the job.
The appointment was announced to the press on February 28, just four
days before the inauguration. Molly Dewson got her political plum, but
with precious few days to spare.[14]

Frances Perkins, who became a trusted and influential member of
Franklin Roosevelt's cabinet, was especially proud for the women of the
country: "I have always felt that it was not I alone who was appointed to
the Cabinet, but that it was all the women of America; and I have been
happy that so many women have shared with me the sense of gratifica-
tion that this time has come." She struck a similar note to the suffrage
leader Carrie Chapman Catt: "The overwhelming argument and
thought which made me do it in the end in spite of personal difficulties
was the realization that the door might not be opened to a woman again
for a long, long time, and that I had a kind of duty to other women to
walk in and sit down on the chair that was offered, and so establish the
right of others long hence and far-distant in geography to sit in the
high seats." Molly Dewson's argument that "she owed it to the women"
had carried the day.[15]

Frances Perkins remained grateful to her friend Molly Dewson for
laying the groundwork and convincing her to accept the challenge. She
soon found a poignant way of expressing her appreciation. Perkins's

husband, Paul Wilson, suffered periodically from mental depression and could not be subjected to the strain of appearing in public at Roosevelt's inauguration. So Perkins asked Dewson to represent her family alongside her daughter, Susannah Wilson, at the private swearing-in ceremony at the White House. How proud Molly must have been to stand up for Frances Perkins at this moment of national consecration.[16]

After devoting several years to getting Franklin Roosevelt elected, Molly Dewson had quite a time at the inaugural festivities. Coworkers Lavinia Engle and Emily Newell Blair gave a luncheon in her honor at the Mayflower Hotel on March 2, and that evening she was the honored guest at a dinner hosted by the Women's National Democratic Club in Washington. Somewhat ignorant of Washington's social customs, she did not realize that as guest of honor she should seat herself first. Finally a labor woman she had known for years leaned over and said, "My feet are tired, aren't you ever going to sit down?" Dewson retorted as she started her soup, "Can't anybody eat until I begin?" After dinner, Dewson asked all those who had been born Democrats to rise, and a sizable portion of the audience responded. She said, "I, myself, am a convert and I envy you your natural advantage. But I warn you we have been a minority party for some time and since we want to stay in office long enough to carry out our plans, you have just two alternatives: each of you must have twelve children and so increase our numbers, or you must make a lot of converts like me."[17]

On the day of Roosevelt's inauguration, March 4, 1933, Molly was "so all fired excited and pleased I was beside myself." She attended the official inauguration on that cold and dreary day, watched the inaugural parade, and then went to the cabinet's swearing-in at the White House. Her next engagement was a dinner given in her honor by Mary Anderson, chief of the Women's Bureau. Her watch said six, so she figured she had plenty of time. When she finally hailed a cab, the driver told her it was eight o'clock: in all the excitement, she had forgotten to wind her watch. Fortunately, everyone understood her late arrival, which was just as well, because "no one could have shaken me down at that moment."[18]

Dewson's exhilaration at Roosevelt's inauguration was muted when, upon returning to New York, she learned that her sister, Ellen, had been taken ill and rushed to a Boston hospital. Through much of March and early April, Dewson stayed with her brother in Milton while visiting her sister daily in the hospital. This was a difficult time for her. She was very close to Ellen, and it was agony to watch her slip away.

Although Molly was healthy and energetic at fifty-nine, Ellen's illness was a disturbing reminder of her own mortality. And, marooned in Boston during the excitement of the early days of the New Deal, she felt torn between devotion to her sister and loyalty to the Roosevelt cause. When she wrote Louis Howe for news in late March, she supplied as a return address "The Side Lines."[19]

Dewson did not completely divorce herself from Democratic politics in Boston. A full-page story about her ran in the *Boston Sunday Globe*, then the Democratic paper. The headline read, "Story Told for First Time how Quincy Girl and Wellesley Graduate Ran Roosevelt Campaign among Women—Learned How to Handle Politicians by Raising Cattle."[20] Although Ellen was a Republican, Molly hoped she would be diverted by the story. Her sister's only comment was, "I wish it had been in the *Transcript* or at least in the *Herald*"—Boston's staid Republican newspapers. Ellen's condition continued to deteriorate, and she died early in April at the age of sixty-two. After her sister's death, Dewson quickly threw herself into ever-widening circles of Democratic politics and reform in New York and Washington.[21]

Franklin Roosevelt quickly made good on his inaugural pledge of "action, and action now." In the first hundred days of his administration, legislation was enacted to put the banking system back on a sound basis, stimulate business recovery through a system of industrial self-government under the National Recovery Act, deal with the agricultural crisis, and begin federal programs of relief and public works to put the unemployed back to work. The Congress adopted the Tennessee Valley Authority, an innovative scheme for regional resource planning and conservation, and agreed to send thousands of young men to Civilian Conservation Corps camps. Equally important to building public confidence, Franklin Roosevelt established a warm rapport with the American people through his inaugural address and radio "fireside chats."[22]

Molly Dewson found herself right at home, philosophically as well as politically, with Roosevelt's initiatives in the early New Deal. "The New Deal has three tasks," she wrote early in the first term. "First, to care for the human misery created by the general collapse; second, to get the wheels started; and third, to work out a better ordered society."[23] To be sure, she occasionally questioned some of the decisions made in Washington, but in general she accepted Roosevelt's political wisdom and was willing to follow whatever course he took. A remark to Felix Frankfurter in 1933 summed up her stance towards the New Deal and its popular leader: "Anyway it's very exciting to me and I have faith in FDR. He always has a trick up his sleeve to give time for his main plans to mature. . . . The People want something different from the Past. Old stuff is all wrong in their eyes. They want action."[24] Roosevelt gave it to them.

Molly Dewson made sure that she was part of the action, although for a time the exact dimensions of her role in the new administration remained undefined. In the spring of 1933, she operated like a minister without portfolio, using her old stationery from the now-defunct Democratic National Campaign Committee to promote causes of interest to her. This arrangement gave her a base of operation, but it was not a long-range solution. When, in the spring of 1933, Eleanor Roosevelt convinced the president and Jim Farley to make the Women's Division of the Democratic National Committee a full-time operation, Dewson was everyone's first choice to head the division, even though she insisted that she wanted to stay in New York. Jim Farley and the Roosevelts convinced Dewson to spend the summer thinking about alternative arrangements. By early October, a compromise emerged. "In the end I gave in as I always did whenever the Roosevelts asked me to do anything," Dewson recalled.[25]

Molly Dewson set the terms of her appointment. "My main duty is to build up the organization of the women, not to speak in behalf of the Party," she announced emphatically when she accepted the position of director of the Women's Division of the Democratic National Committee at a salary of $7,500 a year. She was to have offices both in New York City (her old haunt at the Biltmore Hotel) and in Washington; although she planned to spend three days a week in Washington, she would operate mainly out of New York. She also had her summers off, to spend in Castine with Polly.[26] Dewson's New York staff would be built around her trusted secretary, Harriet Allen, a recent graduate of Mount Holyoke who had worked for her during the presidential campaign. In effect, Molly would be running women's Democratic politics from an outpost in New York, a highly unusual arrangement that underscored how valuable she had become to the Roosevelts.

Why did Molly Dewson decide to take on this challenge? Friends warned her she might not enjoy full-time political work: "it is what one makes of it, of course," observed Sue Shelton White, "but there is a deadly routine to political organization."[27] Making something of a job, however, was just what Molly Dewson excelled at. She planned to avoid the routine by delegating the day-to-day responsibilities to an assistant director and staff in Washington, leaving herself free to act as a gadfly, a facilitator, an organizer.

Molly must also have secured Polly Porter's support for this 1930s equivalent of a commuting marriage, at least on a trial basis. It was clear to Polly by this time that her partner's enthusiasm for Democratic politics was more than just a passing fancy. Sensitive to her partner's concerns, Molly Dewson used her special relationship with the Roosevelts to create a niche that accommodated both her private and public needs. While Molly played Democratic honcho in Washington for three days a week, Polly spent time at the kennel in Connecticut; the two still had long weekends together in New York and summers in Castine. Yet Dewson was aware that her commuting would probably strain the partnership, writing to Felix Frankfurter, "I don't know how long I can stick that, or will." She added tellingly, however, "Think certain opportunities make it worthwhile."[28] This compromise worked successfully until after the 1934 election.

Two further considerations lay behind Dewson's decision to accept the position. One was her desire to maintain her close association with Eleanor Roosevelt. "I miss seeing you. Politics seems sort of endless without you around," complained Molly from New York in the spring of 1933. "I really hate to have you Mrs. Pres.," she sighed soon after. "It absorbs you too much for your friends' satisfaction." By accepting the Women's Division post, Dewson hoped to regain the intimacy she and Eleanor had enjoyed when they shared an office at Democratic headquarters.[29]

The final reason she took the job is perhaps the most obvious: she hated to be on the sidelines. "It sure is fun to have the hand on the plow," Molly exclaimed to Eleanor after several days on the job. The New Deal was her "twentieth century crusade" and she wanted to be part of the action. Her appointment as director of the Women's Division provided her with an institutional base of power and the personal satisfaction of being a member of the Roosevelt team.[30]

Eleanor Roosevelt captured the style and energy of the new Women's Division chief when she commented, "Miss Dewson became director simply by sitting down at her desk and going to work." Dewson's first task in 1933 was patronage. She pursued a definite strategy in winning jobs for political women: "The sine qua non of my ideas was that women competent to be leaders in politics must be given responsibility and power in their party's organization." She continued, "If I had not done my best to get recognition for women few would have been interested in any plans of mine to carry through a program that would win support for the New Deal and put ginger into the Democratic women workers." She wrote more bluntly to Emily Newell Blair, "Anyhow I am going to paddle right ahead and wring as many jobs out of the men for the women who will help build up the Party, as I can."[31]

Requests from women for jobs had been pouring in since the November election, but, with the exception of Frances Perkins, Dewson did nothing about them until the spring of 1933. Finally, in mid-April, Eleanor Roosevelt, Molly Dewson, Nellie Tayloe Ross, and Sue Shelton White convened a meeting to set priorities for women's patronage. While male lawyers or business executives could easily be slotted into New Deal agencies, women with diverse professional and volunteer backgrounds were much harder to place. Democratic women leaders also realized "how much more clamorous the men are," so they kept their list deliberately short—barely one hundred names. Once these women were taken care of, especially the fifteen identified as most deserving of recognition, the Women's Division hoped to help appoint as many other women as possible.[32]

Molly Dewson was deputized to take this list to the men at the Democratic National Commmittee. On April 27, 1933, she met with Jim Farley and another aide. Pencilling at the top, "About the most important letter I ever wrote you!" Molly reported to Eleanor on the conference. "I think they are '100%' friendly toward recognizing the work of the women and that they will probably do it," although "continuous pressure" will have to be brought on behalf of women. "As I look over the ten women whom it is absolutely imperative to give recognition to and the thirteen who are hardly second to this first group in the importance of their work to the Party, it seems to me that both lists could be taken care of in a morning by Mr. Farley in consultation with the Senators and Cabinet officers who would have to be consulted." Unfortunately, winning patronage for these women took far longer than a morning. No matter how much they pared down their lists, the Women's Division had to fight for every appointment.[33]

By mid-May, Dewson was already discouraged. "What is the use of organizing the women at all if their leaders who take responsibility and work hard are not recognized," she complained to Jim Farley. "Don't let the men fool you, Jim. If others have to be recognized, let them be recognized *also.*" By June, only seven women had been appointed, and Dewson griped to Louis Howe, "Women believed that it was a 'New Deal' for our sex but since then nothing has happened more than a few routine appointments." By July, Dewson was writing to Jim Farley, "Heads you win. Tails I lose"—while adding in a postscript to Eleanor, "Heavens but the nicest of men are slippery as eels."[34]

Dewson became angrier as the summer and fall progressed. She wrote to Farley from Castine, "You know, Jim, you have told me at least bi-monthly since November to leave my short list of women workers for the national ticket to you and that you would look after them. So I have not done anything for any of them except nag you which I must have done so pleasantly you have hardly noticed it!!!" She was even franker with Eleanor Roosevelt: "I am like the Jewish Wailing Wall and the wails come thicker and thicker as the Forgotten women see their chances lessen and press closer to the wall." She finally approached Missy LeHand about a meeting with the president himself: "I do not like to seem ungrateful for the few nice positions that have been given the women but if anyone asked me to be frank, I certainly could not say that they were getting anywhere near what seems to me their due, or, in fact, what it would be good politics to give them."[35]

Despite these frustrations, Molly Dewson proved herself especially well suited to the task of patronage politics. She sincerely believed that what she was doing was crucial to women's advancement in politics: not only would it demonstrate to Democratic women that they were taken seriously, but it would offer women the opportunity to show that they could handle the jobs when given the chance. Yet she tried not to appear too strident when dealing with her male counterparts. "Mac, I am not a feminist," she told White House aide Marvin McIntyre. "I am a practical politician out to build up the Democratic Party where it sorely needs it."[36] She could badger the men, but if things did not turn out quite as expected, she did not hold a grudge; she approached her work with an infectious combination of humor, idealism, and pragmatism, which aided her causes, especially since male politicians knew she was not out for herself. Most of all, she was persistent. Molly Dewson was developing into a superb politician, and patronage was one of the things that she did best.

She first turned her attention to a small group of women whom she described as "important personalities in the Party and who reflect a great deal of credit on it." As she had reminded Eleanor Roosevelt in the early days of the New Deal, "In this changing world I feel that the women's vote is going to be more important four years from now and that we must look after our able organization women." Nellie Tayloe Ross, vice-chairman of the Democratic National Committee, received a prominent and not too taxing position as director of the mint, a first for women. Marion Glass Banister, "one of our ablest Democratic politicians"—and not coincidentally the half-sister of the powerful senator Carter Glass of Virginia—was named the assistant treasurer of the United States. Jo Coffin, head of the Labor Advisory Committee for the 1932 campaign, accepted a job as assistant to the public printer at the Government Printing Office.[37]

It was more difficult to find the right spots for two other trusted political workers. Sue Shelton White, who had grown tired of being a "political hack," stood near the top of every Women's Division list, but only in the fall of 1933 did she finally land a position in the Consumers' Division of the National Recovery Administration. When the NRA folded, White joined the legal staff of the Social Security Administration.[38] Emily Newell Blair, vice-chairman of the Democratic National Committee in the 1920s, also posed a problem. "My heart is set on having Emily Blair's services in this campaign as well as during the past ten years recognized," Molly told Eleanor. In the end, Blair's husband, Harry, was named an assistant attorney general, and Emily joined the Consumers' Advisory Board of the NRA. Securing a position for the husband of a loyal Democratic worker proved a successful tactic in other cases as well.[39]

Despite the excitement that had greeted Frances Perkins's nomination, placing more women in the cabinet was never a realistic possibility. But Dewson found plenty of other precedent-breaking appointments for prominent Democratic women on her list. She played a role in the selection of Ruth Bryan Owen as minister to Denmark, the first woman sent abroad to represent the United States. She was especially pleased with this appointment because it "broke new ground." In Roosevelt's second term, she engineered the appointment of Daisy Harriman as minister to Norway.[40]

She was less successful in securing ambassadorial positions for other women. "If Mrs. Olesen had been a man," she observed about one of her top Midwestern organizers, "she would have been offered an ambassadorship." Dewson pushed for appointments of women as delegates to an international conference in South America, only to be told by the State Department that they would appoint only one woman and that the delegate must be fluent in Spanish. "Getting near my limit," she exclaimed in exasperation to Frances Perkins following this setback.[41]

One of Dewson's hardest fights involved appointments to the Veterans' Board of Appeals. She originally asked for three of the fifteen appointments, but nothing happened. The matter dragged on for so long that Roosevelt's aide Marvin McIntyre threatened to lock the main protagonists in a room to let them fight it out. One day on the train down from New York, Dewson recognized General Hines of the Veterans' Administration, the main obstacle to the women's appointments. She introduced herself, and things finally began to happen. "Gallantly the General offered to drive me to the Mayflower Hotel and at last he surrendered." Dewson's three hand-picked candidates, all active workers in the 1932 campaign, soon arrived in Washington. "Yes I am pleased enough at women getting this opening," Dewson confided to new board member Lucy Somerville Howorth of Mississippi. "I had to fight for it like a bag of cats."[42]

Occasionally, too, Molly Dewson and Eleanor Roosevelt found themselves in the anomalous position of opposing women's appointments, especially when Jim Farley failed to honor his pledge to check all women's appointments with Eleanor. Dewson realized that the men would have female candidates of their own—"the most pressing importunities of the boys for their girl friends," she sarcastically labeled these requests—but she wanted her carefully screened organization women to have priority. "The wearisome thing is that our only aim is to get some of the workers in instead of the drones," Molly complained to Eleanor.[43]

While the Women's Division always portrayed patronage in noble terms as a tactic to build up the Democratic organization and give positions to women of outstanding merit, Molly Dewson had one or two small requests that had nothing to do with women's politics. She suggested Gilbert S. Leach for the Postmaster of Castine, calling this "Miss Dewson's one personal request." "I am bold as a lion about trying to get recognition for the women who did the hardest work because I know it is essential for the success of the party in 1934 and 1936," she told Farley, "but when it comes to asking something for myself I feel very modest because I will do just as well by the Party whether or not I get these bits of personal pull." She was persistent just the same, reminding Farley in August, "Don't you think America's Sweetheart deserves anything personal?"[44]

Immersing herself in the nitty-gritty of political patronage, Dewson aimed to recognize at least one woman Democratic worker in every state. She also wanted state Democratic leaders to have a few "plums" to distribute, "not so much on account of the work they did during the campaign but to solidify the leadership of these women." She helped

find women jobs as collectors of customs, registrars in district land offices, and clerks in district courts; she also had a hand in the naming of
some six thousand women as postmasters. She even placed three
women aviators at the Bureau of Air Commerce. Molly commented to
Eleanor about these jobs, "Many of them are minor ones, but they seem
large to the women."[45]

Looking back on the patronage fight, Dewson claimed, "I do not
think I was hindered by my quaint political belief that no Democratic
women of political status had to be 'cleared' by whoever Farley considered the head man of her state. I never cleared a single one." She added
smugly, "Incidentally no man leader ever complained."[46]

On patronage matters, Molly Dewson was not just working for the
Democratic party. She balanced her efforts on behalf of loyal Democratic women with plans to increase the representation of professionally
trained social workers who, she believed, could help pull the country
out of the depression. She was guided in her efforts by her desire to increase opportunities for professional women in public life. "I am a firm
believer in progress for women coming through appointments here and
there and a first class job by the women who are the lucky ones chosen to
demonstate." Frances Perkins was just the first in a long line of talented
women whom Dewson helped to bring into the New Deal administration. She always believed that the work of such women "compared well
with that of the best men and was much better than the average man's
performance."[47]

After her Frances Perkins coup, Dewson was most proud of the appointment of Florence Allen to the Circuit Court of Appeals, which
was the highest position a woman had obtained in the federal judiciary.
To push Allen's candidacy, Dewson used a favorite tactic: she mobilized
social reformers and political leaders across the country in a letter-
writing campaign to President Roosevelt. She was pleased with the
growing momentum of the campaign but realistic about the remaining
hurdles: "There are so many slips twixt the cup and the lip." When
Allen's appointment became official she told Attorney General Homer
Cummings how much it had meant to the women of the country: "I do
not expect there will be many Florence Allens but her appointment
serves as a high water mark such as they have on the banks of the Seine.
It registers the great floods."[48]

Some appointments required no action at all: career women like
Mary Anderson of the Women's Bureau, Grace Abbott of the Chil-

dren's Bureau, and Louise Stanley of the Bureau of Home Economics knew that their positions were safe under Roosevelt. But when Grace Abbott resigned from the Children's Bureau in the spring of 1934, Dewson naturally had a say in naming her successor. "But darling count yourself lucky that you are out of Washington as I understand that nearly fifty of your girls are after it," one of Molly's friends warned her. Dewson sought Frances Perkins's ear with her own suggestion: Clara Beyer, who currently headed the Division of Industrial Standards of the Children's Bureau. "Really Clara is miles ahead of practically any possibility," Molly told Frances. "She is rare. She has brains, judgment, common sense, sense of values, balance, energy, and friendliness. *And she cares.*" In the end, Katharine Lenroot won the Children's Bureau job, but Beyer was named associate director of the Labor Department's new Division of Labor Standards. Beyer was just one of the many talented women that Frances Perkins gathered around her in the Labor Department.[49]

Dewson did not push only women for jobs in the labor standards field—she also promoted an occasional man. She was instrumental, for example, in getting Arthur Altmeyer named assistant secretary of labor, where he served until he joined the Social Security Board in 1935. Both Beyer and Dewson thought Altmeyer would be a great help to Perkins in the department, and Dewson suggested the idea to Perkins. She seemed interested, but did nothing about it. Altmeyer was about to return to his teaching position at the University of Wisconsin when Dewson caught sight of him on the street one day. She pleaded with Altmeyer to wait a few more days. The next morning before breakfast Molly woke Frances Perkins with a phone call. "I am coming over to see you. It's very important or I should not get you or myself up at this hour." Dewson made her pitch for Altmeyer, and her forceful presentation carried the day.[50]

Molly Dewson also had a hand in several appointments of women to prominent New Deal agencies created to meet the emergency needs of the Depression. Her proudest placements were Ellen Sullivan Woodward, appointed to head Women's and Professional Projects at the Works Progress Administration, and Mary Harriman Rumsey, named to chair the Consumers' Advisory Board of the NRA. (Rumsey, who shared a home with Frances Perkins in Washington, was killed in a riding accident in late 1934.) In addition to pushing women for top administrative positions in the relief field, Dewson suggested women qualified to work in the middle ranks of the expanding New Deal bureaucracy.[51]

In her autobiography, Molly Dewson listed more than one hundred women who served in prominent positions in the New Deal. She did not claim personal responsibility for all of them, but she played a part in most. When she totaled up the list, she realized what a breakthrough it represented for women in public life. "In Roosevelt's day women were recognized as never before. . . . The change from women's status in government before Roosevelt is unbelievable." She added, "If he had not been absorbed night and day in his recovery plans, I believe even more would have been appointed."[52]

A vignette dramatically illustrates this transformation. One day in 1935, Mary Anderson and Molly Dewson were seated next to each other at a luncheon at the Women's University Club in Washington. Dewson said, "This is a pleasant dining room for private parties." Anderson replied with a tinge of nostalgia, "I have very pleasant memories of this place. The women in the top government positions used to lunch here regularly on certain days. Now there are so many of them they would need a hall."[53]

The reasons behind Molly Dewson's successes in securing patronage for women range from the personal to the institutional. Her perseverance was certainly a powerful factor. Jim Farley paid tribute to it at a breakfast honoring the Women's Division director: "Molly was a doggone persistent woman and hard to manage. If I said 'yes' to one of her big ideas, she ran off in a hurry for fear I would change my mind. If I said 'no' she stayed around a while until I said 'yes.'" (Dewson commented wryly as she recounted this story, "Farley was always most agreeable at gatherings of this kind.") White House aide Marvin McIntyre saw it from a different perspective: "Molly Dewson is back on my neck," he once complained to Farley, the chair of the DNC.[54]

Molly Dewson also profited from the support of several key allies, starting with President Roosevelt himself. Roosevelt had developed a positive view of women's capabilities in New York State in the 1910s and 1920s. His respect for women like Frances Perkins, Nancy Cook, Marion Dickerman, and Caroline O'Day, many of whom he met through Eleanor, made him far more openminded toward them than the typical male political leader. When Roosevelt was planning to appoint Frances Perkins as industrial commissioner in 1929, Perkins questioned whether her appointment would be popular with women. Franklin replied, "Oh yes, it will. . . . I asked Nancy Cook and she thinks so, and Caroline O'Day." Perkins continued, "These were women he saw all the time. He didn't have to go out on the highways and byways. He saw them personally all the time."[55]

Roosevelt's ability to work with women had limits, however. He never invited women into his inner circle of advisers: Frances Perkins and Molly Dewson, and even Eleanor, were excluded. "I was not one of his brain trust," Dewson admitted.[56] Moreover, Roosevelt only went so far in entrusting major responsibilities to women. He liked the drama that surrounded the appointment of the first woman to the cabinet, but he never seriously considered appointing another woman on that level. He selected Florence Allen for the Circuit Court of Appeals but remained unmoved by pleas to elevate her to the Supreme Court when vacancies occurred in the late 1930s. And he tried actively to keep women *out* of certain "sensitive" areas in the administration. When Daisy Harriman was in the running for a diplomatic post in 1937, Roosevelt told Dewson that he could send a woman only to a country not likely to be drawn into a European conflict. He settled on Norway. When the international situation changed dramatically in 1940, Dewson reminded Roosevelt of his lack of faith in women's capabilities: "Daisy Harriman in Norway and doing all right has been my only chuckle these days."[57]

At base, Franklin Roosevelt treated women politicians in the same pragmatic and instrumental manner as civil rights advocates, conservationists, Southern politicians, labor leaders, and the rest of the New Deal coalition. Sometimes they got what they wanted; more often than not, they had to settle for less. But, since women politicians had rarely been listened to at all before, they remained grateful—perhaps more so than other pressure groups—for this measure of attention and flattery.

Another important ally, of course, was Eleanor Roosevelt. "What would the Democratic women of America do without you there on the spot," Molly cooed to Eleanor in 1933.[58] One reason that Molly Dewson accepted the directorship of the Women's Division was to be close to Eleanor Roosevelt, and her instincts were richly rewarded. Molly and Eleanor's bonds of friendship were at their strongest in 1933. During the early New Deal, Molly often stayed at the White House when she was in Washington and she and Eleanor collaborated almost daily on their joint plans to win patronage for women and build up the Women's Division of the Democratic National Committee. Never again would Dewson be as close either personally or politically to Eleanor Roosevelt as she was in the heady early days of the New Deal.[59]

In her drive for patronage, Molly Dewson took advantage of broader trends which enhanced her pleas for women's recognition. The Democrats were returning to power after twelve years, and, at least in the early New Deal, they had plenty of federal positions at their disposal. The growing professional status of women meant a larger pool of women qualified to serve. Finally, the groundwork had been laid by a small cadre of women pioneers in the federal bureaucracy (Dewson counted twelve pre–1933), who demonstrated that women could perform in high-level government jobs.[60]

Dewson's efforts were also fundamentally affected by the Depression and its impact on the federal bureaucracy. In the 1930s, the federal government took on new responsibilities. It provided work relief, social security, and unemployment compensation and regulated wages and hours and other working conditions. Since women made up the majority of trained social workers, they were often the leading candidates to staff these new agencies. Women's Bureau studies show that the percentage of women government employees rose from 14.3 percent in 1929 to 18.8 percent in 1939. Furthermore, women's rate of federal employment increased twice as rapidly as men's in the decade.[61]

The other salient aspect of women's employment in the federal government in the 1930s was its concentration in certain areas of the bureaucracy. Women found jobs more readily in the recently established New Deal agencies than in older, tradition-bound departments like State and Commerce. Women employees made up almost 45 percent of the Works Progress Administration, whereas their proportion in executive departments hovered around 15 percent. Generally, women did better in newer agencies where traditional prejudices against using women's talents were put aside in the excitement of creating new programs and administrative structures. Once the bureaucracy became more routinized, however, sexist attitudes and barriers reasserted themselves, and women's progress slowed. This is precisely what happened during Roosevelt's second term.[62]

The early 1930s were an exciting time for all the New Dealers who flocked to Washington—"men with long hair and women with short hair."[63] Molly Dewson said Washington "was as lively as an ants' nest that has been split open." She found herself so busy that "personal social life was out for these months": "Rarely was I in my room at the

Mayflower Hotel before eleven o'clock." This hectic and experimental climate proved especially hospitable to women. Suddenly, instead of fitting comfortably into Mary Anderson's small private dining room, they needed a hall. Instead of being ignored or patronized, they were invited to Eleanor Roosevelt's garden parties or asked to her press conferences to discuss their work. With Franklin and Eleanor Roosevelt in the White House, women had an administration that supported their feminist and social welfare goals.[64]

As more and more talented women gathered in Washington, the nation's capital seemed like a changed place. Now, former League of Women Voters president Maud Wood Park noted, women were "sitting in the seat of the mighty." The suffrage leader Carrie Chapman Catt, writing to Eleanor Roosevelt, elaborated: "For some time I have had a collection of statesmen hanging upon my wall, but, under the new administration, I have been obliged to start a new collection and that is one of stateswomen. Now it is ready and you are at the center of it all. . . . You, Miss Perkins, Mrs. Owen, Miss Woolley, Miss Abbott, Miss Anderson, and some others, make a fine looking group—the beginning of the grand display of stateswomen we are going to have after a time." Emily Newell Blair linked this progress directly to Molly Dewson: "It's a monument to you, Molly—all your work and such work—and really worth while from the feminist view-point, I think."[65]

Molly Dewson took personal pride in the Roosevelt administration's recognition of women. The New Deal represented an opening, a chance for women to show what they could do: "At last women had their foot inside the door. We had the opportunity to demonstrate our ability to see what was needed and to get the job done while working harmoniously with men." She concluded dramatically, "The opportunities given women by Roosevelt in the thirties changed our status."[66]

Molly Dewson overstated the long-term effects of the New Deal on the status of women in twentieth-century America, but it is true that the women New Dealers were at the cutting edge of one of the most important changes in modern America: the entrance of women into positions of public leadership and responsibility. Since the nineteenth century, women had been moving away from complete identification with the domestic realm and taking positions in the professions, politics, and government, areas traditionally reserved for men. By the 1930s, women had a crack at national power and influence for the first time. The thirties did not complete the process—it is still incomplete. But women's participation in the New Deal was part of this broader pattern.[67]

Women's experience in the New Deal also addresses the fortunes of feminism in the post-suffrage era. Feminism did not die after 1920: one place where it took hold, however tentatively, was in the politics and government of the New Deal. Molly Dewson was basically a political boss with a feminist twist. Although she was concerned about rewarding her faithful workers, building up her organization, and winning their loyalty to the Democratic party, her real agenda was a feminist commitment to giving women a chance in public life, politics, and the professions. Throughout the 1930s, New Deal women like Molly Dewson, Frances Perkins, and Eleanor Roosevelt self-consciously carried forward the suffrage banner, trying to forge permanent roles for women in politics and government as the next step beyond suffrage.

The collective experience of women in the New Deal demonstrates the importance of women's networks in shaping access to and conduct of power. The women in the New Deal acted both individually and collectively in pursuit of feminist and social welfare objectives. They combined personal friendship with professional activism in a way that fundamentally shaped Democratic politics and the development of the New Deal's social welfare policies. They wielded more power because they cooperated with each other. Molly Dewson captured this spirit: "We girls are not politicians; we're just girls who have done things together for years and years."[68]

Their feminist activism did not go unnoticed. In 1938, Drew Pearson posited in a "Washington Merry-Go-Round" column the existence of a "Ladies' Brain Trust." Pearson cited Frances Perkins, Clara Beyer, Mary LaDame, Mary T. Norton, and Molly Dewson as the nucleus of this group, noting that Frances Perkins "seems happier about taking her hair down with members of her own sex." The syndicated columnist reserved special praise for Molly Dewson, whom he described as "Miss Perkins' most capable advisor." "In fact she is probably the shrewdest lady around the New Deal high command."[69]

The women's network did not usually show up in the newspapers, nor did it seek such publicity. In fact, its members preferred to function behind the scenes. In November of 1933, Molly Dewson participated in an all-day conference at the White House on the Emergency Needs of Women, along with many of the women administrators who had flocked to Washington. Later that day, she mused about the implications of so many women on the verge of assuming positions of power: "I am proud that we have Frances Perkins in a most prominent place in the policy making group and Mrs. Rumsey, Emily, Belle Sherwin, Mrs.

Poole and Yours Truly on the Consumers' Committee and Rose Schneiderman on the Labor Committee. Unofficially, Mrs. Roosevelt is on
the spot and Mrs. Woodward is near the top of the F.E.R.A. which is a
policy making group of a kind."[70] Mobilizing women friends in the
New Deal bureaucracy to influence policy was one of Dewson's most effective tools in the 1930s. The three main actors in this collective undertaking were Eleanor Roosevelt, Frances Perkins, and herself. As
early as November 1933, she had drawn up a blueprint for the operation
of a women's network in the New Deal.

Molly Dewson always saw winning positions for talented women as
only the first step in her wider plans for women's participation in the
New Deal. That larger perspective kept her spirits up as she struggled
with the vicissitudes of patronage throughout 1933. Finally, by early
1934 the end was in sight: "Pretty near all the leaders who wished for
appointments have been taken care of. A few wait on final developments but I consider the patronage issue as closed except for casual hap-
penings. The government has settled down to its stride." Molly confessed her great sense of relief to Eleanor Roosevelt: "The real joy will
be that I will not have to pester you and Franklin about these dashed
jobs. I have set my jaw and gone through with it but I was not born to
nag and I *hate* it."[71] Now Dewson could turn her attention to her next
goal: building up the women's side of the Democratic party and promoting a clear and widespread understanding of the New Deal.

CHAPTER TWELVE

Campaigns Are Won Between Elections

"ODAY is to me a milestone in woman's evolution," Molly Dewson told a group of women Democrats in Richmond, Virginia, in 1935. All her life—as the head of a state department, a suffragist, a member of the boards of civic organizations, and a Democratic politician—she had been observing women expand their roles in public affairs. In the 1930s, something new was happening among women: "at last the women of a great national political party have decided to understand and explain as their first duty and function, and to do so as a recognized part of their party organization." She concluded dramatically, "No woman is too busy, too tired, or too dumb to help."[1]

This Richmond speech encapsulated the political philosophy that Molly Dewson promoted at the Women's Division throughout the 1930s. Education and issues, not patronage and power, were women's real concerns. Recently enfranchised women expected more out of politics than just a rousing speech or the promise of a job: they wanted the government to act as a positive and constructive force in society. Dewson was hardly alone in this orientation: it was the hallmark of women who entered the political sphere after 1920.

The crisis brought on by the Depression made these concerns even more pressing. By and large, the women Dewson met "were far more concerned with the dreadful conditions existing in the early thirties" than the men. She hoped to put women's energy and idealism to work promoting what she referred to as "the human aspects of the New Deal." This crusade became her obsession.[2]

In her plans for organizing women, Dewson wavered about the degree to which women's interests should be singled out. Like many of her contemporaries, she believed that women were fundamentally different from men, primarily because women shared a stronger interest in social betterment and humanitarian justice. "The outstanding feminine contribution is a sense of relatedness," she reasoned, "as opposed to the masculine grasp of facts." This orientation defined women's roles in politics. "The suffragists were right in believing women would act differently from men because we are not so individualistic as they are, but cooperative. Our fundamental interests are security of the home, a chance for the children, and peace. Our natural instinct for cooperation makes women easily interested in the security of other's homes, a chance for all children, and universal peace."[3]

Given a political philosophy based on differences, Dewson welcomed the idea of a Women's Division functioning as a base of operations separate from the main Democratic hierarchy. "If the men wrangle over prestige and patronage, we cannot change their attitude, but we certainly do not need to copy it," she pointedly explained to one California leader. The Women's Division concentrated attention on "a few fundamentals that I believe the ordinary run of man interested in politics has overlooked." These fundamentals concerned both values and tactics. "Most important of all, the genius of women, and distinctly not the genius of men," she argued, "is to make paper plans a reality through faithful, intelligent, persistent attention to single acts, small in themselves but in the aggregate overwhelming."[4]

At the same time that she was pleading the special concerns of her sex, Dewson often reiterated that there was no political issue in which women did not have as legitimate an interest as men. She reminded Eleanor, "Now as to Franklin speaking to women; I daresay I am wrong about this but I have a hunch that his treating us as people without special feminine interests is more in tune with his whole program." Dewson thought that men and women should be equally interested in economic and social welfare: "Even as I write this I stutter because if any man is not interested in youth and children, it is just too bad." Throughout the 1930s, Dewson juggled the separatist and integrationist approaches, trying to have it both ways. She mirrored the tensions between different strands of feminism in postsuffrage America.[5]

Molly Dewson called her educational approach to politics the Reporter Plan. "My basic conviction," Dewson explained, "was that everyday women could be deeply interested in specific plans to care for the
human misery created by the general collapse, to get the wheels started,
to remove existing evils, and to work out a better-ordered society." Appropriately, the program was launched on January 15, 1934, at one of
Eleanor Roosevelt's press conferences for women journalists. Dewson
did not clear the plan in advance with Jim Farley, Louis Howe, or even
the president himself. "Things were marching so fast and every one was
so busy that even Mrs. Roosevelt had never heard of it or anyone else
before it was presented." Yet Eleanor agreed, "sight unseen, or rather,
hearing unheard" to let Molly present the plan: "She did not even remind me that politics were 'out' at her press conference."[6]

The Reporter Plan was an ambitious attempt to link women's
issue-oriented approach to politics with the more traditional concern of
building an active grassroots organization. It encouraged Democratic
women to learn how government programs affected their communities,
and to spread this information to their friends and neighbors. Every
county Democratic organization selected women to serve as Reporters,
each one assigned to cover an agency such as the Agricultural Adjustment Administration, the Reconstruction Finance Corporation, or the
Civilian Conservation Corps. Fortified with facts, Reporters presented
their findings before civic groups, clubs, and other organizations,
thereby spreading the New Deal message throughout the community.[7]

The women journalists at Eleanor Roosevelt's press conference
gave the Reporter Plan good coverage, highlighting Dewson's statement that "if the Administration policies are really understood by Republican women, they will discover that at heart they have been Democrats all along." But the newspaperwomen had a little fun at Dewson's
expense. She introduced the plan by saying that women Democrats had
long hoped for such a grassroots organization and were finally on the
verge of achieving it "for many reasons." The reporters all knew that
Eleanor Roosevelt, sitting demurely on the sofa beside Dewson, lay behind this success, but United Press reporter Ruby Black mischievously
blurted out, "Name three." Eleanor remained silent (and amused), but
Molly responded vigorously: "This Democratic Party really believes in
women, and the plan was presented to it properly." Emma Bugbee of
the *New York Herald-Tribune* teased, "That is old stuff under a new
name—just another paper plan." Dewson replied, "Wait and see." By
the summer of 1934, five thousand women had signed up for the Re-

porter Plan. The number grew to fifteen thousand by the 1936 election, and thirty thousand by 1940.[8]

Although the Reporter Plan found inspiration in the League of Women Voters's program of issue-oriented study and education, in the end the plan followed a different course. Even though Dewson said glibly, "it isn't politics to understand what your government is doing," she definitely intended to pursue partisan objectives. The November 1934 elections were just ten months away, and the Reporters were in a position to disseminate pro-Roosevelt information in communities whose newspapers opposed the New Deal.[9]

One potential obstacle stood in the way of the Women's Division plans: the rapid expansion of the New Deal bureaucracy, which made getting information out of Washington a maze of frustration. "Just to locate an agency in that beehive was a sixty-four dollar question," Dewson admitted. But without facts and figures the Reporter Plan would be a dud. So the Women's Division devised a tool to meet this need—a magazine called the *Democratic Digest.* The divison took over a bulletin previously published by the Women's National Democratic Club and hired Mary Chamberlain, who had been responsible for the Rainbow Fliers, as the new magazine's editor. "Thumbs were down on promoting any man's personal interest," Dewson recalled, and she made a rule that no woman was to be mentioned in the *Democratic Digest* except in connection with what she had done. The magazine played an especially important role in "feeding facts to the hungry Reporters and Democratic women in general."[10]

The Reporter Plan not only increased women's understanding of how government operated but functioned as a force to build political support for the Democratic party. The plan emphasized reporting the facts, not just studying them, which put "ginger" into Democratic workers by giving them something interesting and worthwhile to do. "A practical objective is like vitamins to party workers," Molly Dewson often said. Of course, none of her organizational plans would have worked without the ferment and excitement generated by the early New Deal. Roosevelt's programs made political work "a recreation," she later recalled: "It was like picking quinces on a crisp, sunny day in the fall."[11]

Molly Dewson spent much of the spring of 1934 traveling around the country promoting the Reporter Plan and trying to build up local women's Democratic organizations. This cost money, as did the New York and Washington headquarters that the Women's Division now staffed, and by April Dewson realized that the Women's Division needed a larger budget. Jim Farley disagreed. "Why waste money between campaigns when we are down to the bone," he argued, wearing an expression Dewson called "the Tammany snarl." The battle lines were drawn for their first major confrontation. Molly finally announced, "Oh come, Jim, we've always gotten on so well it's a pity to quarrel now. Let's go to the Boss and let him decide."[12]

On the day of the meeting, Farley appeared glum, Dewson cautiously optimistic. She handed the president a one-page summary of Women's Division accomplishments and a list of reasons to increase its yearly appropriation to fifty thousand dollars. (By way of comparison, the Women's Division budget for the entire 1932 campaign had been forty-two thousand dollars.) Dewson offered to contribute one extra worker at seventy-five hundred a year by resigning as director and becoming an unpaid volunteer. Looking over the total request, the President smiled at Dewson and said, "Will you settle for three thousand a month?" Dewson, the pragmatic politician, quickly agreed. "Obviously the President thinks it is worth our effort," she glowed after the meeting, "for even though the Democratic National Committee is in debt he is willing to have us go ahead for such an end and we are to have the money."[13]

Despite her personal victory, Dewson was quite serious about resigning as director of the Women's Division, just one year into the New Deal. "You cannot know how disappointed I am to give out and not be able to help Franklin to the limit," she explained to Eleanor. "What he is doing is so far seeing and inspired he must succeed anyway. Of course, I love you as I always have so I hate to think of losing even the fleeting glimpses that have lightened the job so much." Molly simply realized she had pushed herself too hard. "I felt I had to get certain things done to be happy and it was such a job to accomplish them I tore myself to bits doing so." More to the point, the regular commute to Washington was proving too much of a strain on her partnership with Polly Porter. Once again, she used exhaustion and overwork to extricate herself from an unsatisfactory professional situation.[14]

Despite her resignation, Molly Dewson continued to be the most important woman politician in the Roosevelt administration. Even though she loved her summers in Castine and winters in New York with Polly, she could not keep away from New Deal politics. "When I told you a year ago spring I was through I meant it," she confessed to Eleanor Roosevelt in 1935, "but since FD gave us so much more opportunity last

fall I weakened and went right back on the job." Under this new compromise, Dewson gave up commuting to Washington and made the
New York office her base of operations; this allowed her to keep what
she referred to as her "home arrangements" intact. Back on volunteer
status, she felt much happier: "I guess I'm queer. I really love not to be
paid when I am working for an ideal. Expensive tastes!"[15]

The only drawback was that her resignation left her without an official title. She finally decided to call herself chairman of the Advisory
Committee of the Women's Division. But this Advisory Committee
had no other members! Did anyone ever question her about his anomaly? "Experienced women are astute," she observed tongue-in-cheek.[16]

The new arrangement obviously demanded a strong Women's
Division director in Washington. Dewson's assistant in 1933–34,
Maybelle Fickel, had proven a competent organizer in the farm belt,
but Dewson did not consider Fickel the kind of "truly liberal" woman
she wanted to head the Women's Division. Molly told Eleanor that her
choice was Carolyn Wolfe of Utah, the wife of a Utah supreme court
justice whom Dewson had tapped as a regional advisor in 1933. Wolfe
also attracted Dewson's attention with a plan she developed for educational study groups for Utah Democratic women. Wolfe later suspected
that it had given Dewson the idea for the Reporter Plan.[17]

Once Dewson made up her mind to have Carolyn Wolfe for her
organization, she subjected her to the same intensive treatment previously directed at Frances Perkins. The objections that Wolfe raised—
leaving her husband and five children in Utah—"didn't seem to bother
[Dewson] so much," Wolfe recalled. Husbands and children, as Clara
Beyer had learned in the 1920s, were not acceptable to Molly Dewson
as reasons for turning down opportunities for public service. When
Wolfe arrived in Washington, Dewson greeted her with, "Now I'll tell
you all about the different states." They finished three days later. Wolfe
served with distinction through the 1936 election.[18]

The 1934 reorganization increased the legitimacy and effectiveness of the Women's Division: the successful battle to increase the budget gave official sanction to Molly Dewson's central tenet that elections
are won between campaigns. As she reminded Louis Howe, "You know
I am not a spender and do not mean anything extravagant. But every
dollar spent NOW in developing enthusiastic women workers down to
the grass roots will be more effective than 25 times as much just before
election." With the 1936 election just two years away, it was time to get
to work.[19]

The Women's Democratic organization grew steadily in 1934 and 1935. The Reporter Plan did especially well, catching on everywhere but the South. Soon the Women's Division realized the need for a staff member who could discuss the New Deal with Reporters and other local Democratic groups across the country. Neither Dewson nor Carolyn Wolfe was an especially inspirational speaker, but Molly was an excellent talent scout. Sometime in the early New Deal, she marked Harriet Elliott, who was dean of women and professor of political science at the University of North Carolina at Greensboro. Elliott was Dewson's kind of woman: straightforward, unmarried, and a former suffragist committed to increasing women's roles in politics and public life. Her background in economics and sociology fit Dewson's job specifications perfectly.[20]

Now all Molly Dewson had to do was to convince Elliott to take a leave of absence and come to Washington to work for the Women's Division. She began her campaign of persuasion in late December 1934, while she and Polly Porter were spending Christmas at Castine, as they often did in the 1930s. She appealed dramatically to Elliott's sense of civic duty: "We are in the midst of a great movement of national forces which often lie dormant or are controlled by finances. I hope that big things will be accomplished before everything settles down again. Certainly the President has in mind to do a lot to secure a more 'abundant life' for the average man and will if he has the country's support for long enough." The Women's Division, Molly told Harriet, aimed to generate just such support.[21]

When Dewson returned to Washington after her Christmas holiday, Carolyn Wolfe informed her that Harriet Elliott had said no. Dewson was aghast that any teacher of government would turn down such an opportunity, and she got Elliott on the phone. "Harriet Elliott, you aren't telling me that you are going on, all your life, teaching government, when you don't know the first thing about it, except theoretically, and refusing a chance like this, that few teachers have, to learn from experience." Silence on the other end of the line. "I'll do it," she said meekly. Dewson editorialized, "There is no pleasure greater than dealing with sensible persons." Later Elliott told Dewson that she had been with the college's president when the call came through, and she had asked him to listen in. After the conversation, the president observed, "You were right to say you would do it. Someday I want to meet that woman."[22]

Dean Elliott lectured extensively about the New Deal for the

Women's Division between February and August 1935, when she resumed her academic duties in Greensboro. She enjoyed her taste of national government so much that she returned to Washington in 1940 to serve on the National Defense Advisory Commission and stayed for the duration of the war.[23]

As an adjunct to the Reporter Plan, Molly Dewson instituted yearly regional conferences throughout her Democratic domain. The 1935 conference in Richmond, Virginia, featured the talent available to the Women's Division for these occasions. Molly Dewson welcomed the delegates, Harriet Elliott discussed the Reporter Plan, and Carolyn Wolfe spoke on party organization. Maryland Democrat Lavinia Engle addressed unemployment insurance, and Ellen Woodward, the highest-ranking woman in the Federal Emergency Relief Administration, described the women's relief program. Frances Perkins gave the keynote address on the Social Security bill, then pending in Congress.

Regional conferences, with their combination of politics, government, and education, stirred up interest both in the Democratic party and the New Deal. These forums proved especially useful in maintaining enthusiasm during the long spells between national elections. They also helped local women forget the "saddle galls of local politics" by promoting the Democratic party as an organization concerned with national problems of government. As Dewson said to the Pennsylvania leader Emma Guffey Miller, "Local problems are forgotten and they can get a pure, good Democratic thrill."[24]

Occasionally the regional conferences provided the Women's Division with new ideas for women's politics. When one speaker at a Kansas City conference mentioned penny collection boxes for feeding the poor during the Depression, Dewson rose to say, "Mrs. Brown, you have given me a welcome idea. The Democratic women in every locality can raise their 'gas money' themselves by putting a penny a week in a little box and asking their friends and neighbors now and then to chip in a penny or a nickel, and men coming to the house might not miss a dime even. We all know about Peter's Pence and what a force it is." The idea caught on instantly, with the only disagreement being whether the money should be collected in mite boxes or metal donkeys. The donkeys won, and by March 1935 the Women's Division had shipped twenty-seven thousand Donkey banks to Democratic women. Donkey Round Ups took place twice a year to collect the money. All proceeds stayed at the local level—not one of the pennies collected was sent to national headquarters.[25]

The Donkey Bank plan had all the ingredients of Dewson's innovative approach to politics: keep women's activities separate from men's, make women self-supporting, and decentralize control of women's politics to the local level. Yet like the Reporter Plan, it did little to help women rise to positions of authority within the regular party structure. The Women's Division achieved great success in energizing women, but that energy tended to find its outlets outside the main party structure rather than within it.[26]

Dewson's inability to gain more substantial roles for women in the party hierarchy reflected her ambivalence over where to focus women's activities. She dubbed her plan for increasing women's representation "fifty-fifty organization." She hoped to convince each state to mandate selection of both a man and a woman for every party position, thus creating positions such as a national committeewoman, state vice chairwoman, county vice chairwoman, and so on down to the local level. By 1939, seventeen states had adopted equal representation on all party committees, either by law or by party regulation. Twenty-two mandated equal representation on some, but not all, committees, while nine states provided no guarantee of equal representation.[27]

Dewson was quick to rationalize her lack of success in winning more equal representation in party affairs. "If at first this is not as much as the women would wish, they must remember that we have had the vote for only a comparatively short period and, moreover, the women have only recently taken a place in public life outside of the home. They must be patient and not expect too quick advancement."[28] For someone so committed to breaking down all barriers to women's advancement in politics, Molly Dewson was often a little too quick to make excuses when things did not quite work out as she had hoped: dwelling on setbacks, major or minor, was counterproductive. Her philosophy no doubt kept up her spirits in the give and take of Democratic politics, but it certainly muted her ability—or, more to the point, her inclination—to criticize the party when women's interests were ignored.

Molly Dewson was happiest when she was proselytizing for New Deal programs ("You know the Women's Division is Dead Sea Apples to me unless it is working tooth and nail for the Roosevelt program," she told Carolyn Wolfe), but she devoted much of her time to more prosaic matters. She continued to handle patronage requests, deal with factionalism among women leaders, and mediate feuds between men's and women's organizations in the states. And she continued to have difficulty with the men at the Democratic National Committee, especially Postmaster General Jim Farley. "Really, I cannot understand the male politician," Dewson chided Farley. "He is so anxious to win and yet he does not take the most ordinary precautions in regard to securing the women's vote. He leaves it all to campaign time just as if the women reacted like the men and he gives no power or authority to the women who really could help him win the woman's vote."[29]

More often than not, Molly Dewson turned to the White House for help and support. "You are very patient to listen to all my ideas," Molly thanked Eleanor on numerous occasions. Molly also enjoyed access to Franklin Roosevelt, although she was careful not to abuse this privilege. She did, however, regularly send Franklin an assortment of articles and letters for his "bedtime basket," telling Missy LeIland, "Sometimes, I think my prattlings and the Women's Democratic Digest will divert him almost as much as stamps." If she had a routine matter that she wanted brought to his attention, she let the request go through regular channels. But when Molly really needed to talk to the president, she just alerted Eleanor and things happened quickly. "When I wanted help on some definite point, Mrs. Roosevelt gave me the opportunity to sit by the President at dinner and the matter was settled before we finished our soup."[30]

Dewson was often a guest at the White House when she was in Washington. She usually stayed in the Lincoln bedroom. "The initial time I slept there was one crowded night and E.R. apologized," she recalled, "but afterwards I asked to sleep there." She always considered it "one of the privileges of the White House" to spend the night in that "enormous, homely bed, hard as a board, where Abraham Lincoln regularly slept." Spending the night often meant she enjoyed the treat of a private breakfast with Eleanor.[31]

As a trusted member of the Roosevelt entourage, Molly regularly attended such White House social events as Eleanor Roosevelt's tea parties for women executives and the annual Gridiron Widows party, which came into being in response to the formal stag dinner for members of the administration sponsored by the men in the press corps. The first year, Dewson went disguised as The Forgotten Man, wearing khaki pants, a yellow shirt, and ranch hat. No one penetrated her disguise.[32]

Eleanor Roosevelt also served as something of a Mother Confessor for Molly Dewson. At times even the naturally optimistic Dewson felt disappointed in Roosevelt's leadership or the results of the New Deal.

In the spring of 1934, she got herself into what Eleanor described as a "kind of panic" over opposition to FDR's policies in Congress. Eleanor Roosevelt passed along a message from her husband: "The ups and downs in peoples' feelings, particularly on the liberal side, are an old, old story. The liberals always get discouraged when they do not see the measures they are interested in go through immediately. . . . Franklin says, for Heaven's sake, all you Democratic leaders calm down and feel sure of ultimate success. It will do a lot in satisfying other people."[33]

Another low point occurred on the eve of the 1936 campaign. In a letter signed "Your Gloomy Gus," Dewson confessed exasperation over her inability to get an audience with the president: "Yet sometimes to be perfectly frank with you I wonder whether some of the persons the papers say he sees are more important to see than I am." She was especially disappointed about the slow progress of the women's Democratic organization, concluding, "I am not positive at all about what next."[34] Such moments of frustration, however, were fairly rare, and publicly Molly maintained the cheerful and even-tempered demeanor she affected when she tangled with Jim Farley: "I am a good sailor and accept the view of the skipper."[35] In fact, there were few more loyal members of the Roosevelt administration than Molly Dewson.

A more typical solution for dealing with setbacks and disappointments was to retreat to Polly Porter. This pattern became more pronounced in the 1930s, especially after Polly's displeasure convinced Dewson to drop her commuting arrangement in 1933–34. No matter how busy things were at the Women's Division, Molly never missed an extended summer in Maine, where she rebuilt her physical and mental strength with Polly's help. "Here I am in Castine and it seems like Heaven!" she wrote to Eleanor in June 1935. "I don't see why I get tired on this political job. I guess it's temperamental for every unturned stone challenges me." She sounded the same theme to Carolyn Wolfe, who was minding the Women's Division in Washington: "I have been here 2 1/2 weeks and gone in strong for painting—house painting—and not churned over and over what we could do more and better and my old head feels less like an over ripe pear. I wish I was not so darned interested in what the Pres. is trying to do. But then if I was not I certainly would be doing something else." Molly admitted to Eleanor, "I feel a million miles away and have settled into the bucolic life with great personal profit."[36]

There was a negative side to this bucolic life, however. Much as Molly Dewson needed to rest and unwind with Polly, she hated to be too far away from the action. Every summer she maintained an active correspondence from her Castine retreat. (It was a good thing she had gotten her Democratic friend appointed postmaster—she was his biggest customer.) She frequently bombarded Carolyn Wolfe for information and pleaded with Clara Beyer, "Can't you stop to write a poor woman the news." Dewson knew that the only way she could keep her mind alive was to keep in touch: "Just crack my head against the job and I get notions. In a vacuum nothing scratches sparks off me. Alas!"[37]

In the summer of 1934, her pent-up energies found an outlet in the Maine gubernatorial campaign of Louis J. Brann. This was a first for Dewson: "No one before had asked me to interfere with men politicians." In 1932 Maine had elected Brann as its first Democratic governor in years, and he was up for reelection in September of 1934. The Maine contest was a potential indicator of Democratic fortunes in the upcoming congressional elections, and the Democratic National Committee took an active interest in the race. Farley had feuded with Governor Brann over patronage, however, so he turned the campaign over to Louis Howe, who in turn passed the assignment along to Dewson. That at least was her interpretation of the chain of events, which she viewed with "considerable private amusement."[38]

Although Dewson worked with the men in the Brann headquarters, she quickly turned her attention to the women's side of the campaign, which had been completely neglected. Louis Howe received two thousand dollars earmarked for women's work from Henry Morgenthau, Sr., the father of the secretary of the treasury and a summer resident of Bar Harbor. Dewson realized that active women leaders needed gas to get around their districts, as well as money for telephone calls and postage, so she allocated a hundred dollars each to the state vice-chairman and the Democratic women leaders in populated districts and twenty-five dollars each to the sixteen county chairmen. She figured that the Maine women could not spend any more money advantageously in the six weeks remaining until the election. She did, however, leave the door open for more funds if the women came up with innovative campaign ideas. None did.[39]

When the campaign ended, $715 was left in her war chest. "To give the women workers more expense money would be senseless," she told Louis Howe, adding, "maybe you would like to use it for cigars on election day." After Brann's successful reelection, Howe told her to send him two hundred dollars and keep the rest: "It is the wish of those who contributed the money, as well as myself, that you accept it as an inadequate expression of our appreciation of what you have done." Dewson, however, could see no reason to keep the money, and she promptly returned it. When Henry Morgenthau heard about the left-over cash, he was greatly amused: "This is a brand new experience for me."[40]

"Men's politics" was just one of the activities that Molly Dewson dabbled in during 1934 and 1935 in addition to her primary work at the Women's Division. "There are just two things I think I know a lot about," she told Franklin Roosevelt in May 1933: "how to get women to vote right" and "how to get a halfway reasonable wage for workers." Throughout the early New Deal, she stole time from politics to work on a variety of social welfare measures, not just the minimum wage. She dubbed these "my private concerns."[41]

During 1934 and 1935, the New Deal underwent a period of con-solidation. If the measures taken during Roosevelt's first hundred days had ended the Great Depression, the rest of his New Deal plan probably would not have been put into effect. The intolerably high unemploy-ment and stagnated business production continued, however, despite such initiatives as the NRA, the Agricultural Adjustment Administra-tion, and the Federal Emergency Relief Administration. When the emergency relief measures of the early New Deal failed to alleviate the economic problems, the Roosevelt administration turned to struc-tural reforms.

The most notable New Deal measures during this period covered labor, social insurance, and relief. The National Labor Relations Act of 1935 (also known as the Wagner Act) placed the weight of the federal government on labor's side in the struggle for unionization. The Social Security Act of 1935, the cornerstone of the American welfare state, provided for a system of old-age insurance and unemployment compen-sation through a federal-state pension fund to which both employers and employees contributed. And the Works Progress Administration (WPA) expanded the federal commitment to providing work for the nation's unemployed. Between 1935 and 1943, the WPA employed 8.5 million Americans on the federal rolls and spent $10.5 billion, an ex-travagant sum by the standards of the 1930s.[42]

Dewson's reform activity in the first term continued to be linked with the National Consumers' League, and she used her friendship with the Roosevelts to advance its program. When the league found gross violations of labor standards in NRA codes, she wrote directly to Franklin with the facts, adding this note to Eleanor: "You may be too busy for this but honestly it is rotten to put Franklin in this hole. It will make 1000s of his supporters so mad."[43]

Because of her long association with the National Consumers' League and her standing as a member of the Roosevelt's unofficial family, Molly Dewson was asked to serve on two advisory committees in the early New Deal. The first was the citizens' advisory committee to the Consumers' Advisory Board (CAB) of the National Recovery Administration. The CAB was established to balance the viewpoints of the NRA's Industrial and Labor Boards, and it was headed by Mary Harriman Rumsey, Frances Perkins's friend and housemate in Washington. In June 1933, Molly Dewson received a telephone call from NRA administrator General Hugh Johnson, asking her to serve on the advisory committee. "It is not merely a scenery committee," he told her. The National Consumers' League was eager to have its viewpoint represented on the committee, and Dewson gladly accepted the assignment.[44]

She later described the frustrations of working on this committee: "Indeed it was nothing as concrete as scenery. We walked in a mist, and no objective was clear-cut." Representing the interests of consumers within the broad industrial program promoted by the NRA proved to be a murky task indeed. Although sympathetic to the public's viewpoint, Dewson the pragmatist did not want to sabotage plans for industrial recovery in the name of consumers. As she told her fellow committee member Paul Douglas, "Roosevelt has ploughed a lot of untilled ground and told us what to plant; it's up to us to raise crops if we can. This is no time to discourage the administration in any way."[45]

Molly Dewson also sat on the Advisory Committee on Economic Security, which played a supporting role in the development of the Social Security Act of 1935. The committee's first action was to call a National Conference on Economic Security in Washington on November 14, 1934. Unemployment insurance, child welfare, employment provisions, old age pensions, and medical care were discussed in roundtable format; Dewson led the session on old age security. In early December, the advisory committee convened in Washington for a solid week of meetings. Dewson had never before participated in such an endurance test. Although the committee was "closely divided on all controversial points," she confessed to Eleanor Roosevelt her desire for any bill that would pass: "I don't care how much the tax is or when it begins. Subsidy vs. Federal-state is settled for me by whatever the administration wants. . . . I'd take it any how it's drafted."[46]

In these two instances, as in virtually ever other aspect of the New Deal, Dewson felt confident enough of the general contours of Roosevelt's commitment to recovery and reform that she cheerfully accepted whatever short-term compromises were necessary. She was the same kind of reformer as Frances Perkins, whom a lifelong friend called "a half-loaf girl: take what you can get now and try for more later."[47] Dewson approached the passage of legislation with the same pragmatism that guided her political behavior, and with a spirit and temperament very similar to that of her trusted leader, FDR.

Reinforcing Dewson's pragmatism was a strong element of personal loyalty to Franklin Roosevelt. She felt that the people on whom Roosevelt depended, of which she counted herself one, should stand by the president, even if he did not always take their advice. When Lewis Douglas, director of the budget, criticized the mounting federal deficit, Dewson told him, "Here we are in a violent depression with a real leader not a do-nothing Coolidge or a do-nothing-right Hoover and if you do not agree with Roosevelt on certain points, you should stick by him and keep giving him your best advice whether he takes it in toto or not."[48] Douglas continued to speak out against what he considered reckless federal spending, and he finally resigned in 1934. Molly Dewson never considered such a course; indeed, she never really let herself disagree with the president. She never felt that Franklin Roosevelt had let her down.

Looking over the New Deal legislation passed during the first term, Dewson was especially proud of the role that Frances Perkins played in the Social Security Act, one of the New Deal's most far-reaching reforms. Perkins's part in the passage of this law exemplifies the many contributions that women reformers made to the social welfare policies of the New Deal. At a 1948 reunion with Molly Dewson, Clara Beyer, and Arthur Altmeyer, Frances Perkins stated boldly, "You and I, Mary, made Roosevelt's labor policy." That labor policy had its origins in earlier Progressive era initiatives to improve labor standards and working conditions for Americans. "I have always thought we were the forerunners of the New Deal," Perkins said. "In fact, I am sure that it was the humanitarian, active and effective action of social workers who turned to legislation as a method of overcoming social disabilities, who made possible the effective action and administration under the political New Deal."[49]

Molly Dewson saw the connections as well. "In short, Roosevelt took advantage of long years of study, research and experimentation in labor legislation and utilized those responsible for it. He brought to realization many goals striven for over twenty years." She had participated in this struggle throughout her professional career, and she seized the opportunities presented by the New Deal to push for implementation of these goals on a national level. Much as she loved being a politician, she had been a social reformer for far longer. "You know about the leopard's spots," she jested to Carolyn Wolfe.[50]

Molly Dewson's faith in Franklin Roosevelt and the New Deal was well founded. The New Deal set in motion a major expansion of presidential power and engendered a dramatic growth in the federal bureaucracy. The national government was no longer a distant or insignificant factor in American life: it now occupied a central position in the nation's political and economic activity. In addition to accepting responsibility for managing the economy, the government guaranteed a whole range of social and economic benefits for citizens. For the first time, the federal government was a force in everyday life through mortgage guarantees, farm subsidies, NRA codes, social insurance, and work relief.

Molly Dewson referred to these programs as the "human aspects of the New Deal," and they go a long way in explaining why she was such an ardent New Dealer. The compassionate and enlightened leadership of Franklin Roosevelt produced reforms that activists like Molly Dewson and Frances Perkins had been advocating for almost three decades. "I think he sensed that a new force was gathering head the world over," Dewson mused: "the desire of humble persons for a decent life and basic security." She saw FDR "as a great and good physician" who "intended to make the birth as painless as possible."[51] The birth he oversaw was the founding of the modern welfare state.

CHAPTER THIRTEEN

The 1936 Campaign

OLLY DEWSON never doubted that Franklin Roosevelt would run for reelection in 1936. She had been planning for that eventuality almost since Inauguration Day, March 4, 1933. Roosevelt's bid for a second term would give her the chance to demonstrate that her efforts to organize Democratic women between campaigns had not been wasted. And she was eager for one last campaign before retirement: "I expect by next November I will have taught the Dem. gals all I know, and can sit in the sun awhile." But most compelling was her continued faith in Roosevelt and the New Deal. "I am not a hero worshipper and I think Roosevelt has had enough glory for any one man," she told Assistant Treasury Secretary Josephine Roche midway through the first term, "but when I think back over those dreary years since women had the vote, I cannot bear to go without another four years under New Deal leadership."[1]

The Women's Division was in strong shape as it entered the 1936 campaign. "The increase of organization and the better comprehension of how to work compared with what we found in 1932 is amazing," Molly boasted to Eleanor Roosevelt. Regional conferences had been held across the country, and the fifty-fifty plan was making headway. Fourteen thousand Reporters, in every state but Louisiana and New Hampshire, were spreading the word about the accomplishments of the

Roosevelt administration to their friends and neighbors; thousands more were reading about the New Deal in the expanded *Democratic Digest*. With great anticipation, Dewson looked forward to a campaign where women could work on issues of their own choosing—"instead of plugging along on men's political theories."[2]

As the time to kick off the campaign approached, members of the Women's Division staff met with the president to discuss women's roles in the upcoming election. In one of those small gestures which meant so much to Democratic women in the New Deal, Eleanor Roosevelt arranged a dinner at the White House in December 1935. Molly Dewson, Maybelle Fickel, and Carolyn Wolfe were invited. The consensus of the meeting was clear: "continue past plan of work to vitalize and make effective the Women's Democratic organizations and to increase the use of the Reporter Plan." Demonstrating once again Dewson's ability to garner financial support for women's activities, Roosevelt agreed to provide the Women's Division with two more rooms at headquarters starting in January and to increase its budget to four thousand dollars a month.[3]

Absent from this planning meeting was Louis Howe, who was seriously ill in a Washington hospital: he did not live to participate in the 1936 campaign. Howe had always been a great friend to women in politics, countering the indifference or lack of understanding demonstrated by Jim Farley and the men at the Democratic National Committee. Without Howe, the chain of political command was less clear. Molly told Eleanor after this White House dinner, "I miss Louis Howe awfully."[4]

The opening salvo of the women's campaign was a two-month Western tour, which Molly Dewson undertook between January 20 and March 26, 1936. The Women's Division always counted its greatest strength in states west of the Mississippi, so Dewson concentrated her efforts there. In her perennial role as talent scout, she was on the lookout for promising recruits for the national staff. She also reckoned that local leaders would like her personal attention, "as they all know me by name." Most important, she wanted to see for herself how well these women understood the political and educational plans the Women's Division had promulgated for the past three years.[5]

The Western trip surpassed Molly's wildest dreams. It was arduous—two solid months on the road, with only a two-week stopover with Lucy Stebbins in Berkeley—but she never doubted whether it was worth the time and trouble. "I have experienced all kinds of temperature on this trip from 40 degrees below in North Dakota to 80 degrees above in the Nevada desert, but there has been no variation in any single place in the temperature of the enthusiasm for Roosevelt. It always broke the thermometer." By the time she returned, she was convinced that Roosevelt would be reelected and that women would play a major role in his victory.[6]

Molly Dewson left New York by train on January 20. She admitted, "Winter is not usually selected for campaigning in the Northwest, but that is because people have not tried it. Winter is the time for studying, thinking, preparing. There is not so much competition for attention." Her instinct proved correct. In Bismarck, North Dakota, a crowd waited until ten o'clock at night "with a temperature of 40 below for a personally unknown speaker, a woman at that, coming on a delayed train." This leg of the trip was characterized by long train rides and unremitting cold: "During my stops, it was so cold I drew my head into my fur coat like a turtle."[7]

Short on time before her departure, she had impetuously requested a general speech from the Democratic National Committee in case she were called on to speak along the tour. As her train headed west from Chicago, she took out the speech and read it with great dismay: "a regular typical politician's speech, which read cold without warmth or personality, delivery, or prestige . . . very wordy, unspecific and drab." She knew at once she could not give it. Fortunately, her trusted secretary had assembled a looseleaf binder of newspaper clippings which Dewson used to draw up a speech that could be adjusted to meet local needs and conditions. By the time she reached Minneapolis, she had a draft that some Democratic friends typed up between trains. For the rest of the trip it occupied the center spot in her looseleaf notebook.[8]

She gave the speech so many times that it took on a patina. No matter how many times she spoke, however, Dewson realized that as an orator she was only third-rate. In her next incarnation, Molly decided, she would study public speaking.[9]

Her first stops were Fargo and Bismarck, North Dakota. She survived her first blizzard but caught such a bad cold that only a hot water bottle and a bottle of whiskey loaned by the male state Democratic chairman got the normally teetotalling Dewson through the night. She next hit Glendive, Montana, finding confirmation of one of her main rationales for the trip: since few politicians ever made their way to isolated Glendive, everybody turned out for her speech, men as well as women.[10]

The next day it was on to Billings, Montana, for a big meeting. "I want to report that even this super-cautious woman considers Montana will deliver in November," she reported to Eleanor Roosevelt. From there she traveled to the state of Washington, where, unfortunately, "personalities seemed to be the chief concern in Seattle, not the gains from the New Deal." Dewson found the atmosphere in Portland as warm as Seattle's had been tense, and she spoke eight times in a single day.[11]

After several weeks on the road, Molly (who celebrated her sixty-second birthday on the trip) needed time to catch her breath. What better place than at the home of Lucy Stebbins? As soon as she hit Berkeley, "I was clapped into bed—to shake my bronchitis and alas to rest my heart." Knowing Eleanor would be concerned, she added, "That item is just for *us*. I have always been an imprudent worker for anything I cared about and now I am caught up with. However I am going to rest here a little longer and go back a little slower."[12]

Just like on Molly's Western swing in 1931–32, Lucy's hospitality provided a perfect base for political activity in California. The state, divided into northern and southern halves (which were as different as Massachusetts and Virginia, Dewson observed) and without city bosses or organized machines, presented a complex political landscape. Among the women, Dewson found enthusiasm and interest, but little actual organization: "The general understanding of government problems and interest in them seemed to me above the average among Eastern women but cooperation in the party organization is on the whole considerably less." As for campaign plans, "it was like pouring ideas on a sandy soil. They soaked them up."[13]

At the end of February, Dewson took to the road again. Her three-week itinerary took her from Los Angeles to Las Vegas, Salt Lake City, Cheyenne, Denver, Grand Island, Nebraska; and on to Lincoln, Omaha, Sioux Falls, Minneapolis, Des Moines, Kansas City, Topeka, Chicago, and finally home to New York on March 23. The only untoward event was a gall bladder attack she suffered while in the lower berth of a sleeper going east.[14]

Dewson found the women on this leg of her trip just as alert and active as those she had met on the way out. "It was really thrilling," she concluded. "There is a new feeling everywhere among the women, a feeling such as I have not known since the suffrage days. Women now are taking the enthusiastic interest in government that we thought then they would."[15]

As in 1932, the reports that Molly wrote nightly to Eleanor were read and analyzed by the men in Democratic headquarters and by Franklin Roosevelt himself. "You'll do as you think wise about giving them to the President," she told Eleanor modestly. Eleanor, of course, promptly passed Molly's colorful reports on to Franklin and relayed back reactions such as "Franklin is much interested" and "Don't get too weary." Dewson treasured these small words of encouragement: "My New England nature approved of the Roosevelts' reaction to this strenuous trip. To me it meant they considered me one of their team. Why a lot of words?"[16]

One final bit of unfinished business remained from this campaign swing. Remembering Franklin Roosevelt's suggestive teasing about her low expenses in 1932, she sent a pointed message to the president: "Tell F.D.R. if he thinks I get unworthy help while travelling. I've been gone *eleven* days, and my round-trip railroad fares cost $210."[17]

When she returned to New York in late March, the Democratic convention was less than three months away. As early as January, the Women's Division had detailed its needs to Forbes Morgan of the DNC: a large reception room, an inner office for conferences, rooms for eight members of Dewson's staff, and reserved places on the platform for selected women delegates. Reminding Morgan of the inadequate support she received at the 1932 convention, Dewson told him that she wanted recognition of women "consonant with the dignity of their organization and their vote-getting ability."[18]

More specifically, Dewson raised the issue of women's representation on the platform committee, a bastion of male privilege on which no woman had ever served. She prodded the Democratic National Committee to encourage states to choose women, but, as she reminded Forbes Morgan tellingly, the "right" kind of woman. "We are not just interested in feminine representation. We wish women who will be recognized as representing woman's point of view." Penning a "Can You Help!" appeal to Eleanor, Molly added, "I expect the women would die of joy if they received this recognition. We don't ask for much in the way of patronage or power but we do think we should have a say in what the party stands for."[19]

Molly's next step was to designate a Women's Advisory Platform Committee in the spring of 1936. Its mandate was to identify the issues of greatest concern to women in public life. The committee's members comprised a virtual who's who of women in politics and government in the 1930s, with Congresswoman Caroline O'Day at its head. Dewson recalled, "Looking over the list, I am proud again of these fourteen women, fine, intelligent, informed, competent and human."[20] The Women's Division kept these early preparations under wraps: "We want to be sure first that the men will receive us." Molly spoke more candidly to one of the committee members: "I am not for staging any petty revolutions and if we were not to be heard, I, myself, would not be for having the committee. This would sound spineless to any feminist but I am practical and am concentrated on a Democratic victory this fall."[21]

One potential hitch marred her plans: if no woman was selected for the regular platform committee, could they depend on male allies to present their carefully drafted suggestions? "Thinking over the situation in 1936, I became filled with wile," Dewson recalled. She conceived an "entering wedge": a resolution to change party rules so that, for every member of the platform committee, each state would designate an alternate of the opposite sex. Since delegates often missed committee meetings due to conflicting convention business, alternates could expect to play substantial roles. She tried the ploy at the convention's first business meeting, and the resolution passed without discussion, lost in a maze of DNC detail. But it did not escape the notice of the journalist Bess Furman, who wrote on the front page of the *New York Times*, "What is called the biggest coup in years so far as women in politics are concerned materialized at the Democratic Convention this afternoon as softly and smoothly as a Summer Zephyr."[22]

The story had an anticlimactic ending. Women such as Caroline O'Day, Harriet Elliott, Ellen Woodward, and Nellie Tayloe Ross were quickly named as alternates to the platform committee. They presented their planks on peace, ratification of the Child Labor Amendment, recognition of Roosevelt's record on women, consumers' rights, civil service, housing, education, and civil liberties. Although the ideas behind these planks made their way into the platform, they appeared only in very general ways. Dewson felt, however, that the final document reflected the essence of women's suggestions. "Well, what matter—the words presenting the desired aim," she told Bess Furman.[23]

Molly Dewson overestimated women's impact on the platform. Two issues of vital concern to them were ignored or glossed over. First, the Child Labor Amendment did not receive a specific endorsement. And, although the platform supported civil service reform, it ignored section 213 of the 1932 National Economy Act. Section 213, the bête noire of women's organizations in the 1930s, stipulated that both members of a married couple could not be employed by the federal government. While sex-neutral in its wording, this measure, intended to create employment opportunities during the Depression, in fact forced sixteen hundred women—and no men—to resign from their jobs. Dewson had always opposed the law: she called it "that dumb clause" and the "one black mark" against the Roosevelt record on women. As she told Eleanor Roosevelt, "I myself think we handled dynamite when we passed 213 of the National Economy Act."[24]

She got herself into trouble, however, when she hinted that the law might be repealed. When she sounded out the White House, Roosevelt raised no objections. But then she could not deliver on her pledge. "Well F.D.R. did say it and poor harassed man he has let me down. It's embarrassing but not fatal." She did not think the Republicans had done any better with their plank on Section 213, which was so broad as to be almost meaningless. "We are against man eating sharks, too," she observed facetiously. Dewson, however, was not going to let disappointment over one issue stand in the way of her pride at the other breakthroughs in political representation for women at the 1936 convention. "Don't you think that, for one not a feminist, I get in some pretty good licks for the girls?" she told Ruby Black afterward.[25]

Four years later, Molly reflected on the 1936 platform coup to Dorothy McAllister, her successor at the Women's Division. "I had the Platform Comm. in '36 because girls like Lavinia Engle wanted it. No harm and a little pleasant importance to a few. I'm not much for that sort of futile stuff but I did want to have good women ready to get themselves appointed alternates to the Platform Com. if I could pull off the scheme as a first step toward what you are now after." Dewson's victory in 1936 did lead to a permanent change. In 1940, the Democratic National Committee adopted new rules which mandated the selection of both a man and a woman from each state for the platform committee. This resolution was adopted without opposition.[26]

One final incident—lasting but a few minutes but with ramifications that reverberated for much longer—made the 1936 convention memorable. At a late night session, Jim Farley approached Molly Dewson and said, "You have always said you would resign if you had to work with Emma Guffey Miller," who was a powerful Pennsylvania Democrat who did not see eye-to-eye with Dewson on women's politics. "Well, I can't help it, I have to make her vice-chairman of the committee. I give you five minutes to decide what you will do."

Dewson was flabbergasted. "This was a totally unexpected double-cross with a vengeance." She quickly proposed an alternative to Farley. "Well, Jim, I will keep on if you will make as many women vice-chairmen of the Democratic National Committee as there are men vice-chairmen." (Currently no woman served in this prestigious position.) Farley agreed, telling Dewson she would be one and asking her to name seven others. In her remaining three minutes, she selected seven women, including Daisy Harriman and her own rival Emma Guffey Miller. The nominating committee then accepted the names of the ten men and eight women, not quite up to Dewson's demand for equal representation but close.[27]

Newspaper accounts contained a slightly more frenzied account. When Jim Farley read the expanded list of women nominated as vice-chairmen, he omitted the name of Molly Dewson. Was this just a slip, or had she been dumped from the committee, Democratic women demanded to know. "Oh, it's there at the top of the list—I just overlooked it," Farley answered nonchalantly.[28]

Perhaps a little too quickly, Dewson absolved Jim Farley from blame. He had once again broken his promise that he would always consult with her and Eleanor Roosevelt about matters concerning women in the Democratic Party. Emma Guffey Miller, an active and persistent Democratic politician whose influence was increased through her brother, Senator Joseph Guffey of Pennsylvania, had forced his hand. But Molly refused to dwell on the "double-cross" for long: "I truly think Farley hated the part he had somehow been forced into and was glad to find a way out." Did this spat affect their working relationship? "Farley and I never spoke of this unpleasant moment. We ignored it."[29]

She also extended a peace pipe to Emma Guffey Miller. "It was a fair fight and, of course, I am glad my idea of how women can contribute best to reelecting Roosevelt won," she wrote to Miller. "But that fight is over and so far as I am concerned it will have no back wash." Dewson could afford to be gracious, however, because her control over women's activities in the Democratic party remained untouched. Newly selected vice-chairman Daisy Harriman well understood the way things stood: "Of course the rest of us are only window-dressing. Molly Dewson will continue to do all the work." But in reality the fight was far from over. This 1936 episode was just the opening skirmish of a more serious disagreement over women's roles in the Democratic party that erupted between Dewson and Miller during the second term.[30]

Immediately after the Democratic convention in Philadelphia, a "bevy" (Eleanor Roosevelt's word) of top Democratic women retired to Hyde Park for rest, recuperation, and strategizing. Nancy Cook played hostess at Val-Kill to a crew that included Caroline O'Day, Frances Perkins, and of course Molly Dewson. Molly treasured the time she spent with Eleanor during the excitement of the convention and campaign: "It has been lovely seeing you so much lately. You are sort of my Mother Earth that I need to touch once in a while."[31]

After this conclave, Eleanor Roosevelt passed on her assessment to the men at Democratic headquarters. "My impression is that the women are further along in their organization and more ready to go than any other unit as yet." The male politicians were much more likely to listen to the First Lady's opinion than they had been four years earlier. Molly Dewson described the men's new respect: "As a matter of course I was expected to be present at staff meetings. When state leaders were called into headquarters, region by region, the women were notified to attend without comment. And a surprising number of leaders who came to see Farley also called on me."[32] To Molly, this meant that she was a full member of the team.

Molly Dewson was in excellent spirits in the summer of 1936, blessed with good health and seemingly unlimited energy for the upcoming campaign. Her spirits improved even further after she had made time for several months in Castine with Polly. In September, she returned to New York to resume her political work, while Polly stayed on in Castine, taking care of the garden and the pets and spending time with her circle of Castine friends. But immediately after the election Molly Dewson was on her way back to Maine "to help bring her family of dogs, cats, and Miss Porter back to New York," as Carolyn Wolfe reported.[33]

The Women's Division planned to run its campaign along the lines of the 1934 Reporter Plan. Roosevelt would be elected if independent voters, the crucial 15–20 percent uncommitted to either major party, knew the achievements of Roosevelt's administration. The best way to win over these independent voters was by "grasstromping," Molly's word for door-to-door canvassing. This very personal style of campaigning would be conducted by the eighty thousand women she counted as active precinct, county, and state Democratic leaders. As she said later, "We had informed woman power enough to cover every locality and go after every vote. It was only a question of organization and the superb vitality of the grasstrompers."[34]

In 1936, the Women's Division once again wrote and distributed

Rainbow Fliers, which comprised more than 90 percent of the publicity material prepared by the Democratic National Committee. The Rainbow Fliers were the local party workers' ammunition as they paid neighborly visits to promote the New Deal. "Democratic Visitors Get Inside That Door. Discuss the Facts on the Fliers and Leave Them" was a favorite Women's Division motto. Eighty-three million fliers were distributed on topics such as farmers, home insurance, taxes, tariffs, civil service, and relief.[35]

The Rainbow Fliers also played a role in rebuffing a last-minute Republican attack on the recently passed Social Security bill. Two Saturdays before the election, many industrial workers received notices in their pay envelopes from management falsely claiming that they would never receive their social security benefits money back, that the federal government was merely holding an empty bag. By Monday morning, the Democratic response was ready: "The Truth about Social Security," "Don't Believe the Labor Spy in Your Pay Envelope," and "Notice of Pay Increase to All Employees." Three and one-half million copies of these fliers were distributed. "The women's great coup in the campaign was turning the Republicans' last-minute blitzkrieg into a rout," Dewson concluded triumphantly.[36]

Since the Rainbow Fliers played such an important role in the national campaign (Charles Michelson claimed these fliers saved the party a million dollars in 1936, because they were much cheaper to produce than the usual glossy publicity material), Molly Dewson made sure their cost came out of the DNC budget, not hers.[37] As in 1932, however, the fliers were stamped with the imprint of the Democratic National Committee rather than that of the Women's Division. The practical politician won out over the feminist: "I was still afraid some men would prefer man-made statements and I considered whatever kudos might have come to the women did not offset the risks," Dewson wrote. Yet she later remarked coyly, "I still wonder what men would have thought if they had known the Fliers were planned and written by a woman."[38]

In addition to Rainbow Fliers geared toward independent voters, Molly Dewson wanted to create and distribute campaign material that would excite women already committed to the Democratic party. When she came home from her Western trip, she complained to Carolyn Wolfe, "Our mimeographed advice on every angle of organization is sound and wise, but it is very dull. Oh dear! I wish we could get out something with snap and humor like *The New Yorker*." Molly put the idea in her mind to percolate, and one Saturday morning she woke up early and rushed to her study. "And so on, for a couple of hours, as fast as I could write and make scribblings of the illustrations, when Mary Porter came to the door and said, rather acidly, 'are you or are you not going to Connecticut this weekend?'" Molly leapt up, took a shower, resumed her work, and was so preoccupied with her ideas that she was back under the shower before she realized what she was doing. "Written between showers," she recalled.[39]

The resulting pamphlet, "Democratic Victory: Dedicated to Mrs. County Leader," had a snappy style and cute illustrations. For example, a slender Democratic woman fishing from "Born Democrat Land" glances over at a stout and stuffy matron on the "rock ribbed Republican land." Corny—but Democratic women loved it, including Molly. "It's my baby and I'm like all mothers," she gushed to Eleanor. "It has the cutest envelope. This is *proof.*"[40]

"Mrs. County Leader" was a popular mail order item from the Women's Division: more than a quarter of a million copies were distributed. Not only did the pamphlet build enthusiasm and loyalty among Democratic workers, but it gave them suggestions about campaign techniques. Along with its cartoons and homilies, the pamphlet conveyed such practical information as how to organize radio parties to listen to President Roosevelt's speeches and how to subscribe to the *Democratic Digest* for news on the Women's Division and the New Deal. The staff irreverently dubbed it "the Ten Commandments of the woman politician."[41]

Letter-writing continued to be the most important weapon in the Women's Division arsenal. Dewson never forgot that the strength of the women's organization lay in the states, not in the Women's Division headquarters in Washington and New York. "Everyone from State Vice Chairman and National Committeewoman down needs appreciation from headquarters and quick response to requests and speedy suggestions on how to solve problems, in order to get the heartiest cooperation and the best work," she reasoned. "If a campaign leader has anything more important to do, once the plans are laid, I do not know it."[42]

Since it was campaign time, the Women's Division added several programs specifically geared towards Roosevelt's reelection. Dewson assembled an impressive array of prominent women who supported Roosevelt. Her task, she believed, had been made easy by Roosevelt's record: "I say without fear of contradiction that never before has the program of the government and that of the great women's civic, social and peace organizations so nearly coincided." Grace Abbott headed a social workers' committee; Mildred Thompson of Vassar, Lucy Stebbins of Berkeley, and Virginia Gildersleeve of Barnard chaired the education committee. Alice Duer Miller headed the author's committee, along with Molly Dewson's close friend Fannie Hurst. Dorothy Bellanca rounded up labor support. There was even an aviator's committee which drew Amelia Earhart into her first political campaign.[43]

Molly Dewson was proudest of the prominent Republican women —such as Mary Woolley of Mount Holyoke, suffrage leader Maud Wood Park, and Mrs. Curtis Bok of the publishing family—who announced their intention of voting for Roosevelt in 1936. During the summer, the president had suggested that Molly put together a committee of independent and Republican women (one of the few specific suggestions he ever made to her), but she beat him to the punch. When she sent him the favorable clippings this committee had already earned, she joked, "The only way for you ever to know the amount of work that has been done for you is for you to get defeated, which would give you time to hear about it. However, I prefer that you should be reelected and not know what is going on."[44]

Another election-year addition was a Speakers' Bureau headed by Gladys Tillett of North Carolina, who was asked back to Washington in the 1940s to head the Women's Division. Women speakers were equipped with a kit prepared by Mary Chamberlain that was so informative that Democratic men begged for copies. The bureau sent one hundred speakers all over the country; one of the most popular was Ruth Bryan Owen, the former minister to Denmark. The Women's Division provided her with a car and trailer, which were driven by Captain Micki Rohde, whom she had married that summer in a small ceremony at Hyde Park with Eleanor Roosevelt looking on. Other women speakers were provided not with a car, but with a plane: Phoebe Omlie's Roosevelt Fliers piloted women speakers around the country in a small two-seater with "Roosevelt" painted on the wings.[45]

Dewson later described her own part as "a calm center in the vortex of a national campaign." She delegated much of the routine work to Carolyn Wolfe and her assistants at the Washington headquarters, leaving herself free to act in her favorite role as troubleshooter. "I spent the day keeping things running smoothly, untangling situations, aiding the staff on decisions and seeing out-of-town Democratic leaders, usually about bothersome problems." "Just a thousand and one small acts," she claimed modestly.[46]

These acts often went on all day and well into the night. After a late supper, a fresh stenographer arrived and Molly spent two or three more hours dictating letters to Democratic women around the country. Fortunately she stayed healthy throughout the long and arduous campaign. "I have stood up awfully well physically under the pressure here," she told Emily Newell Blair—she only lost half a day to bronchitis. She could not resist adding, "The boys took at least three days out to see the world series so my batting average for persistence and diligence is high."[47]

Such dedication earned her the devotion of her staff, who called her "Queen Molly" or "The Colonel." One of them remembered, "I don't think there was anyone who worked with her who wasn't greatly attracted to her." Dewson, in turn, said of her loyal workers, "The headquarters staff was a great team and worked without enough friction to light a match."[48]

A large measure of Dewson's effectiveness lay in her unorthodox approach to getting things done. "Don't ever talk to anybody. Just Act." That is how May Thompson Evans of the Women's Division described Molly's philosophy. "Just make your decision and then move right on with it."[49] Her network of friends and allies throughout the Washington bureaucracy gave her an enormous range of influence and power. "She knew everybody, you know," observed Carolyn Wolfe. "She knew *all* the top people. . . . It is almost impossible to define the power that she had in the political organization, as you look back and see the things that an ordinary person never could have done without her connections." Since few women politicians had Dewson's contacts, it proved difficult for Democratic women to maintain this level of influence and access once she left Washington.[50]

Another component of Molly Dewson's effectiveness lay in her personal demeanor. Like Frances Perkins, she had decided early on that the best way for a woman to function in politics was to get men to think of her as an aunt or mother. A mature woman in her early sixties at the height of her power, Dewson dressed and acted, one news reporter commented, "like a nice Boston aunt," favoring silk prints with matching jackets, low-heeled shoes, and suits with pockets. She did not come across as a befuddled old lady, however. Helen Essary of the *Democratic Digest* reported the advice going around at Republican headquarters: "they don't want any old, heavy dowager stuff; just try to be as much like Molly Dewson as she could."[51]

"Language is funny," the *Boston Herald* noted in 1936. "Seemingly it is all right to call Molly Dewson 'the female Jim Farley' but would it be all right to call him 'the male Molly Dewson'?" Other reporters called her "a Jim Farley in petticoats." Did she mind the comparison? Dewson always saw such things as harmless fun.[52]

In turn, Jim was quite taken with Molly personally, even if he did not always understand her plans for women in public life. "He liked her enormously," Frances Perkins commented. "She was a New England spinster of the blue blood and was just a total surprise to him. He had never met anybody that was remotely like her. Her impulses were intellectual and humanitarian impulses. Her breeding was very superior. Her manners were very superior. But she was capable of the most informal and friendly relationships with him and other politicians." Perkins even thought that Farley sent his daughter to Wellesley primarily because Molly Dewson had graduated from that school.[53]

It was precisely this ability to get along with men as well as women that made Molly Dewson such an effective politician during the New Deal. With an ease that few other women have duplicated, she bridged male and female political worlds and felt at home in either one. As Eleanor Roosevelt's biographer Joseph Lash put it, Dewson was "a reformer who nevertheless understood the political game," adding, "men liked Molly's down-East saltiness." A contemporary admirer of Dewson's was Charles Michelson, the director of publicity for the Democratic National Committee and one of the few men whose advice Dewson sought on political matters. He inscribed a picture he gave her, "To the greatest politician in our gang."[54]

Molly Dewson's warm friendship with Franklin Roosevelt is final testimony to her ability to work with men. Molly and Franklin really enjoyed each other—they could be frank and outrageous, because each knew where the other stood.[55] Few other women felt free to needle the president of the United States with friendly but pointed statements like this: "You know my loyalty to you and I don't need to sugar coat my ideas to you so I dare say that when I heard your speech to the Chamber of Commerce I thought one of Hoover's speeches must have been left in your desk drawer and you had put your hand on it by mistake." Dewson did not have much day-to-day contact with the president, nor did he often consult with her about his plans, but he knew what she was up to. "I hear a lot more about it than you have any idea of," he wrote disarmingly to her during the 1936 campaign. Molly recalled, "What I was conscious of was warm, continuous and constant support and a feeling that he liked me, had confidence in me and my ideas, and was sometimes as amused at my 'goings on' as I was myself."[56]

Eleanor Roosevelt's love and support was more demonstrative but the result was the same: Molly felt part of the team. As the lawyer Dorothy Kenyon wrote to Eleanor after the 1936 election, "I said I thought of the presidency as a collective affair, yours and his. *Actually* I think of it as a triumvirate, he and you and Molly. . . . It's a lucky country that by one stroke gets all three of you."[57]

The electoral results of November 3, 1936, surpassed even Molly Dewson's optimistic hopes. Roosevelt's overwhelming victory demonstrated the political clout of the new Democratic coalition that had been building since the late 1920s. In addition to traditional support among white Southerners, the Democratic party could now count on a potent urban coalition of ethnic groups, city dwellers, organized labor, blacks, and a cross-section of the middle class. Dewson captured Roosevelt's broadbased appeal: "Here was a man who had given work relief instead of apples, who had established C.C.C. camps, who had helped save the mortgaged home and the mortgaged farm, who had given labor the right to organize, unemployment relief and social security, and who had protected bank deposits." This Democratic coalition forged during the New Deal dominated national politics until the 1960s.[58]

Molly Dewson knew that women had played a vital role in the developing New Deal coalition. In fact, she was certain that the contributions of her eighty thousand Democratic women had meant the difference between a narrow Roosevelt victory and the landslide that occurred. "In our hearts we believe that the women re-elected Roosevelt," she told her faithful followers after the election.[59] Like FDR, she was at the peak of her political power.

CHAPTER FOURTEEN

A Just Measure of Social Decency

OOSEVELT'S second term opened on a somewhat frivolous note for Molly Dewson. Immediately after FDR's inauguration, Democratic women got together for a "Molly Dewson Round-Up." Led by Eleanor Roosevelt and Jim Farley (who had to crash the party because men were not invited), Democratic women joined together to heap praise on their beloved leader. Practically every prominent women in the Roosevelt administration was there. Before the gathering broke up, the assembled women had nominated Molly Dewson for president in 1940.[1]

Dewson had a chance for more public fun in mid-February. At Franklin Roosevelt's suggestion, Molly was deputized to give Jim Farley a kiss at a large Democratic dinner honoring him for his part in the 1936 campaign. She protested she was not exactly the flirtatious type, but since she always did what FDR wanted, she soon agreed.

When the alloted time came, she spoke for a few minutes and then went over to Farley. She pinned a rose on his coat, and planted a kiss on his cheek. The audience went wild. She recalled, "The more Jim blushed, the louder the uproar." General Hugh Johnson of the NRA was heard to remark, "I did not think it was in her." Dewson remained calm amidst the commotion, later explaining that there were twenty-two men in her immediate family and such affectionate greetings were standard. President Roosevelt loved it, telling Molly that from where he was sitting, she looked like a spangled Christmas tree because her evening dress had caught the lights. He added with a huge grin that Bess Farley had looked a bit sour. Molly replied, "Oh, it's all right with Mrs. Farley, I asked her permission beforehand. You did not bring me up to be a politician for nothing."[2]

That Dewson participated in this public ritual suggests her complete confidence in her position in the Democratic party. She personally thanked Franklin for suggesting it, adding that almost every letter she was receiving now mentioned the incident. When she called up Mayor Fiorello LaGuardia of New York, whom she had never met, his first words to her were, "Is it a rose or kiss for me?" Newsreel photographers captured the performance on film and spread it across the country. One of Molly's nieces saw the newsreel in a movie theatre and hurriedly left before anyone recognized her![3]

This charade was considered hilarious in part because it was so heavily laden with sexual innuendo. She was "not a shameless wench," Dewson demurred, but merely "a modest maiden who sacrificed her modesty at the President's suggestion."[4] The Democratic men in the audience knew that she claimed eighty thousand followers at the Women's Division, joked with Franklin Roosevelt on easy terms, and battled with Jim Farley on less friendly ones. But could she kiss a man? Molly, secure in her relationship with Polly Porter, must have gotten a good laugh out of this attention to such a token of heterosexuality.

In the second term, Molly Dewson began to cut back on her political activity. Few Democrats were anticipating a third term for Roosevelt, and she was primarily concerned with handing over the strongest possible women's organization to his successor. In the spring of 1937, she broke in a new Women's Division director, Dorothy McAllister, the dynamic head of Michigan's Reporter Plan, whom she described as "a genuine believer in FDR's program, a telling speaker, clear and forceful, and an indefatigable worker."[5]

In fact, the Women's Division had grown so much that the Democratic National Committee authorized Dewson to hire an assistant director as well. She chose May Thompson Evans of the North Carolina Department of Labor, who had been recommended by Harriet Elliott. She subjected Evans to the famous Dewson rush that so many others found impossible to resist. One evening about nine o'clock, soon after the election, Evans received a telephone call in her office. Since Dewson knew that Evans's husband was a reporter in Washington, she figured that May would not turn down the offer of a trip to the nation's capitol. "We want you to come tonight. There's a midnight train. Take it." On Evan's arrival at the Women's Division the next morning, Dewson welcomed her by telling her that she and Eleanor Roosevelt wanted her as the new assistant director of the Women's Division. "This was a bombshell to me," Evans recalled. Soon they were on their way to the White House (with Evans struggling to keep up with Molly's brisk pace) for a meeting with Eleanor Roosevelt and Jim Farley. Everything seemed settled after the half-hour meeting, except that no one had yet asked Evans whether she would accept the job. She later realized that this was characteristic of Molly Dewson's working philosophy: "Make up your own mind, decide, and move right on."[6]

The Women's Division, and the country, confronted a different set of political issues during Roosevelt's second term than those on the agenda of the early New Deal. Roosevelt's second inaugural address had spoken movingly of the one-third of the nation "ill-housed, ill-clad, ill-nourished"—testimony to the hard times that still gripped the nation despite the New Deal's emergency measures. But several weeks later the political focus changed. Unexpectedly, the president submitted a proposal to Congress to enlarge the size of the Supreme Court to fifteen justices. It was a thinly disguised effort to shortcircuit the Court's tendency to strike down New Deal legislation. Displaying an uncharacteristic lack of political sensitivity, Roosevelt consulted neither Congress nor leading politicians before announcing his plan. The proposal immediately met with substantial opposition, both from politicians and from a skeptical American public, who saw the proposal as a politically motivated attack on the constitutionally mandated role of the Supreme Court.[7]

Roosevelt's court-packing plan posed problems for Molly Dewson and the Women's Division. She thought Franklin was "off base" on this issue because it sidetracked attention from the more pressing problems of welfare and reform; furthermore, she thought its presentation had been "bungled." She recognized the problem Roosevelt meant to confront—and, indeed, had been heavily involved in a 1936 National Consumers' League effort to draft a constitutional amendment to exempt social legislation from the scrutiny of the Court—but she disagreed with his methods of solving it. She made sure that Roosevelt knew of her disapproval. It was one of the few times she questioned his judgment during her years of service to the New Deal.[8]

Telling Franklin in private about her doubts was one thing, but letting the Women's Division publicly oppose judicial reorganization was quite another. Her solution was to follow a middle course: she kept the Women's Division from taking a formal stand on the plan but encouraged discussion and debate on the issue. Afterwards she felt she had acquitted herself well in this troubled period: "Heaven knows," she told Eleanor, "I have done a plenty in what I considered the wise and effective way." She may have felt she was being fair, but May Thompson Evans realized how much she was holding back. "Going just so far, and no farther" was Evans's accurate description of the actions of the Women's Division on the court issue.[9]

The Women's Division's lack of enthusiasm for the court plan did not escape the notice of the White House. Eleanor wrote Molly in May, "Will you write James [Roosevelt] and explain. He says you told him you didn't think it wise to get women in on the court issue. He doesn't see your point. I told him in all probability you don't think Democratic women are for it but I don't know." Responding spiritedly that she had "pretty well established my record as being 100% for the New Deal and your father," Molly told James, "I think you would be thoroughly satisfied with what the women have done for the Supreme Court plan if I could tell you about it in detail." She claimed that Democratic women were learning more by studying and debating the issue than by passing resolutions or gathering signatures on petitions: "My general idea is based on the principle of throwing a stone in the water and having ripple after ripple follow the impact." Because of these educational efforts, Dewson asserted, Democratic women now opposed the plan by only a 3 to 1 margin, down from 50 to 1 several weeks earlier.[10]

Dewson's heart was not in this fight. She told Dorothy McAllister candidly, "I have been sort of stubborn about not having the Women's Division take a public stand in the *Digest* for the President's Court Plan. The reason is that forty Senators are opposed to it and I don't want forty Senators in over twenty states opposed to our organization work. I think what we can do for the Party if we do not get them opposed by taking a stand is worth more than coming out publicly, for I believe the Pres. plan will carry and we are doing a lot anyway." Much as she admired Franklin Roosevelt, her private thoughts probably echoed Congressman Hatton Summers's reaction to the plan: "Boys, here's where I cash in my chips."[11]

Dewson's unenthusiastic response to the president's court plan exacerbated another problem she faced early in the second term: a challenge to her authority from Pennsylvania National Committeewoman Emma Guffey Miller. A powerful force in Democratic politics (she had seconded Roosevelt's nomination at the 1936 Democratic convention), Miller stepped up her criticism of Dewson after her selection as vice-chairman of the Democratic National Committee. Miller's complaints concerned patronage, Dewson's handling of members of Congress, and the fact that National Committeewomen had not been consulted about the selection of the new Women's Division director. Her most legitimate grievance concerned Dewson's style of operation: she did not agree with Dewson's tactic of "peaceful penetration." Miller felt that women had to fight publicly for their causes, not just lobby quietly behind the scenes.[12]

Molly Dewson refused to acknowledge the validity of Emma Guffey Miller's charges, choosing instead to see them as a personal attack on her power over the Women's Division (which in part they were). Some of the bitterness between the two women dated back to the brouhaha at the 1936 convention.[13] Another source of acrimony stemmed from Miller's ongoing efforts as a member of the National Woman's Party to promote the Equal Rights Amendment.[14] But at base Dewson seemed unwilling to realize that other women might have different views on how best to increase women's participation in partisan politics and that they might choose different styles of leadership to accomplish their goals. So, instead of paying attention to Miller's criticisms, Dewson portrayed her as playing the kind of personal politics that she associated with men. "Nobody would care about Emma's activities except she can make our Women's Division work ineffective and reduce the women from active workers for the New Deal to a bunch of schemers for personal advancement in which none of our type are interested."[15]

The controversy was soon resolved, although the outcome was never really in doubt. Franklin and Eleanor Roosevelt naturally took Molly Dewson's side. While admitting that Dewson occasionally soft-pedaled direct confrontation, the First Lady reminded Miller, "One of the blessed things about being more or less free, as you have been, is that you can fight for the things you believe in, in the way you wish to, because you do not have the responsibility of the bigger picture constantly before you. . . . If you were in for a year, the very same women would have complaints against you." She therefore encouraged Miller to keep on fighting for the things she believed in: "You can do it where Molly can't, but in a quiet way, I think you will find that she will back you up in many of your more open crusades."[16]

"Thank God I don't see it my duty to have to participate after June first," Molly casually told her confidante Eleanor in the midst of these machinations. Her resignation so soon after Miller's spirited challenge to her hegemony at the Women's Division suggests at first glance that she was driven from office. But Molly Dewson did not quit because of outside attacks, nor did she leave because of dissatisfaction with Franklin Roosevelt's handling of the court-packing plan. The Roosevelts knew that 1936 was Molly Dewson's last campaign—she was tired, sixty-two years old, and ready to let go. As she told Eleanor, "1931-1937 is enough to give to a cause." She had devoted all her energies to nominating, electing, and reelecting Franklin Roosevelt; since no one yet anticipated a third term for him, she assumed that any further work would only benefit his successor.[17]

Her fatigue was coupled with a nagging sense of stagnation, even boredom. The success of the Women's Division in the 1936 campaign reflected the well-tuned structure she had built over the past four years. "And a swell organization and two swell girls—women of experience aged 38 & 36 to build on if the men want it," she told Eleanor. What was exciting in 1932, however, now seemed routine. Following a pattern that stretched back to her days on the Parole Board for the Lancaster School, she began to look for new challenges once the Women's Division was running smoothly. After she broke in Dorothy McAllister and May Thompson Evans, she headed for Castine. "I was free!"[18]

Dewson continued her own story. "Released from harness, I was thoroughly enjoying the summer of 1937 in Castine, Maine, when in August one of the White House staff telephoned me asking whether my legal address was New York or Maine. Something was brewing. Soon the President called me, saying, 'I am sending your name to the Senate for confirmation as a Member of the Social Security Board. I want you to come right down to be sworn in and then you can return for a few days to settle your affairs.' 'Heel, Fido', is my comment on F.D.R.'s remarks."[19]

"Heel, Fido" was Dewson's public description of her appointment to the Social Security Board. In fact, Molly played a far more instrumental role in her nomination than she later let on. Consider this letter to Eleanor Roosevelt right after the November election: "I have been having a very interesting talk with Grace Abbott who came in to see me. I told her I had told you that if there was an assistant secretaryship with an interesting piece of work attached the President wanted me to do I should be glad of the chance." The Social Security Administration appealed, although she also had her eye on a position under Frances

Perkins in the Labor Department. "That would interest me enormously but with a woman as Secretary probably a woman assistant would be too much." Even though writing to Eleanor about her ambitions made her "quite dizzy," she figured that she could talk to her candidly without being misunderstood.[20] Eleanor got the point. She promptly wrote Jim Farley, "Don't forget that Molly wants a job either on the Social Security Board or as an assistant secretary doing some kind of work she is fitted for."[21]

Several factors shaped Dewson's request for a high-level position in the New Deal administration, the very course she strenuously rejected in 1932–33. After working so hard to secure positions for prominent women in government, she wondered what it would be like to serve herself. Her success in the face of the rigors of the 1936 campaign convinced her that she did in fact have the physical stamina to undertake a federal position. Probably her most compelling reason, however, was a desire to return to her old field of labor legislation as her career neared its end. "I cannot believe I have lived to see this day," she exclaimed to Arthur Altmeyer when the Social Security Act passed in 1935. "It's the culmination of what us girls and some of you boys have been working for for so long it's just dazzling."[22]

Throughout her career, Molly Dewson had always made professional decisions based on how they would affect her relationship with Polly Porter. This was one time when she broke the rule. When she accepted the Social Security job, she knew full well that she would have to move to Washington: the three-day-a-week commute she tried in 1933–34 would not suffice for a full-time government position. Perhaps she hoped that Polly would join her in Washington—Eleanor Roosevelt and others had certainly assumed so.[23] But Polly did not come: she remained in New York. That her decision involved intense disappointment and possible recrimination can only be surmised.

When Dewson accepted Franklin Roosevelt's offer to serve on the Social Security Board, she immediately resigned her position as vice-chairman of the Democratic National Committee, since she did not feel it appropriate to oversee political work for the Democratic party while serving on a nonpartisan government board. She said goodbye in a Democratic Digest article entitled "A General Bids Farewell to Her Troops," calling the Democratic party "the best cause any woman ever gave her heart and mind to."[24]

Behind the scenes, she arranged her leave-taking more deliber-

ately. She went straight to the president to make sure that Emma Guffey Miller would not be able to use her departure to grab power in the
Women's Division. Should Miller ask to be put in charge, the men at
the Democratic National Committee were to say that Dorothy Mc-
Allister was entirely satisfactory and that no change was contemplated.
She explained this scenario to Farley, adding, "I was not quite so long-
winded as this to the President, but he caught the idea and said I'll tell
Mrs. Miller myself if necessary." With these details taken care of, she
felt only a nagging sense of anticipation before she actually went to
work at the Social Security Board. She confessed to Clara Beyer in late
August, "I always HATE a job until I get into harness so I'm pretty
glum."[25]

Dewson began her first day on the job amidst a flurry of publicity.
She was a bit rumpled from a train ride down from New York, and the
news photographers snapped a picture of her running a comb through
her hair before the swearing-in ceremony. This photograph went out
over the major wire services, and even *Time* magazine carried it. The
next time she saw the President, he joked, "Molly, you have been having some fine publicity." Dewson asked, "Which picture are you referring to? Me kissing Jim Farley at your command or me combing my hair
in my office the day I was inducted as a member of the Social Security
Board?" "Both!" he answered with a broad smile.[26]

Dewson felt right at home in her new job. As the journalist
Geno Herrick said to Eleanor Roosevelt when the nomination was announced, "It is almost dramatic, isn't it, to have had her prepare for
years for a job that didn't exist while she was preparing for it."[27] But
the Social Security Administration itself was not quite so well prepared
for its first woman member. Her fellow board members, George O.
Bigge and former Assistant Secretary of Labor Arthur Altmeyer, had
full restroom facilities on the seventh floor where the board offices were
located, but nothing comparable existed for women. At age sixty-three,
Molly Dewson had to trot down a flight of stairs to a bathroom used by
the agency's secretaries and typists.[28]

Molly Dewson approached the social security system as a vehicle
to put into practice the reform goals she had sought since 1900. She
hoped social security would soon be "as inconspicuous and effective a
part of our life as a pure water supply or an adequate fire system." Her
conception of it went far beyond old age insurance or unemployment
compensation: "The things that go to make up social security include a

wholesome childhood, adequate education, a job at a healthy and decent wage, proper housing, and some sort of insurance against the inevitable 'rainy days.'" Americans deserved no less than this "just measure
of social decency."[29]

The new board member found her work a mixture of policy formulation and the "bundle of chores" which were the lot of a government
bureaucrat.[30] Despite thirty years experience in the field, she still felt
overwhelmed by the technical nature of much of her work. She often
took material home at night to study, though she admitted that reading
these statistical reports was about as exciting as looking over her insurance policies. Fortunately, the Social Security Administration had assembled an excellent staff of technical experts, including Wilbur J.
Cohen, who became assistant secretary of Health, Education and Welfare under Lyndon Johnson. If she had trouble with some point, she
told Cohen, "I am not a technical expert. Think of me as having the
mind of the average Congressman. Practice on me." She later remi-
nisced to him: "Don't you remember when I came on the Board and was
short of factual understanding . . . how I pressed a button and you stood
beside me very respectfully. I never rose from my seat, grandmothers
never do, do they? And you explained the technicality that confounded
me in words of one syllable."[31]

She used the expertise of Jack Tate, head of the legal division of
the Social Security Administration, in a similar way. One discussion of
a Massachusetts plan became so complicated that she drew Tate aside
and handed him a piece of paper about two inches by four. "You write
down on this just what I'm to say to the governor," she told Tate.
He later recalled, "I did, and she did, and everything got straightened
out."[32]

Jack Tate became one of Molly Dewson's closest friends in the Social Security Administration. Like many others, he greatly respected
her ability to cut to the heart of an issue: "She had a wonderful power of
finding the jugular. She'd just reach right in and catch an issue." Right
after she joined the board, she bluntly asked him how many women
lawyers he had on his staff. "Jack, now you think I'm a politico, and I
guess I am," she began. "But I'll make a deal with you. If you will take
on your staff as high a peccentage of women as there are women in the
legal profession, then I'll leave you alone about appointments." (Retell-
ing the story, Tate interjected at this point, "She was very much a
woman's rights woman.") When Tate demonstrated to her that the So-

cial Security Administration in fact had a higher percentage of women lawyers on its staff than the national ratio, she never mentioned the issue again.[33]

Molly's sense of humor and joie de vivre infected her colleagues at Social Security. If the lawyers got too serious, she joked with them about their striped pants; if Arthur Altmeyer started running on, she just looked at him and said, "Oh, Arthur!" which always cut him off. Staff members delighted in the supply of Hershey bars that she kept in her desk drawer in the board room and passed around during long sessions. Like her former coworkers at the DNC, the members of the Social Security Administration appreciated her unique style.[34]

Many of Dewson's contributions to Social Security were, in her words, "on the personal side."[35] Frank Bane, the executive director of the agency, recalled, "Molly, bless her heart, was a grand old trouper. She'd been in public offices of one kind or another for many, many years. She'd been in top bracket politics. . . . She was a definite asset from the standpoint of the making of policy and from the standpoint of contacts up on the Hill. She knew everybody in town." And Jane Hoey, head of the Bureau of Public Assistance, noted how the contacts Molly Dewson had built up through the National Consumers' League were a great help in dealing with the labor administrators who ran Social Security programs on the state and local levels. "We thought she was quite an asset," Hoey recalled.[36]

Especially important were Dewson's close ties to the White House. Her friendship with the Roosevelts was no secret in official Washington, and board minutes show that she was often asked to use her access to the White House for official Social Security business. When the matters were fairly minor, she went through James Roosevelt, who had become his father's administrative assistant in the second term. If necessary, however, Molly went straight to the president himself.[37]

Molly's residence in Washington gave her new opportunities to spend time with Eleanor Roosevelt. When Dewson's nomination was first announced, Frances Perkins had telegraphed, "Put up with me if you want to." But she settled, alone, in a tiny house with a cheerful garden at 3264 N Street in Georgetown. Eleanor Roosevelt managed to slip away for dinner there fairly often. After one such evening, she shared a description of Dewson's "family" with readers of her column, "My Day": "two very beautiful Persian cats, two dogs, herself and a very efficient colored maid who realizes Miss Dewson knows how to delegate authority and that her job is to remember all the things about the house which Miss Dewson doesn't remember."[38] Whenever possible, Molly returned to New York for the weekend, but, given the press of Social Security business, this was not always possible. So, for the first time in twenty-five years, Molly and Polly were separated for long periods of time. Molly's excitement at serving in the New Deal was tempered by this wrenching reorientation of her personal life.

Molly Dewson's active service on the Social Security Board lasted only until June 1938—a nine-month period. In the late spring, she visited her doctor in New York and received this prognosis: "No disease had attacked me, nothing was wrong, but he strongly advised me to stop work or else—! The work on the Board had not been too heavy. My condition was a hangover from my political activities." She spoke more pointedly about her medical condition to her fellow board member Arthur Altmeyer: "When I was in New York May 22 I saw my Doctor who said emphatically that I was all washed out and was a darn fool if I did not give up work. It is not merely that I had blood pressure very much lower than my normal and also was quite anaemic, but that my heart was not so hot." She was a bit surprised at her "cheerful acceptance of a perpetual vacation considering my life-long habits of perpetual activity" and could only conclude in her letter to Altmeyer, "I guess the good fairy that stood at my cradle was the one that hands out equitable dispositions."[39]

The next step was to see the president. She dreaded telling Franklin she was calling it quits, but he was entirely sympathetic. "You work too hard and never stop," he told her. "You should have done as I do for I am like a cat. I make a quick stroke and then I relax." The president then gently and tactfully inquired into her financial situation, a gesture she never forgot. "As I could get along without working he did not have to make any plans for me, but I have always wondered what his warm, fatherly interest would have led him to do." Roosevelt asked her not to resign immediately but to take a leave of absence starting in July. He thought a summer in Castine might restore her strength, and he wanted her on hand in the fall when a congressional committee was scheduled to evaluate the Social Security Administration. She quickly acceded, and then left for Maine.[40]

As always, Castine proved the perfect place to ruminate about her future. "The old frame is rattling—no matter what the spirit," she told Clara Beyer. "I can't believe you are only ten years younger than I am," she confessed to Eleanor. "I feel a thousand years older." She expanded: "Do you know what Maine folks call a 'dosey' log of wood. I'm that just eaten through with the dry rot of fatigue. I kept on doing more than I felt like doing too long. However I am glad I did. When you are lucky enough to have the chance to do something you believe in awfully it's well to make the most of it." By this point, she obviously felt her active days in politics and government were over.[41]

Publicly, Molly Dewson attributed her resignation to her declining health. Her official letter to the president opened, "I no longer have the physical endurance for a great Federal post." But, whether she admitted it to herself or not, she had other reasons for giving up her position, the principal one being Polly Porter's refusal to move to Washington, which placed too heavy a strain on their partnership. Some of Dewson's friends even hinted that Polly suffered a nervous breakdown.[42] Molly never publicly (or privately) cited this as a factor in her decision. For a final time, she used the excuse of being "all washed out" to extricate herself from a job that no longer offered satisfaction.

On top of Polly's unhappiness and her own health problems, Molly could no longer hide her frustrations with her job. No doubt she hoped her service on the Social Security Board would provide the crowning achievement in a lifelong commitment to social reform, but the position gave her no such deep-seated pleasure. She supported the New Deal (rumors that she resigned because of a policy disagreement were unfounded) and was very fond of her colleagues, especially Arthur Altmeyer. But there was an undeniable monotony to a bureaucrat's life, which involved too much of the kind of routine administration that had driven her out of similar jobs before. Once social security turned from a visionary goal into specific legislation, the technical experts replaced social reformers as the main policymakers. Clara Beyer once asked Arthur Altmeyer what Dewson did on the board, and Altmeyer admitted that she left no clear signature on the program. Dewson herself reached a similar conclusion: "I must put my best foot forward. I am proud of some things I was able to do on the Social Security Board but when you get to be one of a Board you become anonymous."[43]

Before Dewson officially terminated her relationship with the Social Security Board in December of 1938, she worked diligently to ensure that her successor would be a woman. She and Arthur Altmeyer decided on Ellen Sullivan Woodward, whose job as head of Women's and Professional Projects at the Works Progress Administration was winding down. (Dewson confided to Clara Beyer, "Yes she was Arthur's and my pick out of—not Heaven—but available humans.") Franklin Roosevelt, however, was leaning toward a congressman who had just been defeated for reelection. When Dewson wangled a private session with the president, he seemed preoccupied with other matters. Finally she exclaimed in frustration, "Franklin, if you knew what a job it is to get an appointment with you, you would, at least, let me have my say now I am here." Although he listened to her pleas, he seemed more unsympathetic than usual. "Molly, you argue your case too much, but I'll think it over."[44]

She continued to press Woodward's case with the president by mail—"It would send the old war mare to the pasture so happy and confident"—while confessing to Eleanor, "Oh dear Oh dear I hope I did nothing to put the President off Ellen Woodward by being so eager to work out a perfect team mate for Arthur Altmeyer. . . . He must hate pestiferous people and I am awfully sorry to go out under a cloud so far as he is concerned, after ten years of sunshine. What a wail! But I feel quite sad."[45] In the end, she got her way. The president publicly accepted her resignation on December 14 and announced Woodward's nomination at the same time. "That was a love of an acceptance," Molly thanked Franklin, even though she admitted "I was afraid you would be after wanting to kick this persistant old 'she-male' in the seat of me skirt." (Saucily, she signed the letter "Heigh-Ho.") After a farewell dinner in late January attended by more than one hundred friends and colleagues, Molly Dewson officially ended her association with the Social Security Board.[46]

Molly planned to spend her winters in New York and Westport, Connecticut (where Polly ran her kennel), and then decamp to Castine. Her health and spirits showed dramatic improvement. Despite her initial rush of joy at having executed a tough personal and professional decision, however, she soon realized how much she missed both Washington and Eleanor Roosevelt. "When you are shopping in N.Y.C. sometime couldn't I go along and hold your purse? Or chauffeur you to a meeting in the Bronx?" Molly pleaded plaintively to Eleanor just one month into her retirement.[47]

In the spring of 1940, the still homesick Dewson was lured back to Washington for a few days of glory at a National Institute of Government planned by the Women's Division. The National Institute of Government represented the culmination of the Reporter Plan Molly Dewson had first introduced in 1934. It brought together some five thousand Democratic women from forty-five states to meet with the government officials responsible for the New Deal programs they were studying. The Democratic women astounded the government officials with the sagacity and insight of their questions. The journalist Emma Bugbee covered the event, and Dewson reminded her of her original reaction to the plan at Eleanor Roosevelt's press conference. "And now do you think the Reporter Plan was just 'another paper plan?'" she twitted Bugbee.[48]

For Dewson, the high point of the National Institute of Government came at a gala dinner on the last night. Molly Dewson served as toast-mistress, Eleanor Roosevelt was the featured guest, and the speakers' table included the most important women in politics and government in the New Deal. Dewson's heart "thrilled with pride" as she introduced the long line of "intelligent, competent, well-balanced women" who bore testament to Franklin Roosevelt's confidence in women's ability.[49]

At the time he addressed the National Institute of Government gathering, Roosevelt's mind was on two major political dilemmas: whether to seek a third term, and what course to chart with regard to American participation in World War II. While staying at the White House, Dewson noticed how strained and tired he looked, and she told Eleanor with feeling that the country should not expect Franklin to subject himself to the pressures of a third term. Eleanor soon conveyed a message from Franklin: "Tell Molly that as things look I do not think it will be necessary for me to run."[50] Four days later, Hitler's troops marched into Belgium, and Roosevelt and the country began to reevaluate their antipathy toward a third term.

Molly Dewson sat out the 1940 Democratic convention in Chicago from the sidelines in Castine, the first time since 1932 that she was not in charge of women's activities on the convention floor. She listened to most of the sessions on the radio and received telephone reports from Dorothy McAllister and May Thompson Evans. "It almost makes me homesick," she confessed to Eleanor Roosevelt, who herself played a major role in securing the vice-presidential nomination for Henry Wallace. Eleanor reassured her that she had made the right decision: "I can imagine you must have had a feeling of homesickness listening to the Chicago convention. I know that you are very much missed, and particularly by the men, but I think you were wise to take care of yourself."[51]

Once again, Molly Dewson's retirement from Democratic politics proved premature. The Women's Division director, Dorothy McAllister, was a strong public speaker (at Roosevelt's suggestion, she had addressed the full Democratic National Convention at Chicago), but, in Dewson's words, male politicians were "inclined to push her around a little." So Eleanor Roosevelt made Molly an offer she could not refuse: "if you could be at the office to meet people and do some of the work with the men, it would be a great help. That is where Dorothy is weak."[52]

Dewson's only hesitation was that she had not received a formal invitation from the men at the Democratic National Committee. Her worry was soon laid to rest. The reply from its head, Eddie Flynn, was brief and to the point: "Dear Molly: I am not going to write a long letter to you. If you don't come down and do what you're told, I'll go up with a gun and bring you down. And that's that." So, after putting her Castine flower bed in shape for the winter, Molly Dewson headed down for what she described as "a small part" in the 1940 campaign.[53]

When she reported to the Women's Division headquarters in September ("Yes, all of us war horses answer the bell"), she judged its educational program in excellent shape, but found its quarters cramped and clerical help inadequate. Dorothy McAllister had asked for a larger budget, but the men told her that the DNC was short of money. Molly told Dorothy that money was always scarce in Democratic campaigns, and that the men never hesitated to go into debt for what they considered necessary. She was preparing for an all-out assault on Eddie Flynn and company at the DNC when an angel literally walked in the door in the person of Mrs. Anthony J. Drexel Biddle. Molly explained the difference five thousand dollars would make to the Women's Division, and Biddle wrote a check on the spot. "What a wonderful feeling it must be to scribble off such a check without hesitation!" Dewson marveled.[54]

Improvements were immediate. "With a well balanced staff and room to work efficiently peace settled on headquarters like a dove." After two weeks, Dewson felt free to return to Castine. She received from the grateful staff a silver tray engraved "The General."[55]

As the 1940 campaign drew to a conclusion, one final piece of Women's Division business remained unsettled. Dorothy McAllister's husband, like Carolyn Wolfe's four years earlier, was tired of having an absentee wife, and she planned to resign after the election. The choice of a successor was part of the larger dilemma the Women's Division faced of how to maintain women's political momentum now that Molly Dewson was no longer part of the picture. Dewson had never thought that her Women's Division program would be etched in stone; at times, she talked about it going "full blast" only through 1940, when Roosevelt ordinarily would have retired. Whether her initiatives would find a permanent place in the Democratic party remained an open question.[56]

Part of the problem lay in the changing nature of the New Deal. The first term produced an exciting outpouring of relief and reform measures designed to combat the crisis of the Great Depression, but the second term was characterized by retrenchment, controversy, and stalemate. Roosevelt's ill-considered court-packing plan left a legacy of distrust, even after retirements on the Supreme Court altered its philosophical balance and made the issue moot. Far more disastrous was Roosevelt's attempt in 1937 to balance the budget by slashing federal expenditures for relief. The stock market promptly collapsed, and unemployment soared to almost 20 percent again. The administration quickly increased its levels of spending, but not before creating what came to be called the "Roosevelt recession." Moreover, a conservative coalition in Congress blocked or impeded most social legislation throughout the second term. By 1938, therefore, the New Deal had essentially run out of steam.[57]

The changing nature of the New Deal adversely affected women's fortunes. Since so many women administrators were involved in social welfare programs under attack in Congress, they too faced a period of retrenchment. In general, women have done better in government bureaucracies and agencies that are in their infancy; when the initial sense of emergency or challenge has passed, these institutions often become more rigid and hierarchical, and opportunities for women diminish.[58]

The enactment of the Hatch Act, which curtailed political activity by government workers, exacerbated the problems for women in politics. Since the Women's Division relied heavily on prominent women in government to publicize the New Deal's accomplishments, this new restriction cramped women's campaign style. The Hatch Act also forbade payment to political organizations for printed matter, which meant that the Women's Division could no longer sell subscriptions to the *Democratic Digest*. Once the Democratic National Committee took over the expensive proposition of running the magazine, which had been so important to women's political mobilization, it was an inviting target for cutbacks and editorial control.

This impasse in Democratic women's politics in 1940 highlights the mixed legacy of Molly Dewson's accomplishments in the 1930s. On the one hand, women's roles had undeniably increased in the Democratic party and the Roosevelt administration. Much of this progress could be traced directly to Molly Dewson, and she justifiably took pride in these exciting accomplishments for women in public life. Since she had started practically from scratch, it was easy for her and her supporters to delude themselves that remarkable progress had been made overnight.

Yet by the late 1930s the momentum was slowing. "These changes are tentative beginnings," Dewson realized. "They have not stiffened into custom." As long as Dewson was on the job, she could use her forceful personality and unorthodox approach to politics to dicker with and badger the men until she got results. Yet it was difficult to translate such *individual* influence into permanent *institutional* change. When no obvious successor surfaced at the Women's Division ("Well we both agree there is no embarrassment of riches," Molly confided to Eleanor Roosevelt), women's politics went into a holding pattern.[59]

It was also difficult to assure continuation of the special access to the White House that women in politics had enjoyed for nearly a decade—what the historian Ingrid Scobie has dubbed more broadly "the Roosevelt connection."[60] None of the women Dewson groomed to take over the Women's Division could ever hope to take advantage of the intimacy and access she had enjoyed: the people in the White House were the President and Mrs. Roosevelt to them, not Franklin and Eleanor. Furthermore, in the second term, Eleanor began to give more attention to concerns such as civil rights, youth, and international developments at the expense of time previously devoted to women's concerns. Once the Women's Division lost the favored spot in the White House's affections it had enjoyed through the influence of its director, women's politics suffered.

Dewson's approach to politics depended not only on personal connections, but also on the reform atmosphere of the early New Deal. This was both its greatest weakness and its greatest strength. The early New Deal offered unprecedented opportunities for the kind of issue-oriented approach to politics that former suffragists like Dewson knew best. And the Reporter Plan, growing from this approach, proved itself uniquely adapted to circumstances in force during the early 1930s; through the plan the Women's Division was able to spread understanding of the social and economic changes emanating from Washington at the same time that it built support for the Democratic party. But once social welfare programs became accepted, the need for political consciousness-raising diminished. In general, the Women's Division approach was much better suited to positive goals, such as fostering support for New Deal Reforms, than to negative ones, such as defending existing legislation from conservative attack. When the excitement of the first term gave way to the stalemate of the second, enthusiasm waned. The political agenda of the 1940s could not support or sustain the kind of programs that Molly Dewson and the Women's Division had carefully nurtured earlier in the decade.

As Dewson prepared to return to Castine in late 1940, a new factor clouded the future of the Women's Division. American involvement in the European war now seemed a distinct possibility. What impact the war might have on women in politics, or politics in general, was uncertain. She later confessed that in her "heart of hearts," she was glad she never had to face politics during wartime. Unlike in the 1930s, when everything had been so "clear cut," she did not believe she would have functioned very smoothly in the turmoil of such a period. Nevertheless, Molly Dewson the feminist wanted women to play major roles in the upcoming war mobilization. By late 1941 she was writing, "There is much more to a total war beside fighting tactics or bearing arms. . . . Women have talked a lot about equal rights. Let us seize the equal right to serve." As she sat writing her credo for the *Democratic Digest* one bright Sunday afternoon in early December, word came of the Japanese attack on Pearl Harbor. Dewson was, in a way, glad of it: "No more shilly-shallying. Now for action in behalf of our ideals."[61]

CHAPTER FIFTEEN

Castine Revisited

"I THINK when you have to slow up it's hard to do it halfways," Molly Dewson admitted to Frances Perkins in 1939. "If you get far enough away for perspective you lose driving force. If you stop for long enough to get rested you lose momentum." While Dewson believed that "few die of overwork compared with those who die of boredom," by the late 1930s she felt she could no longer actively participate in public life without seriously jeopardizing her health. Consequently, she cut back on politics and embraced domesticity. And her emotional life entered a final distinctive phase: "Polly and I are going through a brand new and really interesting experience—mostly inward," she told Eleanor Roosevelt in 1945. In many ways, the years between 1931 and 1938 had been an aberration in which politics temporarily took priority over partnership. After 1938, the relationship returned to its former equilibrium. Once again, Polly Porter became the center of Molly's life, and they remained constant companions until the end.[1]

Dewson drew an analogy to Caesar's commentaries when describing her life in the early 1940s.. "I am still like Gaul divided in three parts." She and Polly maintained their cooperative apartment in New York, Polly's Bagaduce Kennel in Westport, Connecticut, and Moss Acre in Castine. They planned to divide their time between these three establishments, with occasional trips out to California to visit old friends like Lucy Stebbins. But it was wartime, and Molly and Polly, like many other Americans, found their options diminished by the homefront sacrifices necessary to aid the war effort.[2]

Few were more enthusiastic supporters of home defense than Molly Dewson. "You would think I took this to heart if you had seen me poking around on my necessary errands at forty miles an hour ever since economy on gas was requested; darning old stockings for my venerable shanks; eating cheap-cut stews, and what not," she told readers of the *Democratic Digest*. She even wanted to buy a bicycle to avoid wearing down the tires of her car, but her doctor vetoed that. The result? "I am nursing my tires," she lamented.[3]

For an avid motorist like Dewson, gas rationing was the hardest sacrifice to bear. In the spring of 1942 she and Polly saved their gasoline allotment so that they could drive to Castine—at thirty miles per hour instead of their usual seventy. They arrived with hardly any gas left for the rest of the month. Dewson told her former secretary Harriet Kerr, "When we get home we won't be able to do any shopping for a week or two. Have to live on dandelion roots and bark."[4] They passed a quiet summer, with Molly's flower bed planted as a victory garden. The only untoward event occurred in September, when Molly underwent an operation in which she had "all the useless scrap removed from my abdominal cavity." (She was referring to her appendix and uterus.) The doctor's first words to his seventy-year-old patient were, "You'll feel a lot better," followed by, "you are good for twenty-five years."[5]

It was not always easy for Molly and Polly to keep their spirits up. "War is a dour affair even for the spectator in the last row," Dewson confessed to Supreme Court Justice Stanley Reed. The low point came during the winter of 1942–43, which they spent "marooned" in Georgetown. Since Polly's kennel was located near the busy munitions center of Bridgeport, help was hard to find, and they were forced to work like "galley slaves" to maintain the kennel. Still worse, their fuel ration allowed them to heat only a few rooms at a time, and those at 55 degrees. The two women and seventeen dogs spent the winter huddled in two small rooms.[6]

In the hopes of winning an increased gas allotment and the chance to relocate to Maine, Dewson appealed to the local Westport, Connecticut, rationing board—describing, among other things, the "house maid's knee" she had acquired while maintaining their living quarters! This unabashed plea for sympathy worked, and by early May 1943, she, Polly, and their menagerie of pets were settled in at Castine. They spent the rest of the war years there, renting out their apartment in

New York. With the burner set at 63 degrees, the house well caulked, and additional heat supplied from open fires in Moss Acre's ample fireplaces, they were able to survive several harsh Maine winters.[7]

It was something of an adventure. One winter storm blew down two hundred of Moss Acre's spruce trees and left them without power for three days and without telephone service for six weeks. Fortunately, they were remarkably self-sufficient: a cow and chickens provided fresh milk and eggs every day, and ample stocks of canned vegetables and fruits from the summer's victory garden supplemented their twice-weekly shopping trips. Because of the wartime labor shortage, they could only find one couple to work part-time running the house. Never strangers to manual labor, Molly and Polly pitched in themselves.[8]

Puttering around doing domestic chores was a quaint change after Molly's years of frenzied political activity. To fill their time, Porter and Dewson joined the Women's Alliance and the Grange, memberships they kept for the rest of their lives. Molly especially liked the Grange, where she and Polly were accepted without pretension or affectation. "Good old Maine folks they just KNOW they are anyone's equal," she observed with admiration. She added tellingly, "Of course without Polly's companionship I should prefer a third floor back hall bedroom in New York or some other closely settled spot."[9]

The peace and companionship that the partners found in their old age did not dim Dewson's interest in the world beyond her own personal landscape. Keeping in touch with old friends continued to be a favorite pastime: "Up here in the peace of winter letters are quite exciting, sort of like meeting a friend on the Rue St. Honore in the old days." Dewson often indulged herself by writing what she called "love letters" to Eleanor Roosevelt. When Molly turned seventy in 1944, she told Eleanor, in a phrase she had used often, that "it was like touching mother earth to see you again" and thanked her for "fifteen years so interested and satisfying that all my previous years seem pale things in comparison." Once Dewson left official Washington, however, she lost the intimacy of her earlier friendship with Eleanor Roosevelt. Molly finally subscribed to the Portland Press Herald, which carried "My Day," in order to keep up with Eleanor's activities.[10]

Although Molly had not missed an inauguration since 1932, Maine's winter weather and wartime travel restrictions kept her from attending the simple ceremonies in January 1945 that marked Franklin Roosevelt's fourth term. She was still in Maine when she heard the news of his sudden death on April 12, 1945. She was proud that she was one of the two hundred friends invited to the private services at the White House.[11] Molly tried to express her sense of loss to Eleanor: "The deepest satisfaction and happiness of my life is that I had a chance to help him a little bit at the beginning. . . . I swore my allegiance to you both almost twenty years ago and it has grown more and more steadfast." She treasured the reply that she received from Eleanor, a note that captured the warm relationship Dewson had enjoyed with the president: "You always gave Franklin so much joy—he admired the direct way in which you approached things and he counted on your friendship and loyalty." To this day, her letter hangs in what was Molly Dewson's study in Castine, enduring testimony to Molly's close connections to Eleanor and Franklin.[12]

Franklin Roosevelt's death and the end of the Second World War brought to a close a vital and important chapter in American history. In the next era, which the publisher Henry Luce confidently predicted would be remembered as the "American Century," Molly Dewson played no role. Without the Roosevelts in the White House, she lost her last shred of political influence, and she settled into a life of friendships and professional contacts that centered around Castine and New York. She looked back on her days in the New Deal with increasing nostalgia but did not wallow in the past.

After the isolation of Connecticut and Castine winters during wartime, New York seemed an exciting and stimulating place in the late 1940s. Molly served on the boards of the National Consumers' League and the International Migration Service and frequented the Tuesday members' lunch at the Cosmopolitan Club. Get-togethers with Frances Perkins and Eleanor Roosevelt, while not frequent, were always a special treat. And a steady stream of old New Dealers—from Clara Beyer to Dorothy McAllister, Gladys Tillett, India Edwards, and Florence Kerr—came through New York for a meal or to spend the night at the Dewson-Porter apartment. Rarely a week went by in which Molly did not connect with her professional and political associates from the glory days of the New Deal.

"It's a new world," Dewson observed to the executive director of the International Migration Service in 1950, and that sentiment applied to postwar politics as well. It was not an especially happy time for liberal causes. Anti-Communist hysteria gripped the country, and Dewson was appalled at the excesses committed in its name. "However the real noise here is over Truman's going in for witch hunting," she told Women's Division head India Edwards in 1947. "All the Democrats of quality I have met are aghast, appalled. They consider it has more danger to America than atom bombs." She complained in writing to President Truman in early 1949, "We need another freedom. Freedom from taking slander too seriously."[13]

Despite her spirited defense of freedom, Molly Dewson was concerned about the role of Communists in political life. Much of her venom was directed against the presidential aspirations of Henry Wallace in 1948. She had first-hand evidence of Communist collaboration with the Wallace campaign through Grace Hutchins and Anna Rochester, whom she described as "high up Communists." The Porter-Dewsons were about the only bourgeois friends Hutchins and Rochester had left, and the friendship survived because they usually avoided discussion of politics. But in the spring of 1948, they did talk politics. When Dewson heard them "drool" over Henry Wallace, she was deeply disturbed. "Oh dear I am too old, and too Yankee," she complained darkly to Carolyn Wolfe, "I just dread a government based on a politburo."[14]

Their friendship with Grace Hutchins and Anna Rochester brought Molly and Polly as close as they came to suspicion in the McCarthy era. In early 1953, Eleanor Roosevelt asked Dewson if she remembered making a plea for better treatment of the Communist leader Earl Browder when he was imprisoned in a federal penitentiary in Atlanta. (The issue had been raised in a query to Eleanor Roosevelt's column in McCall's.) Dewson only vaguely recalled such intercession, mistakenly placing it early in the first term. In fact, she had passed a letter from Grace Hutchins to Eleanor Roosevelt in 1941. She made the gesture in the spirit of friendship, not out of familiarity with the case: to her, Earl Browder "was only a newspaper name." Later that year, Dewson forwarded a petition to the Roosevelts, again without endorsing it, asking that Browder be released from prison by Christmas.[15]

Dewson was upset that Eleanor Roosevelt had to defend herself for helping a Communist leader well before anti-Communism became a national obsession. "Have those misled persons who are willing to sacrifice the freedoms and decencies of this country and turn it into a Hitler land or a Totalitarian State, turned their venom onto you? It makes me heart sick." At the same time, she added rather belligerently, "I never thought socialism was practical and therefore believed the 'Russian experiment,' as we called it then, would not work out. As the days past and totalitarians took over the experiment, I became rather intemperately anti-communist as I still am."[16]

To suggest that Molly Dewson was caught up in the McCarthy hysteria would be too harsh a judgment. She was clearly no fan of the Soviet Union, and never had been. But she was never seriously worried about Communist infiltration into the federal government: her faith in democracy made her confident that good and free government would render Communism impotent in the American political system. And her antipathy toward the Wallace campaign was as much a product of her loyalty to the Democratic party as it was fear of Communist subversion.[17]

What about Polly Porter? Did her professions of Communist and anarchist leanings in the 1920s bring her to the attention of the witch hunters in Washington in the 1940s and 1950s? Her name was never mentioned in connection with any investigation, nor did the Federal Bureau of Intelligence keep a file on her.[18] Yet people she knew did suffer. Their friend and lawyer, Dorothy Kenyon, was one of the first people hauled before McCarthy's Senate subcommittee in 1950. And Polly realized the precarious position that Grace Hutchins and Anna Rochester were in, writing, "Going to prison [is] always very much on their minds, I think. No joke to be a Communist these days." Probably more than her partner, Polly Porter was profoundly troubled by the excesses of this period.[19]

Through the 1940s, Molly Dewson occupied herself with a project that often afflicts those who have just retired from public life: she set out to write her memoirs. The very day she resigned from the Social Security Board, she exclaimed, "Now what ho for writing my book." She mentioned casually to Eleanor Roosevelt, "Two publishers have asked me to. But I don't believe I should be good at it. I am a born doer and whereas I can often make a telling statement, a book is very different."[20]

That, in fact, was the gist of the comments that she received from friends who read the early chapters on Dewson's childhood, college, and suffrage experiences. The most devastating critique came from the novelist Fannie Hurst, who became an intimate friend of Dewson's around the time of the 1936 presidential campaign. "You, who are one of the most alive persons I know, are not alive in this narrative. Neither are your friends and experiences. . . . This curious treachery of a pen is not unusual, but the very devil to surmount." Two months after Molly began writing, Fannie Hurst was telling her to start over from scratch. Soon Dewson was telling friends, "I toyed with writing my life history but it turned out rather dull."[21]

Yet she never entirely abandoned the idea of writing an autobiography. A new spur came in 1947 from the Franklin D. Roosevelt Memorial Foundation, which asked her to prepare a "memorandum" with supporting documents describing her association with Franklin Roosevelt. Dewson jumped at the chance to set the record straight on women's contributions to the New Deal. "I am proud to say I think I slipped a lot of first class fundamental ideas over on the men." She set her sights lower this time, however, concentrating on "background stuff" from 1928 to 1940, adding, "I preferred not to try to write a popular book and to try to get it published. The 'record' is what interests me." Unfortunately, Dewson found writing about the New Deal just as much of a chore as chronicling her early years. "I would rather organize the planetary system than write a book," she complained to FDR's former secretary Grace Tully, who ran the foundation.[22]

As her spirits began to sag once again, she received new impetus from an unlikely source: the publication of the second volume of Jim Farley's autobiography. She found *Jim Farley's Story* "so sordid and so psychopathic it has thrown me into a deep gloom." She was appalled at Farley's preoccupation with personal advancement and his lack of interest in the reform ideals of the Roosevelt era and angered that women rated only eighteen words in the entire book. She annotated her copy with sarcastic comments like "Poor Jim," "Oh yeah," and "Pah." When Farley intoned, "History will deliver its judgment when all the testimony is in," she scribbled in the margin, "YOU BET IT WILL." Afterward, she redoubled her efforts to tell her, and women's, side of the story.[23]

In the summer of 1949, Molly Dewson completed the first volume of her political autobiography, which she titled "An Aid to the End." (Polly, with her characteristic vagueness about political matters, was wont to refer to it as "A Means to the End.")[24] Eighteen months later, Dewson finished a draft of a second volume, bringing the completed manuscript to nearly four hundred pages. Unfortunately by 1951 the Roosevelt Foundation was barely functioning, the victim of Cold War hysteria; and the manuscript sat in Grace Tully's office untyped due to lack of secretarial assistance. Dewson began to feel desperate: "Truly Grace I can't bear to let the thing wait for who knows when my 'borrowed time' may run out." Her doctor had told her she was a "piker" if she did not live to be ninety, but she was taking no chances.[25]

Dewson finally took matters into her own hands, retrieved the manuscript from the Roosevelt Foundation, and asked Governor Herbert Lehman of New York for a contribution of 150 dollars to cover typing and binding of the manuscript. Lehman graciously agreed.[26] After thirteen years of intermittent work, Dewson's political autobiography was completed, to her great relief: "Not even a word from Heaven from FDR could make me undertake it again," she told her trusted helper, Harriet Kerr. Historians of the New Deal can be grateful that Dewson persevered and got her story down on paper. Literary stylists have less to applaud. Fannie Hurst was right.[27]

Once Dewson had finally finished the manuscript, she and Polly put into effect a plan they had been considering for some time. In 1952, they sublet their apartment in New York and moved permanently to Maine. The change was prompted in part by their weakening financial situation. The partners were now living on a fixed income of between ten and twelve thousand a year, which Molly described as "just enough to scratch along on." Maintaining two residences put an unnecessary strain on their dwindling resources.[28]

Molly Dewson lived in many places during her life, but she always considered Castine her real home, her steady address. At every crossroad in her life she was drawn there, where she assessed her options, regained her strength, and decided what to do next. It was fitting, therefore, that she and Polly chose to retire there.

Life in Castine settled into a pleasant routine shaped by the seasons and the advancing years of the residents of Moss Acre. "We call this the Old Folks Home," Molly joked, "and all duties, hours, etc. are cut appropriately to the moment's energy." Moss Acre was staffed by a couple, who took care of the house and grounds, and a cook, Ethel Leach, who was the mainstay of the household. Mrs. Leach had come to Moss Acre in 1909 as a young bride—she even predated Molly Dewson's arrival there by several years—and she stayed with Polly after Molly's death. (It was Mrs. Leach's husband whom Dewson had appointed the postmaster of Castine in the 1930s.) This domestic arrangement was eminently comfortable for the Porter-Dewsons. "Much to be personally thankful for! Little to personally complain about! A life completely suited to our years!" Polly exclaimed.[29]

As always, Molly and Polly maintained an active social life, especially during July and August when Castine overflowed with summer residents. Between the Grange, the Women's Club, the Unitarian Alliance, and their network of friends and acquaintances, they usually attended at least one social gathering a day at the height of the season. Polly and Molly had known many of these people since before World

War I—Dorothy Blake, for example, visited the Berlin farm during their suffrage years. So many of their friends were women (parts of Castine were referred to as "No Man's Land") that their Castine social network at times replicated their New York lifestyle in the 1920s and 1930s.[30]

To old friends were added new ones, such as William and Leah Scarlett, who retired to Castine from St. Louis in 1954. Bishop Scarlett, a close friend of Eleanor Roosevelt and a former vice-president of the National Consumers' League, was "100% of my line of thought," Dewson asserted, a welcome change from the predominantly Republican tone of the Maine town. Soon the Scarletts' Friday afternoon gatherings became a regular item on the Dewson-Porters' social calendar.[31]

Just as important company were the steady stream of out-of-town guests who visited Moss Acre each summer. Rarely were Dewson and Porter without friends or family. Before his death in 1951, Joseph P. Chamberlain came up every summer, often with Dewson's Wellesley classmate B. Z. Scott. Polly's friend Irma Lerner visited every year, as did Constance Churchyard, "the very last of my really old friends that survives," Polly noted in 1961. In 1952, Dewson and Porter greeted their old World War I friend, social worker Marie-Thérèse Vieillot.[32]

Molly and Polly also welcomed a host of immediate and extended family members who enriched their retirement years. Polly's brother Bill settled into the household's routines for an extended visit each summer. (He remained the joint owner of Moss Acre until 1952, when he deeded his interest to his sister.) Molly entertained assorted nieces and nephews (she claimed fifty-nine), but her favorite was Virginia Weis Bourne, the granddaughter of Dewson's sister, Ellen. Virginia Bourne, her husband, Standish, and an expanding brood of children paid yearly visits during the 1950s to "Aunt Moll" and "Aunt Poll," often camping out by the shore. The Bournes became such a treasured part of life in Castine that Polly willed Moss Acre to Virginia and Standish.[33]

A typical summer day at Moss Acre might have included gardening, a luncheon or cocktail party, a trip to Bucksport or Bangor for supplies, followed by a light supper on the veranda. Molly and Polly did a remarkable amount of gardening for women of their years. During one season, they harvested almost one hundred quarts of strawberries. "I am glad I am not a migrant worker," quipped the seventy-nine-year-old Dewson after picking and stemming twelve quarts one morning. They worked just as hard around the house, even though they had a hired couple to do the cleaning and heaviest chores. "All my attention now is on living on our income and making plants grow," Molly told an old colleague in 1951.[34]

Evenings were a special, quiet time. Since Porter and Dewson took their main meal at lunch, after a light supper they spent the evening together in the living room, doing crossword puzzles or playing games such as chili, samba, or cribbage. (Polly always lost.) They pasted pictures into their photo albums and wrote letters. They usually listened to the radio for a while. More often, Polly would read aloud while Molly did some sewing or mending. Dewson developed such a passion for mending their old oriental rugs that Polly wondered if she were part Armenian.[35]

Another regular chore was taking care of the pets, which remained primarily Polly's responsibility. When they first came up during the war, they had so many dogs and cats that it was hard for guests to find a seat in the large living room because the animals usurped all the comfortable spots. Gradually the dogs grew old and were put to sleep, so that by the late 1950s only four remained. In 1958, they bought a standard poodle puppy which they named Sophie Vieillot in honor of their French friend. "She's a terror," Polly confessed. "Bright, loving, always on the rampage, and most disconcerting to a slow going elderly household!" Polly's love of animals did not slacken as she grew older: "I should honestly call them the interest and adornment of my days!"[36]

In this last decade of their life together, Molly's and Polly's lives were intertwined in a way they had not been since the Berlin farm in the 1910s. Fannie Hurst once referred to this blending as "the happy territory that exists between the two of you." And Molly captured their harmony when she joked, "The difficulty about putting a postscript on a letter of Polly's is that she has already written everything on my mind to say. Please just multiply it by two (2)." Each year Dewson bragged to her friends about the number of years she and Polly had spent together —they marked their anniversaries the way married couples do. (The final tally was fifty-two.)[37]

Yet each woman retained her own interests and activities. Dogs, cats, friends, and gardening shaped Polly's life, all observed with a wry sense of humor that kept her on the outside of more conventional lives. She remained hostile to organized religion, and her left-wing politics shocked many of their Castine friends. Though she talked less frequently about Communism, her continued support for civil rights,

Alger Hiss, labor unions, international peace, and accommodation with the Soviet Union set her apart from her Down East neighbors.

While she once admitted, "Sometimes it annoys me that I seem fated always to be 'at outs' with my pleasant and worthy associates," on the whole Polly cherished her eccentricity. She cultivated an amused aloofness at social gatherings: "Everyone very gay and amused, except MGP who is rather a sour puss at that sort of an affair," she wrote of one Unitarian potluck. After enduring another such occasion, she wrote sarcastically, "They were all kind men, all of them were long winded men, and most of them were fat men!" She remained skeptical about public affairs: "Well, the space man actually got off and back safely." But she saved her most biting words for Maine's hunting season, which she tagged "death stalking in the woods." With perhaps a small bit of glee, one year she tallied the number of hunters who had been killed or seriously injured during this annual slaughter.[38]

Polly remained indifferent to mainstream politics, although living with Molly she did not dare to be quite so wicked about politicians as she was about deerhunters. She classified all of Molly's political discussions as "highbrow" and rarely participated. On the other hand, politics remained one of Dewson's favorite pastimes. She was the reigning doyenne of Maine Democratic politics in the 1950s and state leaders trooped to Moss Acre to seek her advice. "It's quite amusing to have unknown men again calling me Molly altho I do not know their names even," she chuckled to Clara Beyer.[39]

New faces appeared on the Maine Democratic scene in the 1950s —those of Edmund Muskie, Frank Coffin, and Paul Fullam—and Dewson befriended all three men. She grew especially close to senatorial candidate Fullam, a Colby College government professor who personified her ideal of a concerned and enlightened public official. (She no doubt was swayed by his fulsome praise of her autobiography, especially when he claimed "there is nothing in the field except De Toqueville.") Fullam was a frequent visitor to Moss Acre. Reminiscent of Alice B. Toklas, who talked with the wives of the great while Gertrude Stein held forth with the men, Polly chatted amiably with Mrs. Fullam about dogs on these occasions.[40]

Much as Dewson dabbled in Maine Democratic politics, her heart remained in the New Deal past. After attending a reunion of "the old crowd" in Washington, she sighed nostalgically, "There is a lot of warmth in the ashes of the Roosevelt Days." She still felt close to her old comrades: "After all when two persons have had a warm and strong contact, because they had worked hard over a common interest, they do not forget each other." As she observed to her Social Security colleague Maurine Mulliner, "From my experience the joy of keeping in close touch with one's family and friends is life supporting."[41]

Dewson's closest link with the New Deal was Clara Beyer, who remained with the Division of Labor Standards into the 1960s. "You are my only warm contact with the Roosevelt Era," Molly told Clara. "Temperature 90° even in the shade of Castine." Eleanor Roosevelt also continued to hold a special place in Dewson's heart. Dewson reached out to Eleanor with messages from "this old octogenarian friend who loves you very much." Molly at first feared that she might never see Eleanor Roosevelt again after she retired to Maine, but Eleanor's friendship with William and Leah Scarlett provided frequent excuses for get-togethers in Castine when she was on her way to and from Campobello. The last of these reunions took place just two months before Dewson died.[42]

Molly Dewson and Frances Perkins continued to exchange poignant letters as they neared the end of their lives. (Perkins died in 1965.) Although illness or other commitments always seemed to doom their attempts to get together, the affection remained. Dewson summed up their relationship in historical terms: "I have always felt that our lives were tied together in a way although our social intercourse was limited. We were on the same boat, going to the same port."[43]

As Molly settled into a life of old friends and nostalgic memories, ceremonial occasions took on special importance. Her seventieth birthday occurred during wartime, "but minding the Government I am restricted," she told Eleanor Roosevelt. A more lavish gathering marked her eightieth in 1954. Her Castine friends arranged a surprise party, and Dewson was inundated with telephone calls and letters from old cronies. She was delighted by, if a bit skeptical about, the many people who congratulated her on the major role she had played in the New Deal. "Now we can all sink back until my 90th," she joked to Harriet Kerr.[44]

The nicest gift Dewson received in 1954 had nothing to do with her birthday: it occurred when Eleanor Roosevelt and Lorena Hickok dedicated their book on women in politics, *Ladies of Courage*, to her. Molly cherished this public recognition of her accomplishments in the New Deal period. She had never sought fame or fortune, but in her declining years she became somewhat obsessed with her place in history. She repeatedly urged acquaintances ranging from Adlai Stevenson to Polly's goddaughter to make the trip to Hyde Park or the Women's Archives at Radcliffe to read "An Aid to the End."[45]

She entered her ninth decade in a philosophical mood: "I am 80, heart slower, kidneys lazy etc. but not complaining about life—still agreeable but not my choice like the old fighting days." She joked that she still went on thinking even if she was too old to do anything about it: "No matter how many years fly by and how your wind diminishes and your leg muscles weaken and you are pigeon holed in the beautiful country, your interest does not flag, and you can read yourself into touch." She told Maurine Mulliner, "When you are an octogenarian you may be 'a good influence' and a clarifier of thought and any such, but it is not so satisfying as a more active part—take it from me. Dear me that sounds gloomy," she added, "and I'm happy, healthy, and comfortable, Heaven knows! Thank you Heaven!"[46] Dewson worried that she was not growing old with much éclat. "My spirit feels decked out in some one else's second hand clothes," she told Clara Beyer. "Sometimes I get sort of lonesome for my old friends of the FDR period," she confided to her on another occasion. "There is not any friend of my retired years that means as much as many of my working comrades of the old days."[47]

While nothing compared to the heady days of the New Deal, life continued to hold old pleasures, like driving, and new ones, like watching programs on the television that she and Polly purchased in 1959. At first they had been dubious about the new invention, but it soon became an accepted part of their daily routine. Watching television even began to supplant their fifty-year tradition of reading aloud in the evenings.

The television came in most handy for one of Dewson's favorite pastimes: observing the fortunes of the Democratic party. She actively followed the 1960 presidential campaign, and stayed awake until 2:15 A.M. watching the Democratic convention. She was a great admirer of Adlai Stevenson but thought John F. Kennedy had a better chance of beating Richard Nixon, whom she abhorred. "I'm so against Nixon," she told Clara Beyer, "if I was not so well, considering my years, I'd offer to bump his grinning face with an axe." (She never forgot that Nixon got his start in politics by using dirty tricks to defeat her close friend, Helen Gahagan Douglas.) According to Dewson, Kennedy's one weakness was that he did not realize what a help women could be to him politically. Yet unlike Eleanor Roosevelt, who made just that point to Kennedy during the early days of his administration, Dewson was content to remain on the sidelines. As she surveyed the political challenges of the 1960s, she sighed to Clara Beyer, "What a period to begin life in. I thank the Lord for scheduling me for an earlier time."[48]

Molly Dewson had a final brief fling with politics in 1960: at the venerable age of eighty-six, she ran for the Maine state senate. Although Hancock County had never elected a Democratic state senator, local Democrats did not want to concede the election. So Castine's political leader, Jimmie Sawyer, "teased" the old New Dealer into putting her name on the ballot as the Democratic candidate, even though in her three decades in politics she had never given any thought to running for office herself.[49] Dewson did not exactly hit the campaign trail, but she did make "the best speech of my life and kept the 65 Dems in a state of mirth for ten minutes" at a political gathering in Ellsworth. On the Saturday night before the special election, Dewson's Castine neighbor Frank Hatch organized a torchlight parade reminiscent of Roosevelt election nights in Hyde Park. A grand total of twenty people marched from the Grange Hall to Moss Acre, their torches attracting clouds of mosquitoes. They carried placards that read "If DUZ won't clean up, DEWSON will" and sang ditties composed by Hatch, who was well known in Castine for his tendency to versify at the slightest provocation. The revelers serenaded the candidate with tunes the likes of "Molly Bagadewson will do / She's the girl who'll carry us through / Greatest liberal who ever, ever ran / Molly's the Friend of the Common Man!"[50]

Molly Dewson received 725 votes to her Republican opponent's 4,140, not a bad showing in this overwhelmingly Republican stronghold. She was pleased that in Castine itself enough Republicans voted for her to produce a 28–28 tie. Even more gratifying were the tributes that came in once her candidacy was picked up by the national wire services. One of the nicest came from Felix Frankfurter. "My dear Senator," he began, "can it be that you are the good old girl I used to know—one of those rare reformers who was gay in the service of righteousness, gay and shrewd. What I've read of the Miss Mary Dewson who is trying to break into the Senate from Hancock County of the old Democratic state of Maine sounds like my old Molly. I'm wholly out of politics but wish for you."[51]

The state senate nomination was something of a lark, but it proved a highlight of Dewson's retirement years. The publicity brought her into contact with old workers from the New Deal, rekindling her warm association with that earlier period. By 1960, however, there were not many New Dealers left. Dewson's carefully preserved scrapbooks became necrologies of friends and colleagues with whom she had worked over the years. Nelle Schwartz died in 1955 and B.Z. Scott in 1958. Lucy Mason passed away in 1959, several years after her mind had gone. Dewson found it "pathetic to see such a valiant soul going through a final period when she is not her self. Like Belle Sherwin. Like so many." Perhaps the saddest loss was that of Lucy Ward Stebbins, who died in 1955 after a long illness. On her trip to California in 1952, Molly knew that she was seeing Lucy for the last time. "One by one we surrender," she mourned.[52]

Unlike Lucy Stebbins and Lucy Mason, Molly Dewson was blessed with good health until the end of her life.[53] Well into her eighties, she remained mentally sharp and suffered no real physical infirmities other than weak knees. She passed a driving test at the age of eighty-seven, although it took her two tries, and said she felt younger behind the wheel than at any other time. (Castine residents were less confident: they feared she would back her Buick down the town's steep streets right into the harbor.) She almost died from an acute attack of peritonitis in 1957, but recovered quickly enough to attend her sixtieth reunion at Wellesley later that spring. She sped her recovery by reading Arthur Schlesinger Jr.'s new book, *The Crisis of the Old Order.*[54]

Molly's Wellesley reunion was one of the last extended trips she made away from Castine. Undaunted by the compromises necessitated by old age, she claimed she had inherited a "tough strain" from her "old Injun fighting" great-great-grandfather Colonel Joe Williams, and she went on record as planning to live to ninety, by far the longest anyone had lived in her family for generations. "You can't lose me!" she exclaimed to Clara Beyer. "My address is permanent until the last day."[55]

Molly and Polly hit a spell of ill health in 1961 and 1962. In February, Polly slipped on the ice and broke her hip. She spent a month in the hospital, and it was November before she could come downstairs without the help of a walker. Dewson nearly exhausted herself with sixteen-hour days as she took charge of the household, the pets, and Polly's daily needs.[56] Just as Polly's hip healed in early 1962, calamity struck again. The day had gone well (Molly had passed her driver's test in Ellsworth), but after they went to bed, Polly awoke with chest pains. To make matters worse, one of the dogs urgently needed to go out. When Dewson got out of bed to take the dog downstairs, she slipped on the rug and cracked her collar bone. Meanwhile, Polly was having a heart attack. "The next thing anyone knows M.W.D. and I are in the Castine Hospital!" Dewson's injury was not serious, but Porter had another several-month convalescence before she could resume her normal routines. To top it off, their faithful housekeeper, Mrs. Leach, fell down the stairs and cracked two ribs. Not until late spring was Moss Acre back to normal.[57]

The summer of 1962 followed the patterns and rhythms that Polly and Molly had established during the more than fifty previous summers they shared in Castine. Dorothy Blake organized expeditions to Mt. Desert to see the rhodora in bloom; Castine friends picnicked on their shore. Bill Porter and Irma Lerner came for their annual summer visits. Molly cut back to one party a day, but Polly sometimes went to two. Still something of a political celebrity, Molly showed off her study (affectionately called "the FDR room" to this day) to visiting Democratic leaders, including the gubernatorial candidate who paid a courtesy call with Castine political leader Jimmie Sawyer. Molly had lunch with Eleanor Roosevelt at Bishop and Mrs. Scarlett's, and she and Polly went almost every Saturday night to the Grange. Dewson described her lifestyle as "just pleasant passing of the time," adding, "Of course to me it is a poor excuse for living and I envy my old working days . . . but at 87 one must be a philosopher."[58]

In mid-October, she had a real treat: a visit from her old Democratic buddies Clara Beyer, India Edwards, and Bea Stern. "The 4 Democrats," as Polly dubbed them, took a long drive to see the fall foliage and reminiscence about the 1930s. Polly told Clara Beyer soon after, "Your visit here was a real joy to M.W.D. She is devoted to you, but besides that, she loved to hear talk about the old times so very dear to her heart." But at eighty-eight, Molly realized her time was running out. Before her friends left, she took her dearest comrade from the old days aside and confided, "I'm not going to be here much longer, Clara." She could no longer get a driver's license and claimed she could not live without one. But she had no regrets. "I'm ready to go."[59] Eight days later she was dead.

The end came painlessly. Early on Wednesday morning, October 17, Dewson suffered a stroke while climbing out of bed. She was rushed unconscious to the Castine hospital, where she remained in a coma. Molly's capable niece came over from New Hampshire to stay with Polly, and the two women went about their daily routines while paying frequent visits to the hospital. The network of Castine friends that had so enriched their lives rallied around to help. Dewson remained in stable condition, although still unconscious; Polly reported that she looked peaceful and comfortable.

By Sunday, Molly was steadily failing, having developed pneumo-
nia and a high fever. The doctors told Polly that she was not likely to
regain consciousness in her present state, and Polly prayed for a painless
end. "They swear she does not suffer," Polly kept telling herself. She
paid one more visit to Dewson's room after dinner and then returned to
Moss Acre. Around 8:30 that evening came the call telling her that
Molly Dewson had died quietly without regaining consciousness. After
more than fifty years of partnership, Polly Porter was on her own.[60]

Molly Dewson was not the only prominent New Dealer to die in
the fall of 1962. On November 7th, barely two weeks later, Eleanor
Roosevelt died. The massive outpouring of emotion and respect for
Eleanor, the twentieth century's most well-known woman, stood in
stark contrast to the quiet ceremonies that surrounded her friend's end.

It seems uncanny yet strangely fitting that these two women,
whose lives were so intertwined during the New Deal, should have left
this life in tandem. Serving the Roosevelts gave Molly Dewson the
greatest satisfaction of her life; Eleanor and Franklin Roosevelt opened
doors that she could never have entered otherwise. In 1959, she had
joked to her old political comrade India Edwards, "Do you suppose that
by any chance Heaven will arrange get-together days or revival meetings?"[61] If such a heavenly New Deal reunion ever took place, Molly
Dewson would likely be sitting at the right hand of Eleanor and at the
feet of Franklin Delano Roosevelt.

Notes

INTRODUCTION

1. Mary W. Dewson, "An Aid to the End" (unpublished autobiography, 1949), 1:46–47, in Mary Dewson papers, Schlesinger Library, Radcliffe College.

2. Quoted in *The Reminiscences of Maurine Mulliner* (1967), 129, in the Oral History Collection of Columbia University.

3. William L. Riordan, *Plunkitt of Tammany Hall: A Series of Very Plain Talks on Very Practical Politics* (New York, 1963), 3.

4. For example, see Kathryn Kish Sklar, "Hull House in the 1890s: A Community of Women Reformers," *Signs* 10 (Summer 1985): 658–77.

5. Dewson to Mrs. Elizabeth Borden, November 20, 1952, Dewson papers, Schlesinger.

6. See Estelle Freedman, "Separatism as Strategy: Female Institution Building and American Feminism, 1870–1930," *Feminist Studies* 5 (Fall 1979): 512–29. Many of the ideas developed in this introduction were suggested by Freedman's hypothesis. See also Blanche Wiesen Cook, "Female Support Networks and Political Activism," in Nancy Cott and Elizabeth Pleck, eds., *A Heritage of Her Own* (New York, 1979), 412–44.

7. I am using the definition of feminism formulated by Linda Gordon in *Woman's Body, Woman's Right: Birth Control in America* (New York, 1976), xiv: "sharing in an impulse to increase the power and autonomy of women in their families, communities and/or society."

CHAPTER 1: A NEW ENGLAND GIRLHOOD

1. Dewson to Clara Beyer, February 18, 1943, Clara M. Beyer papers, Schlesinger Library, Radcliffe College; Dewson to Lorena Hickok, November 21, 1952, Mary Dewson papers, Schlesinger.

2. Dewson to Clara Beyer, February 18, 1943, Beyer papers, Schlesinger.

3. Dewson to Felix Frankfurter, December 14, 1932, Felix Frankfurter papers, Library of Congress.

4. Mary W. Dewson, "My Little Mother," 14–15, MS in Dewson papers, Schlesinger. For a more complete genealogy, see "Family Portraits of Mary W. Dewson," scrapbook in possession of Virginia Bourne, Moss Acre, Castine, Maine.

5. Dewson, "My Little Mother," 14, 16. Material for reconstructing Dewson and Williams family history can be found at the Quincy Historical Society and the Quincy Public Library.

6. Dewson, "My Little Mother," 2.

7. Ibid., 13.

8. Henry Adams, The Education of Henry Adams (1918; repr. Boston, 1961), 8.

9. Charles Francis Adams, Three Episodes of Massachusetts History (Boston, 1892), 2:644, 927–28, 954. For further background on Quincy, see William S. Pattee, A History of Old Braintree and Quincy (Quincy, 1878); and William Churchill Edwards, Historic Quincy Massachusetts (Quincy, 1957).

10. Edgar Hoover, Jr., Location Theory and the Shoe and Leather Industries (Cambridge, 1937), 135, 269; John A. Garraty, The New Commonwealth, 1877–1890 (New York, 1968), 82; Alan Dawley, Class and Community: The Industrial Revolution in Lynn (Cambridge, 1976).

11. A trade journal, The Shoe and Leather Reporter Annual of 1886 (Boston, 1886), 379, listed Dewson on the board of the New England Shoe and Leather Association, a leading trade group. For family connections, see Quincy City Directory, 1868–1912; and listings in the Shoe and Leather Reporter for the same period.

12. Dewson, "My Little Mother," 13, 17; Pattee, A History of Old Braintree and Quincy, 440–43.

13. For contemporary descriptions of such diseases and their manifestations, see William Alexander Hamilton, A Treatise on the Diseases of the Nervous System (New York, 1876); and S. Weir Mitchell, Lectures on Diseases of the Nervous System, especially in Women (Philadelphia, 1881). See also Charles E. Rosenberg, "The Place of George M. Beard in Nineteenth Century Psychiatry," Bulletin of the History of Medicine 36 (1962): 245–59.

14. When Edward Dewson died in 1898, the cause of death was listed as a chronic ulcer. Vital Records, August 11, 1898, Clerk's Office, Quincy, Massachusetts.

15. Most recent historical writing along these lines has focused on female illness: the historian Carroll Smith-Rosenberg and others have argued that female

invalids used diseases like hysteria as a revolt against the roles of wife, mother, and domestic slave decreed for their sex in nineteenth century America. Alice James, for example, retreated into a life of female invalidism when she was unable to reconcile being a woman with being a member of the talented James family.

Neurasthenia was not just a woman's disease, however: many late nineteenth-century neurasthenics were men. Perhaps these men used such illnesses to avoid gender definitions as well. As Barbara Sicherman has pointed out, "If women were sometimes expected, and perhaps even encouraged, to be weak and sickly, an ethos of fortitude made it difficult for men to exhibit weakness of any kind. Illness, in all its presumed objectivity, was one of the permissible exceptions." For further discussion, see Carroll Smith-Rosenberg, "The Hysterical Woman: Sex Roles and Role Conflict in 19th Century America," *Social Research* 39 (Winter 1972): 652–78; Carroll Smith-Rosenberg and Charles Rosenberg, "The Female Animal: Medical and Biological Views of Woman and Her Role in Nineteenth Century America," *Journal of American History* 60 (September 1973): 332–56; Jean Strouse, *Alice James: A Biography* (Boston, 1980); Barbara Sicherman, "The Uses of a Diagnosis: Doctors, Patients, and Neurasthenia," *Journal of the History of Medicine* 32 (January 1977): 33–54.

16. For general background, see Barbara Welter, "The Cult of True Womanhood, 1820–1860," *American Quarterly* 18 (1966): 151–74; Kathryn Kish Sklar, *Catharine Beecher: A Study in American Domesticity* (New Haven, 1973); Nancy F. Cott, *The Bonds of Womanhood* (New Haven, 1977); Ann Douglas, *The Feminization of American Culture* (New York, 1977).

17. Dewson, "As I Remember My Mother," 8, MS in Dewson papers, Schlesinger. This seems to have been an earlier draft of "My Little Mother" and contains some quotations and vignettes not found in the other version.

18. Ibid., 14; Dewson, "My Little Mother," 5.

19. See Douglas, *The Feminization of American Culture*; and Sandra M. Gilbert and Susan Gubar, *The Madwoman in the Attic* (New Haven, 1979).

20. Dewson, "My Little Mother," 16.

21. Ibid., 18.

22. For example, Mr. Dewson helped to organize the celebration of the church's 250th anniversary in 1889. See "The 'Chappel of Ease' and Church of Statesmen: Commemorative Services of the Completion of 250 years since the gathering of the First Church of Christ in Quincy" (Quincy, 1890), 133.

23. Dewson, "My Little Mother," 20–21.

24. Ibid., 17.

25. Dewson to Lorena Hickok, November 21, 1952, Dewson papers, Schlesinger.

26. Dewson, "As I Remember My Mother," 14.

27. Quoted in a fragment of a biography begun by Dewson's niece, Virginia Stone, in the 1930s. Currently in the possession of Virginia Bourne, Castine, Maine.

28. Dewson, "As I Remember My Mother," 9–10; Dewson, "My Little Mother," 17–18.

29. Dewson, "My Little Mother," 10; Dewson, "As I Remember My Mother," 1.

30. Dewson, "As I Remember My Mother," 2; Dewson, "My Little Mother," 8–9. Molly described the onset of a menstrual period to her sister in a note not intended for family consumption: "Yesterday was my 1st day week too early ditto the time before. I went to recitations then to bed early and cut today as they were not so important." Molly Dewson to Ellen Dewson, October 1893, Wellesley College letters, in possession of Virginia Bourne, Moss Acre, Castine, Maine.

31. The four brothers and one sister led completely conventional lives; their sister's choices stand out in stark contrast.

32. Dewson, "My Little Mother," 17; Dewson to family, late January 1894, and n.d. [1893–94], Wellesley College letters, Moss Acre.

33. *The Reminiscences of Frances Perkins* (1955), 3:180, 490–91, in The Oral History Collection of Columbia University.

34. Dewson cited by name Cousin Carrie Lane, Miss Abbie Gourgas, Cousin Frannie Whitcher, Cousin Sarah Preston, Mrs. George Wendell, Mrs. Henry Johnson, Mrs. Joseph Brewer, Mrs. James Barr Ames, Mrs. Charles Putnam, and Miss Julia Eastman. See "My Little Mother," 22; Dewson, "As I Remember My Mother," 20.

35. Dewson, "As I Remember My Mother," 19, 20.

CHAPTER 2: THE EDUCATION OF MOLLY DEWSON

1. Dewson to Lorena Hickok, November 21, 1952, Mary Dewson papers, Schlesinger Library, Radcliffe College.

2. Warren Leon, "High School: A Study of Youth and Community in Quincy, Massachusetts" (Ph.D. diss., Harvard University, 1979).

3. Records of Adams Academy, Quincy Historical Society; obituary of Edward H. Dewson, Jr., February 10, 1939, *Quincy Patriot Ledger*; obituary of George Badger Dewson, April 28, 1939, *Quincy Patriot Ledger*; Resume, Dewson papers, Schlesinger. See also Dewson to Lorena Hickok, November 21, 1952, Dewson papers, Schlesinger.

4. Emily Greene Balch, "Catharine Innes Ireland, 1838–1925: A Memorial" (1929), in Erin Go Bragh [Ireland Forever] papers, Schlesinger. Balch, winner of the 1946 Nobel Prize for Peace, was one of Miss Ireland's most illustrious graduates. Balch went directly from Miss Ireland's in 1886 to the newly opened Bryn Mawr College, and she always credited her later academic success to the superior academic training she had received at Miss Ireland's. In 1896, she joined the Wellesley faculty, where she was one of Molly Dewson's favorite professors. See Barbara Miller Solomon, "Emily Greene Balch," in Barbara Sicherman and Carol

Hurd Green, eds., *Notable American Women: The Modern Period* (Cambridge, 1980), 41–45.

5. Anna Putnam to Ellen Dewson, 1892; and Edward Dewson to Molly Dewson, April 19, 1894, Wellesley College letters in the possession of Virginia Bourne, Moss Acre, Castine, Maine.

6. The best general introduction to the history of higher education for women in America is Barbara Miller Solomon, *In The Company of Educated Women* (New Haven, 1985); pp. 119–22 discuss marriage rates for educated women at the turn of the century. For further background, see Mable Newcomer, *A Century of Higher Education for American Women* (New York, 1959); and Helen Lefkowitz Horowitz, *Alma Mater: Design and Experience in the Women's Colleges from Their Nineteenth-Century Beginnings to the 1930s* (New York, 1984).

7. See the letter cited below (Edward Dewson to Molly Dewson, April 13, 1894, Wellesley College letters, Moss Acre), in which he tells his daughter he is "no lunatic except on the subject of equal rights for women." See also an unpublished 1896 essay on Abigail Adams in Edward Dewson's handwriting, which includes this statement: "At this season, when our institutions of learning are turning out thousands of well equipped women ready to stand by the side of man on equal terms, and share with him in the duties and responsibilities of life . . ." Moss Acre, Castine.

8. Material on Dana Hall found in "Family Portraits" scrapbook, Moss Acre; Archives of the Dana Hall School, Wellesley, Mass.

9. Material on the Eastmans found in Dewson papers, Schlesinger, including an obituary of Julia Eastman from the *Boston Transcript*, January 2, 1911; *Bulletin*, 1891, Dana Hall Archives.

10. "Memorabilia, 1944–1948" and "Family Portraits" scrapbooks, Moss Acre; Dewson to Family, fall 1893, Wellesley College Letters, Moss Acre. In Dallas after the 1936 election she happened to meet one of the other five members of the Dana Hall political club. This woman too was still active in Democratic politics. Dewson to Hickok, November 21, 1952, Dewson papers, Schlesinger; Mary W. Dewson, "An Aid to the End" (unpublished autobiography, 1949), 2:189, Dewson papers, Schlesinger.

11. General background on Wellesley has been drawn from Florence Converse, *The Story of Wellesley* (Boston, 1915); Converse, *Wellesley College: A Chronicle of the Years 1875–1939* (Wellesley, 1939); Jean Glasscock, ed., *Wellesley College, 1875–1975: A Century of Women* (Wellesley, 1975); and Horowitz, *Alma Mater*.

12. Dewson to Family, September 28, 1893; Molly Dewson to Ellen Dewson, n.d. [fall 1893]; Dewson to Family, n.d. [late January 1894] and May 30, 1895, Wellesley College Letters, Moss Acre.

13. Dewson to Family, January 1894, and November 1893, Wellesley College Letters, Moss Acre.

14. Dewson to Family, October 1895, Wellesley College letters, Moss Acre.

15. Converse, *The Story of Wellesley*, 119.

16. Note on letter from Kendall to Dewson, December 17, 1939, Dewson papers, Schlesinger; "Memorabilia, 1944–1948," scrapbook, Moss Acre; Dewson to Family, n.d. [fall 1893] and November 1893, Wellesley College letters, Moss Acre. Further biographical material on Kendall can be found in the Wellesley College Archives.

17. Dewson to Family, September 17, 1893; November 1893; January 1894, Wellesley College letters, Moss Acre. Dewson and Kendall remained in contact until Kendall's death at the age of ninety-seven in 1952. In her will, Dewson left five thousand dollars (her largest bequest) to Wellesley to establish a lecture series in Kendall's name. It is currently administered by the political science department.

18. Dewson to Family, n.d. [fall 1895], Wellesley College letters, Moss Acre.

19. Allen Davis, "Katharine Coman," in Edward T. James and Janet James, eds., *Notable American Women: A Biographical Dictionary, 1607–1950* (Cambridge, 1971), 1:365–67.

20. Catalogue, 1895–96, Wellesley College Archives.

21. This course, which she took first semester her senior year, and Social Pathology, taught by Coman's protégé Emily Greene Balch second semester, were both graduate-level courses for which Dewson needed special permission from the faculty council to count toward her undergraduate degree. Her friend Mary Woolley, later the president of Mount Holyoke College but then a popular young instructor in the Bible department, "spoke of the lovely way in which Miss Coman presented my cause. Made me feel quite stuck up." Her petition was granted. Dewson to Family, undated [fall 1896], Wellesley College letters, Moss Acre.

22. Dewson quoted in Converse, *The Story of Wellesley*, 144–45.

23. Denison House papers, Schlesinger. Dewson's name is never included in the lists of student volunteers, although other classmates like Belle Sherwin and Mary Haskell were mentioned.

24. Patricia Ann Palmieri, "In Adamless Eve: A Social Portrait of the Academic Community at Wellesley College, 1875–1920" (Ph.D. diss., Harvard University, 1981), esp. pts. 4 ("A Social Portrait of Academic Women at Wellesley College, 1900–1910") and 6 ("The Communal Experience"). See also by the same author "Patterns of Achievement of Single Academic Women at Wellesley College, 1880–1920," *Frontiers* 5 (1980); and "Here Was Fellowship: A Social Portrait of Academic Women at Wellesley College, 1880–1920," *History of Education Quarterly* 23 (Summer 1983).

25. This is a variation of the term *Boston Marriage*, used to describe such relationships. For further discussion of this phenomenon, see chaps. 4, 6.

26. Dewson to Family, fall 1896, Wellesley College letters, Moss Acre. Although Dewson never had Mary Woolley as a professor, she knew her well enough to be invited down to the Woolley family home in Pawtucket, Rhode Island, the

summer before her junior year. See note in Mary Dewson papers, Franklin D. Roosevelt Library, Hyde Park, New York.

27. Dewson to Family, February 19, 1896; October 1895, Wellesley College letters, Moss Acre.

28. Dewson to Family, November 1896, Wellesley College letters, Moss Acre. Dean Stratton was asked to leave at the end of the 1896–97 academic year.

29. Dewson to Family, December 1895, Wellesley College letters, Moss Acre. For example, she worked especially hard on a paper about early trade unions that she was to deliver to a college social club, because she knew Vida Scudder would be there. She admitted, "I was glad she noticed me at all enough to remember me, for I'm that mercenary everything counts and I did be extra particular on her account." She approached her relationships with Kendall and Coman in a similar fashion. See Dewson to Family, n.d. [fall 1896], Wellesley College letters, Moss Acre.

30. This idea is developed by Joyce Antler, "'After College, What?': New Graduates and the Family Claim," *American Quarterly* 32 (Fall 1980): 409–34. See also chap. 4.

31. Edward Dewson to Molly Dewson, April 13, 1894, Wellesley College letters, Moss Acre.

32. Molly Dewson to Ellen Dewson, October 1893, Wellesley College letters, Moss Acre.

33. *Classbook—Wellesley, '97* (Wellesley, Mass., 1897), 30, Dewson papers, Schlesinger.

34. Horowitz, *Alma Mater*, contains a good discussion of such rituals at the Seven Sisters colleges.

35. Glasscock, *Wellesley College: A Century of Women*, 240–43.

36. Dewson to Family, November 23, 1896, Wellesley College letters, Moss Acre.

37. Dewson to Family, late January 1894, Wellesley College letters, Moss Acre.

38. Dewson to Family, April 14, 1894, and April 29, 1894, Wellesley College letters, Moss Acre.

39. Horowitz, *Alma Mater*, 162–66.

40. Nancy Sahli, "Smashing: Women's Relationships before the Fall," *Chrysalis* 8 (Summer 1979), 21. See also Horowitz, *Alma Mater*, 64–68, 166–69.

41. Dana Hall and Wellesley scrapbook, 1891–97, Moss Acre.

42. Material on Phi Sigma is found in the records of Phi Sigma, Wellesley College Archives.

43. Molly Dewson to Frank Dewson, undated [1895–96], Wellesley College letters, Moss Acre.

44. Dewson to Family, September 28, 1893, Wellesley College letters, Moss Acre. Molly Dewson did not have an allowance: she simply asked her parents for

money when she needed it, usually two or three dollars at a time. Since she sent all her laundry home, had all her clothes made by her sister, and relied primarily on library books for her course reading, her main cash expenditure was the train fare between Wellesley and Quincy.

45. Dewson to Family, n.d., Wellesley College letters, Moss Acre.

46. Minutes of Phi Sigma, May 15, 1895, Phi Sigma records, Wellesley College Archives; Dewson to Nell Dewson, undated, Wellesley College letters, Moss Acre.

47. Molly Dewson to Frank Dewson, September, 1895, Wellesley College letters, Moss Acre. For Dewson's activism on campus toward improving the athletic facilities, see her article in *The Wellesley Magazine* 4 (May 1896): 463–64.

48. Dewson to Nell Dewson, October, 1893; Dewson to Family, undated [fall 1893], Wellesley College letters, Moss Acre.

49. For descriptions of these matches, see *The Wellesley Magazine*, June 1894, November 1894, and November 1895, Wellesley College Archives. For Dewson's book-buying, see Wellesley College letters, Moss Acre.

50. Dewson to Family, undated [late October 1895], Wellesley College letters, Moss Acre.

51. Dewson to Family, October 29, 1895; May 26, 1896, Wellesley College letters, Moss Acre.

52. Class of 1897 records, Wellesley College Archives. Although there was no official student government until 1901, each class had its own organization, by-laws, and officers. The 1897 class constitution is in Dewson's handwriting.

53. Note by Molly Dewson pencilled in *Classbook, Wellesley '97*; class minutes, March 3, 1894, March 14, 1894, October 11, 1894, and October 12, 1895, Class of 1897 records, Wellesley College Archives.

54. Geneva Crumb scrapbook, Class of 1897 records, Wellesley College archives.

55. Dewson to Family, May 10, 1896, Wellesley College letters, Moss Acre.

56. Dewson to Family, May 27, 1896, Wellesley College letters, Moss Acre; *Classbook, Wellesley '97*, 32. To reconstruct the deadlock, see the class minutes from May, 1896, Class of 1897 records, Wellesley College archives.

57. Edward Dewson to Molly Dewson, May 30, 1896, and June 2, 1896, Wellesley College letters, Moss Acre. South Street, in the heart of Boston's leather district, was the location of her father's business.

58. *Classbook, Wellesley '97*, 65.

CHAPTER 3: A PROGRESSIVE APPRENTICESHIP

1. *Wellesley '97 Classbook* (1910), 15, found in Mary Dewson papers, Schlesinger Library, Radcliffe College.

2. Daniel T. Rodgers, "In Search of Progressivism," *Reviews in American History* (December 1982): 113–32, provides an overview and attempt at synthesis.

Paula Baker, "The Domestication of Politics: Women and American Political Society, 1780–1920," *The American Historical Review* 89 (June 1984): 620–47, provocatively compares male and female political culture in the period. A recent book that stresses the moral idealism of the Progressive generation is Robert M. Crunden, *Ministers of Reform: The Progressives' Achievement in American Civilization, 1889–1920* (New York, 1982).

3. Elizabeth Cabot Putnam to Elizabeth Glendower Evans, August 24, 1903, Elizabeth Glendower Evans papers, Schlesinger.

4. Ibid.

5. Dewson to Barbara Miller Solomon, October 20, 1959; Dewson to Lorena Hickok, November 21, 1952; Katharine Coman to Dewson, May-June, 1897; resume, all in Dewson papers, Schlesinger.

6. Dewson to Family, n.d. [December 1896], Wellesley College letters in the possession of Virginia Bourne, Moss Acre, Castine, Maine. Dewson asked her Wellesley professors Katharine Coman and Elizabeth Kendall to write her letters of recommendation, which were so flattering that she boasted, "Bless the old ladies souls but they were more than kind," as she sent copies home to her family. Dewson was so proud of these letters that she mounted them in her scrapbook and later made copies for her papers at the Schlesinger and Roosevelt Libraries.

7. Dewson to Family, n.d. [December 1896], Wellesley College letters, Moss Acre; Wellesley College scrapbook, Moss Acre; Charles E. McLenegan to Dewson, July 10, 1897, Dewson papers, Schlesinger. Frances Perkins, whose family background and career development were similar to Dewson's, taught briefly after her graduation from Mount Holyoke. After several years, she decided her interests lay in social reform and settlement work rather than teaching. Molly Dewson might have followed a similar route. See George Martin, *Madam Secretary: Frances Perkins* (Boston, 1976).

8. Dewson to Elizabeth Glendower Evans, October 10, 1936, Evans papers, Schlesinger. See also Dewson to Alice Goldmark Brandeis, November 30, 1935, Evans papers, Schlesinger, where she asserts that Evans "really gave me my start in life."

9. Biographical material can be found in the Elizabeth Glendower Evans papers at Schlesinger and in Paul C. Taylor, "Elizabeth Glendower Evans," in Edward T. James and Janet James, eds., *Notable American Women: A Biographical Dictionary* (Cambridge, 1971), 1:588–89.

10. Elizabeth Glendower Evans to Dickinson Miller, February 20, 1933, Evans papers, Schlesinger.

11. The influence of Elizabeth Glendower Evans far outweighed that of Elizabeth Cabot Putnam, the same "Miss Lizzie" whose bonnet the young Molly Dewson used to retrieve from under dusty sofas as a child. Putnam had neither the forceful personality nor the wide-ranging connections to match Evans's ability to launch a career. For examples of biography structured around the role of mentors in a woman's life, see Elisabeth Griffith, *In Her Own Right: The Life of Elizabeth*

Cady Stanton (New York, 1984); and Ellen Condliffe Lagemann, *A Generation of Women: Education in the Lives of Progressive Reformers* (Cambridge, 1979).

12. Background on the WEIU is found in the extensive Women's Educational and Industrial Union papers at the Schlesinger Library; and in Karen J. Blair, *The Clubwoman as Feminist: True Womanhood Redefined, 1868–1914* (New York, 1980), esp. pp. 73–91. See also Agnes Donham, "The History of the Women's Educational and Industrial Union" (MS, 1955), WEIU papers, Schlesinger.

13. "History of the Domestic Reform League" (1903), WEIU papers, Schlesinger.

14. Despite her impressive credentials in economics and statistical research, Dewson had given little thought to domestic service as a social or economic issue. A recurring topic in the letters back and forth between Quincy and Wellesley was the inadequacy of the servants in the Dewson household. The only time Molly did any domestic work herself was at Wellesley, where the young women were expected to take care of their own rooms as well as do four hours a week of domestic work at the college. "I am learning more thoroughly than any thing else here how to be a first class second girl, between the dusting, sweeping, washing and waiting on table, not to mention chamberwork," she complained half-humorously after a month of classes. When domestic work was abolished her senior year, Molly was delighted: "I want to tell you how grand it is to have the maids. It's like living on roses." Dewson's sympathy for the life of the domestic worker was obviously incomplete. See Dewson to Family, October 8, 1893, and October 26, 1896, Wellesley College letters, Moss Acre. For Mrs. Dewson's complaints, see letters from Elizabeth Dewson to Molly Dewson, n.d. [1891–93], in the possession of Peter Hall.

15. Mary W. Dewson, agent, "The Effort to Attract the Workers in Shops and Factories to Domestic Service" (1897), WEIU papers, Schlesinger. For further background on domestic service in New England, see Faye Dudden, *Serving Women* (Middletown, Conn., 1982); and Carol S. Lasser, "Maid, Mistress, and Market" (Ph.D. diss., Harvard University, 1982).

16. "The Hours of Labor in Domestic Service," *Massachusetts Labor Bulletin* 8 (October 1898); "Social Conditions in Domestic Service," *Massachusetts Labor Bulletin* 13 (February 1900).

17. Dewson to Lorena Hickok, November 21, 1952, Dewson papers, Schlesinger. Dewson, however, never became so enamored of statistics and research to contemplate an academic career, as did Edith Abbott. See Lela Costin, *Two Sisters for Social Justice: A Biography of Grace and Edith Abbott* (Urbana, Ill., 1983), which portrays Edith as the scholar and Grace as the activist who translates knowledge into policy. Although she combined elements of both, Molly Dewson was far closer in temperament and style to Grace Abbott than to her sister Edith.

18. "The School of Housekeeping," catalogue and prospectus, Dewson papers, Schlesinger. For more background, see the WEIU papers at Schlesinger and Donham, "A History of the WEIU."

19. Janet Wilson James, "Ellen Swallow Richards," *Notable American*

Women, 3:143–46. For background on the Home Economics movement, see Margaret Rossiter, *Women Scientists in America: Struggles and Strategies to 1940* (Baltimore, 1982).

20. Dewson to Barbara Miller Solomon, October 20, 1959, and note, Dewson papers, Schlesinger. Both Schlesinger and the Roosevelt Library contain copies of the expense book.

21. Dewson to Herman Kahn, January 29, 1959, Dewson papers, Schlesinger.

22. Ibid.

23. Mary W. Dewson, "My Little Mother," 11, MS in Dewson papers, Schlesinger.

24. For background on Lancaster, see Barbara Brenzel, *Daughters of the State* (Cambridge, 1983), and Brenzel, "Lancaster Industrial School for Girls: A Social Portrait of a Nineteenth Century Reform School for Girls," *Feminist Studies* 3, 1/2 (1975): 40–53. For general background on the history of juvenile delinquency, see Robert M. Mennel, *Thorns and Thistles: Juvenile Delinquents in the United States, 1824–1940* (Hanover, N.H., 1973), and Steven L. Schlossman, *Love and the American Delinquent: The Theory and Practice of "Progressive" Juvenile Justice, 1825–1920* (Chicago, 1977). See also Joan Jacobs Brumberg, "'Ruined' Girls: Changing Community Responses to Illegitimacy in Upstate New York, 1890–1920," *Journal of Social History* 18, 2 (Winter 1984), 247–72.

25. Elizabeth Cabot Putnam to LeBaron Briggs, February 3, 1909, Radcliffe Archives; Elizabeth Glendower Evans, unpublished article on Elizabeth Cabot Putnam, 1904, Evans papers, Schlesinger.

26. Elizabeth Cabot Putnam to LeBaron Briggs, 1909, in Dewson papers, Schlesinger. Dewson worked out of Boston rather than Lancaster because one of her main responsibilities was to find employment for girls released on probation. Since most girls were placed in domestic service, Boston and its suburbs provided the best job opportunities.

27. See *Trustees' Report of the Lyman and Industrial Schools*, 1902–1910, passim. Molly Dewson donated a set of these reports, carefully annotated wherever she is mentioned, to the Schlesinger Library.

28. Her initial salary was around $1,400. By 1906, she was earning $1,500, and by 1911, her salary reached $2,000 a year.

29. Mary W. Dewson, "The Social Worker," *Wellesley Magazine* 13 (February 1905), 174–75.

30. Dewson to Lorena Hickok, November 21, 1952, Dewson papers, Schlesinger.

31. Dewson, "Public Work: Visitors for Children and Girls and Officers of the State Industrial School," speech, n.d., Dewson papers, Schlesinger; Dewson, "Report of the Superintendent," *Trustees' Report of the Lyman and Industrial Schools* (December 1907), 92; ibid. (December 1909), 70.

32. *Wellesley '97 Classbook* (1910), 15, Dewson papers, Schlesinger; Eliz-

abeth Glendower Evans and Mary W. Dewson, "Feeblemindedness and Juvenile Delinquency: A Study from Experiences," *Charities and the Commons* (May 2, 1908), 186; Dewson, "Report of the Superintendent," *Trustees' Report of the Lyman and Industrial Schools* (October, 1905), 84.

33. Barbara Miller Solomon, *Ancestors and Immigrants: A Changing New England Tradition* (Cambridge, 1956), 145–51; John Higham, *Strangers in the Land: Patterns of American Nativism, 1860–1925* (Rutgers, 1955), 150–53. See also Daniel J. Kevles, *In the Name of Eugenics: Genetics and the Uses of Human Heredity* (New York, 1985).

34. Evans and Dewson, "Feeblemindedness and Juvenile Delinquency," 185, 188.

35. Brenzel, *Daughters of the State*, identifies a similar pattern. See also Ruth Rosen, *The Lost Sisterhood: Prostitution in America, 1900–1918* (Baltimore, 1982), 22–23, for the application of the label *feebleminded* to prostitutes.

36. See Sophonisba Breckinridge to Dewson, May 22, 1911; February 23, 1912; and September 30, 1912, in Dewson papers, Schlesinger. Dewson admired Breckinridge tremendously: "She registered slightly below Jane Addams" (Moss Acre scrapbook).

37. On Radcliffe, see letters from Elizabeth Cabot Putnam and Charles Putnam to LeBaron Briggs, March 22, 1909, and April 29, 1909, Radcliffe Archives. Material on Dewson's other job offers and social work contacts is found in Dewson papers, Schlesinger.

38. Mary W. Dewson, "An Aid to the End" (unpublished autobiography, 1949), 1:14, in Dewson papers, Schlesinger.

39. For general background, see James T. Patterson, *America's Struggle Against Poverty, 1900–1980* (Cambridge, 1981), and Robert H. Bremner, *From the Depths: The Discovery of Poverty in the United States* (New York, 1956).

40. Background appears in Josephine Goldmark, *Impatient Crusader: Florence Kelley's Life Story* (Urbana, Ill., 1953); Dorothy R. Blumberg, *Florence Kelley: Social Pioneer* (New York, 1966); and Judith A. Baer, *The Chains of Protection: The Judicial Response to Women's Labor Legislation* (Westport, Conn., 1978). See also "The Development of Minimum Wages Laws in the United States, 1912–1927," *Women's Bureau Bulletin* 61 (Washington, D.C., 1928).

41. Elizabeth Glendower Evans, "Interesting People I Have Known: Florence Kelley, Always a Pioneer," newspaper article, 1934, Evans papers, Schlesinger.

42. The Massachusetts political scene is well described in Arthur Mann, *Yankee Reformers in the Urban Age* (Cambridge, 1954); Richard Abrams, *Conservatives in a Progressive Era: Massachusetts Politics, 1900–1912* (Cambridge, 1964); and H. LaRue Brown, "Massachusetts and the Minimum Wage," *Annals of the American Academy of Political and Social Science* 48 (July 1913), 13–21.

43. Dewson, Ford Hall Memorial Tribute to Elizabeth Glendower Evans, January 28, 1938, Dewson papers, Schlesinger.

44. *Report of the Commission on Minimum Wage Boards* (January, 1912), published by the Commonwealth of Massachusetts. The final report ran to 326 pages, over 200 of which were devoted to Molly Dewson's statistics and analysis. See also Mary W. Dewson, "Pay Rolls and Profits," *The Survey* (November 9, 1912), 174–75.

45. *Report of the Commission on Minimum Wage Boards*, 9–10; Baer, *The Chains of Protection*, 73.

46. *Report of the Commission on Minimum Wage Boards*, 188–89. Evans's article about Florence Kelley in the "Interesting People I Have Known" series confirms that Molly Dewson did the interview, although she is not cited by name in the final report.

47. H. LaRue Brown, "Massachusetts and the Minimum Wage," 15.

48. Ibid., 15–16, discusses the components of the law as it finally passed.

49. James T. Patterson, "Mary Dewson and the American Minimum Wage Movement," *Labor History* 5 (Spring 1964), 134–52. See also Goldmark, *Impatient Crusader*.

50. Mabel Gillespie to Dewson, December 31, 1912, Dewson papers, Schlesinger.

51. James Patterson first developed this idea in his 1964 article, "Mary Dewson and the American Minimum Wage Movement."

CHAPTER 4: POLLY

1. *Wellesley '97 Classbook* (1910), 15, Mary Dewson papers, Schlesinger Library, Radcliffe College.

2. For discussions of the difference that supportive families could make to women's professional aspirations, see Joyce Antler, "'After College, What?': New Graduates and the Family Claim," *American Quarterly* 32 (Fall 1980): 409–34, and Patricia A. Palmieri, "Patterns of Achievement of Single Academic Women at Wellesley College, 1880–1920," *Frontiers* 5 (Spring 1980), 63–67.

3. Mary W. Dewson, "As I Remember My Mother," 22, MS in Dewson papers, Schlesinger.

4. For Stebbins's view of social work, see "Opportunities for Social Service," *Radcliffe Magazine* 12 (April 1910), 133–36. Biographical material on Stebbins can be found in the Radcliffe Archives.

5. This characterization was supplied by family friend Dorothy Blake in an interview in her Castine, Maine, home, October 4, 1980. Blake had known Polly Porter since the 1890s.

6. She worked with Joseph Lee on the playground movement and served under Lee on a committee of social workers who volunteered in the aftermath of the Chelsea Fire of 1907. She belonged to the Monday Evening Club (an organization of Boston's paid social workers) and often spoke to women's clubs on domestic service and female juvenile delinquency. Dewson was also active in alumnae affairs

through Wellesley College, presiding over class reunions and keeping up with Phi Sigma affairs. She was also a member of the Boston branch of the Association of College Alumnae, the forerunner of the American Association of University Women. See Dewson papers, Schlesinger; Wellesley College archives.

7. William Inglee Dewson, formerly of the family leather business, now listed his occupation as superintendent. He died in 1923, and the house was sold soon after.

8. Guest Book, and Theater Scrapbook, Moss Acre, Castine, Maine; catalogue in Dewson papers, Schlesinger.

9. Elizabeth Glendower Evans, "Interesting People I Have Known—Florence Kelley, Always a Pioneer," newspaper article (1934), in Elizabeth Glendower Evans papers, Schlesinger. Dorothy Blake provided the vignette about Polly no longer needing a chaperone in her October 4, 1980, interview.

10. Dewson, "As I Remember My Mother," 13.

11. Note, Dewson papers, Schlesinger.

12. Scrapbooks in the possession of Peter Hall contain real estate brochures from the spring of 1911.

13. See Jane Addams, "Filial Relations," in Anne F. Scott, ed., *Democracy and Social Ethics* (Cambridge, 1964); and "The Subjective Necessity for Social Settlements," in Jane Addams, *Twenty Years at Hull House* (New York, 1910). Elizabeth Dewson's obituary appeared in the *Quincy Patriot Ledger*, December 29, 1912.

14. Registry of Deeds, June 6, 1912, bk. 1996, p. 246, Worcester County Courthouse, Worcester, Massachusetts; Ruby A. Black, "Mary W. Dewson," *Equal Rights* (August 8, 1936), found in Dewson papers, Schlesinger.

15. The December 25, 1912, inscription was found in a book by Katharine Lee Bates entitled *Spanish Highways and Byways*, which is found in the living room at Moss Acre.

16. For sharing recollections and material on Polly Porter, I am greatly indebted to her godchildren, Marion Hall Hunt and Peter Hall. Virginia Bourne also helped me to understand her "Aunt Poll." Other background was supplied by interviews with Dorothy Blake, October 4, 1980, Castine, Maine; and James Barr Ames, July 28, 1981, Boston.

17. *William Deering, 1826–1913* (privately printed, Chicago, 1914), Moss Acre. The Northwestern University Archives contain extensive material on the Deering family.

18. The Deering genealogy was reconstructed from the application of Charles Deering to the Chicago Historical Society, found in Deering Family papers, Northwestern University Archives. See also the 1907 manuscript by Charles Deering about his father's life, Deering Family papers, Northwestern. Polly Porter's daybook of March 9, 1955 [Moss Acre], records that date as the 107th anniversary of her father's birth. The family connections may have been even stronger, since

William Reed Porter and Deering's first wife, Abby Reed Barbour, shared a common middle name, suggesting they were cousins.

19. James Deering later built Villa Vizcaya, a grand Italian palazzo on the Biscayne Bay in Florida. He was Polly's distant cousin, and she kept clippings about his doings in her scrapbook. See "The Deerings . . . A First View," *Miami Herald*, March 23, 1958.

20. Deering Family papers, Northwestern; *Evanston City Directory* (Chicago: R. R. Donnelly and Sons), 1879–95.

21. Conversation with Peter Hall, June, 1981; Katharine Beebe to Peter Hall, n.d. [c. 1972], in the possession of Peter Hall.

22. Katharine Beebe to Peter Hall, undated [c. 1972], in the possession of Peter Hall.

23. Interview with Dorothy Blake, October 4, 1980, Castine, Maine.

24. Records of the estate of William D. Porter are found in the Hancock County Courthouse, Ellsworth, Maine, filed October term, 1905 (vol. 130, p. 365) and April term, 1906 (vol. 130, p. 453).

25. This phrase was supplied by Standish and Virginia Bourne in October, 1980. Molly Dewson commented much later to a friend about Bill: "He really is a lamb poor old chap. Everytime I thought of life without Poll I ended up thinking—you old cad. Remember Bill and where he would be." Dewson to Fannie Hurst, no date [1930s], Fannie Hurst papers, University of Texas.

26. Interview with James Barr Ames, July 28, 1981. Mr. Ames, the son of the former Harvard Law School dean and himself a Boston lawyer, graciously provided me with a copy of the trust agreement from the files of Ropes and Gray, Boston. The trust agreement is dated September 20, 1905; the document was amended in 1931 to include Molly Dewson. Polly also had a smaller trust fund from her paternal grandfather, William Reed Porter.

27. Interview with James Barr Ames, July 28, 1981, Boston.

28. Scrapbooks in the possession of Peter Hall, covering the period from 1895 on, are full of pictures of young men who were friends of the Porter family at Castine and presumably were candidates for romantic involvement.

29. One set of photographs documents a week that Bunny and Polly spent in 1906 camping on the beach, during which they passed the time by reading to each other from the Oxford Book of English Verse. See scrapbooks in possession of Peter Hall.

30. *Cambridge Blue Book* (1908), Moss Acre; Polly Porter daybooks, September 26, 1952, Moss Acre.

31. For background on the early years of the Boston School for Social Workers, see the Harvard University Archives; the quotation comes from a 1904 circular. See also Sally Herman Lunt, "The Professionalization of Social Work: The History of Education for Social Work, with special reference to the School for Social Workers" (Ph.D. diss., Harvard University, 1974); and Nathan Huggins,

Protestants Against Poverty: Boston's Charities, 1870–1900 (Westport, Conn., 1971).

32. Course catalogue, 1909, Boston School for Social Workers, Harvard University Archives. Polly's underlined textbooks are still on the shelves of the living room at Moss Acre.

33. Simmons College Archives and Alumnae Offices contain no mention of Porter's graduation.

34. Interview with Dorothy Blake, October 4, 1980, Castine, Maine.

35. The historian Jean Christie, who interviewed Dewson near the end of her life, recalled a private moment at Moss Acre when Polly said to her ("with such pride" as Christie recalled), "Molly might have married, you know—she had plenty of chances—there were men who wanted her—but she chose me." While I have uncovered absolutely no evidence of men who were interested romantically in Dewson, I agree with Christie that the key words were "but she chose me." Personal correspondence from Jean Christie to author, October 25, 1983.

36. A general historical overview of women's friendships is presented in Lillian Faderman, *Surpassing the Love of Men: Romantic Friendships and Love between Women from the Renaissance to the Present* (New York, 1981). A pathbreaking article surveying women's relationships was Carroll Smith-Rosenberg, "The Female World of Love and Ritual: Relationships between Women in Nineteenth-Century America," *Signs* 1 (Autumn 1975): 27; see also "The New Woman as Androgyne: Social Disorder and Gender Crisis, 1870–1936," in Carroll Smith-Rosenberg, *Disorderly Conduct* (New York, 1985). Helen Howe cited several Boston marriages in *The Gentle Americans, 1864–1960: Biography of a Breed* (New York, 1960). The Lesbian History issue of *Frontiers* (vol. 4, Fall 1979) also contains material on female couples from the past. For a fictional treatment, see the Henry James's description of the relationship between Olive Chancellor and Verena Tarrant in his 1888 novel, *The Bostonians.*

37. For biographical material on these women, see Edward T. James and Janet James, eds., *Notable American Women* (Cambridge, 1971); and Barbara Sicherman and Carol Hurd Green, eds., *Notable American Women: The Modern Period* (Cambridge, 1980).

38. For these changing perceptions, see Faderman, *Surpassing the Love of Men*, 239–53, 297–340; Linda Gordon, *Woman's Body, Woman's Right* (New York, 1976), 193–94; Estelle Freedman, "Separatism as Strategy: Female Institution Building and American Feminism, 1870–1930," *Feminist Studies* 5 (Fall 1979): 512–29; and Carroll Smith-Rosenberg, "The New Woman as Androgyne."

39. The derivation or translation of the French nickname "Puisye" remains obscure. It may be a variant of Pussy.

40. Polly Porter to Molly Dewson, undated letters [1917–18], Moss Acre. The letter that sparked this response has not survived, but the context of Porter's reply suggests that Molly may have raised fears about Polly leaving her or growing less dependent on her. I have never located a similar "love letter" from Molly to

Polly, so I have no way of knowing how she addressed her partner. My guess is that Dewson's letters combined humor, sarcasm, and some sprinklings of affection, but were basically what most Dewson letters were: a description of her current activities and commitments.

41. Blanche Wiesen Cook, "Female Support Networks and Political Activism," in Nancy F. Cott and Elizabeth H. Pleck, eds., *A Heritage of Her Own* (New York, 1979), 412–44.

42. In this same letter, she even referred to one of their dogs as "Fu T'ou Porter-Dewson." Dewson to Maud Wood Park, March 12, 1920, League of Women Voters papers, Library of Congress.

43. Dewson to Mary Hutchinson Page, February 14, 1938, Dewson papers, Franklin D. Roosevelt Library, Hyde Park, New York.

44. Polly Porter to Marion Hall, 1963, letter in the possession of Marion Hall Hunt. Polly's eloquence confirms an observation Molly Dewson once made to her friend Fannie Hurst: "Polly's letters are much more revealing than her conversation. She is more articulate by pen." Letter, n.d. [1930], Fannie Hurst papers, University of Texas at Austin.

45. Such a formulation is reminiscent of an 1892 letter from one woman to another about their relationship, quoted in Carroll Smith-Rosenberg, "The Female World of Love and Ritual," 27: "To me it seems to have been a closer union than that of most marriages. We know there have been other such between two men and also between two women. And why should there not be. Love is spiritual, only passion is sexual."

CHAPTER 5: THE FARMER-SUFFRAGETTES

1. A detailed description of the farm, prepared when Porter and Dewson put it up for sale after World War I, is found in the Mary Dewson papers, Schlesinger Library, Radcliffe College. Their second car was a serviceable Ford.

2. Moss Acre scrapbook in the possession of Virginia Bourne, Castine, Maine. See also Leland Maynard to Molly Dewson, March 7, 1934, Mary Dewson papers, Franklin D. Roosevelt Library, Hyde Park, New York [hereafter FDRL].

3. Description of farm, Dewson papers, Schlesinger.

4. Moss Acre Library. After they moved to the farm, they embossed their books with "Porter and Dewson Farm."

5. Ibid.

6. "The Farm, 1912–1917," scrapbook in possession of Peter Hall.

7. Looseleaf notebook, "Dairy Farm, 1913–1917," Moss Acre.

8. Dewson to Harriet Allen Kerr, June 16, 1940, Harriet Allen Kerr papers, Schlesinger; Mary Chamberlain interview with Molly Dewson, *Boston Sunday Globe*, March 19, 1933, Moss Acre.

9. Farm description, Dewson papers, Schlesinger.

10. For general background, see Eleanor Flexner, *Century of Struggle* (Cam-

bridge, 1959); and Anne F. Scott and Andrew M. Scott, *One Half the People: The Fight for Woman Suffrage* (Philadelphia, 1975).

11. Aileen Kraditor, *The Ideas of the Woman Suffrage Movement, 1890–1920* (Garden City, N.Y., 1971).

12. Mari Jo Buhle, *Women and American Socialism, 1870–1920* (Urbana, Ill., 1981); Sheila M. Rothman, *Woman's Proper Place* (New York, 1978); Karen J. Blair, *The Clubwoman as Feminist: True Womanhood Redefined, 1868–1914* (New York, 1980).

13. The oral histories gathered in Sherna Gluck, *From Parlor to Prison: Five Suffragists Talk about Their Lives* (New York, 1976), convey this sense of excitement.

14. *The Reminiscences of Frances Perkins* (1955), 1:200–01, in the Oral History Collection of Columbia University.

15. Dewson to Herbert Kahn, December 4, 1958, Dewson papers, Schlesinger.

16. The organizational records of the College Equal Suffrage League and the Boston Equal Suffrage Association for Good Government are found in the Women's Rights Collection [hereafter WRC], Schlesinger. The CESL minutes of January 27, 1911 (vol. 112, WRC), describe the tea.

17. Roosevelt had heard of her work with delinquent girls and thought she might have some first-hand observations on the interest of working women in suffrage. (She didn't.) Dewson gave Roosevelt's letter to a nephew, who lost it.

18. Dewson to Theodore Roosevelt, February, 1912, Dewson papers, Schlesinger.

19. The scrapbook is vol. 5 in the WRC, Schlesinger.

20. Sharon Hartman Strom, "Leadership and Tactics in the American Woman Suffrage Movement: A Perspective from Massachusetts," in Jean E. Friedman and William G. Shade, *Our American Sisters* (Lexington, Mass., 1982), 372–92.

21. Suffrage scrapbook, WRC, Schlesinger.

22. Ibid.

23. Ibid.

24. Ibid. See the *Boston Sunday Herald*, October 17, 1915, for press coverage of the suffrage parade.

25. Minutes of the Executive Board, Massachusetts Woman Suffrage Association, July 25, 1916, WRC, Schlesinger; *Proceedings of the NAWSA Convention*, December 14–19, 1915, Washington, D.C., found at Schlesinger. The Massachusetts delegation included many women with whom Dewson would soon be working on the MWSA board: Alice Stone Blackwell, Mary Hutchison Page, Margaret Foley, Gertrude Leonard, and Dewson's mentor and old friend, Elizabeth Glendower Evans, who had joined the suffrage movement in 1909.

26. Dewson to Helen Gahagan Douglas, February 23, 1944, Dewson papers,

FDRL; Dewson note on letter from Carrie Chapman Catt to Molly Dewson, July 26, 1934, Moss Acre.

27. Susan Ware, *Beyond Suffrage: Women in the New Deal* (Cambridge, 1981), 31; Dewson to Clara M. Beyer, February 3, 1934, Clara M. Beyer papers, Schlesinger; Dewson to Florence Armstrong, October 11, 1958, Sue Shelton White papers, Schlesinger.

28. Flexner, *Century of Struggle*, 271.

29. Minutes of the Executive Board, MWSA, September 28, 1916, WRC, Schlesinger. See also minutes from March 30, 1916 and June 22, 1916, for Dewson's growing involvement.

30. Minutes of the Executive Board, MWSA, September 28, 1916, and October 26, 1916, WRC, Schlesinger.

31. Minutes of the Executive Board, MWSA, November 9, 1916, and November 23, 1916, WRC, Schlesinger.

32. Minutes of the Executive Board, MWSA, November 23, 1916, WRC, Schlesinger, cover the wide-ranging debate.

33. Grace Johnson to Teresa Crowley, November 20, 1916, WRC, Schlesinger.

34. Carrie Chapman Catt to Mrs. Charles Sumner Bird, May 31, 1918, WRC, Schlesinger.

35. *Proceedings of the MWSA Annual Meeting*, May 9–11, 1917, WRC, Schlesinger; Minutes of the Executive Board, MWSA, March 22, 1917, April 13, 1917, and August 17, 1917, WRC, Schlesinger; Minutes of the Executive Board, Boston Equal Suffrage Association for Good Government, April 11, 1917, WRC, Schlesinger.

CHAPTER 6: WOMEN AT WAR

1. Dewson to Lucy Stebbins, January 30, 1919, WWI letters in the possession of Virginia Bourne, Moss Acre, Castine, Maine.

2. David M. Kennedy, *Over Here: The First World War and American Society* (New York, 1980), links the war to the Progressive spirit and describes its domestic and international impact.

3. For the story from the militants' viewpoint, see Doris Stevens, *Jailed for Freedom: The Story of the Militant American Suffragist Movement* (1920; repr. New York, 1976). Eleanor Flexner, *A Century of Struggle* (Cambridge, 1959), surveys the suffrage scene, and Kennedy, *Over Here*, describes the general pattern of domestic repression.

4. Dewson to Lucy Stebbins, September, 1917, Moss Acre.

5. Minutes of the Executive Board, Massachusetts Woman Suffrage Association, October 11, 1917, Women's Rights Collection [hereafter WRC], Schlesinger Library, Radcliffe College; auction handbill, Moss Acre. Porter and

Dewson tried to sell the farm when they returned from France, but the worldwide glut of agricultural products in the aftermath of World War I made it an inopportune time to sell a farm. Registry of Deeds records, Worcester County, show they finally sold the farm in 1924.

6. Dewson to Lucy Stebbins, September 17, 1917, and October 15, 1917, Moss Acre.

7. American Red Cross, *The Work of the American Red Cross During the War: A Statement of Finances and Accomplishments, 1917–1919* (Washington, D.C., 1919), 51, 61–64; Ruby Black, "Mary W. Dewson," *Equal Rights* (August 8, 1936), in Mary Dewson papers, Schlesinger.

8. Dewson to Grace Johnson, October 13, 1917, WRC, Schlesinger; bill from Abercrombie and Fitch saved in Dewson papers, Schlesinger.

9. Dewson to Lucy Stebbins, November 18, 1917, Moss Acre; Dewson to Grace Johnson, November 20, 1917, WRC, Schlesinger; Dewson to William D. Porter, Jr., December 3, 1917, Moss Acre.

10. Round Robin, November 6, 1917, Dewson papers, Schlesinger. Dewson had little free time to write to all her siblings, so she continued the family custom of round robins, in which a single letter was circulated to the entire family. The only other people she regularly corresponded with while in France were Lucy Stebbins and Bill Porter. Dewson apprised all her correspondents that her letters were probably read by a censor and might not be allowed through if too frank.

11. Dewson to Lucy Stebbins, November 18, 1917, Moss Acre; Dewson to William D. Porter, Jr., December 3, 1917, Moss Acre.

12. Dewson to Lucy Stebbins, January 23, 1918, and November 18, 1917, Moss Acre.

13. Resume, Dewson papers, Schlesinger.

14. Dewson to Lucy Stebbins, October 11, 1917, Moss Acre; Round Robin, July 3, 1918, Dewson papers, Schlesinger. When Polly was posted to Bourg with Molly, she told her brother, "I have joined your Aunty Whitewash at last—isn't that nice?" (Polly Porter to William D. Porter, Jr., December 25, 1917, Moss Acre.) But then she learned they were to be separated: she felt "perfectly awful" about leaving "Aunty W" and was not happy about the choice of St.-Etienne either. (Polly Porter to William D. Porter, Jr., January 27, 1918, Moss Acre.)

15. Round Robin, October 28, 1918, Dewson papers, Schlesinger. See also Edward Devine to Mary G. Porter, April 9, 1918, Moss Acre, describing the transfer.

16. Dewson to Lucy Stebbins, May 19, 1918, Moss Acre.

17. Mary G. Porter to William D. Porter, Jr., February 27, 1918, and February 20, 1918, Moss Acre.

18. Round Robin, March 1, 1918, Dewson papers, Schlesinger; Dewson to Grace A. Johnson, June 2, 1918, WRC, Schlesinger.

19. Round Robin, March 1, 1918, Dewson papers, Schlesinger.

20. Round Robin, April 7, 1918, Dewson papers, Schlesinger.

21. Dewson to Lucy Stebbins, January 23, 1918, Moss Acre; Dewson quoted in *Quincy Patriot Ledger*, August 24, 1918; Dewson to Lucy Stebbins, April 19, 1918, Moss Acre.

22. Dewson quoted in Alice Stone Blackwell, "International Viewpoints," *The Woman Citizen* (April 12, 1919), 963, in WRC, Schlesinger.

23. Round Robins, July 3, 1918, and September 3, 1918, Dewson papers, Schlesinger.

24. Mary G. Porter to Edward Devine, April 5, 1918, Moss Acre; Mary G. Porter to William D. Porter, Jr., January 1, 1918, Moss Acre.

25. Mary G. Porter to William D. Porter, Jr., January 27, 1918, Moss Acre; Dewson to William D. Porter, Jr., June 30, 1918, Moss Acre; Letter, n.d. [1918], from American Red Cross assistant to Edward Devine, Moss Acre.

26. Polly Porter to Dewson, n.d. [November 1918], Moss Acre.

27. Mary G. Porter to William D. Porter, Jr., December 25, 1917, Moss Acre; clipping, WRC, Schlesinger.

28. Mary G. Porter to William D. Porter, Jr., December 25, 1917, Moss Acre; Round Robin, September 3, 1918, Dewson papers, Schlesinger.

29. Round Robin, September 3, 1918, Dewson papers, Schlesinger; 1897 Classnotes, *Wellesley Alumnae Quarterly*, 1919, in Dewson papers, Schlesinger.

30. Dewson to Lucy Stebbins, January 23, 1918, Moss Acre; Round Robin, September 3, 1918, Dewson papers, Schlesinger; Dewson to Lucy Stebbins, June 15, 1918, Moss Acre.

31. Round Robin, September 3, 1918, Dewson papers, Schlesinger.

32. Kennedy, *Over Here*, 212.

33. Dewson to Lucy Stebbins, January 23, 1918, Moss Acre; Round Robins, September 3, 1918, and April 7, 1918, Dewson papers, Schlesinger.

34. Dewson to Grace Johnson, June 2, 1918, WRC, Schlesinger.

35. Polly Porter to Molly Dewson, n.d. [November 1918], Moss Acre.

36. Bound scrapbook, "The War, 1917–1919," Moss Acre.

37. Interview with Dorothy Blake, October 4, 1980, Castine, Maine.

38. Porter to Dewson, n.d. [November 1918], Moss Acre; Report from Dewson to Major Coulston, November 26, 1918, Dewson papers, Schlesinger. See also Dewson report of November 11, 1918, Dewson papers, Schlesinger.

39. Dewson, "Two Days in Laon with the American Red Cross Eight Weeks After the Germans Were Driven Out," December 12, 1918, Dewson papers, Schlesinger.

40. Margaret Curtis to Molly Dewson, December 21, 1918, Dewson papers, Schlesinger.

41. Round Robin, December 2, 1918, Dewson papers, Schlesinger.

42. Dewson to Grace A. Johnson, December 7, 1917, WRC, Schlesinger.

43. Other ties continued even without supportive networks engendered by a shared professional commitment to social work. Despite profound political differences, Polly and Molly kept in touch with their fellow Red Cross worker Helen

Frick, daughter of the steel magnate Henry Clay Frick, well into the 1950s. Helen Frick to Dewson, April 20, 1959, Memorabilia scrapbook (1957–1959), Moss Acre.

44. Polly Porter daybook, July 28, 1952, Moss Acre. The association between American and French professional women had an impact on the course of social work in France after 1920. For women like Marie-Thérèse Vieillot, wartime collaboration marked the beginning of a period of interaction and professional cooperation between French and American social workers in the years between the wars. For background see the Marie-Thérèse Vieillot papers, Schlesinger, which were gathered and deposited by Marion Hall Hunt. See especially Vieillot's speech, "Alumnae Day" (n.d., 1950s), which describes these transatlantic connections.

45. Round Robin, October 28, 1918, Dewson papers, Schlesinger.

46. Dewson to Lucy Stebbins, May 19, 1918, Moss Acre; Round Robin, October 28, 1918, Dewson papers, Schlesinger.

CHAPTER 7: "WHEN RED ROSES ARE GREEN": THE NATIONAL CONSUMERS' LEAGUE

1. My interpretation of the 1920s has been shaped by the work of Nancy Cott, especially her questioning of the year 1920 as a major turning point for women in a presentation to the Russell Sage Foundation/New School of Social Research colloquium on Women in twentieth-century American politics. Cott's ideas will be developed further in her book *The Grounding of Modern Feminism* (forthcoming, Yale University Press).

2. J. Stanley Lemons, *The Woman Citizen: Social Feminism in the 1920s* (Urbana, Ill., 1973); Sheila M. Rothman, *Woman's Proper Place* (New York, 1978).

3. Jane Addams, *Woman Citizen* (April 19, 1924), 14–16.

4. Paul Kleppner used regression analysis to conclude that women's voting patterns did not cause the sharp drop in voter participation that occurred in the 1920s; instead, he points to "political-environmental conditions" prevailing for both sexes when women were enfranchised. (Paul Kleppner, "Were Women to Blame? Female Suffrage and Voter Turnout," *Journal of Interdisciplinary History* 12 [Spring 1982]: 621–43.) Sara Alpern and Dale Baum confirm Kleppner's argument and provide data to challenge the common assumption that women were apathetic about voting. (Sara Alpern and Dale Baum, "Female Ballots: The Impact of the Nineteenth Amendment," *Journal of Interdisciplinary History* 14 [Summer 1985]: 43–67.)

5. Suzanne LaFollette, *Concerning Women* (New York, 1926), 268.

6. See, for example, William L. O'Neill, *Everyone Was Brave: A History of Feminism in America* (Chicago, 1971). More judicious interpretations, but ones

that still suggest a backslide occurred in the 1920s following suffrage mobilization, include: William H. Chafe, *The American Woman* (New York, 1972); Lemons, *The Woman Citizen*; Estelle Freedman, "Separatism as Strategy: Female Institution Building and American Feminism, 1870–1930," *Feminist Studies* 5 (Fall 1979): 512–29; and Paula Baker, "The Domestication of Politics: Women and American Political Society, 1780–1920," *The American Historical Review* 89 (June 1984): 620–47.

7. Molly Dewson to Lucy Stebbins, January 30, 1919, letters in the possession of Virginia Bourne, Moss Acre, Castine, Maine.

8. See Dewson to Fannie Hurst, n.d. [1939], Fannie Hurst papers, University of Texas at Austin; invitation, March 7, 1919, Women's Rights Collection [hereafter WRC], Schlesinger Library, Radcliffe College.

9. Dewson to Lucy Stebbins, January 30, 1919, Moss Acre; Class notes, 1897, *Wellesley Alumnae Quarterly* (1919), in Mary Dewson papers, Schlesinger. Pictures of this trip are found in the scrapbook marked "California and Castine, 1919–1920," Moss Acre. For a history of automobile touring in America, see Warren James Belasco, *Americans on the Road: From Autocamp to Motel, 1910–1945* (Cambridge, 1979).

10. Harriet Anderson to John Shillady, July 26, 1921, Dewson papers, Schlesinger.

11. Homer Folks to Dewson, January 3, 1921, and June 17, 1921; Helen Rogers to Dewson, July 8, 1919, Dewson papers, Schlesinger. Dewson discusses the job offer from Maud Wood Park to Barbara Miller Solomon, January 21, 1960, and in a note on a letter from Park to Dewson, December 21, 1953, Dewson papers, Schlesinger. Dewson explained that the League of Women Voters did not want two national leaders from the same state, and said that she had other "irons in the fire," meaning her National Consumers' League job.

12. Florence Kelley to Dewson, June 16, 1919, Dewson papers, Schlesinger. Reflecting how the two women were already identified as a couple, Kelley had written, "My love to Miss Porter, and tell her that the prospect for next winter seems much more cheerful with you both in the offing." See also Kelley to Dewson, June 27, 1919; July 18, 1919; and July 31, 1919, all in Dewson papers, Schlesinger.

13. For biographical material, see Josephine Goldmark, *Impatient Crusader: Florence Kelley's Life Story* (Urbana, Ill., 1953); Louise C. Wade, "Florence Kelley," in Edward T. James and Janet James, eds., *Notable American Women: A Biographical Dictionary, 1607–1950* (Cambridge, 1971), 316–19. Kathryn Kish Sklar is currently writing a biography of Florence Kelley.

14. A partial list of alumnae includes Frances Perkins, Molly Dewson, Nelle Schwartz, Clara Beyer, Dorothy Kenyon, Josephine Roche, Jeannette Rankin, and Elinore Herrick. See Josephine Goldmark, "Fifty Years—The National Consumers' League," *The Survey* 85 (December 1949): 674–76.

15. Frances Perkins speech, "My Job," WRC, Schlesinger; Frances Perkins,

Memorial Tribute to Florence Kelley (1932), in National Consumers' League papers [hereafter NCL], Library of Congress [hereafter LC]; Goldmark, *Impatient Crusader*, viii.

16. See Goldmark, "Fifty Years—The National Consumers' League," 674–76; Allis Rosenberg Wolfe, "Women, Consumers and the National Consumers' League in the Progressive Era, 1900–1923," *Labor History* 16 (Summer 1975): 378–92; Clement E. Vose, "The National Consumers' League and the Brandeis Brief," *Midwest Journal of Political Science* 1 (November 1957): 267–90.

17. Clarke A. Chambers, *Seedtime of Reform: American Social Service and Social Action, 1918–1933* (Minneapolis, 1963), covers this period.

18. Dewson to Dorothy Blumberg, July 14, 1958, Dewson papers, Schlesinger; Dewson to Ramona Mattson, April 1, 1954, Dewson papers, Schlesinger; Dewson speech, National Consumers' League Proceedings in honor of Florence Kelley, December 8, 1939, NCL, LC.

19. Florence Kelley to Felix Frankfurter, October 10, 1921, Felix Frankfurter papers [hereafter FF], LC.

20. For general background on this complicated issue, see Chafe, *The American Woman*; Lemons, *The Woman Citizen*; Susan Becker, *The Origins of the Equal Rights Amendment: American Feminism Between the Wars* (Westport, Conn., 1981).

21. Although the two sides were polarized over this issue, there was actually more common ground than usually recognized. Dewson told one former NWP member, "Outside of this one enormous point I sympathize with what they had in mind altho being a practical old humdrummer I did not care for their dramatic methods." (Dewson to Sue Shelton White, October 13, 1939, Sue Shelton White papers, Schlesinger.) Florence Kelley sounded a similar theme: "My debates with the Woman's Party are one percent against an Amendment which will never be adopted and 99% for women judges and a responsible Court." (Kelley to Dewson, February 17, 1924, Dewson papers, Schlesinger.) In other words, reformers like Kelley and Dewson did not view women as passive, weak, and completely dependent on men. They agreed with many items on the feminist agenda of the National Woman's Party, including increasing the representation of women in elected office and removing legal discriminations against women. However, they continued to believe, contrary to the National Woman's Party, that labor legislation benefited women, and this major disagreement overshadowed whatever common ground the two sides may have shared.

22. Minutes of the Executive Board of the National Consumers' League, April 4, 1922, NCL, LC.

23. A good overview of the minimum wage and the courts is found in Judith A. Baer, *The Chains of Protection: The Judicial Response to Women's Labor Legislation* (Westport, Conn., 1978), 91–101. See also "Minimum Wage Commissions: Current Facts," compiled by Mary W. Dewson (New York, 1921), in Dewson papers, Schlesinger.

24. Florence Kelley to Dewson, July 7, 1921, Dewson papers, Schlesinger.

25. Dewson to Barbara Miller Solomon, October 20, 1959, Dewson papers, Schlesinger. Recent books on Frankfurter include H. N. Hirsch, *The Enigma of Felix Frankfurter* (New York, 1981); and Bruce Allen Murphy, *The Brandeis/ Frankfurter Connection* (New York, 1982).

26. Resume, Dewson papers, Schlesinger; Dewson to Clement Vose, February 11, 1956, Dewson papers, Schlesinger; Dewson to Felix Frankfurter, September 23, 1923, FF, LC.

27. Felix Frankfurter to Dewson, February 28, 1921, FF, LC; Felix Frankfurter to Florence Kelley, February 28, 1921, FF, LC.

28. Dewson to Felix Frankfurter, November 14, 1922, FF, LC; Florence Kelley to May Carson, November 24, 1922, NCL, LC.

29. Dewson to Felix Frankfurter, December 14, 1922, FF, LC.

30. Dewson to Eleanor Roosevelt, March 5, 1940, Eleanor Roosevelt papers [hereafter ER], Franklin D. Roosevelt Library, Hyde Park, New York [hereafter FDRL]; Dewson to Florence Kelley, February 10, 1923, NCL, LC. See also Dewson's handwritten timesheet in Dewson papers, Schlesinger.

31. Florence Kelley to Adolph Berle, quoted in Chambers, *Seedtime of Reform*, 68; Dewson to Florence Kelley, February 10, 1923, NCL, LC. The $6,500 bill for printing the brief, a sum which ordinarily would have swamped the Consumers' League budget, was paid out of a special fund donated by Mrs. Willard Straight. Memorandum of Florence Kelley–Molly Dewson talk, March 22, 1923, NCL, LC, with an accounting of the fund attached.

32. Dewson to Felix Frankfurter, November 20, 1920, NCL, LC. Frankfurter's legal analysis, which was sixty-six pages long, centered around the procedural propriety of the rehearing and the constitutionality of the statute itself, arguing that such regulation was a valid exercise of the state's police power. The rest of the brief was given over to factual material compiled by Dewson. It included descriptions of the operation of minimum wage laws in the United States and in Europe and Australia and material to rebut claims that workers were displaced or industries hurt when the minimum wage was instituted. More broadly, it marshalled evidence to describe the terrible working conditions and low wages under which many women toiled, conditions which made a healthy and happy life impossible. The brief concluded with a recitation of the positive social benefits derived from a stronger state role in guaranteeing the health and welfare of American citizens, especially women. See *Adkins v. Children's Hospital, 261* U.S. 525 (1923).

33. Florence Kelley to Dewson, June 8, 1924, NCL, LC.

34. Dewson to Marion Denman Frankfurter, March 18, 1923, FF, LC.

35. The opinions are excerpted in "The Development of Minimum Wage Laws in the United States, 1912–1927," *Women's Bureau Bulletin* 61 (Washington, D.C., 1928); and in Egbert R. Nichols and Joseph Baccus, eds., *Selected Articles on Minimum Wages and Maximum Hours* (New York, 1936).

36. Dewson to Clement Vose, February 11, 1956, Dewson papers, Schlesinger.

37. Nichols and Baccus, *Selected Articles*, 143−56; Chambers, *Seedtime of Reform*, 93−94; Baer, *The Chains of Protection*, 93−94.

38. Especially distressing to her was the amicus curiae brief filed by the National Woman's Party, which opposed the minimum wage for women. This probably explains why Dewson felt "sour" about this group for the rest of her life. Dewson to Sue Shelton White, October 13, 1939, Sue Shelton White papers, Schlesinger.

39. National Consumers' League, *The Supreme Court and Minimum Wage Legislation, Comment by the Legal Profession on the District of Columbia Case* (New York, 1925), 264.

40. Dewson to Isador Lubin, April 16, 1957, Mary Dewson papers, FDRL; Dewson to Clement Vose, February 11, 1956, Dewson papers, Schlesinger.

41. A copy of the amicus brief in *Gainer v. Dorhman* is found in the Women's Rights Collection, Schlesinger. Norris C. Hundley, Jr., "Katherine Philips Edson and the Fight for the California Minimum Wage, 1912−1923," *Pacific Historical Review* (August 1960): 271−85, supplies important background. See also Edson to Dewson, August 17, 1923, Katherine Philips Edson papers, UCLA; Dewson to Frankfurter, October 18, 1923, FF, LC; Edson to Florence Kelley, April 3, 1924, NCL, LC; Dewson to Clement Vose, February 11, 1956, Dewson papers, Schlesinger.

42. The plaintiff admitted that she had been hired by a detective agency to make a false application for a job (she offered to work for six dollars a week, well below the minimum wage and therefore illegal) and that she had lent her name to the court challenge without realizing its significance. See Dewson to Isador Lubin, April 16, 1957, Dewson papers, FDRL; Katherine Edson to Florence Kelley, January 7, 1925, FF, LC; Warren Pillsbury to Florence Kelley, January 12, 1925, NCL, LC.

43. Baer, *Chains of Protection*, 96. Arizona had a flat weekly rate covering all women's industries. This type of minimum wage differed from the model supported by the National Consumers' League, which suggested that commissions be set up and empowered to set specific rates for individual industries. Although the NCL saw the uniform rate as too inelastic to cover women's varied working conditions, such an across-the-board standard was the approach adopted by the Fair Labor Standards Act of 1938.

44. Baer, *Chains of Protection*, 99−101.

45. Dewson had had a chance in 1922 to become assistant chief of the Children's Bureau, but had turned it down because she was in the thick of the minimum wage battle. With the warmth and friendship that often bound professional women in this period, Children's Bureau chief Grace Abbott had told Dewson, "Do come—I'll do everything I can to make you happy and comfortable and can promise to keep you hard at work." Grace Abbott to Dewson, February, 1922, Dewson papers, Schlesinger.

46. Dewson to Florence Kelley, February 13, 1924, Dewson papers, FDRL.

47. Florence Kelley to Dewson, February 17, 1924, Dewson papers, Schlesinger; minutes of the Executive Board, National Consumers' League, May 22, 1924, NCL, LC.

48. Dewson to Felix Frankfurter, October 8, 1923, FF, LC; Florence Kelley to Katherine Philips Edson, April 15, 1925, NCL, LC.

49. Dewson to Florence Kelley, February 13, 1924, Dewson papers, FDRL; Florence Kelley to Dewson, October 13, 1924, Dewson papers, Schlesinger.

CHAPTER 8: A SMALL WORLD: NEW YORK IN THE 1920s

1. Dewson note on letter from Eleanor Roosevelt to Dewson, 1926, Mary Dewson papers, Franklin D. Roosevelt Library, Hyde Park, New York [hereafter FDRL].

2. *Wellesley '97 Classbook* (1927), 22–23, in Mary Dewson papers, Schlesinger Library, Radcliffe College.

3. Ibid.

4. Interview with Clara Beyer, November 19, 1980, Washington, D.C.

5. For floor plans and pictures of the apartment, see bound scrapbook, 1931–1935, and Memorabilia, 1957–1959, Moss Acre. Dewson willed the Chauncy Ryder painting to Wellesley College, where it hangs in Cazenove Hall.

6. Dewson to Clara Beyer, May 4, 1921, Clara M. Beyer papers, Schlesinger.

7. Pictures of these extended trips were carefully mounted in scrapbooks which are still found at Moss Acre or in the possession of Peter Hall.

8. The diary of this 1927 trip is found in the Dewson papers, Schlesinger.

9. Dewson to Lucy Stebbins, October 29, 1928, Lucy Stebbins papers, Schlesinger.

10. Dewson to "Vic," April 25, 1928, Dewson papers, Schlesinger; Dewson to Jean Tillier, February 24, 1928, and March 20, 1928, Dewson papers, Schlesinger.

11. Note, Dewson papers, Schlesinger; Dewson to "Vic," April 25, 1928, Dewson papers, Schlesinger. For an account of this trip, in which they visited France, Germany, the Balkans, Switzerland, and Italy, see Dewson to Family, September 3, 1929, Moss Acre. See also bound scrapbook, 1929, Moss Acre, for photographs of the trip, including some of the steep mountain passes Molly loved to drive. "One of them the Stelvic is over 9000 feet high and believe me it gave me a thrill—80 hair pin turns and where they were enlarging the corners of the steepest part we had to back five times."

12. Interview with Clara Beyer, November 19, 1980, Washington, D.C.

13. Interview with Tommy Thomas, August, 1981, Castine, Maine; interview with Clara Beyer, November 19, 1980, Washington, D.C.

14. Interview with Peter Hall, October 17, 1983, New Haven, Conn.

15. For more information on Pioneer Youth, see *The New York Times*, May

26, 1924, and February 15, 1925; and scrapbook entitled "New York and Castine, 1924–1927," in the possession of Peter Hall.

16. Interview with Clara Beyer, April 18, 1981, Cambridge, Mass. The Moss Acre library contained a commentary by Harold Laski on *The Communist Manifesto*, but the book belonged to Dewson, not Porter.

17. The characterization came from Joseph Lee, a leader in the playground movement. See Memorabilia, 1938–1944, Moss Acre.

18. Dewson wrote in her autobiography: "Never a 'fellow-traveler' or even a Socialist, I, like many other thoughtful American citizens, blushed at certain conditions in 'the American way of life,' and while I was an advocate of step by step progress, I was interested in the wholesale attack by the Russians in their 'noble experiment,' as it was commonly called in the Twenties, until the experiment became the tool of a handful of ambitious, autocratic, unscrupulous men." Mary W. Dewson, "An Aid to the End" (unpublished autobiography, 1949), 2:36, in Dewson papers, Schlesinger.

19. Historians often use the word *homosocial* to describe such a lifestyle. This label connotes the primary importance of women's emotional and professional relationships, but differentiates such a lifestyle from a more specifically lesbian or homosexual culture. The term was probably first used in Carroll Smith-Rosenberg's article "The Female World of Love and Ritual," *Signs* 1 (Autumn 1975): 1–30.

20. For example, Polly—herself once a ward of adults—was the legal guardian of Eleanor Remy Hall, arranging for her schooling and overseeing her care after she caught tuberculosis. Polly (and to a lesser extent Molly) always remained closely involved in the lives of the Halls and their offspring. See the scrapbooks for the role that such extended family played in the Porter-Dewson life.

21. *Wellesley '97 Classbook* (1927), 22–23. Dewson indicated her awareness of Freudian theories of sexuality to her New Deal colleague Sue Shelton White in 1939: "After all us old maids have been repaid in our secret hearts for what we sacrificed to some principles and standards thro' which I suppose we sublimated the sex instinct!!" Dewson to Sue Shelton White, October 13, 1939, Sue Shelton White papers, Schlesinger. Citations listed in chap. 4 notes about women's friendships discuss changing attitudes towards women's sexuality, esp. Carroll Smith-Rosenberg, "The New Woman as Androgyne," in *Disorderly Conduct* (New York, 1985).

22. Dewson to Clara Beyer, August 10, 1920, and May 4, 1921, Clara M. Beyer papers, Schlesinger.

23. Dewson to Clara Beyer, October 7, 1931, and Clara Beyer to Dewson, October 9, 1931, Beyer papers, Schlesinger.

24. Minutes of the Board of Directors, June 4, 1924, July 2, 1924, August 6, 1924, Women's City Club records, New York City. The job paid $4,000 a year, and Dewson stipulated that she expected two months of vacation each summer.

25. Frances Perkins to Dewson, July 29, 1924, Dewson papers, FDRL.

26. Invaluable background on the Women's City Club is supplied in Elizabeth Perry, "Training for Life: Eleanor Roosevelt and Women's Political Networks in the 1920s," in Joan Hoff-Wilson and Marjorie Lightman, eds., *Without Precedent: The Life and Career of Eleanor Roosevelt* (Bloomington, Ind., 1984), 28–45.

27. Mary W. Dewson, "Report of the Civic Secretary," *Bulletin of the Women's City Club* (June 1925), 26–27.

28. Frances Perkins to Dewson, July 29, 1924, Dewson papers, FDRL.

29. Quoted by Dewson in the *Bulletin of the Women's City Club* (June 1925): 26–27.

30. *Bulletin of the Women's City Club* (June 1925): 19; Mary W. Dewson, "Report of the Civic Secretary," Minutes of the Board of Directors, December 3, 1924, Women's City Club records, New York City.

31. See Minutes of the Board of Directors, October 1, 1924, Women's City Club records, New York City; *Bulletin of the Women's City Club* (June, 1925), 21–27; Minutes of the general meeting of the Ratification Committee, January 9, 1925, in Eleanor Roosevelt papers [hereafter ER], FDRL.

32. *Bulletin of the Women's City Club* (June 1925): 26–27. The other three issues were extension of the merit system in the Department of Education (no action); the right of illegitimate children to father's support (enacted); and the inclusion of boys under the Wayward Minors Act (enacted).

33. *Bulletin of the Women's City Club* (June 1925): 26–27; minutes of the Board of Directors, January 7, 1925, and April 1, 1925, Women's City Club records, New York City; *Bulletin of the Women's City Club* (June 1926): 17. See also Clarke A. Chambers, *Seedtime of Reform* (Minneapolis, 1963), 65–66.

34. Minutes of the Board of Directors, May 6, 1925, Women's City Club records, New York City; Frances Perkins to Dewson, July 29, 1924, Dewson papers, FDRL. Dewson's experience at the Women's City Club was quite different from Eleanor Roosevelt's: the historian Elizabeth Perry has argued convincingly that the club was a key element in Eleanor's political education in the 1920s. Perhaps the difference is that Dewson had been professionally active for twenty-five years at that point, whereas Eleanor Roosevelt was just learning (albeit very quickly) her way around public life and thus had more to gain from the Women's City Club's brand of politics.

35. Minutes of the Board of Directors, May 6, 1925, Women's City Club records, New York City.

36. Dewson, "An Aid to the End," 1:5.

37. Minutes of the Board of Directors, March 4, 1925, Women's City Club records, New York City.

38. Dewson, "An Aid to the End," 1:5–6.

39. Eleanor Roosevelt to Dewson, December 23, 1925, Dewson papers, FDRL.

40. Eleanor Roosevelt to Dewson, 1926, Dewson papers, FDRL. For a description of this camping trip, see Joseph P. Lash, *Eleanor and Franklin* (New York, 1971), 399.

41. Dewson, "An Aid to the End," 1:90. See also Frances Perkins to James T. Patterson, March 9, 1961, Frances Perkins papers, Schlesinger.

42. Frances Perkins to Dewson, June 23, 1931, Dewson papers, FDRL.

43. Joseph P. Lash, *Love, Eleanor: Eleanor Roosevelt and Her Friends* (Garden City, N.Y.,1982), 84–85.

44. *The Reminiscences of Frances Perkins* (1955), 2:87–88, in The Oral History Collection of Columbia University. The coalition was modeled on the Women's Joint Congressional Committee, which served similar functions on a national level in Washington in the postsuffrage years. Other members included Rose Schneiderman, Maud Swartz, Mary Dreier, and Mabel Leslie of the Women's Trade Union League; George Hall, George Alger, and Jeanie Miner of the Child Labor Committee; Nelle Schwartz and Florina Lasker from the Consumers' League; and Bernard Shientag from the New York Department of Labor. For details on the New York group, see Lash, *Eleanor and Franklin*, 415.

45. Frances Perkins, "My Job," Women's Rights Collection, Schlesinger.

46. Dewson to Eleanor Roosevelt, February 7, 1929, ER, FDRL.

47. Frances Perkins to Dewson, February 16, 1929, Frances Perkins papers, Columbia.

48. For examples of these changing attitudes, see Dorothy Dunbar Bromley, "Feminist—New Style," *Harper's* 155 (October 1927); and Elaine Showalter, ed., *These Modern Women: Autobiographical Essays from the Twenties* (Old Westbury, N.Y., 1978).

49. Dewson, "An Aid to the End," 1:6.

50. Ibid.

CHAPTER 9: BAPTISM INTO POLITICS

1. Mary W. Dewson, "An Aid to the End" (unpublished autobiography, 1949), 1:21, 2:1–2, in Mary Dewson papers, Schlesinger Library, Radcliffe College.

2. Carrie Chapman Catt, "Political Parties and Women Voters," address to the League of Women Voters, 1920. Other former suffragists were not so sure that women should work within the parties. Anne Martin of Nevada argued that such a strategy would put women right where male political leaders wanted them: "bound, gagged, divided, and delivered to the Republican and Democratic parties." Anne Martin, "Feminists and Future Political Action," *The Nation* (February 18, 1925).

3. For an excellent introduction to the league's philosophy and mode of

action in the 1920s and 1930s, see Marguerite Wells, "A Portrait of the League of Women Voters at the Age of Eighteen" (Washington, D.C., 1938).

4. J. Stanley Lemons, *The Woman Citizen: Social Feminism in the 1920s* (Urbana, Ill., 1973), 111–12.

5. Sophonisba P. Breckinridge, *Women in the Twentieth Century* (New York, 1933), 313–24.

6. Belle Moskowitz, "Junio Politics and Politicians," *Saturday Evening Post* 203 (September 6, 1930): 6.

7. This argument differs from the one proposed by Paula Baker in a recent article entitled "The Domestication of Politics." Baker's formulation compares developments in male and female political cultures of the nineteenth century in order to draw conclusions about the changing political structures of modern American life. Yet, when Baker ventures into the postsuffrage era, she underestimates the degree to which women maintained a separate political culture as a tool for political mobilization and action. See Paula Baker, "The Domestication of Politics: Women and American Political Society, 1780–1920," *American Historical Review* 89 (June 1984): 620–47.

8. See Joseph P. Lash, *Eleanor and Franklin* (New York, 1971); and Susan Ware, "Eleanor Roosevelt and Democratic Politics: Women in the Postsuffrage Era," in Joan Hoff-Wilson and Marjorie Lightman, eds., *Without Precedent: The Life and Career of Eleanor Roosevelt* (Bloomington, Ind., 1984).

9. Frances Perkins noted that these women injected a new element into politics: "These were well bred women, nice, polite women, a cut above the usual Tammany wives and machine politicians." *The Reminiscences of Frances Perkins* (1955), 2:568–69, in the Oral History Collection of Columbia University.

10. Dewson laid out her reasons for supporting Smith in twenty-two pages of handwritten scrawl to Lucy Stebbins, who was trying to build support for Smith in California. See Dewson to Lucy Stebbins, July 22, 1928, Lucy Stebbins papers, Schlesinger.

11. Dewson to Eleanor Roosevelt, September 16, 1928, Mary Dewson papers, Franklin D. Roosevelt Library, Hyde Park, New York [hereafter FDRL]. In order to keep her impressions confidential, Dewson typed the letter herself. She sent a copy to Polly, with this melodramatic note penned at the top: "Polly—No One in the world must see this nor say anything about this part of the situation to a soul until after election. For God's sake. Just wanted you to know what I was up against."

12. Dewson, "An Aid to the End," 1:6, 62, 7. Memorabilia from the 1928 campaign is found in the Dewson papers, FDRL.

13. Dewson to Frances Perkins, May 25, 1959, Frances Perkins papers, Columbia; Dewson, "An Aid to the End," 1:50. For the 1928 election, see Oscar Handlin, *Al Smith and His America* (Boston, 1958); David Burner, *The Politics of Provincialism* (1967); Alan J. Lichtman, *Prejudice and the Old Politics* (1979); and

Kristi Andersen, *The Creation of a Democratic Majority, 1928–1932* (Chicago, 1979).

14. Dewson to Lucy Stebbins, October 28, 1928, Stebbins papers, Schlesinger; Dewson to Lavinia Engle, November 16, 1932, Dewson papers, FDRL.

15. Dewson, "An Aid to the End," 1:7–8.

16. Ibid.

17. Quoted in Lash, *Eleanor and Franklin*, 433.

18. Dewson, "Should Women of the Leisure Class Follow Gainful Occupations?" n.d. [1920s], Dewson papers, Schlesinger. One organization to which Dewson devoted time as a board member was the International Migration Service (IMS), later known as International Social Service, which dealt with social work problems that crossed national boundaries, such as relocating refugees or reuniting families separated by war or political unrest. Close associates on the IMS board included the Columbia professor Joseph P. Chamberlain, Margaret Curtis of the YWCA in Boston, and Homer Folks of the New York State Charities Aid Association. For background, see the International Social Service Papers, Social Welfare History Archives, University of Minnesota.

19. "Facts about the Consumers' League of New York" (1927), found in Dewson papers, Schlesinger. Further material on the Consumers' League of New York is found at the Martin P. Catherwood Library of the New York State School of Industrial and Labor Relations, Cornell University. Some correspondence is also located in the papers of the National Consumers' League [hereafter NCL], Library of Congress [hereafter LC].

20. Dewson to Charlotte Carr, April, 1929, Dewson papers, FDRL.

21. Minutes of the Executive Committee of the Consumers' League of New York, November 16, 1928, CL of NY papers, Cornell. The candy industry may also have been chosen in part because of Dewson's familiarity with the industry from the 1912 minimum wage report. Unfortunately, conditions in New York in 1928 were barely better than they had been in Massachusetts sixteen years earlier.

22. Dewson to Katherine Wiley, May 29, 1928, NCL, LC.

23. *Proceedings of the National Consumers' League Annual Convention, November 15–16, 1928* in NCL, LC; Dewson to Katherine Wiley, May 29, 1928, NCL, LC.

24. See aims listed in the final document, "Candy White List, 1928–1932," NCL, LC. Attempts, primarily spearheaded by Dewson, to establish a national candy list failed. See *Proceedings of the National Consumers' League Annual Meeting, November 15–16, 1928*; Executive Committee Minutes, National Consumers' League, January 31, 1929, April 23, 1929, May 29, 1929, September 27, 1929, and February 11, 1931, NCL, LC.

25. Minutes of the Executive Committee of the National Consumers' League, December 13, 1932, January 21, 1933, January 23, 1934, NCL, LC.

26. Mary Hughes to Thomas Stamm, January 13, 1938, NCL, LC. See

chap. 10 for a discussion of the National Consumers' League initiatives on labor standards in the early 1930s.

27. Frances Perkins to Florence Kelley, January 30, 1929, NCL, LC.

28. Minutes of the Executive Committee, October 2, 1931, NCL, LC; Dewson to Grace Abbott, October 4, 1931, Dewson papers, Schlesinger. The two other women Dewson wrote to were Frances Perkins and Mary Van Kleeck.

29. Grace Abbott to Dewson, October 11, 1931; Dewson to Grace Abbott, December 4, 1931, Dewson papers, Schlesinger.

30. When Kelley suspected the seriousness of her illness, she summoned "Sister Dewson" to her bedside: "Do come. . . . There are things I must tell you, but cannot write." Dewson later portrayed this episode dramatically: "She called me to her death bed to arrange for her successor in the National Consumers' League." Florence Kelley to Dewson, October 2, 1931, Dewson papers, FDRL; Dewson to Dorothy Blumberg, July 14, 1958, Dewson papers, Schlesinger.

31. Dewson to Grace Abbott, October 4, 1931, Dewson papers, Schlesinger. For material on Mason, see Nancy Ann White, "Lucy Randolph Mason," in Barbara Sicherman and Carol Green, eds., Notable American Women: The Modern Period (Cambridge, 1980), 461–67.

32. Mary Anderson quoted in Clara Beyer to Pauline Goldmark, April 19, 1932, Beyer papers, Schlesinger; note, Dewson papers, FDRL.

CHAPTER 10: F.R.B.C.: FOR ROOSEVELT BEFORE CHICAGO

1. Mary W. Dewson, "An Aid to the End" (unpublished autobiography, 1949), 1:8–10, in Mary Dewson papers, Schlesinger Library, Radcliffe College.

2. Ibid., 1:17; 2:206.

3. Ibid., 1:1.

4. Ibid., 2:206–07.

5. The one exception was Roosevelt's Supreme Court packing plan in 1937. See chap. 14.

6. Standard sources are Frank B. Freidel, Franklin D. Roosevelt: The Triumphs (Boston, 1956); and Arthur Schlesinger, Jr., The Crisis of the Old Order, 1919–1933 (Boston, 1957). They can be supplemented by Kenneth S. Davis's recent biography focusing on FDR's years as governor.

7. Dewson quoted in Elizabeth Glendower Evans to Dickinson Miller, February 20, 1933, Elizabeth Glendower Evans papers, Schlesinger.

8. Dewson, "An Aid to the End," 2:226, 1:11.

9. Ibid., 1:11.

10. Ibid.; Dewson to Lorena Hickok, November 21, 1952, Dewson papers, Schlesinger; note, Dewson papers, Schlesinger. Dewson's autobiography contains a complete set of the Rainbow Fliers for 1932 and 1936.

11. *The Reminiscences of Frances Perkins* (1955), 3:476–77, in the Oral History Collection of Columbia University, hereafter cited as Perkins, OHC.

12. Dewson, "An Aid to the End," 1:12.

13. Ibid., 19–20. The response to these letters was, in Dewson's words, "not impressive."

14. Perkins, OHC, 3:474.

15. Eleanor Roosevelt to Dewson, March 11, 1931, Mary Dewson papers, Franklin D. Roosevelt Library, Hyde Park, New York [hereafter FDRL]; Eleanor Roosevelt to Molly Dewson, August 4, 1932, quoted in Joseph P. Lash, *Eleanor and Franklin* (New York, 1971), 467.

16. Dewson, "An Aid to the End," 1:24.

17. Ibid., 24–25.

18. Ibid., 27, says Franklin Roosevelt; Lash, *Eleanor and Franklin*, 452, cites Eleanor.

19. Women who stood out included Carolyn Wolfe of Salt Lake City, whom Dewson later brought to Washington to head the Women's Division of the Democratic National Committee; Grace Westerhouse of Pasadena, who was a devoted Roosevelt follower; and Mrs. Carroll Stewart, "the one woman I met on my trip who was a strong leader in her own right." Dewson later arranged Stewart's appointment to the Board of Veterans' Appeals. See Dewson, "An Aid to the End," 1:27–28.

20. Ibid., 30–31.

21. Dewson to Family, December 4, 1931, Dewson papers, FDRL.

22. Ibid.; note, Dewson papers, Schlesinger.

23. Dewson report, January, 1932, Dewson papers, FDRL; Dewson, "An Aid to the End," 1:32.

24. Dewson, "An Aid to the End," 1:32–33.

25. Ibid., 33.

26. *Democratic Bulletin* (August 1932), 21. Her ideas at the time can be found in Mary W. Dewson, "Some Suggestions for a Democratic Platform," *Democratic Bulletin* (December 1931).

27. Dewson, "An Aid to the End," 1:34.

28. Ibid.

29. Ibid., 37.

30. Ibid., 43–44, 41.

31. Ibid., 46–47.

32. Perkins, OHC, 3:474.

33. Dewson, "An Aid to the End," 1:37.

34. Ibid., 70.

35. Ibid., 70–71. Mary Norton later became a close friend of Dewson, as well as an important Democratic ally in Congress. She played an important role in the passage of the 1938 Fair Labor Standards Act.

36. Ibid., 69.

37. Ibid., 61, 55.

38. Ibid., 41–42, 66.

39. Quoted in Lash, *Eleanor and Franklin*, 468.

40. Dewson, "An Aid to the End," 1:65.

41. Ibid., 63–65.

42. Ibid., 65.

43. 1932 Campaign Letterbook, Dewson papers, FDRL; Dewson, "An Aid to the End," 1:65–66.

44. Dewson, "An Aid to the End," 1:67.

45. Ibid., 71, 72.

46. See Robert S. McElvaine, *The Great Depression* (New York, 1984), for background on the 1932 election; the quote from Roosevelt is found on p. 117.

47. She continued in a more partisan vein, "If the Farmer-Labor people and the Progressive Republicans can be satisfactorily amalgamated with the Democrats there is no reason why the Middle West should not be Democratic for many years." Dewson, "An Aid to the End," 1:72.

48. Ibid., 2:181.

49. Dewson to Family, December 16, 1932, letters in possession of Virginia Bourne, Moss Acre, Castine, Maine.

50. Dewson report, November 24, 1932, Official File 300, FDRL.

51. Dewson, "An Aid to the End," 1:77; Franklin Roosevelt to Dewson, December 12, 1932, Dewson papers, Schlesinger.

52. Dewson, "An Aid to the End," 1:77.

CHAPTER 11: PATRONAGE POLITICS

1. William Leuchtenburg, *Franklin D. Roosevelt and the New Deal* (New York, 1963); and Robert McElvaine, *The Great Depression* (New York, 1984), provide historical overviews; Studs Terkel, *Hard Times: An Oral History of the Great Depression* (New York, 1970), describes the human impact of the Depression.

2. Mary W. Dewson, "An Aid to the End" (unpublished autobiography, 1949), 1:92, in Mary Dewson papers, Schlesinger Library, Radcliffe College. See also the National Consumers' League papers at the Library of Congress for more material on this conference, including a transcript of the proceedings.

3. Speech prepared for the Conference on the Breakdown of Industrial Standards sponsored by the National Consumers' League, December 12, 1932, in Dewson papers, Schlesinger.

4. Campaign speech, 1936, Dewson papers, Schlesinger; interview with James Barr Ames, July 28, 1981, Boston, Mass. See chap. 15 for further discussion of their financial situation.

5. Dewson, "An Aid to the End," 1:91; Dewson to Emily Newell Blair, November 25, 1932, in Patronage Letterbook, Mary Dewson papers, Franklin D. Roosevelt Library, Hyde Park, New York [hereafter FDRL].

6. *The Reminiscences of Frances Perkins* (1955), 3:528, in the Oral History Collection of Columbia University [hereafter Perkins, OHC].

7. Dewson, "An Aid to the End," 1:78, 79; Dewson to Franklin D. Roosevelt, December 24, 1932, Official File 300 [hereafter OF], FDRL. Perhaps Roosevelt realized that Dewson was involved in this campaign, and brought up the Woodring letters to tease her.

8. Dewson to Clara Beyer, December 23, 1932, Clara M. Beyer papers, Schlesinger.

9. Perkins, OHC, 3:517; Frances Perkins to Lillian Wald, July 11, 1932, Frances Perkins papers, Columbia. See also Perkins, OHC, 3:359.

10. Perkins, OHC, 3:521, 525.

11. Ibid., 521, 544, 523, 525.

12. Note from Felix Frankfurter, Memorabilia 1957–1959, scrapbooks in the possession of Virginia Bourne, Moss Acre, Castine, Maine; Perkins, OHC, 3:526.

13. Perkins, OHC, 3:570. Clara Beyer recounted Roosevelt's objections in an interview, November 19, 1980, Washington, D.C.

14. Perkins, OHC, 3:581.

15. Frances Perkins, speech to the American Women's Association, November 24, 1933; and Frances Perkins to Carrie Chapman Catt, June 11, 1945, Frances Perkins papers, Columbia.

16. Dewson, "An Aid to the End," 1:107.

17. Ibid., 106.

18. Dewson to Mary Winslow, January 26, 1945, Winslow papers, Schlesinger. See also Dewson, "An Aid to the End," 1:107.

19. Dewson to Louis Howe, March 27, 1933, President's Personal File [hereafter PPF] 5689, FDRL.

20. Mary Chamberlain interview with Molly Dewson, *Boston Sunday Globe*, March 19, 1933.

21. Dewson, "An Aid to the End," 1:108.

22. For an overview of this period, see Frank B. Freidel, *Franklin D. Roosevelt: Launching the New Deal* (Boston, 1973).

23. "The Human Aspects of the New Deal" (March 1, 1934), in Dewson, "An Aid to the End," 2:234.

24. Dewson shared her reactions on the early New Deal with Felix Frankfurter, who was spending a sabbatical year in England. "Don't you find it pretty stuffy in England with all our old prejudices awash," she twitted him. See Dewson to Felix Frankfurter, November 30, 1933, Felix Frankfurter papers [hereafter FF], Library of Congress [hereafter LC].

25. Joseph P. Lash, *Eleanor and Franklin* (New York, 1971), 513; Dewson, "An Aid to the End," 1:123.

26. Dewson to James Farley, October 5, 1933, Eleanor Roosevelt papers [hereafter ER], FDRL. Dewson decided not to volunteer her time for a consciously

feminist reason: "Since Mrs. Ross had accustomed the men to paying a decent salary, I could not set the women back by making their one regular position voluntary." (Dewson, "An Aid to the End," 1:123.) Given the financial losses she and Polly had suffered early in the Depression, however, the salary may have been more welcome than she let on here.

27. Sue Shelton White to Dewson, October 11, 1933, 1929–1940 Letterbook, Dewson papers, FDRL.

28. Dewson to Felix Frankfurter, November 30, 1933, FF, LC. The description of her new job was an afterthought, written on the back of the envelope.

29. Dewson to Eleanor Roosevelt, May 23, 1933, July 30, 1933, and October 10, 1933, ER, FDRL.

30. Dewson to Eleanor Roosevelt, October 20, 1933, ER, FDRL; Dewson, "An Aid to the End," 1:121.

31. Dewson, "An Aid to the End," 1:123, 124, 2:1–2; Dewson to Emily Newell Blair, August 13, 1933, Patronage Letterbook, Dewson papers, FDRL.

32. Dewson to Jim Farley, April 28, 1933, ER, FDRL.

33. Dewson to Eleanor Roosevelt, April 27, 1933, ER, FDRL.

34. Dewson to James Farley, May 15, 1933, ER, FDRL; Dewson to Eleanor Roosevelt, May 15, 1933, ER, FDRL; Dewson to Louis Howe, June 5, 1933, Patronage Letterbook, Dewson papers, FDRL; Dewson to Jim Farley, July 2, 1933, OF 300, FDRL (the postscript is on the copy of this letter that she sent to Eleanor Roosevelt, ER, FDRL).

35. Dewson to James Farley, August 21, 1933, Women's Division of the Democratic National Committee papers [hereafter WD-DNC], FDRL; Dewson to James Farley, September 5, 1933, WD-DNC, FDRL; Dewson to Eleanor Roosevelt, August 21, 1933, ER, FDRL; Dewson to Missy LeHand, January 5, 1934, WD-DNC, FDRL.

36. Dewson to Marvin McIntyre, February 5, 1934, Patronage Letterbook, Dewson papers, FDRL.

37. Dewson to Eleanor Roosevelt, April 27, 1933, and March 23, 1933, ER, FDRL; Susan Ware, *Beyond Suffrage: Women in the New Deal* (Cambridge, 1981), 52.

38. Dewson to Eleanor Roosevelt, October 30, 1933, OF, FDRL; Dewson to Franklin Roosevelt, October 30, 1933, OF, FDRL. The differences in the tone of these two letters capture Dewson's working relationships with both the Roosevelts. See Ware, *Beyond Suffrage*, 51–52.

39. Dewson to Eleanor Roosevelt, March 28, 1933, ER, FDRL. Dewson arranged a job in the Post Office department for the husband of the well-regarded Kansas leader Mrs. Harrison Parkman in what was definitely a two-for-one deal: "She undoubtedly would give her time if her husband were well taken care of." (Dewson to Eleanor Roosevelt, April 27, 1933, ER, FDRL.) Similarly, she found a job for the husband of Maybelle Fickel, whom she then tapped for the Women's Division staff in Washington. Fickel was paid a nominal salary and devoted herself

full-time to building up the women's Democratic organization in the farm belt. See Dewson, "An Aid to the End," 1:138; and revised patronage list, June 13, 1933, ER, FDRL.

40. Dewson to Carrie Chapman Catt, January 3, 1934, WD-DNC, FDRL.

41. Dewson to Henry Wallace, January 18, 1934, WD-DNC, FDRL; Dewson to Frances Perkins, October 23, 1936, Perkins General Subject File, Department of Labor records, National Archives; Dewson to Eleanor Roosevelt, August 21, 1933, ER, FDRL; Eleanor Roosevelt to Dewson, August 30, 1933, ER, FDRL.

42. Dewson, "An Aid to the End," 1:136–37; Dewson to Lucy Somerville Howorth, July 1, 1934, Lucy Somerville Howorth papers, Schlesinger. See also Dewson to Howorth, March 7, 1934, WD-DNC, FDRL.

43. Eleanor Roosevelt to James Farley, September 20, 1933, ER, FDRL; Dewson to Eleanor Roosevelt, August 18, 1933, ER, FDRL. See also Dewson, "An Aid to the End," 1:126.

44. Dewson to James Farley, May 23, 1933, and August 15, 1933, Patronage Letterbook, Dewson papers, FDRL. See also the Women's Division list of June 13, 1933, in ER, FDRL.

45. Dewson to Eleanor Roosevelt, April 27, 1933, ER, FDRL; James Farley to Carolyn Wolfe, September 25, 1935, WD-DNC, FDRL.

46. Dewson, "An Aid to the End," 1:125.

47. Dewson to Lucy Somerville Howorth, August 21, 1949, Lucy Somerville Howorth papers, Schlesinger; Dewson, "An Aid to the End," 1:140.

48. Dewson to Florence Caspar Whitney, March 5, 1934, WD-DNC, FDRL; Dewson to Homer Cummings, March 9, 1934, WD-DNC, FDRL. On retiring from the federal bench in 1959, a grateful Florence Allen told Molly Dewson, "As I wrote Mrs. Roosevelt none of this would have happened if President Roosevelt had not defied tradition by putting a woman on this bench. And *you* had a lot to do with that!" Allen to Dewson, December 4, 1959, Dewson papers, Schlesinger. For further background on Allen's career, see Beverly Blair Cook, "Florence Ellinwood Allen," in Barbara Sicherman and Carol Hurd Green, eds., *Notable American Women: The Modern Period* (Cambridge, 1980), 11–13.

49. Lavinia Engle to Dewson, June 27, 1934, WD-DNC, FDRL; Dewson to Frances Perkins, May 3, 1934, Frances Perkins papers, Columbia.

50. Dewson, "An Aid to the End," 1:85–86.

51. Ware, *Beyond Suffrage*, 53–54; Dewson to Harry Hopkins, September 12, 1933, ER, FDRL.

52. Dewson, "An Aid to the End," 1:135, 139, 124.

53. Ibid., 140–41.

54. Ibid., 2:187; Marvin McIntyre to James Farley, January 14, 1936, OF, FDRL.

55. Perkins, OHC, 2:721.

56. Dewson, "An Aid to the End," 1:1.

57. Dewson to Franklin Roosevelt, spring 1940, Dewson papers, FDRL.

58. Dewson to Eleanor Roosevelt, May 3, 1933, ER, FDRL.

59. The year 1933 also marked the height of Eleanor Roosevelt's intense relationship with the journalist Lorena Hickok; the two women were exchanging daily letters and phone calls that suggest a deep emotional attachment. See Doris Faber, *The Life of Lorena Hickok, E.R.'s Friend* (New York, 1980), the first book to make use of the Hickok papers at FDRL. William H. Chafe's biographical sketch in Joan Hoff-Wilson and Marjorie Lightman, eds., *Without Precedent: The Life and Career of Eleanor Roosevelt* (Bloomington, 1984), 3–27, contains a more sympathetic and balanced view of the relationship.

60. Dewson, "An Aid to the End," 1:140. See also Ware, *Beyond Suffrage*, 57–67.

61. Rachel Nyswander and Janet Hooks, "Employment of Women in the Federal Service, 1923–1939," *Women's Bureau Bulletin* 182 (Washington, D.C., 1941); Mary E. Pidgeon and Janet Hooks, "Women in the Federal Service, 1923–1947," *Women's Bureau Bulletin* 230 (Washington, D.C., 1949).

62. Nyswander and Hooks, "Employment of Women in the Federal Service, 1923–1949," 25. See also Ware, *Beyond Suffrage*, chap. 6.

63. Quoted in a *New York Times* editorial, March 4, 1983, marking the fiftieth anniversary of Roosevelt's inauguration.

64. Dewson, "An Aid to the End," 1:108, 2:3, 34–35.

65. Maud Wood Park to Dewson, November 5, 1933, Moss Acre; Carrie Chapman Catt to Eleanor Roosevelt, August 15, 1933, ER, FDRL; Emily Newell Blair to Dewson, January 7, 1934, 1929–1940 Letterbook, Dewson papers, FDRL.

66. Dewson, "An Aid to the End," 1:140, 20.

67. See Barbara Sicherman and Carol Hurd Green, "Introduction," *Notable American Women: The Modern Period*, xxi.

68. Clipping, n.d., Moss Acre. See Ware, *Beyond Suffrage*, for a fuller discussion of the women's network in the New Deal.

69. Drew Pearson, "Washington Merry-Go-Round," January 17, 1938, clipping found at Moss Acre.

70. Dewson to Lavinia Engle, November 20, 1933, WD-DNC, FDRL.

71. Dewson to Lavinia Engle, May 28, 1934, WD-DNC, FDRL; Dewson to Eleanor Roosevelt, January 26, 1934, OF, FDRL.

CHAPTER 12: CAMPAIGNS ARE WON BETWEEN ELECTIONS

1. Speech by Molly Dewson, January 28, 1935, in Mary Dewson papers, Franklin D. Roosevelt Library, Hyde Park, New York [hereafter FDRL].

2. Mary W. Dewson, "An Aid to the End" (unpublished autobiography, 1949), 1:48; 2:233–39, 7, in Mary Dewson papers, Schlesinger Library, Radcliffe College.

3. Dewson to John Pollard, March 19, 1934, Women's Division of the Democratic National Committee papers [hereafter WD-DNC], FDRL; Dewson, "An Aid to the End," 1:110.

4. Dewson to Mrs. Matison Boyd Jones, May 18, 1936, Dewson papers, FDRL; "Campaign of 1936, Work of the Women's Division," Dewson papers, FDRL; Dewson, speech to Kentucky Democratic Women's Clubs, April, 1933, Dewson papers, FDRL; Dewson, speech, May, 1936, Dewson papers, FDRL. In her autobiography, under the heading "Most Men's Political Theories," Dewson listed: that the candidate's personality, not his or her stand on issues, influences voters; that party platforms can be used during campaigns to influence voters interested in issues but can be ignored after the election; that officers of groups of farmers, labor, veterans, etc., can "turn over" the votes of their memberships; and that almost all campaign workers expect a job or some personal advantage to accrue to them as a result of their work. Dewson, "An Aid to the End," 2:180.

5. Dewson to Eleanor Roosevelt, July 25, 1936, Eleanor Roosevelt papers [hereafter ER], FDRL; Dewson to Herbert Kahn, April, 1950, Dewson papers, Schlesinger.

6. Press release, 1934, WD-DNC, FDRL; Dewson, "An Aid to the End," 2:7, 11. A copy of the original Reporter Plan, dated January 1934, is in WD-DNC, FDRL. See also Susan Ware, Beyond Suffrage: Women in the New Deal (Cambridge, 1981), 70–71.

7. Dewson, "An Aid to the End," 2:7.

8. Ibid., 13; Joseph P. Lash, Eleanor and Franklin (New York, 1971), 513; "Advance of Democratic Women" (1940), 25, in Dewson papers, Schlesinger; Dewson, "An Aid to the End," 2:5, 11–12.

9. Dewson, "An Aid to the End," 2:13.

10. Ibid., 17, 63–64, 90. Starting with a circulation of only 1,600 in 1935, subscriptions rose to 13,000 by 1936; approximately 25,000 Democratic women subscribed in 1940.

11. Ibid., 1:82; 2:205.

12. Ibid., 2:37–38.

13. Dewson to Harriet Elliott, February 27, 1934, WD-DNC, FDRL.

14. Dewson, "An Aid to the End," 2:38–39; Dewson to Carolyn Wolfe, August 8, 1934, Carolyn Wolfe papers, Schlesinger.

15. Dewson to Eleanor Roosevelt, June 11, 1935, ER, FDRL; note, Dewson papers, FDRL; Dewson to Eleanor Roosevelt, December 18, 1934, ER, FDRL.

16. Dewson, "An Aid to the End," 2:39–40.

17. Note, Dewson papers, FDRL; Carolyn Wolfe, "Educating for Citizenship: A Career in Community Affairs and the Democratic Party, 1906–1976" (1978), 62–63, in California Women Political Leaders Oral History Project, Bancroft Library, Berkeley, California.

18. Wolfe, "Educating for Citizenship," 81a, 98, 223.

19. Dewson to Louis Howe, November 22, 1934, in ER, FDRL.

20. Dewson, "An Aid to the End," 2:66; Dewson to Harriet Elliott, December 27, 1934, WD-DNC, FDRL.

21. Dewson to Harriet Elliott, December 27, 1934, WD-DNC, FDRL.

22. Dewson, "An Aid to the End," 2:65–67.

23. Vera Largent, "Harriet Wiseman Elliott," in Edward T. James and Janet James, eds., *Notable American Women: A Biographical Dictionary* (Cambridge, 1971), 1:572–74.

24. Dewson, "An Aid to the End," 2:69; Dewson to Emma Guffey Miller, April 12, 1935, Emma Guffey Miller papers, Schlesinger.

25. Dewson, "An Aid to the End," 2:80–81, 82.

26. Dewson to Caroline O'Day, March 15, 1934, WD-DNC, FDRL.

27. Dewson, "An Aid to the End," 2:5–6. As part of this initiative, Dewson favored the dismantling of women's Democratic clubs outside the regular party structure. "Perhaps we may still be in the stage where we have to do our fighting by clubs formed of selected groups of women," she told Congresswoman Caroline O'Day of New York, "but I think we should try to burst into the Party and count for something in the regular organization." See Dewson to Caroline O'Day, March 15, 1934, WD-DNC, FDRL.

28. Dewson to Blanche Fritz, March 24, 1937, Dewson papers, FDRL.

29. Dewson to Carolyn Wolfe, August 8, 1934, Wolfe papers, Schlesinger; Dewson to James Farley, March 2, 1933, ER, FDRL.

30. Dewson to Eleanor Roosevelt, February 26, 1935, ER, FDRL; Dewson to Missy LeHand, May 29, 1935, Official File [hereafter OF], FDRL; Dewson, "An Aid to the End," 1:2.

31. Memorabilia, 1961, scrapbook in the possession of Virginia Bourne, Moss Acre, Castine, Maine; Dewson, "An Aid to the End," 2:71.

32. Dewson to family, December 12, 1934, Dewson papers, FDRL.

33. Eleanor Roosevelt to Dewson, March 9, 1934, quoted in Dewson, "An Aid to the End," 2:212–13.

34. Dewson to Eleanor Roosevelt, November 5, 1935, ER, FDRL. The letter read in part: "The importance of seeing me of course depends on whether he thinks any real number of voters are gained by anything but great currents of thought started by the acts of the administration and by the President's interpretation of them.

"I am sure I don't know myself whether there has been any sense in Mrs. Wolfe and me working like niggers to try to get the women to inform themselves on the New Deal and be ready to speak on it. However I believed it would give them courage when under Republican attack and even make them vote getters. I also believed it would strengthen their organizations which are needed to keep the Democrats in line and get them to the polls.

"I believed this so thoroughly that I was willing to take the responsibility for an active campaign to this end through 1934 and 1935."

35. Dewson to James Farley, March 20, 1934, WD-DNC, FDRL.

36. Dewson to Eleanor Roosevelt, June 11, 1935, WD-DNC, FDRL; Dewson to Carolyn Wolfe, June 27, 1935, WD-DNC, FDRL; Dewson to Eleanor Roosevelt, June 26, 1935, ER, FDRL.

37. Dewson to Clara Beyer, August 25, 1935, Clara M. Beyer papers, Schlesinger; Dewson to Carolyn Wolfe and Helen Essary, July 21, 1935, WD-DNC, FDRL.

38. Dewson, "An Aid to the End," 2:41, 43.

39. Ibid., 53–54.

40. Ibid., 54–55.

41. Ibid., 1:112, 2:25.

42. For events of this period, see William E. Leuchtenberg, *Franklin D. Roosevelt and the New Deal* (New York, 1963), chaps. 5–8; and Robert S. McElvaine, *The Great Depression* (New York, 1984), chaps. 10–11.

43. Dewson to Eleanor Roosevelt, December 14, 1933, ER, FDRL. Molly had an ulterior motive for keeping Eleanor apprised of Consumers' League doings. As First Lady, Eleanor donated most of the income she earned from speaking and writing to charity. Dewson had first suggested the "dear old grasping National Consumers' League" as a beneficiary in 1934; when Eleanor volunteered to give $3,000 in 1935, Molly was overjoyed. "Eleanor you are too wonderful. $3000!!! I shall have my photograph framed and put on the walls of the N.C.L. by the grateful League." See Dewson to Eleanor Roosevelt, April 22, 1935, and May 1, 1935, ER, FDRL.

44. Dewson, "An Aid to the End," 1:117–18.

45. Ibid., 118.

46. "National Conference on Economic Security, November 14, 1934," Women's Rights Collection, Schlesinger; Dewson to Josephine Roche, December 11, 1934, Dewson papers, FDRL; Dewson to Eleanor Roosevelt, March 13, 1935, ER, FDRL. See also Dewson to family, December 12, 1934, Dewson papers, FDRL, for her reactions to her colleagues on the committee, including Frank Graham, Paul Kellogg, Gerald Swope, and Marion Folsom.

47. Quoted in George Martin, *Madam Secretary: Frances Perkins* (Boston, 1976), 98.

48. Dewson, "An Aid to the End," 1:1; 2:211.

49. Ibid., 1:82; Frances Perkins to James T. Patterson, March 9, 1961, Frances Perkins papers, Schlesinger. For further discussion of women's impact on the social welfare policies of the New Deal, see Ware, *Beyond Suffrage*, chap. 5.

50. Dewson, "An Aid to the End," 1:17; Dewson to Carolyn Wolfe, August 8, 1934, Wolfe papers, Schlesinger.

51. Dewson, "An Aid to the End," 2:233–38, 206.

CHAPTER 13: THE 1936 CAMPAIGN

1. Dewson to Eleanor Roosevelt, February 10, 1936, Eleanor Roosevelt papers [hereafter ER], Franklin D. Roosevelt Library, Hyde Park, New York [here-

after FDRL]; Dewson to Josephine Roche, April 24, 1935, Women's Division of the Democratic National Committee papers [hereafter WD-DNC], FDRL.

2. Dewson to Eleanor Roosevelt, February 10, 1936, ER, FDRL; Mary W. Dewson, "An Aid to the End" (unpublished autobiography, 1949), 2:179, Mary Dewson papers, Schlesinger Library, Radcliffe College.

3. Dewson to James Farley, December 21, 1935, WD-DNC, FDRL.

4. Dewson to Eleanor Roosevelt, December 19, 1935, ER, FDRL. See also Joseph P. Lash, *Eleanor and Franklin* (New York 1971), 578–79.

5. Dewson to Eleanor Roosevelt, November 5, 1935, ER, FDRL.

6. "Campaign of 1936; Work of the Women's Division," in WD-DNC, FDRL.

7. Dewson, "An Aid to the End," 2:97.

8. Ibid., 97–98.

9. Ibid., 108. See also Dewson to Eleanor Roosevelt, November 5, 1935, ER, FDRL.

10. Dewson, "An Aid to the End," 2:106, 107–108; "Report on North Dakota, January 23–25, 1936," WD-DNC, FDRL.

11. Dewson to Eleanor Roosevelt, January 30, 1936, ER, FDRL; Dewson, "An Aid to the End," 2:110; Dewson to Eleanor Roosevelt, February 10, 1936, ER, FDRL; Dewson to Emma Guffey Miller, February 17, 1936, WD-DNC, FDRL.

12. Dewson to Eleanor Roosevelt, February 10, 1936, ER, FDRL; Dewson to Emma Guffey Miller, February 17, 1936, WD-DNC, FDRL.

13. Dewson quoted in Women's Division press release, 1936, WD-DNC, FDRL.

14. Dewson, "An Aid to the End," 2:124. "In the excitement of the campaign I forgot about this episode until ten years later [when] I had another upset which identified the experience on the train."

15. Ibid., 124–25.

16. Dewson to Eleanor Roosevelt, January 27, 1936, Official File [hereafter OF], FDRL; Dewson, "An Aid to the End," 2:208.

17. Dewson to Eleanor Roosevelt, January 30, 1936, ER, FDRL.

18. Dewson to W. Forbes Morgan, January 17, 1936, WD-DNC, FDRL; James Farley to Dewson, June 16, 1936, WD-DNC, FDRL.

19. Dewson to W. Forbes Morgan, January 17, 1936, WD-DNC, FDRL; Dewson to Eleanor Roosevelt, June 19, 1936, ER, FDRL.

20. Its members included: congresswomen Mary T. Norton and Caroline O'Day; Annette Abbott Adams, Harriet Elliott, Jo Coffin, Emily Newell Blair, Lavinia Engle, Dorothy McAllister, Mrs. Bennett Champ Clark, and Mrs. Ben Kizer. Dewson, "An Aid to the End," 2:128.

21. Dewson to Mrs. Bennett Champ Clark, May 21, 1936, WD-DNC, FDRL.

22. Dewson, "An Aid to the End," 2:129.

23. Dewson to Bess Furman, February 25, 1948, Dewson papers, Schlesinger.

24. Dewson to Eleanor Roosevelt, July 25, 1936, Mary Dewson papers, FDRL; Dewson to Eleanor Roosevelt, October 29, 1935, ER, FDRL.

25. Dewson to Carolyn Wolfe, June 16, 1936, WD-DNC, FDRL; Dewson to Eleanor Roosevelt, April 17, 1937, ER, FDRL; Dewson to Charl Williams, July 10, 1936, WD-DNC, FDRL; interview with Dewson by Ruby Black in *Equal Rights* 2 (August 8, 1936): 179–80, in Dewson papers, Schlesinger. The term *feminist* was usually applied in the 1920s and 1930s to members of the National Woman's Party (to which Ruby Black belonged) who supported the Equal Rights Amendment. Since Dewson strongly believed in protective legislation rather than the ERA, she would not generally have used the term feminist to describe herself. Nor would have women such as Frances Perkins or Eleanor Roosevelt.

26. Dewson to Dorothy McAllister, June 5, 1940, WD-DNC, FDRL; Dewson, "An Aid to the End," 2:131.

27. Dewson, "An Aid to the End," 2:151–52.

28. Farley quoted in the *New York Times*, June 27, 1936. Copy of clipping found in Dewson papers, Schlesinger.

29. Dewson, "An Aid to the End," 2:152; 1:53.

30. Dewson to Emma Guffey Miller, June 30, 1936, ER, FDRL; Harriman quoted in *New York Times*, June 27, 1936. For Miller's side of the story, see Miller to Dewson, July 6, 1937, Emma Guffey Miller papers, Schlesinger. See also chap. 14.

31. Eleanor Roosevelt, "My Day," June 30, 1936, ER, FDRL; Dewson to Eleanor Roosevelt, July, 1936, ER, FDRL.

32. Eleanor Roosevelt memorandum, July 16, 1936, ER, FDRL; Dewson, "An Aid to the End," 2:176–77.

33. Carolyn Wolfe to Marion Glass Banister, November 6, 1936, in Marion Glass Banister papers, Library of Congress.

34. Dewson, "An Aid to the End," 2:168. See also "Campaign of 1936; Work of the Women's Division," WD-DNC, FDRL.

35. Dewson, "An Aid to the End," 2:56; "Advance of Democratic Women" (1940), 26, in Dewson papers, Schlesinger.

36. "Advance of Democratic Women," 26; Dewson, "An Aid to the End," 2:172–75.

37. Dewson, "An Aid to the End," 2:156; Dewson to Charles Michelson, July 7, 1936, WD-DNC, FDRL.

38. Dewson, "An Aid to the End," 2:145, 157.

39. Ibid., 145–46.

40. Dewson to Eleanor Roosevelt, May 20, 1936, ER, FDRL.

41. Dewson, "An Aid to the End," 2:156–57.

42. "Campaign of 1936; Work of the Women's Division," WD-DNC, FDRL.

43. Dewson, "What Women Could and Should Do for the Democratic Party" (1936), WD-DNC, FDRL; Dewson, "An Aid to the End," 2:164–68.

44. Dewson to Franklin Roosevelt, September 10, 1936, WD-DNC, FDRL; Dewson, "An Aid to the End," 1:1.

45. Dewson, "An Aid to the End," 2:167, 169; Dewson to Phoebe Omlie, June 30, 1936, Dewson papers, FDRL. Omlie wanted neon lights that flashed "Roosevelt" when she flew at night, but that proved unfeasible.

46. Dewson, "An Aid to the End," 2:177–78; "Campaign of 1936; Work of the Women's Division," WD-DNC, FDRL.

47. Dewson, "An Aid to the End," 2:177–78; Dewson to Emily Newell Blair, October 19, 1936, WD-DNC, FDRL.

48. Anna Dickie Olesen to Dewson, October 2, 1936, WD-DNC, FDRL; Sophonisba Breckinridge to Dewson, August 5, 1936, WD-DNC, FDRL; interview with Virginia Rischel, 18, in Eleanor Roosevelt Oral History Project, FDRL; Dewson, "An Aid to the End," 2:178.

49. Interview with May Thompson Evans (1978), 7, 71, in Eleanor Roosevelt Oral History Project, FDRL.

50. Carolyn Wolfe, "Educating for Citizenship: A Career in Community Affairs and the Democratic Party, 1906–1976" (1978), 100, in California Women Political Leaders Oral History Project, Bancroft Library, Berkeley, California.

51. *Providence Evening Bulletin*, October 30, 1936; Helen Essary quoted in Dewson to Eleanor Roosevelt, October 6, 1936, ER, FDRL.

52. 1936 clipping, Women's Rights Collection, Schlesinger; *Providence Evening Bulletin*, October 30, 1936.

53. *The Reminiscences of Frances Perkins* (1955), 7:492, 493, in the Oral History Collection of Columbia University.

54. Lash, *Eleanor and Franklin*, 432; note, Dewson papers, FDRL. The photograph is found in Dewson papers, Schlesinger.

55. At times, Dewson treated FDR as if he were a child and she his favorite aunt. During a 1940 meeting with leaders of the Women's Division, she told him that she had brought him a present and held out a shut hand. "His face lit up eagerly, but I said he must speak to the others before I showed it to him." The surprise was a nineteenth-century political trinket. Dewson, "An Aid to the End," 2:226.

56. Dewson to Franklin Roosevelt, May 8, 1933, quoted in ibid., 1:112; Franklin Roosevelt to Dewson, September 12, 1936, President's Personal File, FDRL; Dewson, "An Aid to the End," 2:210.

57. Dorothy Kenyon to Eleanor Roosevelt, November 6, 1936, ER, FDRL.

58. Dewson, "An Aid to the End," 2:182.

59. *Democratic Digest* (January 1937).

CHAPTER 14: A JUST MEASURE OF SOCIAL DECENCY

1. Newspaper article by Emma Bugbee, January 27, 1937, in Mary Dewson papers, Schlesinger Library, Radcliffe College. See also the *Democratic Digest* (February 1937).

2. Mary W. Dewson, "An Aid to the End" (unpublished autobiography, 1949), 2:215–16, Dewson papers, Schlesinger; *Democratic Digest* (March, 1937). Dewson thought she had surprised Jim Farley, but the Master of Ceremonies had let the secret out the week before, including the fact that it was FDR's suggestion. See notes, February 15, 1937, James Farley papers, Library of Congress. I am grateful to Frank Freidel for bringing this document to my attention.

3. Dewson to Franklin Roosevelt, February 25, 1937, Mary Dewson papers, Franklin D. Roosevelt Library, Hyde Park, New York [hereafter FDRL]; Dewson, "An Aid to the End," 2:216.

4. Dewson to Emma Guffey Miller, March 27, 1937, Emma Guffey Miller papers, Schlesinger.

5. Dewson, "An Aid to the End," 2:186–87; Dewson to Eleanor Roosevelt, December 24, 1936, Eleanor Roosevelt papers [hereafter ER], FDRL.

6. Interview with May Thompson Evans (1978), 4–7, in Eleanor Roosevelt Oral History Project, FDRL.

7. For background, see William Leuchtenberg, *Franklin D. Roosevelt and the New Deal, 1932–1940* (New York, 1963), and James T. Patterson, *Congressional Conservatism and the New Deal* (Lexington, Ken., 1967).

8. Interview with May Thompson Evans, 14, FDRL; Dewson, "An Aid to the End," 2:214; Dewson note on Dorothy McAllister to Dewson, July 27, 1937, Dorothy McAllister papers in the possession of Ingrid Scobie; Dewson to E.C. Moran, December 13, 1936, Dewson papers, FDRL; Dewson to Elmer Andrews, October 20, 1936, Dewson papers, FDRL; Dewson to Clement Vose, February 11, 1956, Dewson papers, Schlesinger.

9. Dewson to Eleanor Roosevelt, April 17, 1937, ER, FDRL; May Thompson Evans to Dewson, March 29, 1937, Dewson papers, Schlesinger.

10. Dewson to Eleanor Roosevelt, May 18, 1937, ER, FDRL; Dewson to James Roosevelt, June 4, 1937, ER, FDRL; Dewson to Carolyn Wolfe, March 25, 1937, Carolyn Wolfe papers, Schlesinger.

11. Dewson to Dorothy McAllister, March 26, 1937, Women's Division of the Democratic National Committee papers [hereafter WD-DNC], FDRL; Summers quoted in Leuchtenberg, *F.D.R. and the New Deal*, 234.

12. Dewson recited Miller's charges in letters to Eleanor Roosevelt, April 17, 1937, and June 22, 1937, ER, FDRL. See also Emma Guffey Miller to Eleanor Roosevelt, July 12, 1937, Miller papers, Schlesinger.

13. In fact, Miller was still rehashing the incident fifteen years later. See Emma Guffey Miller to Bess Furman, September 5, 1951, Miller papers, Schlesinger.

14. For example, Miller had attempted to put the Equal Rights Amendment on the agenda of the Inter-American Peace Conference scheduled for Buenos Aires in late 1936. Molly Dewson opposed this scheme in a strongly worded communication to Secretary of State Cordell Hull: "Of course, I am for the same civil and political rights for women as for men. Practically every woman is. But behind the demand for a blanket equal rights convention is the desire to remove the protection afforded women from exploitation through working them unconscionably long hours." Miller's attempt failed, but right after the election, Molly warned Eleanor, "I can't believe Emma Guffey is not up to something." To recreate this controversy, see Dewson to Cordell Hull, June 5, 1936, and July 27, 1936, Dewson papers, FDRL; Emma Guffey Miller to Marion Glass Banister, July 18, 1936, Dewson papers, FDRL; Cordell Hull to Dewson, August 3, 1936, Dewson papers, FDRL; Dewson to Eleanor Roosevelt, December 24, 1936, ER, FDRL.

15. Dewson to Eleanor Roosevelt, June 22, 1937, ER, FDRL.

16. Eleanor Roosevelt to Emma Guffey Miller, July 15, 1937, Miller papers, Schlesinger.

17. Dewson to Eleanor Roosevelt, April 17, 1937, ER, FDRL.

18. Ibid.; Dewson to Herbert Kahn, March 6, 1959, Dewson papers, Schlesinger.

19. Dewson, "An Aid to the End," 2:192.

20. Dewson to Carolyn Wolfe, September 20, 1937, Carolyn Wolfe papers, Schlesinger; Dewson to Eleanor Roosevelt, December 11, 1936, President's Secretary's File [hereafter PSF], FDRL. That Dewson's letter ended up in the president's files rather than in Eleanor's personal papers shows that she passed it on to her husband.

21. Eleanor Roosevelt to James Farley, n.d. [late 1936], ER, FDRL.

22. Dewson to Arthur Altmeyer, August 25, 1935, Appointments, Chairman's Files, Records of the Social Security Board, National Archives [hereafter NA].

23. Eleanor Roosevelt to Dewson, August 17, 1937, ER, FDRL.

24. *Democratic Digest* (October, 1937), 4. Although Dewson told her followers that she had "taken the veil" politically when she joined the Social Security Board, May Thompson Evans of the Women's Division left convincing testimony of Dewson's continuing role in Democratic politics in the second term: "But Molly's activities, I'd like to say here, were broad. She was on the Social Security Commission and served in many other capacities. . . . We cleared with her as she had the final responsibility in her partnership with Mrs. Roosevelt to assure effective political activity by the women." Not until after the 1940 election did Molly Dewson's control over the Women's Division end. See interview with May Thompson Evans, 8, FDRL.

25. Dewson to James Farley, September 22, 1937, ER, FDRL; Dewson to Clara Beyer, August 25, 1937, Clara M. Beyer papers, Schlesinger.

26. Dewson, "An Aid to the End," 1:89; 2:216-17.

27. Geno Herrick to Eleanor Roosevelt, August 25, 1937, ER, FDRL. Elsie George, "The Women Appointees of the Roosevelt and Truman Administrations" (Ph.D. diss., American University, 1972), provides much useful information about Dewson's service gleaned from the Social Security Records.

28. *The Reminiscences of Maurine Mulliner* (1967), 152, in the Oral History Collection of Columbia University [hereafter Mulliner, OHC]. Mulliner noted that when Ellen Sullivan Woodward replaced Dewson on the board, she had a private bathroom built on her suite of offices. "There was a difference in the temperament of the women," Mulliner observed pointedly.

29. Dewson to James Farley, September 22, 1937, Dewson papers, FDRL; Dewson, radio speech, "This Social Security—What Is It?" (1938), Dewson papers, Schlesinger; Dewson, "An Aid to the End," 2:200. For her further ideas on Social Security, see "What Social Security Means to Women," October 11, 1937, Social Security Administration papers, NA.

30. Dewson, "An Aid to the End," 2:195. For the minutes of the Social Security Board meetings, see Record Group 47, Social Security Administration, NA.

31. Dewson, "An Aid to the End," 2:192–93; Dewson to Wilbur Cohen, December, 1955, quoted in George, "Women Appointees," 118.

32. *The Reminiscences of Jack Tate* (1965), 19, in the Oral History Collection of Columbia University [hereafter Tate, OHC].

33. Ibid., 18–19.

34. *The Reminiscences of Jane Hoey* (1965), 88, in the Oral History Collection of Columbia University [hereafter Hoey, OHC]; Tate, OHC, 12–13; Mulliner, OHC, 129. See also *The Reminiscences of Bernice Bernstein* (1965), 46, in the Oral History Collection of Columbia University [hereafter Bernstein, OHC].

35. Dewson, "An Aid to the End," 2:192–94. In one case, she personally interceded with the Civil Service Commission on behalf of Eleanor Lansing Dulles, who worked in the research division. When the Social Security Administration had first been set up, civil service confirmation had not been required for top appointments. By 1937, the Civil Service Commission began to certify those administrators already on the job. Approval was withheld from Dulles because of her poor eyesight. Dewson was amazed at this bureaucratic oversight, claiming, "Eleanor Dulles would be more valuable blind with a Chinaman to read to her than most workers who see." She produced medical evidence that Dulles's eye problems were not degenerative, and the appointment went through. But this was not the end of her efforts on Dulles's behalf: at one of her last board meetings, she raised the issue of why Dulles was only the acting director of her division.

36. *The Reminiscences of Frank Bane* (1965), 101–02, in the Oral History Collection of Columbia University; George, "Women Appointees," 117; Hoey, OHC, 88.

37. George, "Women Appointees," 120–21; note, Dewson papers, FDRL; Bernstein, OHC, 39, 47. Director of Personnel William Mitchell supplied another

example of Dewson's intermediary role with the White House. Mitchell claimed that FDR had asked Dewson to look into whether the Social Security Administration was getting filled up with New York Jews. *The Reminiscences of William Mitchell* (1965), 17–18, in the Oral History Collection of Columbia University.

38. File of congratulatory letters on Social Security announcement, Dewson papers, FDRL; Eleanor Roosevelt, "My Day," February 1, 1938, ER, FDRL.

39. Dewson, "An Aid to the End," 2:224; Dewson to Arthur Altmeyer, June 10, 1938, Dewson papers, FDRL.

40. Dewson to Arthur Altmeyer, June 10, 1938, Dewson papers, FDRL.

41. Dewson to Clara Beyer, August 18, 1938, Beyer papers, Schlesinger; Dewson to Eleanor Roosevelt, October 10, 1938, and October 25, 1938, ER, FDRL.

42. Dewson to Franklin Roosevelt, December 10, 1938, Official File [hereafter OF], FDRL; George, "Women Appointees," 102. George cites as sources personal communications from Clara Beyer (October 29, 1970) and Lavinia Engle (November 13, 1971). Family members and Dewson's former secretary Harriet Allen Kerr also found this a plausible explanation.

43. Dewson to Arthur Altmeyer, June 10, 1938, Dewson papers, FDRL; Dewson, "An Aid to the End," 2:192, 200; interview with Clara Beyer, November 19, 1980, Washington, D.C.; Dewson to Edna Stantial, August 19, 1943, Women's Rights Collection, Schlesinger. A further reflection of Dewson's dissatisfaction with this period of her life is the small part it plays in her autobiography. Scarcely 10 pages out of 400 are devoted to Social Security.

44. Dewson to Clara Beyer, January 31, 1939, Beyer papers, Schlesinger; Dewson, "An Aid to the End," 2:225.

45. Dewson to Franklin Roosevelt, December 7, 1938, PSF, FDRL; Dewson to Eleanor Roosevelt, December, 1938, ER, FDRL.

46. Dewson to Franklin Roosevelt, December 14, 1938, PSF, FDRL; Guest list for dinner party, January 20, 1939, Dewson papers, FDRL.

47. Dewson to Eleanor Roosevelt, June 30, 1939, and January 27, 1939, ER, FDRL. As Molly once observed, "If Mrs. Roosevelt did not hit two birds with every one stone, she never could have carried out her schedule." Dewson, "An Aid to the End," 1:13.

48. Dewson, "An Aid to the End," 2:12. For the coverage that the event received in the national press, see *Time*, May 13, 1940, 22–23.

49. Dewson, "An Aid to the End," 2:191.

50. Ibid., 228–29. Dewson wrote later that fall to an old friend, "When I left the White House on May 5th after a short visit there, I believed the chances were nine out of ten that Roosevelt would not accept a nomination for the third term." Dewson to Jane McGinnis, October 4, 1940, WD-DNC, FDRL.

51. Dewson to Eleanor Roosevelt, July 13, 1940, ER, FDRL; Eleanor Roosevelt to Dewson, July 21, 1940, ER, FDRL.

52. Dewson, "An Aid to the End," 2:201–02; Eleanor Roosevelt to Dewson, August 8, 1940, ER, FDRL. See also Dorothy McAllister to Dewson, August 3, 1940, WD-DNC, FDRL.

53. Dewson, "An Aid to the End," 2:203.

54. Dewson to Dorothy Straus, September 21, 1940, WD-DNC, FDRL; Dewson, "An Aid to the End," 2:203–04.

55. Dewson, "An Aid to the End," 2:204.

56. Dewson to Eleanor Roosevelt, December 23, 1938, ER, FDRL.

57. One of the few pieces of reform legislation to win passage was the 1938 Fair Labor Standards Act, which made permanent the minimum wage and maximum hours provisions and abolition of child labor first attempted in the National Recovery Administration codes. For developments during the second term, see Patterson, *Congressional Conservatism and the New Deal.*

58. For women's issues in the second term, see Susan Ware, *Beyond Suffrage: Women in the New Deal* (Cambridge, 1981), chap. 6.

59. Dewson, speech, 1936, Dewson papers, FDRL; Dewson to Eleanor Roosevelt, November 10, 1940, ER, FDRL.

60. See Ingrid Winther Scobie, "Helen Gahagan Douglas and the Roosevelt Connection," in Joan Hoff-Wilson and Marjorie Lightman, eds., *Without Precedent: The Life and Career of Eleanor Roosevelt* (Bloomington, Ind., 1984), 153–175.

61. Dewson to Harriet Allen Kerr, February 24, 1945, papers in the possession of Harriet Allen Kerr; Mary W. Dewson, "Shall we sell our birthright for a mess of potage?" *Democratic Digest* (January 1942), in Dewson, "An Aid to the End," 2:247–49.

CHAPTER 15: CASTINE REVISITED

1. Dewson to Frances Perkins, May 8, 1939, Frances Perkins papers [hereafter FPP], Columbia; Dewson to Lorena Hickok, October 23, 1941, Lorena Hickok papers, Franklin D. Roosevelt Library, Hyde Park, New York [hereafter FDRL]; Dewson to Eleanor Roosevelt, January 15, 1945, Eleanor Roosevelt papers [hereafter ER], FDRL.

2. Dewson to Carolyn Wolfe, January 31, 1942, Carolyn Wolfe papers, Schlesinger Library, Radcliffe College.

3. Mary W. Dewson, "Shall we sell our birthright for a mess of potage?" *Democratic Digest* (January 1942), quoted in Mary W. Dewson, "An Aid to the End" (unpublished autobiography, 1949), 2:249, in Mary Dewson papers, Schlesinger; Dewson to Elizabeth Magee, March 8, 1944, National Consumers' League papers, Library of Congress [hereafter NCL, LC]; Dewson to Carolyn Wolfe, March 25, 1942, Wolfe papers, Schlesinger.

4. Dewson to Harriet Allen Kerr, May 20, 1942, papers in the possession of Harriet Allen Kerr [hereafter Kerr papers]. Mrs. Kerr kindly loaned me copies of these letters, as well as letters Dewson wrote to Douglas Kerr, her godchild.

5. Dewson to Eleanor Roosevelt, October 1, 1942, ER, FDRL.

6. Dewson to Stanley Reed, n.d. [1940s], Mary Dewson papers, FDRL; Dewson to Mary Winslow, January 26, 1945, Mary Winslow papers, Schlesinger.

7. Dewson to the Ration Board of Weston, Conn., April 23, 1943, Dewson papers, FDRL.

8. Dewson to Mary Winslow, January 26, 1945, Winslow papers, Schlesinger; daybooks kept by Polly Porter [hereafter Daybook], February 6, 1945, and June 29, 1945, in the possession of Virginia Bourne, Moss Acre, Castine, Maine.

9. Dewson to Mary Winslow, January 26, 1945, Winslow papers, Schlesinger.

10. Ibid.; Dewson to Eleanor Roosevelt, February 4, 1944, November 10, 1940, and August 16, 1941, ER, FDRL. She also kept up her correspondence with Franklin Roosevelt. Her favorite topic during the war years was military strategy. Based on her driving trip through Yugoslavia and Transylvania in 1928, for example, Dewson suggested that the president consider a surprise landing of troops on the Dalmatian coast. Roosevelt humored her by telling her that he had immediately gotten out a map to look over the terrain. See Dewson, "An Aid to the End," 2:229–30; Dewson to Herman Kahn, n.d. [1950s], Dewson papers, Schlesinger.

11. Dewson, "An Aid to the End," 2:231.

12. Dewson to Eleanor Roosevelt, April 14, 1945, Dewson papers, FDRL; Eleanor Roosevelt to Dewson, May 16, 1945, ER, FDRL.

13. Dewson to Ruth Larned, November 21, 1950, International Social Service papers, Social Welfare History Archives, University of Minnesota; Dewson to India Edwards, March 26, 1947, India Edwards papers, Schlesinger; Dewson to Harry S. Truman, January 8, 1949, Dewson papers, FDRL.

14. Dewson to Carolyn Wolfe, February 15, 1948, March 8, 1948, and March 26, 1948, Wolfe papers, Schlesinger.

15. Dewson to Eleanor Roosevelt, April 1, 1941, and note on letter from Grace Hutchins to Dewson, March 28, 1941, ER, FDRL; Dewson to Eleanor Roosevelt, November 20, 1941, Dewson papers, FDRL.

16. Dewson to Eleanor Roosevelt, December 29, 1952, ER, FDRL (Molly sent two different letters to Eleanor on this day reacting to the request); Eleanor Roosevelt to Dewson, January 3, 1953, ER, FDRL. The January letter contains a draft of Eleanor's response to the query. Ordinarily she would have ignored the challenge, but, given the mood of the times, she did not want to seem to be evading the issue.

17. Dewson preferred to keep the progressive element within the Democratic party, rather than in a third party. For similar reasons, Dewson declined to join the Americans for Democratic Action in the 1950s because she felt it might jeopardize her standing in the Maine Democratic Party. See Dewson to Arthur Schlesinger, Jr., November, 1958, Dewson papers, FDRL.

18. Correspondence, author to the Federal Bureau of Investigation, 1981.

Under the Freedom of Information Act, the FBI informed me that there was no file on Molly Dewson either.

19. Daybook, January 2, 1951, Moss Acre.

20. Dewson to Harriet Allen Kerr, December 13, 1938, Kerr papers; Dewson to Eleanor Roosevelt, October 25, 1938, ER, FDRL.

21. Fannie Hurst to Dewson, April 8, 1939, Fannie Hurst papers, University of Texas; Dewson to Edna Stantial, August 19, 1943, Women's Rights Collection, Schlesinger. Only fragments of this early draft survive. The chapters on her childhood formed the base for the pieces "My Little Mother" and "As I Remember My Mother," which Dewson circulated to friends in early 1946; the suffrage chapter that she sent to Edna Stantial has never been found. One positive result of Dewson's abortive attempt was that it prodded her to catalogue and sort her papers for various archives: the Women's Archives at Radcliffe (later the Schlesinger Library) and the Franklin D. Roosevelt Library were the major repositories.

22. Grace Tully to Dewson, September 22, 1947, Dewson papers, Schlesinger; Dewson to Grace Tully, September 26, 1947, and April 7, 1951, Franklin D. Roosevelt Memorial Foundation papers [hereafter FDR Foundation], FDRL; Dewson to Herbert Lehman, January 17, 1952, Herbert Lehman papers, Columbia.

23. Dewson to Grace Tully, March 12, 1948, FDR Foundation, FDRL. Dewson's annotated version of *Jim Farley's Story* is found in Dewson's papers at FDRL. She saved one final jab for her completed autobiography: "May the Lord forgive you. I cannot." Dewson, "An Aid to the End," 1:53.

Another prod came from Arthur Schlesinger, Jr., then a junior Harvard historian embarking on a multivolume study of Franklin Roosevelt. On her way to Castine in the spring of 1948, Dewson dropped off some eighty pages at Schlesinger's Cambridge home, which he told her he read with "great interest, pleasure and profit." "That lovely statement wiped the sweat from my brow," Dewson told Clara Beyer, "and I am pulling myself together to continue the remaining years." She added to Grace Tully, "I do not think he was buttering me up." See Schlesinger to Dewson, June 8, 1948, ER, FDRL; Dewson to Clara Beyer, December 4, 1948, Clara M. Beyer papers, Schlesinger; Dewson to Grace Tully, June 12, 1948, FDR Foundation, FDRL.

24. Daybook, September 13, 1952, Moss Acre. The awkward title seems to represent an attempt to convey two ideas: that she supported the reform goals of the New Deal, and that she remained loyal to FDR throughout the period.

25. Dewson to Grace Tully, December 30, 1951, and September 29, 1951, FDR Foundation, FDRL.

26. Dewson to Herbert Lehman, January 17, 1952, Lehman papers, Columbia; Herbert Lehman to Dewson, January 21, 1952, Lehman papers, Columbia. That Dewson did not feel she could afford this cost herself is an indication of the deteriorating state of her finances.

27. Dewson to Harriet Allen Kerr, May 29, 1951, Kerr papers.

28. Dewson to Grace Tully, September 26, 1947, FDR Foundation, FDRL. Polly's Daybook for 1961 includes a budget of $10,000; family members mentioned a figure of around $12,000. Even though their income was limited, both women held substantial assets when they died. Molly Dewson left almost $125,000 in assets (mostly trusts and savings accounts), and Polly's estate in 1972 totalled more than $400,000. I am grateful to James Barr Ames, their lawyer and friend, for making this information available to me.

29. Dewson to Arthur Altmeyer, March 7, 1953, Dewson papers, FDRL; Dewson to Harriet Allen Kerr, August 19, 1945, Kerr papers; Daybook, May 1, 1959, Moss Acre; Polly Porter to Marie-Thérèse Vieillot, March 11, 1956, Marie-Thérèse Vieillot papers, Schlesinger. Their servants' wages of only $17 a week did not strain their budget, and in any case they would have been lost without a cook. The daybooks contain details about wages and other financial matters.

30. Betty Nash Nicholson to author, March 8, 1981.

31. Dewson to Harriet Allen Kerr, May 31, 1954, Kerr papers.

32. Daybook, July 24, 1961, and July 24, 1952, Moss Acre.

33. Transference of deed, January 10, 1952, in Hancock County records, Book 1110, page 744, Ellsworth, Maine.

34. Dewson to Elizabeth Magee, June 24, 1953, NCL, LC; Dewson to Ruth Larned, May 15, 1951, International Social Service papers, Minnesota.

35. Polly Porter to Marion Hall, January 25, 1959, papers in the possession of Marion Hall Hunt [hereafter Marion Hunt papers].

36. Polly Porter to Marion Hall, December 14, 1958, Marion Hunt papers.

37. Fannie Hurst to Dewson, July 20, 1936, Fannie Hurst papers, University of Texas at Austin; Dewson postscript on Polly Porter to Marion Hall, February 5, 1961, Marion Hunt papers; Dewson to Maurine Mulliner, August 26, 1955, Maurine Mulliner papers, Schlesinger.

38. Daybooks, November 1, 1957, February 2, 1961, February 1, 1956, May 5, 1961, November 1, 1954, and November 12, 1957, Moss Acre.

39. Dewson to Clara Beyer, December 4, 1954, Beyer papers, Schlesinger.

40. Paul Fullam to Dewson, June 28, 1954, Dewson papers, Schlesinger; Daybook, June 10, 1954, Moss Acre.

41. Dewson to Grace Tully, April 19, 1949, FDR Foundation, FDRL; Dewson to India Edwards, August 18, 1955, India Edwards papers, Schlesinger; Dewson to Maurine Mulliner, September 6, 1962, Mulliner papers, Schlesinger.

42. Dewson to Clara Beyer, December 26, 1957, Beyer papers, Schlesinger; Dewson to Eleanor Roosevelt, October, 1955, ER, FDRL; Daybook, August 20, 1962, Moss Acre. Polly was never invited to these private luncheons, although she was always greeted warmly by Eleanor when she picked Molly up. It tells us something about Eleanor's priorities late in life that she came to Castine primarily to see the Scarletts, with Molly Dewson just an added bonus.

43. Dewson to Frances Perkins, April 7, 1957, FPP, Columbia.

44. Dewson to Eleanor Roosevelt, February 4, 1944, ER, FDRL; Dewson to Harriet Allen Kerr, February 20, 1954, Kerr papers.

45. Note on letter from Lorena Hickok to Molly Dewson, May 10, 1954, Dewson papers, FDRL.

46. Dewson to Lorena Hickok, 1953, Dewson papers, FDRL; Dewson to Maurine Mulliner, March 25, 1956, and January 1, 1956, Mulliner papers, Schlesinger.

47. Dewson to Clara Beyer, December 13, 1947, and December 1, 1959, Beyer papers, Schlesinger.

48. Dewson to Clara Beyer, June 19, 1960, March 9, 1961, and October 16, 1960, Beyer papers, Schlesinger; interview with Clara Beyer, November 9, 1980, Washington, D.C.

49. Dewson to Clara Beyer, June 19, 1960, Beyer papers, Schlesinger; Dewson to Harriet Allen Kerr, May 22, 1960, Kerr papers. See also the article in the *Ellsworth American*, June 11, 1960, found in Dewson papers, Schlesinger.

50. Dewson to Clara Beyer, June 19, 1960, Beyer papers, Schlesinger; Daybook, June 9, 1940, Moss Acre; Dewson to Harriet Allen Kerr, July 10, 1960, Kerr papers; Daybook, June 18, 1960, Moss Acre; Memorabilia, 1960–1961, Moss Acre.

51. Dewson to Harriet Allen Kerr, July 10, 1960, Kerr papers; Felix Frankfurter to Molly Dewson, June 16, 1960, Moss Acre. The *Ellsworth American*, June 22, 1960, contained election results.

52. Dewson to Elizabeth Magee, April 28, 1954, NCL, LC; Dewson to Harriet Allen Kerr, March 10, 1955, and July 10, 1960, Kerr papers.

53. The fact of Dewson's longevity reinforces the difficulty of making a final assessment of the impact of her health on her career. Although I did not have access to her medical records (if they even still exist), it seems that the diagnosis of heart trouble in the 1930s did not significantly limit or restrict her activities during the rest of her life. The work that she and Polly did around Moss Acre was certainly at times physically strenuous. Probably it was the psychological stress of political work that caused her doctor's concern in the 1930s. When her retirement removed the causes of such stress, both professional and personal, her health returned to its normally robust state.

54. Dewson to Harriet Allen Kerr, June 2, 1957, Kerr papers.

55. Dewson to Eleanor Roosevelt, April, 1939, ER, FDRL; Dewson to Clara Beyer, August 17, 1962, Beyer papers, Schlesinger.

56. Dewson to Harriet Allen Kerr, October 26, 1961, Kerr papers; Dewson to Lorena Hickok, August 13, 1961, Hickok papers, FDRL. Polly was very worried about Molly's overexertions, noting that she looked tired, thin, and slightly bewildered as she tried to cope. See Daybooks for February and March, 1961, Moss Acre.

57. Daybooks, beginning January 15, 1962, Moss Acre; Dewson to Clara Beyer, March 10, 1962, Beyer papers, Schlesinger.

58. Dewson to Clara Beyer, November 12, 1961, Beyer papers, Schlesinger.

59. Polly Porter to Clara Beyer, October 18, 1962, Beyer papers, Schlesinger; interview with Clara Beyer, November 19, 1980, Washington, D.C.

60. This description of Dewson's final days was reconstructed from Polly's diary, which starkly recorded the events in the same straightforward style she used for describing trips to Bucksport or gardening in the afternoon. Dewson died on October 21 and was cremated several days later; her ashes were sent to the family plot in the Forest Hills Cemetery in Boston.

61. Dewson to India Edwards, December 27, 1959, Edwards papers, Schlesinger.

Index